Rainbow Edition

Reading Mastery V
Presentation Book B

Siegfried Engelmann • Jean Osborn • Steve Osborn • Leslie Zoref

S R A

Macmillan/McGraw-Hill

Columbus, Ohio

SRA Macmillan/McGraw-Hill
250 Old Wilson Bridge Road
Suite 310
Worthington, Ohio 43085
Printed in the United States of America.
ISBN 0-02-686402-9
        5 6 7 8 9 0 UNG 99

Lesson 61

Lesson 61

PART A   **Word Lists**

1	2	3	4
kennel	ledge	moist	**Vocabulary words**
quail	ridge	moisture	1. kennel
dwarf	edge	chill	2. ridge
Yodeler	nudge	chilly	3. ledge
		tearful	4. quail
			5. dwarf

WORD PRACTICE AND VOCABULARY

EXERCISE 1   Word practice

1. Everybody, find lesson 61, part A in your skillbook. *Wait.* Touch under each word in column 1 as I read it.
2. The first word is **kennel.**
3. Next word. **Quail.**
4. *Repeat step 3 for each remaining word in column 1.*
5. Your turn. Read the first word. *Signal.* **Kennel.**
6. Next word. *Signal.* **Quail.**
7. *Repeat step 6 for each remaining word in column 1.*
8. *Repeat the words in column 1 until firm.*

EXERCISE 2   Word family

1. Everybody, touch column 2. *Check.*
   All those words end with the letters **d-g-e.** Touch under the first word. *Pause.* What word? *Signal.* **Ledge.**
2. Next word. *Pause.* What word? *Signal.* **Ridge.**
3. *Repeat step 2 for each remaining word in column 2.*
4. *Repeat the words in column 2 until firm.*

EXERCISE 3   Word practice

1. Everybody, touch under the first word in column 3. *Pause.* What word? *Signal.* **Moist.**
2. Next word. *Pause.* What word? *Signal.* **Moisture.**
3. *Repeat step 2 for each remaining word in column 3.*
4. *Repeat the words in column 3 until firm.*

EXERCISE 4   Vocabulary development

Task A
1. Everybody, touch column 4. *Check.*
   First you're going to read the words in column 4. Then we'll talk about what they mean.
2. Touch under the first word. *Pause.*
   What word? *Signal.* **Kennel.**
3. Next word. *Pause.*
   What word? *Signal.* **Ridge.**
4. *Repeat step 3 for each remaining word in column 4.*
5. *Repeat the words in column 4 until firm.*

Task B
Now let's talk about what those words mean. Word 1 is **kennel.** A **kennel** is a place where dogs are kept. Often a kennel has a fenced-in place where the dogs can run and an indoor place where they can sleep. Everybody, what do we call a place where dogs are kept? *Signal.* **A kennel.**

Task C
Word 2 is **ridge.** A **ridge** is the top part of a long hill that doesn't come to a point. When you get to the top of a ridge, you can walk along the ridge without going uphill or downhill.

Task D
Word 3 is **ledge.** A **ledge** is a flat shelf on a hill or a cliff.

Task E
Word 4 is **quail.** A **quail** is a bird that is very good to eat. Quails are about as big as pigeons.

Task F
Word 5 is **dwarf.** Another word for **very short** is **dwarf.** Very short grass is called dwarf grass. Everybody, what would you call very short trees? *Signal.* **Dwarf trees.**

Lesson 61

Adventure on the Rocky Ridge
PART 2

When Martha and the other puppies were six months old, they were all interested in hunting, but they weren't allowed to run free. Julie still kept Martha in her room, but Martha's brothers and sisters lived in a kennel with the other hounds.  The hounds in the kennel howled and ran back and forth, trying to get out of the kennel, but the only time Mr. Owl let them out was when he trained them. Even though a hound has a magnificent nose, it takes more than two years to train a hound. The problem that a young hound has is that it wants to hunt everything. The young hound may start out following the scent of a deer. But if the hound comes across the scent of a rabbit or a quail, the hound will quickly forget about the deer and follow the new scent. These young hounds must work hour after hour learning to stay with one scent and ignoring the others.(B)

Martha didn't go hunting with her brothers and sisters because Martha was a pet, and Julie's constant companion. She slept under Julie's bed, went along with Julie in the morning as Julie did her chores around the house, and stayed inside during the days while Julie was in school. When Julie returned after school, Martha became so excited that she could hardly stand it.

She wagged and wiggled and whined. And when Julie left, Martha felt very lonely and sad. She watched and sniffed, and looked outside. The hours seemed to drag until she caught Julie's scent or heard the sound of her voice.(C)

One day after school, Julie had just finished cleaning out the kennel when she saw her father far off on the rocky ridge. The ridge was steep and dangerous. Julie's father did not allow her to go up there because of her leg. As Julie watched her father she knew that he was returning from a training session with Martha's brothers and sisters. He had taken Leader with him. Leader was the best hound in the kennel. Mr. Owl took Leader along so that the other dogs could imitate him and learn from him.(D)

Julie could tell by the way her father was walking that he was disappointed. When he was disappointed, his shoulders drooped and his feet plodded along slowly. As she watched him and the hounds slowly descend the rocky ridge, she knew why he was disturbed. Ever since she could remember, he had talked about the day when he would raise a dog that could track an animal over the rocky ridge. No dog in the country had ever done it. The reason was

234   Lesson 61   Textbook

that the rocky ridge did not hold the scent of animals. There was no long grass or moisture to hold the scent. Instead, there was nothing but hard, polished rock, with tiny patches of dwarf grass here and there.

A constant wind blew over the rocky ridge, and that wind blew away what little scent any animal left on the rocks. Julie

had often watched hounds try to track animals over the ridge. They would easily follow the scent through the long grass below the ridge. Then they would move upward, to places where there were more rocks and less grass. Here, they would become confused. They would whine and run in circles, trying to pick up the scent. Sometimes, the best hounds—like Leader—

Lesson 61   Textbook   **235**

STORY READING

EXERCISE 5   Decoding and comprehension

1. Everybody, turn to page 234 in your textbook. *Wait. Call on a student.*
   What's the error limit for this lesson? **9 errors.**
2. *Call on individual students to read. Present the tasks specified for each circled letter.*
(A) How old are the puppies now?
   Six months old.
● Where does Martha live? *Idea:* In the house.
● Where do her brothers and sisters live?
   In a kennel.
● What's a kennel? *Idea:* A pen where dogs are kept.
(B) How long does it take to train a young hound to be a good hunter? **More than two years.**
● What problem does the hound have? *Idea:* It wants to hunt everything.
● So what does the hound have to practice doing? *Idea:* Staying with one scent.
(C) Name some things that Julie would do everyday. *Ideas:* Do chores; go to school.
● How did Martha feel when Julie went to school? *Ideas:* Sad; lonely.
● How did Martha feel when Julie returned? *Idea:* Excited.
(D) Where was Julie's father when she saw him? *Idea:* On the rocky ridge.
● How often had Julie gone up there? *Idea:* Never.
● Why would it be particularly dangerous for her? *Idea:* Because of her leg.
● Why had her father taken Leader with him? *Idea:* He was the best dog in the kennel and the other dogs could learn from him.
● Everybody, look at the picture on the next page.
   In the distance you can see the rocky ridge with Julie's father and the hounds on it.
(E) The way Julie's father walked indicated how he felt as he returned from the rocky ridge.
● How did he feel? *Idea:* Disappointed.
● Why was he disappointed? *Idea:* None of the hounds could track over the rocky ridge.
● What had he always dreamed about? *Idea:* A hound that could follow the scent over the rocky ridge.
● Could Leader follow a scent over the rocky ridge? **No.**
● Why was it hard for hounds to track animals on the rocky ridge? *Idea:* Because they lost the animals' scent on the rock.
● What would the hounds do when they lost the scent? *Idea:* Whine and run in circles.
● Read the rest of the story to yourselves and be ready to answer some questions.

would run farther, almost to the top of the ridge. But even Leader would lose the scent on the ridge, and run aimlessly this way and that way. (E) ★9 ERRORS★

As her father approached, the dogs saw Julie and Martha. They ran ahead, jumped all over Julie, and began wrestling with Martha. They quickly stopped playing, however, because they were tired from their long outing. Julie's father sat down on the grass next to her. The half-grown hounds climbed on him and licked his face. He laughed and pushed them aside. Then he explained to Julie, "Around noon, I saw a large deer climbing the rocky ridge. I was hoping that one of the young hounds would be able to track it over the ledge. But. . ." His voice trailed off. He continued, "maybe one of them will still be better than Leader." He pointed to one of the half-grown hounds. "Yodeler over there did as well as Leader. But when they got to the top of the ridge, they lost the scent."

• • •

Three months later, when Martha and the other dogs from the litter were nine months old, a terrible thing happened. It was late fall, and the nights were very cold, with raw winds and the smell of winter. Julie came home from school, greeted her mother, and limped into the living room. She sat down to read a book as her mother worked in the kitchen. Martha jumped up into Julie's lap. "Get out of here," she said laughing. "You're not a little puppy any more. You have to stay on the floor." Julie pushed Martha down and returned to the book she was reading. Martha wanted to

236   Lesson 61   Textbook

play, so she grabbed Julie's shoe and started to wrestle with it. "Cut it out," Julie said. "I'm busy." Martha sat down and looked up at Julie with her tail wagging and her eyes bright.

"All right," said Julie. She stood up and walked to a box in the corner of the room. She took a rubber ball from the box. She rolled the ball across the floor. Martha took off after it. She caught the ball and began to wrestle with it. Then she began to chew on it, as Julie sat down and started reading again. After a couple of minutes passed, Martha brought the ball over to Julie and dropped it by her feet. She let out a little, "woof." Julie picked up the ball and rolled it across the floor again.

The game went on for a while. Then Julie played another game with Martha. Julie took one of her old mittens. She let Martha smell it for a few seconds. Then she hid it behind the couch. "Go find the mitten," she told Martha. Martha held her head high and sniffed the air. She trotted in a circle and suddenly stopped. She turned and went directly to the mitten. Julie had hoped that the game would keep Martha busy for a while, but Martha's nose was so good that it took her only a few seconds to find anything inside the house. In fact, when Julie had played the same game outside, Martha would always find the mitten in a few minutes, even when it was hidden far out in the middle of the meadow.

Suddenly, Julie noticed that her mother was standing by the living room door, looking outside, into the darkness. "I wonder what happened to your father,"

she said thoughtfully, still peering into the darkness. "He should have been back hours ago."

"Where did he go?" Julie asked, as she put the book aside.

"I think he went out with Yodeler and the others," she replied. "But I don't think he intended to stay out after dark."

Julie suddenly felt anxious. She limped over to the door and opened it. A raw wind almost pushed the door out of her grip and sent a chilly blast into the room.

"Close the door, honey," her mother said. "I'm sure your father will be home shortly."

Three hours later, the house was silent. Julie and her mother were sitting at the table, but neither had eaten very much. They sat in silence, trying not to think about why Julie's father hadn't yet returned.

They didn't know he had a good reason for not returning. He couldn't walk. He had taken Leader, Boomer, and the other dogs from the litter over the rocky ridge. Two of the young dogs had picked up the scent of a deer and had followed the scent along the steep slopes, where the grass was long. Julie's father had tried calling the dogs back and had followed them for over two miles. Then he had come to a treacherous place where the trail went over a narrow ledge. Her father had tripped on one of the rocks and had fallen over twenty feet. He had landed sharply in an awkward position. The severe pain from his right leg told him that it was broken. It was impos-

sible for him to climb back up the ledge and get home. So he called Boomer and Leader close to him. He curled up with the dogs so that he would be protected from the terrible cold, as he waited and tried to ignore the intense pain of his leg.

Julie looked out the window of the living room. Suddenly, she noticed some forms in the yard.

"Look, Mom," she said, pointing out the window. "There's Yodeler." Julie's mother ran to the front door and opened it. Yodeler and three other dogs from the litter ran into the house. Usually, they weren't allowed inside but neither Julie nor her mother scolded them. Julie and her mother looked outside into the darkness.

"Bill," Julie's mother called. "Bill, are you out there?"

The only response that came was a howl from one of Martha's sisters. Soon, five more of the dogs were inside the house, wagging their tails and sniffing everything.

Julie's mother turned to Julie. With a worried voice, she said, "Julie, I'm afraid something has happened to your father."

Lesson 61   Textbook   237

- How old was Martha on the cold night described in the story? *Idea:* Nine months old.
- After Julie came home, she tried to read a book but somebody kept bothering her. Who bothered her? **Martha.**
- Julie played two games to try to keep Martha busy. What was the first game? *Idea:* Rolling a ball.
- What was the other game? *Idea:* Hiding a mitten.
- Why didn't the game of hiding the mitten keep Martha busy very long? *Idea:* Because she could find the mitten right away.
- As Julie and her mother waited, what had happened to Julie's father? *Idea:* He had fallen off the rocky ridge.
- Why hadn't he come home? *Idea:* He had broken his leg and couldn't walk.
- What did he do to try to stay warm? *Idea:* Curled up with Boomer and Leader.
- When were Julie and her mother certain that Julie's father was in serious trouble? *Idea:* When Yodeler and the other dogs appeared.

Award 4 points or have the students reread to the error limit sign.

EXERCISE 6   Individual reading checkout

1. *For the individual reading checkout, each student will read 140 words. The passage to be read is the shaded area on the reproduced textbook page for lesson 61 in this presentation book.*
2. Today is a reading checkout day. While you're doing your independent work, I'll call on each student to read part of yesterday's chapter.
3. When I call on you, come up to my desk and bring your textbook with you. After you have read, I'll tell you how many points you can write in the checkout box that's at the top of your workbook page.
4. *If the students finishes the passage in one minute or less, award points as follows:*

0 errors . . . . .3 points
1 or 2 errors . . . . .1 point
More than 2 errors . . . . .0 points

5. *If a student takes more than one minute to read the passage, the student does not earn any points, but have the student reread the passage until he or she is able to read it in no more than one minute with no more than two errors.*

INDEPENDENT WORK

Do all the items in your skillbook and workbook for lesson 61.

ANSWER KEY FOR WORKBOOK

Review Items

1. You have read about three dogs.
   a. Which dog lived in California?
   Brown Wolf
   b. Which dog was the runt of the litter? _Martha_
   c. Which dog belonged to Skiff Miller?
   Brown Wolf
   d. Which dog belonged to John Thornton?
   Buck
   e. Which dog pulled a heavy sled all by himself? _Buck_
   f. Which dog belonged to Julie Owl?
   Martha

2. Write **true** or **false** for each item.
   a. When you go up a mountain, the plants change. _true_
   b. Some redwood trees are as tall as a thirty-five story building.
   true
   c. Mexico is a country north of Canada. _false_
   d. California is one of the largest states in the United States.
   true
   e. A hound dog does not have a sensitive nose. _false_

WORKCHECK AND AWARDING POINTS

1. *Read the questions and answers for the skillbook and workbook.*

2. *Award points for independent work as follows:*

   > 0 errors . . . . .6 points
   > 2 errors . . . . .4 points
   > 3, 4, or 5 errors . . . . .2 points
   > 5 or more errors . . . . .0 points

3. *Award bonus points as follows:*

   > Correcting missed items
   > or getting all items right . . . . .2 points
   > Doing the writing
   > assignment acceptably . . . . .2 points

4. *Remind the students to put the points they earned for their reading checkout, in the box labeled* **CO**.

ANSWER KEY FOR SKILLBOOK

PART B

1. *Idea:* The animals in the cave slept for three months.
2. *Idea:* Boats go in the water.
3. *Idea:* John played baseball.
4. *Idea:* The horses ran a race.

PART C

5. a. litter
   b. scent
   c. *Idea:* Follow every scent
   d. *Ideas:* Julie's father; Mr. Owl
   e. No
6. a. Leader
   b. *Idea:* How to track
7. a. The rocky ridge
   b. *Ideas:* No moisture, short grass;
   c. None
8. a. A deer
   b. No
9. a. *Ideas:* Julie's father; Mr. Owl
   b. *Idea:* Late Fall
   c. *Ideas:* Cold; windy
10. a. *Idea:* A ball
    b. *Idea:* A mitten
    c. *Idea:* She had a sensitive nose
11. a. *Idea:* On the rocky ridge
    b. *Idea:* He had broken his leg
    c. *Idea:* Two dogs
    d. *Idea:* To keep him warm
12. a. *Idea:* The dogs
    b. *Idea:* Something had happened to Julie's father

PART D

13. a. very dangerous
    b. witness
    c. bare
    d. miracle
    e. hardships
    f. come back into sight
    g. decisively
    h. misery
    i. intense
    j. afford

Lesson 62

<table>
<tr><td colspan="2">

Lesson 62

</td></tr>
<tr><td colspan="2">

PART A   **Word Lists**

</td></tr>
</table>

1	2	3	4
Johnson	gong	**Vocabulary words**	**Vocabulary words**
receiver	possible	1. ledge	1. stocking cap
alert	possibilities	2. dwarf	2. down
	expected	3. quail	3. receiver
	unexpectedly	4. ridge	
	operation	5. kennel	
	Whitebirds		

WORD PRACTICE AND VOCABULARY

EXERCISE 1   Word practice

1. Everybody, find lesson 62, part A in your skillbook. *Wait.* Touch under each word in column 1 as I read it.
2. The first word is **Johnson.**
3. Next word. **Receiver.**
4. *Repeat step 3 for* **alert.**
5. Your turn. Read the first word. *Signal.* **Johnson.**
6. Next word. *Signal.* **Receiver.**
7. *Repeat step 6 for* **alert.**
8. *Repeat the words in column 1 until firm.*

EXERCISE 2   Word practice

1. Everybody, touch under the first word in column 2. *Pause.* What word? *Signal.* **Gong.**
2. Next word. *Pause.* What word? *Signal.* **Possible.**
3. *Repeat step 2 for each remaining word in column 2.*
4. *Repeat the words in column 2 until firm.*

EXERCISE 3   Vocabulary review

Task A

1. Everybody, touch column 3. *Check.* First you're going to read the words in column 3. Then we'll talk about what they mean.
2. Touch under the first word. *Pause.* What word? *Signal.* **Ledge.**
3. Next word. *Pause.* What word? *Signal.* **Dwarf.**
4. *Repeat step 3 for each remaining word in column 3.*
5. *Repeat the words in column 3 until firm.*

Task B

You've learned the meanings for all these words. Word 1 is **ledge.** *Call on a student.* What's a **ledge?** *Idea:* A flat shelf on a hill or a cliff.

Task C

Word 2 is **dwarf.** *Call on a student.* What does **dwarf** mean? *Idea:* Very small.

Task D

Word 3 is **quail.** *Call on a student.* What's a **quail?** *Idea:* A bird that is very good to eat.

Task E

Word 4 is **ridge.** *Call on a student.* What's a **ridge?** *Idea:* The top part of a long hill that doesn't come to a point.

Task F

Word 5 is **kennel.** *Call on a student.* What's a **kennel?** *Idea:* A place where dogs are kept.

EXERCISE 4   Vocabulary development

Task A

1. Everybody, touch column 4. *Check.* First you're going to read the words in column 4. Then we'll talk about what they mean.
2. Touch under the first line. *Pause.* What words? *Signal.* **Stocking cap.**
3. Next word. *Pause.* What word? *Signal.* **Down.**
4. *Repeat step 3 for* **receiver.**
5. *Repeat the words in column 4 until firm.*

Task B

Now let's talk about what those words mean. The words in line 1 are **stocking cap.** *Call on a student.* What's a **stocking cap?** *Idea:* A long, floppy cap that is shaped like a sock.

Task C

Word 2 is **down.** One meaning of **down** is **soft feathers.** A coat filled with **soft feathers** is filled with **down.** Everybody, what is a coat fill with soft feathers called? *Signal.* **A down coat.**

Task D

Word 3 is **receiver.** The **receiver** of the phone is the part of the phone that you hold in your hand when you're making a call. Everybody, what do we call the part of the phone that you hold in your hand? *Signal.* **The receiver.**

Adventure on the Rocky Ridge

PART 3

Julie's mother pushed the door shut, closing off the wicked wind. She then walked briskly to the telephone. "I'm going to call the Whitebirds," she said, as she picked up the receiver. Julie watched her mother ignore the dogs that were trying to jump on her and lick her face. A few moments later, Julie's mother put down the receiver and said, "The phone line is dead. The wind must have blown the line down."Ⓐ She went to the closet, got her coat, and threw it over her shoulders. "I'm going for help," she explained. "You put the dogs in the kennel. Then you keep an eye open for your father. I may not be back for some time."

As soon as her mother opened the door, the fierce wind blew it out of her hand and it swung all the way open, making a loud banging sound as it struck the wall. Julie's mother grabbed the door, and as she pulled it shut she smiled and said, "Don't worry, honey. Everything is going to be all right."

Julie returned Yodeler and all the other dogs except Martha to the kennel. Then she went inside and waited. She kept looking at the phone, hoping that it would ring any moment and her mother would

tell her that her father was safe.Ⓑ But every time Julie found herself looking at the phone, she would have to remember that the phone wasn't working. "Just be patient," she told herself. She tried to figure out how long it would take before she received some word about her father. The Whitebirds lived three miles away. Possibly, her father had stopped over there to get out of the cold.

No, he would never let the dogs go home by themselves. And besides, not all the dogs had come home. Eight of the dogs from the litter had returned. But Boomer was still out, and so was Leader.Ⓒ

Then she thought that possibly the younger dogs had run away. Maybe they had come home by themselves while Julie's father had stopped off at the Whitebirds.Ⓓ

Then Julie began to imagine darker possibilities.Ⓔ Maybe a bear had attacked her father. Maybe Boomer and Leader had tried to defend her father. Maybe they were . . . No, don't think of that.Ⓕ
★6 ERRORS★

If only the dogs could talk and tell Julie what had happened!

An old clock in the living room rang

STORY READING

EXERCISE 5 Decoding and comprehension

1. Everybody, turn to page 238 in your textbook. *Wait. Call on a student.* What's the error limit for this lesson? **6 errors.**

2. *Call on individual students to read. Present the tasks specified for each circled letter.*

Ⓐ About what time is it when this part of the story is taking place? *Idea:* Seven or eight o'clock at night.

● Why were the dogs inside the house? *Idea:* Because they had come home without Julie's father.

● Were they normally allowed to go into the house? **No.**

● Who was Julie's mother trying to call? **The Whitebirds.**

● What do you think she was going to ask them? *Idea:* If they knew anything about Julie's father.

● What does that mean: **The phone line is dead?** *Idea:* It isn't working.

● What did Julie's mother think had caused the problem? *Idea:* The wind.

Ⓑ What was Julie hoping? *Idea:* That her father was safe.

● Even if he was safe, would the phone ring? **No.**

● Why not? *Idea:* Because it's not working.

Ⓒ Julie is talking to herself. Listen to what was going on in her mind. *Read from* Ⓑ *to* Ⓒ.

● At first, she thought that her father had stopped over at the Whitebirds. How far away did they live? **Three miles.**

● What made Julie think that he hadn't stopped over at the Whitebirds? *Ideas:* Boomer and Leader had not returned; he would never let the dogs go home without him.

Ⓓ What is Julie thinking now? *Idea:* Maybe her father was at the Whitebirds. That's what Julie would like to believe.

Ⓔ Tell me a darker possibility. *Response:* Student preference.

Ⓕ She didn't finish that last thought. What might have happened to Boomer and Leader if they tried to defend Julie's father from a bear? *Idea:* They might be killed.

● Read the rest of the story to yourselves and be ready to answer some questions.

each hour. Julie sat near the window and listened to the clock. Each time it rang, she became more anxious. When it sounded with eleven gongs, she couldn't hold back the tears. She threw her arms around Martha's neck and began to sob. Martha thought that she was trying to play and tried to shake free. "What are we going to do?" Julie said as Martha gnawed playfully on Julie's hand.

Julie knew that she couldn't sleep, so she decided to try reading, but it was no use. She read the same passage over three or four times without understanding what it said. Then she put the book aside and returned to the window.

Shortly after midnight, Julie became so anxious that she opened the front door and called as loudly as she could, "Daddy, Daddy."

Martha cocked her head and became very alert, glancing first at Julie and then at the darkness. Julie's voice was drowned in the sound of the wind.

At one in the morning, Julie couldn't stand it any longer. She knelt down in front of Martha, took Martha's head and held it firmly between her hands. She looked intently into Martha's big brown eyes and said, "You've got to help me find Daddy." Martha let out a playful groan and licked Julie's face. "Please, help me," Julie said. "Please." Martha shook free and attacked Julie's hand with another playful growl.

Julie wrote her mother a note that told where she was going. She got a flashlight and tested it to make sure that the beam was strong. Then she went to her room and dressed in her warmest clothes: a heavy down coat, thick mittens, a thick stocking cap, wool knee socks, and winter boots. She got a leash from the kitchen and attached it to Martha's collar. Then she found a pair of gloves that her father had worn that morning. She knelt down and held the gloves in front of Martha's nose. "Daddy," she said excitedly. "That's Daddy. Go find him."

Martha grabbed the gloves and began to wrestle with them.

"No!" Julie said sharply. She then continued in a softer tone. "Don't play. You must help me find Daddy." She held the gloves in front of Martha's nose for a few moments. Then she put the gloves in her pocket and went outside.

She didn't know which direction her father had gone, so she decided to walk around the meadow that surrounded the house. Before Julie and Martha had gone three hundred feet, Martha caught a scent. Martha held her head up and let out a howl. The dogs in the kennel responded by howling back. They wanted to join her. Martha pulled on the leash and continued to howl. A few minutes later, Julie realized that Martha was tracking something that was moving in a small circle. "It's a rabbit," she said aloud. Rabbits always circle when a hound tracks them. She bent down in front of Martha again, and removed her father's gloves from her pocket. She held the gloves in front of Martha's nose and said, "Daddy. Find Daddy. Please understand. Please."

Lesson 62   Textbook   **239**

And for some reason, the dog did understand. It's hard to say why. Martha hadn't been trained to track. And for Martha, the scent of a person was far less interesting than the scent of a quail or a deer. Of course, Martha had the ability to track a person. Her nose could easily tell one person from another. It could also tell her which direction the person had been moving and how long ago the person had been in a particular place. Martha easily recognized the scent of Julie's father on the gloves. The only thing Martha didn't understand was what Julie wanted her to do. When they had first gone out into the night, Martha had thought that Julie was giving her an unusual treat. It wasn't often that Julie let her sniff the magnificent smells that were in the meadow. But now, something was different. Possibly, the cold wind made Martha become more serious. She really didn't enjoy being in the cutting wind and yet, something about the way Julie behaved told her that there was im-portant business out here. Somehow, Martha knew that neither she nor Julie would go back into the comfortable house until the business had been completed.

Suddenly, Martha sniffed the gloves and looked at Julie with a serious expression, almost as if she was saying to her master, "I understand that we have a job to do."

Julie put her father's gloves back into her pocket and continued to circle the meadow. When they came to the side of the meadow that was closest to the rocky ridge, Martha began to sniff the grass excitedly. Then she raised her head and gave a funny, little bark. It wasn't the kind of howl that she always let out when she caught the scent of animals or birds. Each of those howls was a long, "ooooo" that would sometimes last four seconds. The sound that she let out now in the bitter wind was an excited little bark, as if she was trying to say, "I found it!"

She pulled Julie this way and that way as she tried to decide which way the trail went. Julie tried to keep up, but because of her bad leg she couldn't move very fast. At last, she made a difficult decision. She took off her mittens and unfastened Martha's leash. Julie realized the chance she was taking. If Martha caught the magnificent scent of a deer or some other animal, she might not come back. But she would be able to work faster if she was free. Before releasing Martha, Julie held Martha by her collar and once more presented the pair of gloves. Then she let go of Martha and said, "Go find Daddy."

240   Lesson 62   Textbook

- After Julie waited for a long time, she started to cry. *Call on a student.* How many gongs had the old clock made when she started to cry? **Eleven.**
- Julie couldn't sleep, so what did she first decide to do? *Idea:* Read.
- Did that work? **No.**
- Why not? *Idea:* She was too worried.
- At one o'clock in the morning, what did Julie decide to do? *Idea:* Go find her father.
- Who was going to help Julie? **Martha.**
- What did Julie present to Martha? *Idea:* Her father's gloves.
- Why? *Idea:* So Martha would pick up the scent.
- Shortly after they went outside, Martha began to howl. Had she caught the scent of Julie's father? **No.**
- What was Martha tracking? **A rabbit.**
- How did Julie know that it was a rabbit? *Idea:* Rabbits always lead dogs in circles.
- What did Julie do to remind Martha of what she had to do? *Idea:* Made her sniff the gloves again.
- Did Martha seem to understand? **Yes.**
- What was different about the way Martha behaved when she caught the scent of Julie's father? *Idea:* She gave a short bark.
- Why did Julie let Martha off the leash? *Idea:* So she could go faster.
- There was a chance that Martha would do something that Julie didn't want her to do. What was that? *Idea:* Track an animal.
- What did Julie do just before she released Martha? *Idea:* Made her sniff the gloves again.

Award 4 points or have the students reread to the error limit sign.

INDEPENDENT WORK

Do all the items in your skillbook and workbook for lesson 62.

Lesson 62   **7**

ANSWER KEY FOR WORKBOOK

Review Items

1. Look at the row of pictures.

| A | B | C |

a. Write the letter of the picture that shows a place that would hold an animal's scent well. ___A___

b. Write the letter of the picture that shows a place that would hold a scent, but not too well. ___C___

c. Write the letter of the picture that shows a place that would hold a scent poorly. ___B___

d. Why would this place hold the scent poorly? *Idea: There are no plants.*

2. Write the main use for each animal. Choose from **hunting, food,** or **carrying.**

a. cow	*food*
b. mongoose	*hunting*
c. goose	*food*
d. donkey	*carrying*
e. falcon	*hunting*
f. hound	*hunting*
g. sheep	*food*
h. llama	*carrying*
i. goat	*food*
j. elephant	*carrying*

WORKCHECK AND AWARDING POINTS

1. *Read the questions and answers for the skillbook and workbook.*

2. *Award points for independent work as follows:*

0 errors	6 points
2 errors	4 points
3, 4, or 5 errors	2 points
5 or more errors	0 points

3. *Award bonus points as follows:*

Correcting missed items or getting all items right	2 points
Doing the writing assignment acceptably	2 points

ANSWER KEY FOR SKILLBOOK

PART B

1. *Idea:* The oceans are made of salt water.
2. *Idea:* The cities are in California.
3. *Idea:* Willie mailed a letter.
4. *Idea:* Frank made a phone call.

PART C

5. a. Whitebirds
   b. *Idea:* The phone was dead
   c. *Idea:* Went for help
6. *Ideas:* Put the dogs in the kennel; watch for her father
7. a. One o'clock in the morning
   b. Martha
8. a. *Idea:* A pair of her father's gloves
   b. No
9. A rabbit
10. a. circle
   b. *Idea:* Held the gloves to Martha's nose
11. a. Yes
   b. A deer
12. a. a howl
   b. a short bark
13. a. She was crippled
   b. *Idea:* Take Martha off the leash
   c. *Idea:* Loose the scent
   d. *Idea:* Held the gloves to Martha's nose again

PART D

14. a. toppled
   b. spring
   c. stop
   d. afford
   e. decisive
   f. reluctant to
   g. sensitive
   h. determination

Lesson 63

WORD PRACTICE AND VOCABULARY

EXERCISE 1   Word practice

1. Everybody, find lesson 63, part A in your skillbook. *Wait.* Touch under each word in column 1 as I read it.
2. The words in the first line are **Mr. Taylor.**
3. Next word. **Hoarse.**
4. *Repeat step 3 for each remaining word in column 1.*
5. Your turn. Read the first line. *Signal.*
   Mr. Taylor.
6. Next word. *Signal.* **Hoarse.**
7. *Repeat step 6 for each remaining word in column 1.*
8. *Repeat the words in column 1 until firm.*

EXERCISE 2   Vocabulary review

Task A

1. Everybody, touch column 2. *Check.*
   First you're going to read the words in column 2. Then we'll talk about what they mean.
2. Touch under the first word. *Pause.*
   What word? *Signal.* **Down.**
3. Next word. *Pause.*
   What word? *Signal.* **Receiver.**

Task B

You've learned the meanings for these words.
Word 1 is **down.** *Call on a student.*
What is **down?** *Idea:* Soft feathers.

Task C

Word 2 is **receiver.** *Call on a student.*
What's a **receiver?** *Idea:* The part of the phone that you hold in your hand.

EXERCISE 3   Vocabulary development

Task A

1. Everybody, touch column 3. *Check.*
   First you're going to read the words in column 3. Then we'll talk about what they mean.

2. Touch under the first line. *Pause.*
   What words? *Signal.* **Wild goose chase.**
3. Next word. *Pause.*
   What word? *Signal.* **Cast.**
4. *Repeat step 3 for each remaining word in column 3.*
5. *Repeat the words in column 3 until firm.*

Task B

Now let's talk about what those words mean. The words in line 1 are **wild goose chase.** When you go on a **wild goose chase,** you are going after something you won't find. If somebody goes out looking for Peter Rabbit, they're going on a wild goose chase.

Task C

Word 2 is **cast.** When hunting dogs are trying to find the scent of an animal, they **cast.** That means they go back and forth sniffing the ground. When they find the scent, they stop casting and follow the trail left by the scent. Everybody, what are hunting dogs doing when they go back and forth trying to pick up a scent? *Signal.* **Casting.**

Task D

Word 3 is **hoarse.** This kind of **hoarse** tells how your voice sounds. I'll say something in a hoarse voice. *Talk hoarsely.* This is hoarse. Everybody, what kind of voice did I just talk in? *Signal.* **A hoarse voice.**

Task E

Word 4 is **face.** The **face** of a cliff is the part of the cliff that goes up and down. It's the part you can see from a distance. Everybody, what do we call the part of a cliff that goes up and down? *Signal.* **The face.**

Task F

Word 5 is **unexpectedly.** When something happens **unexpectedly,** it happens when you don't expect it. If you don't think you'll slip, but you do slip, you slip unexpectedly. Everybody, what do you do if you don't think you'll slip, but you do slip? *Signal.* **You slip unexpectedly.**

Task G

Word 6 is **fumble.** When you **fumble** for something, you try to pick it up, but you keep dropping it. Let's see you fumble for your pencil. *Check.*

Task H

Word 7 is **sprawling.** Something that is **sprawling** is all spread out. Everybody, what is something doing if it is all spread out? *Signal.* **Sprawling.**

Lesson 63

Adventure on the Rocky Ridge

PART 4

Martha ran and circled the place where she had first caught the smell of Julie's father. She circled it three times to find out which direction the tracks led. After completing the third circle, she knew the direction. She took off very fast, leaving Julie far behind. From time to time, Martha raised her head and barked. Julie listened for the barks and followed them as quickly as she could, but she couldn't walk very fast. Soon she was far, far behind Martha. (A) Julie could no longer hear Martha's barks, but she knew where Martha was heading—right up the face of the rocky ridge.

When Julie realized that her father had gone up the rocky ridge, a very dismal feeling came over her. Julie had seen Leader and the other dogs with keen noses track animals to the top of the ridge. She had seen them cast aimlessly across the rocks trying to pick up the scent on the bare, windblown rocks. (B)

But she followed in the direction that Martha had gone. It took Julie over half an hour to reach the steep slopes of the rocky ridge. She had turned on her flashlight so that she would not trip over the rocks that jutted out of the grass. She was wearing mittens, but her hands were beginning to ache with cold. She tried not to pay attention to the pain. From time to time, she stopped and called, "Martha, Martha," but she had little hope that the dog would hear her. (C)

Julie continued up the rocks. In some places she had to climb the rocks the way you would climb a ladder. She had trouble holding the flashlight and going up the steep rocks. Once, her bad leg slipped and she crashed into a rock. She hurt her ribs, but even worse, the fall did something to the flashlight. It still worked most of the time, but it would grow dim and go out. By banging it against the palm of her other hand, she could make the beam come on. (D)

For nearly half an hour she climbed up the side of the rocky ridge. She knew that she wasn't following the same path that her father had taken. She knew that he would have led the dogs up a trail that was easier to climb than the one she was on. But she didn't know where that trail was. She knew only that he had probably gone to the top of the rocky ridge, and she figured that as long as she was climbing up, she would get to the top. (E)

At last, Julie reached the top. She limped along easily on top of the smooth

Lesson 63 Textbook   **241**

ridge. Things were brighter up there. The sky was clear and the moon shone so brightly that she could see her shadow. She turned off the flashlight and stuffed it into her pocket. Then she cupped her hands around her mouth and called, "Martha, Martha." She continued to call until her voice started to become hoarse. (F)

★ **8 ERRORS** ★

Suddenly, Julie saw Martha's dark form casting along the flat surface of the ridge. "Martha," she called again. The dog stopped, turned, and ran over to her. Julie could tell from Martha's behavior that she had lost the trail.

Julie took off her mittens, and tried to fasten the leash to Martha's collar. Julie's fingers were becoming so numb that she could hardly feel what she was doing. But finally, she managed to hook the leash onto the metal ring of the collar. Julie was blowing on her hands to warm them, when she noticed two dots of light in the valley to the south. She quickly took out her flashlight, pushed the button forward, and pounded the flashlight four times against her palm until the beam came on brightly. Then she pointed the flashlight in the direction of the lights below and waved it back and forth. Soon, the other lights responded by moving back and forth.

Julie then removed her father's gloves from her pocket, held them in front of Martha's nose, and said, "Daddy. Go find Daddy."

The young hound wagged her tail, turned away, and began to pull on the leash. She was trying to return to the place where she had lost the scent. Martha had followed the trail of Julie's father to a large rocky flat area on top of the ridge, but the scent had become so faint that she couldn't follow it. She led Julie back to the flat area. She sniffed and pulled Julie, first in one direction, then in another. At last, Martha caught a very faint scent. She raised her head and signaled her find with a little yelp. Then she pulled forward with so much power that Julie almost stumbled. "Good dog," Julie said. "Go find Daddy."

Martha followed the scent for about a hundred feet, when she started to move in small circles. She had lost the scent again. She stuffed her nose into cracks between the rocks and sniffed so loudly that Julie could hear the sniffs above the wind. Suddenly, Martha raised her head and gave another little bark. She once more pulled Julie forward.

Suddenly, Julie turned around and noticed that the lights were approaching very fast from the south. She didn't want to stop searching because she was afraid that if Martha lost the faint scent, she might not find the trail again. "Go find Daddy," she said, following Martha who was pulling on the leash again.

As Julie continued to follow Martha, she heard voices calling above the wind. "Bill," a man's voice called. "Is that you, Bill?"

"It's me, Julie!" she shouted, still following Martha.

Within a few minutes, the lights were very close and Julie could recognize the voices. They belonged to Mr. Whitebird,

242   Lesson 63 Textbook

EXERCISE 4   Decoding and comprehension

1. Everybody, turn to page 241 in your textbook. *Wait. Call on a student.* What's the error limit for this lesson? **8 errors.**
2. *Call on individual students to read. Present the tasks specified for each circled letter.*

(A) Could Julie keep up with Martha? **No.**
- Why not? *Idea:* Because she limped.
- How did Julie know where Martha was? *Idea:* She could hear Martha barking.
- How did Julie know that Martha was tracking her father and not some other animal? *Idea:* Because of the sound of the barks.
- What kind of noise would Martha make when she was tracking an animal? *Idea:* Martha would howl.

(B) Why did Julie have a dismal feeling? *Idea:* Because dogs can't track on the rocky ridge.
- Why did Julie have doubts that Martha would be able to find Julie's father? *Idea:* The other dogs had lost the scent of animals on the rocks.

(C) How long did it take Julie to reach the steep slopes of the rocky ridge? *Idea:* Over half an hour.
- Did she have both hands in her pockets to keep them warm? **No.**
- Why not? *Idea:* She had to hold the flashlight.

(D) What happened to Julie when she fell? *Idea:* She hurt her ribs.
- What happened to her flashlight? *Idea:* It broke.
- How did the flashlight behave after that fall? *Idea:* It kept getting dim and then going out.
- What would Julie do to make the light come back on? *Idea:* Slap it against the palm of her hand.

(E) Did Martha follow the same path Julie's father took? **Yes.**
- Was Julie following the same path that her father took? **No.**
- Why couldn't Julie keep up with Martha? *Idea:* Julie was crippled.

(F) What happens to your voice when it becomes hoarse? *Idea:* You can hardly talk.
- What made Julie's voice hoarse? *Idea:* Calling Martha.
- Why did Julie turn off the flashlight when she reached the top of the rocky ridge? *Idea:* She could see in the moonlight.
- The story says, **She limped along easily.** Why was it easier for her to walk now than it was when she was going up the side of the ridge? *Idea:* The top of the ridge was flat and smooth.
- Read the rest of the story to yourselves and be ready to answer some questions.

her mother, and another neighbor, Mr. Taylor. The three of them were trying to find Mr. Owl on the rocky surface. When the party grew close, Julie's mother shouted, "Julie, what are you doing out here?"

Before Julie could answer, Mr. Whitebird asked, "Where's your father?"

"I don't know," Julie said, "but Martha's on his trail."

"She can't be," Mr. Whitebird said as he trotted up to Julie. He caught his breath and then continued, "No dog alive can track over these rocks."

"Martha can," Julie said hoarsely.

Julie's mother threw her arms around

Julie. "Julie, Julie," she said. "What on earth are you doing out here? You'll freeze to death."

"Mom," Julie said, "Martha's on Dad's trail. She's followed him all the way up here."

Julie could see the dim outline of Mr. Taylor shaking his head. "You better get yourself back home," he said flatly. "That dog is just taking you on a wild goose chase."

"No she isn't!" Julie protested. "She's tracking."

At that moment, Martha caught the scent of a rabbit. It was a marvelous scent, the kind that hound dogs dream about. With a great pull on the leash she lunged forward and let out a long, "Oooooooo."

She pulled Julie so hard and unexpectedly that Julie slipped and went sprawling on the rocks. Mr. Taylor helped her up and Mr. Whitebird grabbed Martha's leash.

"No," Julie protested. "That's not the signal she makes for Daddy's trail. She must have picked up a different scent. But I'm telling you she was on Daddy's trail."

The two men looked at each other as Julie's mother knelt down beside her to see if she was all right.

Then Mr. Taylor patted Julie on the shoulder. "You know," he said slowly, "you may be right."

Mr. Whitebird added, "I don't know what that dog was just tracking, but she sure was tracking something. And I've never seen a dog that could track anything up here. So, maybe we should give her a chance to show what she can do."

"She'll do it," Julie said, fumbling in her pocket for her father's gloves. "She'll do it. You'll see." She held the gloves in front of Martha's nose again and told her, "Go find Daddy."

After all students have finished reading:

- Did Julie catch up to Martha on the rocky ridge? **Yes.**
- Was Martha on the trail when Julie found her? **No.**
- Why not? *Idea:* She had lost the scent.
- What did Julie notice in the valley to the south? *Idea:* Lights.
- How did Julie signal to the people? *Idea:* With her flashlight.
- How did they signal back? *Idea:* They waved their lights.
- Did Julie stop and wait for them? **No.**
- Why did Julie encourage Martha to keep sniffing for the trail? *Idea:* She didn't want Martha to lose the scent.
- Name the people in the party that caught up to Julie. *Idea:* Mr. Whitebird, Julie's mother, Mr. Taylor.
- When they first called to Julie, who did they think she was? *Idea:* Julie's father.
- At first did they believe that Martha had tracked Julie's father? **No.**
- Why not? *Idea:* No dog could track a scent on the ridge.
- What scent did Martha pick up when they were talking? *Idea:* The scent of a rabbit.
- How did Julie know that it wasn't the scent of her father? *Idea:* Because Martha howled.
- Why did Mr. Whitebird and Mr. Taylor think that it was possible that Martha was tracking Julie's father? *Idea:* Because they had seen her track the rabbit.

Award 4 points or have the students reread to the error limit sign.

INDEPENDENT WORK

Do all the items in your skillbook and workbook for lesson 63.

ANSWER KEY FOR WORKBOOK

Review Items

1. Write which character could have made each statement. Choose from **Julie, Julie's father, Julie's mother, or Mr. Taylor.**
   a. "You should have stayed home and waited, as I told you to do."
      Julie's mother
   b. "I can tell by Martha's bark that she is on the right trail."
      Julie
   c. "Unless these two hounds stay close to me, I'll freeze from the cold."
      Julie's father
   d. "I've raised a lot of dogs and I know that Martha couldn't be tracking Bill's scent."
      Mr. Taylor

   e. "After I left the house I stopped at Mr. Whitebird's house and then we picked up another man who could help us." *Julie's mother*
   f. "My hand is terribly cold from holding the flashlight, but I'll keep on going."
      Julie
   g. "I hope somebody finds me pretty soon." *Julie's father*
   h. "You lost the scent, so I'll let you smell the gloves again."
      Julie

2. Write whether each statement describes **Martha** or a **brother** of hers.
   a. This dog was a runt. *Martha*
   b. This dog could track a scent on the rocky ridge. *Martha*
   c. This dog lived in a kennel.
      brother
   d. This dog went with Julie's father to be trained. *brother*
   e. This dog has the most sensitive nose in Kentucky. *Martha*
3. Look at the picture of the rocky ridge.

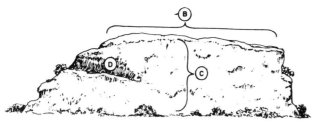

   a. Which letter shows the face? *C*
   b. Which letter shows a ridge? *B*
   c. Which letter shows a ledge? *D*

WORKCHECK AND AWARDING POINTS

1. *Read the questions and answers for the skillbook and workbook.*
2. *Award points for independent work as follows:*

0 errors	*6 points*
2 errors	*4 points*
3, 4, or 5 errors	*2 points*
5 or more errors	*0 points*

3. *Award bonus points as follows:*

Correcting missed items or getting all items right	*2 points*
Doing the writing assignment acceptably	*2 points*

ANSWER KEY FOR SKILLBOOK

PART B

1. *Idea:* Oz promised the characters that he would give them something.
2. *Idea:* The furniture in his house was dusty.
3. *Idea:* People have emotions.
4. *Idea:* Nellie could jump over barriers.

PART C

5. *Idea:* By the sound Martha made
6. a. *Idea:* To the rocky ridge
   b. dogs could not track there
7. a. Her ribs
   b. Her flashlight
   c. *Idea:* Hit it against her palm
8. a. No
   b. *Idea:* At the top of the ridge
9. was on
10. a. *Idea:* Lights
    b. *Idea:* Waved her flashlight
11. a. *Ideas:* Grow cold; fade
    b. Bill
    c. Mr. Whitebird; Julie's mother, Mr. Taylor
    d. No
12. a. A rabbit
    b. *Idea:* By the sound Martha made
13. Yes

PART D

14. a. tore
    b. soiled
    c. hardships
    d. misery
    e. intense
    f. determination
    g. kennel

Lesson 64

WORD PRACTICE AND VOCABULARY

EXERCISE 1   Vocabulary review

Task A

1. Everybody, find lesson 64, part A in your skillbook. *Wait.* Touch column 1. *Check.* First you're going to read the words in column 1. Then we'll talk about what they mean.
2. Touch under the first line. *Pause.* What words? *Signal.* **Wild goose chase.**
3. Next word. *Pause.* What word? *Signal.* **Sprawling.**
4. *Repeat step 3 for each remaining word in column 1.*
5. *Repeat the words in column 1 until firm.*

Task B

You've learned the meanings for all these words. The words in line 1 are **wild goose chase.** *Call on a student.*
What are you doing when you go on a **wild goose chase?** *Idea:* You are going after something you won't find.

Task C

Word 2 is **sprawling.** *Call on a student.*
What does **sprawling** mean? *Idea:* All spread out.

Task D

Word 3 is **hoarse.** *Call on a student.*
Say, "what time is it?" in a **hoarse** voice.
Student should speak in a hoarse voice.

Task E

Word 4 is **cast.** *Call on a student.*
What do dogs do when they **cast?** *Idea:* They go back and forth trying to pick up a scent.

Task F

Word 5 is **unexpectedly.** *Call on a student.*
What does **unexpectedly** mean? *Idea:* Something happens when you don't expect it.

Task G

Word 6 is **face.** *Call on a student.*
What is the **face** of a cliff? *Idea:* The part of a cliff that goes up and down.

Task H

Word 7 is **operate.** *Call on a student.*
What do doctors do when they **operate?** *Idea:* They fix something that is wrong with your body.

EXERCISE 2   Vocabulary development

Task A

1. Everybody, touch column 2. *Check.* First you're going to read the words in column 2. Then we'll talk about what they mean.
2. Touch under the first word. *Pause.* What word? *Signal.* **Intently.**
3. Next word. *Pause.* What word? *Signal.* **Emotions.**

Task B

1. Now let's talk about what those words mean. Word 1 is **intently.** When you do something **intently,** you concentrate on that thing. When you are listening intently, you concentrate on listening. Everybody, what are you doing when you concentrate on listening? *Signal.* **Listening intently.**
2. What are you doing when you concentrate on working? *Signal.* **Working intently.**

Task C

Word 2 is **emotions.** Your **emotions** are the different feelings that you have. Some emotions are anger, fear, and joy. Everybody, what are anger, fear, and joy? *Signal.* **Emotions.**

Lesson 64

Adventure on the Rocky Ridge
PART 5

Mr. Whitebird was holding Martha's leash. Mr. Taylor was next to him. Julie's mother put one arm around Julie as she and Julie tried to keep up with the others. Twice Martha tried to follow the rabbit's trail. Each time Julie shouted, "No!" and again let Martha smell her father's gloves. Ⓐ At last, the dog started to cast about for the scent. She went across the top of the rocky ridge, from one side to the other. Suddenly, she let out a sharp bark. "That's it!" Julie announced. "She's got it again!" Ⓑ

Julie heard Mr. Taylor say, "Look there! She is on a different trail now." Both Mr. Taylor and Mr. Whitebird raised dogs—not as good as those that Julie's father raised, but very good compared to most dogs. The men understood dogs very well, and they knew that Martha was very certain about the scent that she was now following. And they knew that it was not the same scent she had howled over earlier.

Martha went for another two or three hundred feet along the flat surface of the rocky ridge. Then she started down the other side. She was right on the trail that Julie's father had left. And she was only about one thousand feet from where he was lying at that moment. But when she started down the far side of the rocky ridge, Mr. Taylor pulled on the leash and stopped Martha. "I don't know," he said above the wind. "I can't picture Bill going down there. This is a very dangerous place."

Julie and her mother caught up to them. Mr. Whitebird explained. "I don't know if we should try to go down there. Maybe the dog has Bill's scent and maybe the dog doesn't. But there are some treacherous places down there. And I can't imagine why Bill would go down there."

"Martha's on his trail," Julie said in a much sharper tone than she had intended. Ⓒ

"But why would Bill go down there?"

Lesson 64 Textbook **245**

"I don't know," Julie said. "But . . ." Then she said, "Maybe one of the dogs got away and he went after it."

During the moment that followed, the wind blew bitterly. Finally, Mr. Whitebird said, "She may be right. There's some grass down there. Maybe one of the dogs picked up a scent and Bill went after it."

Mr. Taylor shook the leash and said to Martha, "Go find him."

Martha turned around for a moment, then she put her nose to the ground and began trying to find the scent. She was on a narrow, rocky path, so there was only one direction for her to go. She moved forward, stopping every few feet to search the cracks of the rocks for some sign. But the scent of Julie's father was now quite old and was almost gone.

The party moved slowly down the trail, but Martha gave no sign that she was tracking Julie's father. At last, the party came to a place where a large clump of grass grew out of the rocks. When Martha was about four feet from the grass, she suddenly tugged forward. "Yep, yep," she said. Then much more loudly, she announced, "Arrr, arrrr."

A moment later there was a response from somewhere in the darkness ahead of them. This response came just as Julie was saying, "That's it. Martha's got . . ."

The response was a long wail of a hound. "Ooooooo." Ⓓ ★9 ERRORS★

246 Lesson 64 Textbook

STORY READING

EXERCISE 3 Decoding and comprehension

1. Everybody, turn to page 245 in your textbook. *Wait. Call on a student.* What's the error limit for this lesson? **9 errors.**

2. *Call on individual students to read. Present the tasks specified for each circled letter.*

Ⓐ Where were Julie and the others? *Idea:* On the rocky ridge.

● About what time was it? *Idea:* After one in the morning.

● What was the weather like? *Idea:* Cold and windy.

● How could Julie tell whether Martha was on the rabbit's trail or her father's trail? *Idea:* By the sound of her bark.

● What did she do each time Martha started to track the rabbit? *Idea:* Let Martha smell her father's gloves.

Ⓑ What does she have again? *Idea:* The scent of Julie's father.

Ⓒ Say, Martha's on his trail, the way Julie said it. *Idea: Student should speak in an intense tone.*

● Why do you think Julie spoke in a meaner tone than she had intended? *Ideas:* She was cold; tired; worried; she was sure she was right.

Ⓓ Who made that response? *Ideas:* Leader; Boomer.

● Where was that hound? *Idea:* With Julie's father.
So they must be very close to Julie's father.

● Read the rest of the story to yourselves and be ready to answer some questions.

14 Lesson 64

Everybody stopped as Mr. Taylor pulled back on Martha's leash. "Did you hear that?" Mr. Taylor asked.

"I heard something," Julie's mother said. "It sounded like Leader."

"I think it came from ahead of us," Mr. Taylor said. Then he flicked the leash and said, "Get him, Martha."

Martha pulled forward to the next patch of grass. "Arrr, arrr," she announced.

Everybody stood silently and listened intently for some sound above the wind. "Ooooooooooooooooo," came the reply.

"That's Leader, Leader," Julie's mother said. "Leader," she called. "Here, boy. Come here."

"Ooooooooooo," came the reply.

"Let's go," Mr. Whitebird said, and moved forward very cautiously over the jagged rocks.

"Bill, Bill," they called from time to time. "Can you hear us?"

At one time, two dogs howled in response.

"That's Boomer," Julie said. Her feet were numb from cold but she didn't even notice them. And she was almost exhausted because it took extra effort for her to walk. But she wasn't thinking about how she felt. Her mind was concentrating on only one thing—any sounds that could be heard above the wind. She searched every sound of the wind for a familiar voice.

At last the party came to the place where Mr. Owl had slipped. The scent was now very plain to Martha. She could smell

Mr. Owl below her. She could also smell Boomer and Leader. She stood at the edge of the trail, held her head high, and announced with a very loud voice, "Arrr, arrr."

"Help," a dim voice replied from down below.

Julie held onto Martha's leash as Mr. Taylor, Mr. Whitebird and her mother scrambled along the path looking for a place where they could climb safely down to Mr. Owl.

• • •

The trip back to Mr. Whitebird's station wagon was long and cold. The men cut some branches and fastened them to both sides of Bill's broken leg. Then, one man got on each side of Bill and they led him back up on to the flat surface of the rocky ridge. From there, the party moved slowly along the top of the ridge until they came to a path that was not very steep. That path led down to a place that was less than a mile from where Mr. Whitebird's station wagon was parked. Julie's mother ran ahead and drove the station wagon through the field to meet the party.

When everybody was in the station wagon with the heater on full blast, Mr. Taylor asked, "How are you doing, Bill?"

Slowly, Mr. Owl said, "I don't think I would have lasted the night. It was horrible."

Julie's mother put her arms around him and held her face next to his. "It's all right now," she said in a thick voice. "You're going to be okay."

Lesson 64 Textbook 247

Julie sat in the back of the wagon with the three dogs. She was glad and sad at the same time. She kept blinking and with each blink a tear fell down her cheek. Then suddenly, she kissed Martha on her head and said, "Oh, thank you so much."

Everybody turned around and looked at Julie. Then, everybody started to cry, even Mr. Taylor, who never showed any emotion. He patted Julie on the head and said, "Your daddy owes a lot to you, young lady." Then he coughed and pretended not to be crying. Boomer licked Mr. Taylor's hand. Nobody said anything for a long time. They just sat there, with the humming sound of the heater filling the wagon with wonderful hot air.

• • •

The story about Julie and Martha was told thousands of times during the next years. Martha grew up and had many litters of puppies. One time, she had a litter of fourteen. The morning after Martha

delivered that litter, Julie's father picked up the runt from that litter and said, "Don't worry, little one. Nobody's going to give you away. Maybe you'll be as great as your mother."

And that puppy was great, but not as great as Martha. Many people came from far off just to see Martha track. Even Leader knew that Martha was the finest hunting dog in the pack. When Leader lost a scent, he would hold his head up and look at Martha. Then he'd follow her.

Some nice things also happened to Julie. The next year her leg was operated on. The operation helped her walk better. But the doctor told her that she would still walk with a limp.

Julie wasn't disappointed. When the doctor announced that she would still have a limp, she looked at the doctor and said, "I don't mind. You don't have to be born perfect to be outstanding. I learned that from my dog, Martha."

248 Lesson 64 Textbook

- What did Mr. Whitebird and Mr. Taylor do for Mr. Owl's broken leg? *Idea:* Tied some branches to it.
- How did they help him walk? *Idea:* They stood on each side of him and held on to him.
- Who ran ahead to get the station wagon? *Idea:* Julie's mother.
- Did they go down the same way that Julie had gone up the rocky ridge? **No.**
- When they were in the car, who did Julie thank? **Martha.**
- Then what did everybody start to do? **Cry.**
- How did Mr. Taylor try to cover up his crying? *Idea:* He coughed and pretended he wasn't crying.
- Martha grew up and had many litters of puppies. Do you think those puppies were worth a lot of money? *Response:* Student preference.
- Why? *Response:* Student preference.
- Who became the finest hunting dog in the pack that Julie's father raised? **Martha.**
- How did Leader show that he knew that Martha was the best hunter? *Idea:* When Leader lost a scent, he'd look at Martha and follow her.
- Do you think Julie's father made a lot of money from Martha's puppies? *Response:* Student preference.
- What nice things happened to Julie the next year? *Idea:* She had an operation on her leg.
- Did the operation help Julie walk better? **Yes.**
- Did the operation allow her to walk perfectly? **No.**
- What did she tell the doctor when he announced that she would still have a limp? *Idea:* You don't have to be perfect to be outstanding.

Award 4 points or have the students reread to the error limit sign.

INDEPENDENT WORK

Do all the items in your skillbook and workbook for lesson 64.

ANSWER KEY FOR WORKBOOK

Map Skills

1. Look at the map.

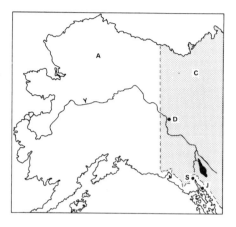

a. What's the name of town D?

Dawson

b. What metal was discovered near

that town? ___ *gold*

c. What's the name of river Y?

Yukon

d. What's the name of country C?

Canada

e. What's the name of state A?

Alaska

Crossword Puzzle

To work the puzzle, read an item and
figure out which word the item describes.
Then write the word in the puzzle.
Complete the entire puzzle.

Across

2. Grass that never grows tall is _____
   grass.
4. The top part of a long hill.
6. The part of the phone that you hold in
   your hand.
8. When you concentrate on something,
   you do that thing _____.
9. Soft feathers.

Down

1. The part of a cliff that goes up and
   down.
3. When you _____ for something, you
   try to keep picking it up.
5. A place where dogs are kept.
7. The different feelings that you have
   are your _____ .

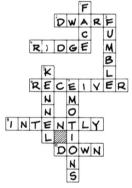

1. *Read the questions and answers for the skillbook
   and workbook.*
2. *Award points for independent work as follows:*

0 errors	....................6 points
2 errors	....................4 points
3, 4, or 5 errors	..............2 points
5 or more errors	.............0 points

3. *Award bonus points as follows:*

Correcting missed items
or getting all items right ....2 points
Doing the writing
assignment acceptably..........2 points

ANSWER KEY FOR SKILLBOOK

PART B

1. *Idea:* Some vehicles can cross the Pacific
   Ocean.
2. *Idea:* Angela liked to play sports.
3. *Idea:* Martha could track the scent of animals.
4. *Idea:* The trees in the park were beautiful.

PART C

5. **a.** *Idea:* A rabbit's scent
   b. let out a sharp bark
6. Leader
7. *Idea:* Made a splint for it
8. **a.** Julie's mother
   b. *Idea:* To get the station wagon
9. They cried
10. **a.** 14
    b. *Idea:* Nobody's going to give you away
11. **a.** Yes
    b. No
12. Martha
13. **a.** beginning
    b. beginning
    c. end
    d. end
    e. end
    f. end
    g. beginning

PART D

14. **a.** reappear
    b. decisively
    c. misery
    d. reluctant
    e. sensitive

Lesson 65

Lesson 65			
PART A	**Word Lists**		
1	**2**	**3**	**4**
airedale	greyhound	**Vocabulary words**	**Vocabulary words**
terrier	bloodhound	1. emotions	1. herding
Negroes	basketball	2. intently	2. biography
biography	football		

WORD PRACTICE AND VOCABULARY

EXERCISE 1   Word practice

1. Everybody, find lesson 65, part A in your skillbook. *Wait.* Touch under each word in column 1 as I read it.
2. The first word is **airedale.**
3. Next word. **Terrier.**
4. *Repeat step 3 for each remaining word in column 1.*
5. Your turn. Read the first word. *Signal.* **Airedale.**
6. Next word. *Signal.* **Terrier.**
7. *Repeat step 6 for each remaining word in column 1.*
8. *Repeat the words in column 1 until firm.*

EXERCISE 2   Word family

1. Everybody, touch column 2. *Check.* All those words are made up of two shorter words. Touch under the first word. *Pause.* What word? *Signal.* **Greyhound.**
2. Next word. *Pause.* What word? *Signal.* **Bloodhound.**
3. *Repeat step 2 for each remaining word in column 2.*
4. *Repeat the words in column 2 until firm.*

EXERCISE 3   Vocabulary review

Task A

1. Everybody, touch column 3. *Check.* First you're going to read the words in column 3. Then we'll talk about what they mean.
2. Touch under the first word. *Pause.* What word? *Signal.* **Emotions.**
3. Next word. *Pause.* What word? *Signal.* **Intently.**

Task B

You've learned the meanings for these words. Word 1 is **emotions.** *Call on a student.* What are **emotions?** *Idea:* Feelings.

Task C

1. Word 2 is **intently.** *Call on a student.* What does it mean when you do something **intently?** *Idea:* You concentrate on doing that thing.
2. Everybody, what are you doing when you concentrate on working? *Signal.* **Working intently.**

EXERCISE 4   Vocabulary development

Task A

1. Everybody, touch column 4. *Check.* First you're going to read the words in column 4. They we'll talk about what they mean.
2. Touch under the first word. *Pause.* What word? *Signal.* **Herding.**
3. Next word. *Pause.* What word? *Signal.* **Biography.**

Task B

Now let's talk about what those words mean. Listen to this sentence and see if you can figure out what the word **herding** means. Everybody, what word? *Signal.* **Herding.** Listen. The collie was so good at **herding** sheep that she could get 100 sheep inside the barn in less than a minute. *Call on a student.* What could **herding** mean? *Ideas:* Rounding up; leading.

Task C

Word 2 is **biography.** The true story of somebody's life is called a **biography.** Everybody, what do we call the true story of somebody's life? *Signal.* **A biography.** So the true story of George Washington's life is a **biography** of George Washington. Everybody, what is the true story of George Washington's life? *Signal.* **A biography of George Washington.**

Lesson 65

Dogs, Dogs, Dogs

Hound Dogs and Sled Dogs

You have read about two kinds of dogs that are very different from each other—sled dogs and hound dogs.Ⓐ The sled dog is a working dog. It is strong. It is able to sleep outside in a snowbank when the temperature is far below zero. The sled dog has so much endurance that it can go for days without food. The sled dog has a nose that is far more sensitive than yours, but that nose is very poor compared to the nose of a good hound dog. A hound dog lives to sniff new smells.Ⓑ You could see the difference between a one-year-old hound dog and a one-year-old sled dog if you were walking in a field with them. Let's say that you crossed the trail left by a rabbit. The hound dog would pick up the trail quickly. The sled dog might follow the hound dog. But if you called the dogs, the sled dog would obey your command while the hound dog would completely ignore you. The hound dog would stay on that trail, and the only way you'd get the hound dog off the trail would be to catch it, put it on a leash, and pull it off the scent.Ⓒ

Hound dogs that have very sensitive noses usually don't make good pets. They may love people, but they love to hunt so much more that they run away. They don't mean to run away. They go outside, pick up a scent, and follow it. Sometimes they don't come home for a day or two. Sometimes they get so far from home that they can't find their way back. When the hound gets to the age of four or five, it stays around home more. But when you let a younger hound outside, you may not see that hound again until the next morning, when it comes in all dirty and exhausted.Ⓓ

Dog Breeding

The hound dog and the sled dog do different kinds of work. The hound dog is very different from the sled dog.Ⓔ At one time there were not different kinds of dogs. The different kinds of dogs developed because people wanted dogs to do different kinds of work.

Here's how people made different types of dogs: They would select the best dogs from each litter. If people wanted a dog that was brave and strong, they would select the bravest and strongest puppies from each litter. When puppies are young you can tell a lot about which puppies will

Lesson 65 Textbook **249**

EXERCISE 5 Decoding and comprehension

1. Everybody, turn to page 249 in your textbook. *Wait. Call on a student.* What's the error limit for this lesson? **8 errors.**
2. *Call on individual students to read. Present the tasks specified for each circled letter.*

Ⓐ Name three ways that they are different in how they look. *Call on individual students. Ideas:* Sled dogs are heavier; stronger; have more fur.

● Name three ways they are different in how they behave. *Call on individual students. Ideas:* Sled dogs are more obedient; don't like to hunt as much; have more endurance.

Ⓑ Is the sled dog's nose more sensitive than your nose? **Yes.**

● How does it compare with the hound dog's nose? *Idea:* The hound dog's nose is better.

● A hound dog lives to sniff new smells. What does that mean? *Idea:* It's the most important thing in the hound dog's life.

Ⓒ Which dog would obey you when you call? **The sled dog.**

● Why wouldn't the hound dog obey you? *Idea:* The hound dog is too fascinated with hunting.

Ⓓ Which hound runs away more, a year old hound or a five year old hound? **A year old hound.**

● What does the young hound sometimes do if you let it run free? *Idea:* Goes away for a day or two.

Ⓔ What does that mean: **they do different kinds of work?** *Idea:* Hound dogs are used for hunting; sled dogs are used for working.

grow up to be brave fighters. You just observe how the puppy behaves when you scold it or spank it. If it rolls over on its back, it probably will not grow up to be a great fighter. If it just yelps and looks at you, without rolling over, it will probably grow up to be a fighter. (F) ★8 ERRORS★

Let's say that people keep only the best fighters from each litter. Let's say that the people keep doing this for a hundred years. At the end of the hundred years all the puppies in a litter will grow up to be far better fighters than the dogs that lived a hundred years earlier. These later dogs will look different from the earlier dogs, and they will behave a lot differently. When people develop a new type of dog they develop a new breed of dog.

By selecting only the dogs that are best for a job, people can develop new breeds of dogs that are friendly, or dogs that look pretty, or dogs that are good at herding sheep. They can develop breeds of dogs that are very tiny or breeds that are very huge. They can develop breeds with long hair or short hair, breeds with long ears or short ears, and even breeds with long tails or short tails.

New Breeds of Dogs

Today, there are about two hundred breeds of dogs. Most of these breeds are only a few hundred years old. Some are less than one hundred years old. If people wanted to develop a new breed, they would use a mixture of the breeds that are alive today.

Here are some dogs that people might use:

The greyhound is one of the fastest dogs. So, if people wanted a new breed of dog that had great speed, they would start with a greyhound.

The airedale is one of the best fighters and probably the bravest dog. So, if people wanted a dog that was so brave it would attack a bear, they could start with an airedale.

Collies and their relatives are the best herding dogs. So, if people wanted a dog to be good at herding animals such as sheep, they might start with a collie.

Hounds have the most sensitive noses, and the bloodhound may have the most sensitive nose of all hounds. So, if people wanted a dog that had a great sense of smell, they could start with a bloodhound.

Poodles may be the smartest dogs. Collies and sled dogs are also very smart, but poodles may be easier to train. So, if people wanted a dog that was very smart, they could start with a poodle.

Let's say that people wanted a dog that was very good at herding and very, very fast. They could start with a mother collie and a father greyhound. Some of the puppies of these parents might have the speed of the greyhound, and the herding ability of the collie.

If people wanted a very brave fighting dog that was extremely smart, they could start with a mother poodle and a father airdale. Some of their puppies might be very smart and very brave.

What could people start with if they wanted a breed of dog that had a very sensitive nose and was very, very fast?

What could people start with if they wanted a breed of dog that was very good at herding and very smart?

If people kept the best puppies from each litter and used those dogs as the parents for each new litter of puppies, they would probably have the kind of breed that they want within twenty or thirty years.

(F) How can you test a young puppy to see how brave it will be when it grows up? *Idea:* Observe how the puppy behaves when you scold it or spank it.

● Read the rest of the story to yourselves and be ready to answer some questions. Read the selection over twice to make sure that you get all the information about the different breeds of dogs.

After all students have finished reading:

● What do we call a new type of dog?
A new breed.

● How many breeds of dogs are there today?
About two hundred.

● If we wanted to make a new breed of dog with great speed, which dog could we start with? **A greyhound.**

● Why would we start with a greyhound? The greyhound is the fastest dog.

● What kind of dog could we start with if we wanted a breed that was very brave?
An airedale.

● What kind of dog could we start with if we wanted a breed that would herd animals very well? **A collie.**

● What does a dog do when it herds sheep? *Idea:* It makes sure they stay together.

● What kind of dog could we start with if we wanted a dog with a great nose? *Idea:* Hound.

● What kind of dog could we start with if we wanted a dog that was very smart? **A poodle.**

● What kind of breeds would we use for parents if we wanted dogs that were very fast and had a very good nose? *Idea:* Greyhound and hound.

● What kind of breeds would we use for parents if we wanted dogs that were good at herding and very smart? *Idea:* Collie and poodle.

● Which kind of breeds would we use for parents if we wanted dogs that were very brave and smart? *Idea:* Airedale and poodle.

● Remember the facts about the different kinds of breeds. You will need to use them later.

Award 4 points or have the students reread to the error limit sign.

INDEPENDENT WORK

Do all the items in your skillbook and workbook for lesson 65.

ANSWER KEY FOR WORKBOOK

Story Items

1. Pretend that you want a brave dog. Put the following events in the right order by numbering them from 1 through 3.

   2 You would select brave puppies from the first litter.
   1 You would begin with two brave parents.
   3 You would select brave puppies from the second litter.

3. Write **fact** or **fiction** for each statement.
   a. Dogs can be very brave.
      fact
   b. Dogs can talk to people.
      fiction
   c. People can go to the Land of Oz.
      fiction

Review Items

2. Write which color each thing is.
   a. The Land of the Munchkins
      blue
   b. The Land of the Quadlings
      red
   c. The Land of the Winkies
      yellow
   d. The Emerald City
      green
   e. Glinda's dress
      white

   d. The Land of Oz is described in a book. *fact*
   e. People looked for gold near Dawson.
      fact

WORKCHECK AND AWARDING POINTS

1. *Read the questions and answers for the skillbook and workbook.*
2. *Award points for independent work as follows:*

0 errors	*6 points*
2 errors	*4 points*
3, 4, or 5 errors	*2 points*
5 or more errors	*0 points*

3. *Award bonus points as follows:*

Correcting missed items or getting all items right	*2 points*
Doing the writing assignment acceptably	*2 points*

ANSWER KEY FOR SKILLBOOK

PART B

1. a. *Idea:* Sled dogs and hound dogs
   b. Sled dog
   c. Hound dog
2. a. Hound
   b. No
   c. Yes
3. a. Greyhound
   b. Airedale
   c. Collie
   d. Hound
   e. Poodle
4. a. Poodle and airedale
   b. Greyhound and collie
   c. Hound and poodle

PART C

5. a. Buck
   b. The Cat that Walked by Himself
   c. The Ugly Duckling
   d. Brown Wolf
   e. A Horse to Remember
   f. The Cat that Walked by Himself
   g. Adventure on the Rocky Ridge
   h. The Ugly Duckling
   i. Dick Whittington
   j. A Horse to Remember
6. a. afford
   b. misery
   c. sensitive
   d. determination
   e. kennel
   f. hoarse
   g. unexpectedly

Lesson 66

WORD PRACTICE AND VOCABULARY

EXERCISE 1   Word practice

1. Everybody, find lesson 66, part A in your skillbook. *Wait.* Touch under each word in column 1 as I read it.
2. The words in the first line are **Ebbets Field.**
3. Next word. **Brooklyn.**
4. *Repeat step 3 for each remaining word in column 1.*
5. Your turn. Read the first line. *Signal.* **Ebbets Field.**
6. Next word. *Signal.* **Brooklyn.**
7. *Repeat step 6 for each remaining word in column 1.*
8. *Repeat the words in column 1 until firm.*

EXERCISE 2   Word practice

1. Everybody, touch under the first line in column 2. *Pause.* What words? *Signal.* **Jackie Robinson.**
2. Next word. *Pause.* What word? *Signal.* **Athlete.**
3. *Repeat step 2 for each remaining word in column 2.*
4. *Repeat the words in column 2 until firm.*

EXERCISE 3   Vocabulary review

Task A
1. Everybody, touch column 3. *Check.* First you're going to read the words in column 3. Then we'll talk about what they mean.
2. Touch under the first word. *Pause.* What word? *Signal.* **Biography.**
3. Next word. *Pause.* What word? *Signal.* **Herding.**

Task B
You've learned the meanings for these words. Word 1 is **biography.** *Call on a student.* What is a **biography?** *Idea:* **The true story of somebody's life.**

Task C
Word 2 is **herding.** *Call on a student.* What does **herding** animals mean? *Idea:* **Rounding up animals in one place.**

EXERCISE 4   Vocabulary development

Task A
1. Everybody, touch column 4. *Check.* First you're going to read the words in column 4. Then we'll talk about what they mean.
2. Touch under the first line. *Pause.* What words? *Signal.* **Major leagues.**
3. Next word. *Pause.* What word? *Signal.* **Plant.**
4. *Repeat step 3 for each remaining word in column 4.*
5. *Repeat the words in column 4 until firm.*

Task B
Now let's talk about what those words mean. The words in line 1 are **major leagues.** The **major leagues** are the professional leagues with the best players.

Task C
1. Word 2 is **plant.** Another word for a **factory** is **a plant.** Another name for **a steel factory** is **a steel plant.**
2. Everybody, what's another name for **an automobile factory?** *Signal.* **An automobile plant.**
3. What's another name for **a tire factory?** *Signal.* **A tire plant.**

Task D
Word 3 is **bold.** When you are **bold,** you are confident. Everybody, what do we call somebody who is confident? *Signal.* **Bold.**

Task E
Word 4 is **daring.** When you are **daring,** you take chances. Everybody, what do we call somebody who takes chances? *Signal.* **Daring.**

Task F
Word 5 is **athlete.** An **athlete** is a person who competes in sporting events. Everybody, what do we call a person who competes in sporting events? *Signal.* **An athlete.**

Lesson 66

Facts about Baseball

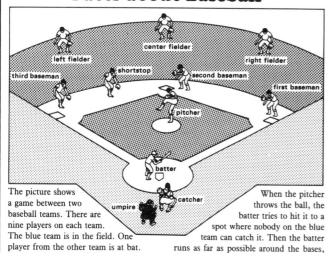

The picture shows a game between two baseball teams. There are nine players on each team. The blue team is in the field. One player from the other team is at bat.

The pitcher on the blue team throws the ball toward the catcher, who plays behind home plate. There are players at first base, second base, and third base. Between second and third base is another player called the shortstop. In the outfield, there are three more players: the left fielder, the center fielder, and the right fielder.

The player from the other team is standing at home plate, holding a bat.

When the pitcher throws the ball, the batter tries to hit it to a spot where nobody on the blue team can catch it. Then the batter runs as far as possible around the bases, starting with first base. If the batter can come all the way back to home plate, the batter scores a run.

The picture also shows an umpire right behind the catcher. The umpire calls out "Strike" for good pitches and "Ball" for bad pitches.

The selection that you will begin reading in this lesson is a biography of a famous baseball player: Jackie Robinson.Ⓐ

Jackie Robinson
by Duane Jefferson
Part 1

The year 1947 was a long time ago, but I can remember some things about that year as if they had happened yesterday. At that time, I worked in a meat-packing plant. The work was hard and I didn't like it very much. But I had one great interest that made the days more interesting. I was a sports fan.Ⓐ

I didn't just enjoy watching good athletes compete in sporting events—I loved it. Every chance I had I'd go to a football game or a basketball game or a boxing match. But my favorite team played right here in Brooklyn, New York. The team is no longer here. It moved to Los Angeles in 1958, and when the team moved I felt as bad as I would have felt if I'd lost my best friend. I loved that team. Today, they're called the Los Angeles Dodgers. But back then, they were the Brooklyn Dodgers.Ⓑ People used to call the Brooklyn Dodgers "the bums," but they sure weren't bums. They were rough and they were good.

I never missed a game on the weekends. The Dodgers used to play in Ebbets Field.Ⓒ And when the Dodgers played on Saturday or Sunday, I'd be there in the stands. I'd be yelling at the umpire. I'd be booing at the players from the other teams.

And I'd be cheering like mad for the Dodgers.

For me, the game wouldn't end when it was over on the field. At work the next Monday, we'd talk about the game. We'd go over every play of the game. I couldn't even begin to count the hours we spent talking about the Dodgers. Sometimes we'd talk about other teams. We'd argue about who was the best hitter, who was the best first baseman, or who was the best pitcher. But we'd always agree on one thing—the Dodgers were the greatest. Even if they didn't win, they were the best team to watch. They were bold and daring. They were tough. And when they played baseball, they played baseball.Ⓓ
★ 6 ERRORS ★

The other day I went to the place where Ebbets Field used to stand. It's not there any more. There's nothing but city there now. But when I stood on the corner where the entrance used to be, I had a very strange feeling. It was almost as if the clock had turned back to the year 1947. I could almost see Ebbets Field, with a line of fans waiting to get in. I could almost hear the great, hoarse roar that came from the stands when a Dodger hit a home run. I

STORY READING

EXERCISE 5   Comprehension passage

1. Everybody, turn to page 252 in your textbook.
2. *Call on individual students to read. Present the tasks specified for the circled letter.*

Ⓐ How many players from one baseball team are in the field? **Nine.**

● Which player plays right behind the batter? **The catcher.**

● How far must a batter move around the bases before a run scores? *Idea:* All the way around.

● Name the bases that a batter goes around, starting with first base. **First base, second base, third base, home plate.**

EXERCISE 6   Decoding and comprehension

1. Everybody, look at page 253 in your textbook. *Wait. Call on a student.* What's the error limit for this lesson? **6 errors.**
2. *Call on individual students to read. Present the tasks specified for each circled letter.*

Ⓐ Today you're going to start reading a biography of a great baseball player named Jackie Robinson.

● Whose biography are you going to read? **Jackie Robinson's.**

● Where did the person telling the story work? **At a meat-packing plant.**

● What made his days more interesting? *Idea:* He was a sports fan.

● How could being a sports fan make your days more interesting? *Idea:* You would enjoy watching sports.

● What year is the person telling this story remembering? **1947.**

Ⓑ What's the favorite sport of the person telling the story? **Baseball.**

● What team was his favorite team? **The Brooklyn Dodgers.**

● What is the team called today? **The Los Angeles Dodgers.**

● How did the person telling the story feel when the team moved? *Idea:* Bad.

Ⓒ Where did the Brooklyn Dodgers use to play? **Ebbets Field.**

● Where was Ebbets Field? **Brooklyn.**

Ⓓ The person telling the story sounds like a real fan. What did he mean when he said that the game didn't end when it was over on the field? *Idea:* People would talk about the game for days.

● His favorite team was the Dodgers. What was the favorite team of the people he'd talk to? **The Dodgers.**

● Where did a lot of the discussions about baseball games take place? *Idea:* At the place he worked.

● Read the rest of the story to yourselves.

must have stood on that corner for ten minutes, thinking back to 1947. A lot of games went through my mind, and I remembered a lot of great players. But as I stood there, the one player that my mind kept going back to was Jackie Robinson. It's amazing, but I can remember a game when the man sitting next to me said, "Why is that man wearing a Dodger uniform?"

I remember I turned to him and said, "Don't you read the papers? That's Jackie Robinson." I'd read about Jackie Robinson. Jackie Robinson was the first black man to play major league baseball, the very first one. And that day in the spring of 1947 was the first time anybody ever saw a black man playing in a major league baseball game.

If I'd known then what I know now, I would have stood up and yelled, "Yea for Jackie!" I would have said, "He's the greatest and we should be shouting for joy that he's in a Dodger uniform!" But most of the Dodger fans were not cheering. They were asking each other why a black man was dressed in a Brooklyn Dodger uniform.

I didn't learn much about Jackie Robinson from that first game. He didn't play very well. He didn't show any daring; he didn't do much of anything. I didn't know it at the time, but he was scared to death. He knew how people felt about him. He knew that everybody was looking for the slightest excuse to throw him out of the major leagues. But there was more to it than what we knew. Jackie Robinson couldn't play well if he felt everybody was against him. And when he walked out there on the first day in Ebbets Field, he felt like the most lonely person in the world. He was the only black player on the team—the only black man in the major leagues.

Some of the other players on the team wouldn't even talk to him. They wouldn't joke with him or help him out, or stick up for him. Can you imagine what that's like—when even the men on your team aren't with you? And your own fans don't cheer for you? And the newspapers are saying that the man who hired you made a terrible mistake and that you have no right to play in the majors? Can you imagine how lonely Jackie must have felt each time he walked up to the plate with his bat? Sometimes, when I think about that day and I realize what a fine, gentle person Jackie Robinson was, I get sort of choked up. But, as I said, I didn't know much about Jackie Robinson then.

- When the person telling the story was standing in front of the place where Ebbets Field had been, he remembered what happened during one year. What year was he remembering? **1947.**
- What person was he remembering? **Jackie Robinson.**
- In one way that person was the first to be in the major leagues. What way? *Idea:* He was the first black player.
- What team was Jackie Robinson on? **The Brooklyn Dodgers.**
- How did the Brooklyn Dodger fans respond to him the first time he came out in a Dodger uniform? *Idea:* They didn't cheer for him.
- How did the other players on the team respond to him? *Idea:* They didn't help him or support him.
- How did Jackie Robinson feel? *Idea:* Very lonely.
- When something happened, Jackie Robinson couldn't play well. When couldn't he play well? *Idea:* When he thought everyone was against him.
- Did he feel that he was alone at first? **Yes.**
- So, how did he play? *Idea:* Poorly.

Award 4 points or have the students reread to the error limit sign.

FACT GAME

FACT GAME SCORECARD

1	2	3	4	5	6	7	8	9	10
11	12	13	14	15	16	17	18	19	20
21	22	23	24	25	26	27	28	29	30

Fact Game

2. Tell which character wanted each thing from Oz.
   a. Courage
   b. A trip back to Kansas
   c. A heart
   d. Brains
3. a. Which metal was discovered near Dawson in 1896?
   b. Which river flows through Dawson?
   c. Which story took place near Dawson?
4. Tell whether each thing is **fact** or **fiction.**
   a. An article about California in an encyclopedia.
   b. A story about a wizard.
   c. A novel about a brave dog.
5. Tell whether each statement is **true** or **false.**
   a. Mount Whitney is in California.
   b. California is one of the smallest states.
   c. Redwoods are shorter than oak trees.
6. Tell whether each animal was used for **hunting, food,** or **carrying things.**

a. elephant
b. sheep
c. dog
d. donkey
7. Tell which dog each statement describes.
   a. This dog saved John Thornton's life.
   b. This dog lived in California.
   c. This dog tracked a person over a rocky ridge.
8. a. What is the name of the horse race that includes barriers and obstacles?
   b. In which country does the Grand National Championship take place?
9. a. What's the class name for animals that do not live with people?
   b. What's the class name for animals that live with people?
10. a. Which breed of dog is very fast?
    b. Which breed of dog is good at herding sheep?
    c. Which breed of dog has the best sensitive nose?
11. Tell which **land** each group of people lived in.
    a. Gillikins
    b. Quadlings
    c. Munchkins
    d. Winkies
12. a. Who was the first black man to play major league baseball?
    b. Which team did he play for?
    c. Which ball park did that team play in?

EXERCISE 7 Fact game

1. Everybody, find lesson 66 in your workbook. *Wait.* You're going to play a game that uses the facts you have learned. Here are the rules: The player rolls the dice, figures out the number of the question, reads that question out loud, and answers it. The monitor tells the player if the answer is right or wrong. If it's wrong, the monitor tells the right answer. If it's right, the monitor gives the player one point. Don't argue with the monitor. The dice goes to the left and the next player has a turn.

2. If the game goes smoothly, all players in that game will earn 5 bonus points. I'll tell the groups whether they earn the bonus points. Each player who gets more than 13 points will earn another 5 bonus points. You'll play the game for 20 minutes.

3. *Divide students into groups of four or five. Assign monitors. Tell monitors the answers are on workbook page 143. Circulate as students play the game. Comment on groups that are playing well.*

4. *At the end of 20 minutes, have all students who earned more than **13 points** stand up. Award 5 bonus points to those players. Award points to monitors. Monitors receive the number of points earned by the highest performer in the group.*

• *Tell the monitor of each game that ran smoothly:* Your group did a good job. Give yourself and each of your players 5 bonus points.

• Everybody, write your game points in box FG on your point chart. Write your bonus points in the **bonus** box.

INDEPENDENT WORK

Do all the items in your skillbook and workbook for lesson 66.

WORKCHECK AND AWARDING POINTS

1. *Read the questions and answers for the skillbook and workbook.*
2. *Award points for independent work as follows:*

> 0 errors . . . . .6 points
> 2 errors .4 points
> 3, 4, or 5 errors . . . . .2 points
> 5 or more errors . . . . .0 points

3. *Award bonus points as follows:*

> *Correcting missed items*
> *or getting all items right* . . . .*2 points*
> *Doing the writing*
> *assignment acceptably* . . . .*2 points*

ANSWER KEY FOR SKILLBOOK

PART B

1. **a.** Nine
   b. The catcher
   c. The umpire
   d. First base
   e. Home plate
2. **a.** Jackie Robinson
   b. 1947
   c. Brooklyn Dodgers
3. **a.** Los Angeles
   b. Ebbets Field
   c. No
4. **a.** In a meat-packing plant
   b. *Idea:* Sports
5. **a.** No
   b. No
   c. No
   d. *Idea:* against
   e. *Idea:* Well

PART C

6. **a.** Poodle
   b. Collie
   c. Hound
   d. Greyhound
   e. Airedale
7. **a.** A
   b. C
   c. B
8. **a.** D
   b. B
   c. C
9. **a.** very strong
   b. reluctant
   c. fumbled
   d. sprawling
   e. intently
   f. emotions

ANSWER KEY FOR FACT GAME

2. **a.** Lion
   b. Dorothy
   c. Tin Woodman
   d. Scarecrow
3. **a.** Gold
   b. Yukon River
   c. Buck
4. **a.** Fact
   b. Fiction
   c. Fiction
5. **a.** True
   b. False
   c. False
6. **a.** Carrying things
   b. Food
   c. Hunting
   d. Carrying things
7. **a.** Buck
   b. Brown Wolf
   c. Martha
8. **a.** Steeplechase
   b. England
9. **a.** Wild animals
   b. Domestic animals
10. **a.** Greyhound
    b. Collie
    c. Hound
11. **a.** Land of the North
    b. Land of the South
    c. Land of the East
    d. Land of the West
12. **a.** Jackie Robinson
    b. Brooklyn Dodgers
    c. Ebbets Field

Lesson 67

Lesson 67

PART A   **Word Lists**

1	2	3	4
inspiration	Pearl Harbor	Branch Rickey	**Vocabulary words**
appreciation	Kansas City	Eddie Stanky	1. bold
narrator	Pittsburgh	lousy	2. plant
	Georgia	fault	3. daring
	Hawaii	articles	4. athlete
	Honolulu	addition	
	Germany	additional	
	Missouri		
	Montreal		
	Kentucky		

5
Vocabulary words
1. steal a base
2. National League Pennant
3. resent
4. dugout
5. talented
6. insult
7. appreciation
8. rookie
9. narrator

WORD PRACTICE AND VOCABULARY

EXERCISE 1   Word practice

1. Everybody, find lesson 67, part A in your skillbook. *Wait.* Touch under each word in column 1 as I read it.
2. The first word is **inspiration.**
3. Next word. **Appreciation.**
4. *Repeat step 3 for **narrator.***
5. Your turn. Read the first word. *Signal.* **Inspiration.**
6. Next word. *Signal.* **Appreciation.**
7. *Repeat step 6 for **narrator.***
8. *Repeat the words in column 1 until firm.*

EXERCISE 2   Word family

1. Everybody, touch column 2. *Check.* The words in column 2 are names of places you'll be reading about.
2. Touch under the first line. *Check.* Those words are **Pearl Harbor.** What words? *Signal.* **Pearl Harbor.**
3. Next line. *Pause.* Those words are **Kansas City.** What words? *Signal.* **Kansas City.**
4. Next word. *Pause.* That word is **Pittsburgh.** What word? *Signal.* **Pittsburgh.**
5. *Repeat step 4 for each remaining word in column 2.*
6. Now let's see if you remember all those words. Touch under the first line in column 2. *Pause.* What words? *Signal.* **Pearl Harbor.**
7. Next line. *Pause.* What words? *Signal.* **Kansas City.**
8. Next word. *Pause.* What word? *Signal.* **Pittsburgh.**
9. *Repeat step 8 for each remaining word in column 2.*
10. *Repeat the words in column 2 until firm.*

EXERCISE 3   Word practice

1. Everybody, touch under the first line in column 3. *Pause.* What words? *Signal.* **Branch Rickey.**
2. Next line. *Pause.* What words? *Signal.* **Eddie Stanky.**
3. Next word. *Pause.* What word? *Signal.* **Lousy.**
4. *Repeat step 3 for each remaining word in column 3.*
5. *Repeat the words in column 3 until firm.*

EXERCISE 4   Vocabulary review

Task A
1. Everybody, touch column 4. *Check.* First you're going to read the words in column 4. Then we'll talk about what they mean.
2. Touch under the first word. *Pause.* What word? *Signal.* **Bold.**
3. Next word. *Pause.* What word? *Signal.* **Plant.**
4. *Repeat step 3 for each remaining word in column 4.*
5. *Repeat the words in column 4 until firm.*

Task B
You've learned the meanings for all these words. Word 1 is **bold.** *Call on a student.* What does **bold** mean? *Idea:* Confident.

Task C

Word 2 is **plant.** *Call on a student.*
What is a **plant?** *Idea:* A factory.

Task D

Word 3 is **daring.** *Call on a student.*
What is a **daring** person? *Idea:*
A person who takes chances.

Task E

Word 4 is **athlete.** *Call on a student.*
What is an **athlete?** *Idea:* A person who
competes in sporting events.

EXERCISE 5   Vocabulary development

Task A

1. Everybody, touch column 5. *Check.*
   First you're going to read the words in
   column 5. Then we'll talk about what they
   mean.
2. Touch under the first line. *Pause.*
   What words? *Signal.* **Steal a base.**
3. Next line. *Pause.*
   What words? *Signal.* **National League Pennant.**
4. Next word. *Pause.*
   What word? *Signal.* **Resent.**
5. *Repeat step 4 for each remaining word in column 5.*
6. *Repeat the words in column 5 until firm.*

Task B

Now let's talk about what those words mean.
The words in line 1 are **steal a base.** When a
baseball player **steals a base,** the player runs
to the next base before the batter hits the ball.

Task C

The words in line 2 are **National League
Pennant.** There are two major league baseball
leagues, the American League and the
National League. The team that wins the most
games in each league wins the pennant for
that league. Then the **National League
Pennant** winner plays the **American League
Pennant** winner in the World Series.
Everybody, what does the team that wins the
most games in the National League win?
Signal. **The National League Pennant.**

Task D

1. Word 3 is **resent.** When you **resent**
   something, you are angered by that thing.
   Here's another way of saying **She was
   angered by his cooking: She resented his
   cooking.** Everybody, what's another way of
   saying **She was angered by his cooking?**
   Signal. **She resented his cooking.**
2. Everybody, what's another way of saying
   He was angered by her dog? *Signal.*
   He resented her dog.

Task E

Word 4 is **dugout.** The **dugout** is the place
that baseball players sit in when they wait for
their turn at bat. The dugout faces the baseball
field. Everybody, what do we call the place
where the players sit while waiting their turn at
bat? *Signal.* **The dugout.**

Task F

Word 5 is **talented.** Somebody is **talented** if
that person has a lot of skill. A violin player
who has a lot of skill is a talented violin player.
Everybody, what's an athlete with a lot of skill?
Signal. **A talented athlete.**

Task G

Word 6 is **insult.** An **insult** is a name or
gesture that is supposed to make you mad.
Everybody, what do we call a name or gesture
that is supposed to make you mad? *Signal.*
An insult.

Task H

Word 7 is **appreciation.** When you show
somebody that you are grateful, you show your
appreciation. When Julie told Martha how
grateful she was, she was showing Martha her
appreciation. Everybody, what was she
showing when she showed how grateful she
was? *Signal.* **Her appreciation.**

Task I

Word 8 is **rookie.** A baseball player who is
playing in his first year is called a **rookie.**
Everybody, what do we call a player who is
playing in his first year? *Signal.* **A rookie.**

Task J

Word 9 is **narrator.** We call a person who tells
a story a **narrator.** Everybody, what do we call
a person who tells a story? *Signal.* **A narrator.**

Baseball

In the last lesson, you learned some facts about the players on a baseball team. Here are more facts about how the game is played:

The game goes for nine innings unless there is a tie. (The number of innings is easy to remember because there are nine innings and nine players on the field.)(A)

For each inning, both teams have a turn at batting. A team can keep on batting until that team has three outs. After the team has three outs, they go to the field and the other team takes a turn at batting.(B)

If a game is tied at the end of nine innings, the teams play additional innings. They continue to play until one team is ahead of the other at the end of an inning.(C)

Look at the scoreboard. It shows the scores made by the Dodgers and the Phillies. The number at the top of each column is the number of that inning.(D) The number in each box shows how many runs the team scored during that inning.

- Which team scored in the first inning? (E)
- How many runs did the Dodgers score in the first inning?(F)
- How many runs did the Dodgers score in the second inning?(G)
- So how many runs did the Dodgers have altogether at the end of the second inning?(H)
- How many runs did the Phillies have altogether at the end of the second inning?(I)
- How many runs did the Phillies have altogether at the end of the fourth inning?(J)
- How many innings did this game last?(K)
- What was the score at the end of nine innings?(L)
- Which team won the game?(M)
- What was the final score?(N)

	1	2	3	4	5	6	7	8	9	10	11
Dodgers	1	5	0	0	0	0	0	0	0	0	3
Phillies	0	0	2	2	0	0	2	0	0	0	0

256   Lesson 67   Textbook

STORY READING

EXERCISE 6   Comprehension passage

1. Everybody, turn to page 256 in your textbook.
2. *Call on individual students to read. Present the tasks specified for each circled letter.*

(A) How many players are on the field? **Nine.** That's how many innings there are in a regular game.

- How long does the game go unless there is a tie? **Nine innings.**
- What score would the two teams have if there is a tie? **The same score.**

(B) How many teams bat during each inning? **Both.**

- How many outs can each team have in an inning? **Three.**

(C) What do the teams do if the score is tied at the end of nine innings? *Idea:* They play additional innings.

- When does the game finally end? *Idea:* When one team is ahead at the end of an inning.

(D) Touch the column for the first inning. That's the column with 1 at the top. *Check.* Touch the column for the fifth inning. *Check.*

(E) What's the answer? **Dodgers.**
(F) What's the answer? **One.**
(G) What's the answer? **Five.**
(H) What's the answer? **Six.**
(I) What's the answer? **Zero.**
(J) What's the answer? **Four.**
(K) What's the answer? **Eleven.**
(L) What's the answer? **Six to six.**
(M) What's the answer? **Dodgers.**
(N) What's the answer? **Nine to six.**

EXERCISE 7   Decoding and comprehension

1. Everybody, look at page 257. *Wait. Call on a student.* What's the error limit for this lesson? **8 errors.**
2. *Call on individual students to read. Present the tasks specified for each circled letter.*

Jackie Robinson

PART 2 Ⓐ

After the first game that Jackie Robinson played, we had a lot of arguments at work. Some of the workers thought that Robinson had every right to be in the majors, but others didn't agree. I remember that one of the men who said that Jackie deserved to be on the team kept saying, "If you're a Dodger fan, you've got to be behind the whole team. That means you've got to be behind every player. When you're against one player, you're against the whole team." What he said kept running around in my head, and later on I admitted to myself that he had a good point. But I still wasn't a big fan of Jackie Robinson. Ⓑ

I began to change my mind after the fourth or fifth game of the baseball season. Ⓒ The way Robinson played sure didn't make me change my mind, because he was playing lousy. He'd been up at bat twenty times and he still didn't have one hit. What made me start changing my mind was the Phillies. Ⓓ The players on the Phillies would yell at Jackie Robinson from the dugout and call him names. Jackie never batted an eye. He didn't yell back. He just ignored them. Ⓔ

At first, we thought that Jackie Robinson had no fight in him. But then we started to find out the true story, Jackie had made a deal with the general manager of the Dodgers. Ⓕ The general manager at that time was named Branch Rickey, and he wanted to see black players have a chance to compete in major league baseball. He didn't like the idea that talented black athletes could not play in the major leagues. So he picked Jackie Robinson to be the first black player. Rickey knew that if Jackie failed, other black players would have a tough time getting into the majors. Ⓖ

Rickey also knew that the other major league teams didn't want black players. A couple of teams had said that they wouldn't play the Dodgers because there was a black player on the team. Branch Rickey knew that there would be problems—big problems. So he selected a player who was strong enough to take insults without fighting back. The player was Robinson. Before Jackie Robinson put on a Dodger uniform, he had agreed that he wouldn't fight or argue or cause any kind of trouble. Branch Rickey made Robinson promise all that because Rickey knew that if anything happened, nobody would consider who was really at fault. People would just say, "Robinson is a troublemaker. Throw him out of the majors." Ⓗ

Can you imagine how much courage it

Lesson 67 Textbook **257**

---

took _not_ to fight back and argue? Can you imagine what it would be like to know that you're as good—maybe better—than any other player on the field, and listen to them call you names? But Robinson kept his bargain with Branch Rickey. Ⓘ

★8 ERRORS★

Jackie Robinson just played ball, the best he could—which wasn't really very good when he felt that everybody was against him. But in one of those games with the Phillies, something happened that changed things.

The players from the Phillies were yelling at Jackie Robinson. Everybody on the Dodgers team knew that Robinson had made a bargain with Rickey. And they could see that Robinson had a lot of courage because he was keeping the bargain. So one time, when the Phillies were calling him names, the second baseman for the Dodgers—Eddie Stanky—yelled at the Philly players, "Why don't you yell at somebody who can answer back?"

Then the Dodger shortstop—Pee Wee Reese—went over and put his arm around Jackie's shoulder. He was showing everybody that he was on Jackie Robinson's side.

I started to get on his side, too. I'll tell you what it was like. Do you know how you can argue with your brother or sister and get mad at them? But if somebody else gets mad at them, you get mad at that person. That's how I felt. It was all right for me to be mad at Robinson. But there was no way that the Phillies could call him names. Robinson was a Dodger and as far as I was concerned, I was going to stick up for him against the whole Philly team.

Ⓐ In what year did the first black player play in major league baseball? **1947.**

● Who was that player? **Jackie Robinson.**

● How did the fans like him at first? *Idea:* They didn't like him.

● Did Jackie Robinson play well in his first game? **No.**

● Why not? *Idea:* Because he couldn't play well when he thought people were against him.

Ⓑ After the first game, someone at work said something that kept running around in the narrator's head. What did that person say? *Idea:* If you're a Dodger fan, you've got to be behind the whole team.

● If you're a fan, how would you show that you're behind a team? *Ideas:* Cheer for the whole team; go to all the games.

Ⓒ What did the narrator change his mind about? *Idea:* Being a Jackie Robinson fan.

Ⓓ The Phillies is the nickname for the Philadelphia baseball team. The narrator says the Phillies helped him change his mind about Jackie Robinson.

● Was Robinson playing well yet? **No.**

● How many times had he been up to bat? **Twenty times.**

● How many hits did he have? **None.**

Ⓔ What would Jackie Robinson do when the players on the Phillies called him names? *Idea:* Ignore them.

Ⓕ The general manager is the boss of the whole team.

Ⓖ What was the name of the general manager of the Dodgers? **Branch Rickey.**

● Why was it important for Jackie not to fail as a major league player? *Idea:* If he failed, other black players would have a tough time getting into the majors.

Ⓗ What had Branch Rickey made Jackie Robinson promise? *Idea:* Not to fight back.

● If Robinson got into a fight, would people care about who was really at fault? **No.**

● What would they say? *Idea:* Robinson is a troublemaker.

● If Jackie Robinson had been thrown out of the majors for being a troublemaker, would it have been easy for other black players to get into the majors? **No.**

● If Jackie Robinson did a good job, would it be easier for other black players to get into the majors? **Yes.**

So Branch Rickey didn't want to give anybody the chance to say that Jackie Robinson was a troublemaker. That must have been very, very difficult for Jackie Robinson to listen to insults from other players without saying anything.

Ⓘ Robinson kept his bargain, what did he do? *Ideas:* He didn't say anything; he didn't fight back.

But after the first few games, every Dodger fan had a reason for sticking up for Robinson. I already said he couldn't play well when he felt everybody was against him. But when he felt that somebody was on his side, he didn't just play well. He played like a fireball! After that day with the Phillies, he knew that the players on the Dodger team were on his side. And once he knew that, nothing could stop him.

He was something to watch. He seemed to stir up the whole team and make all the players play better. He could hit the ball. But when he got on base, that's when the action really started. He could steal a base as fast as you could blink your eye. He'd drive the pitchers on the other team crazy. One of them said that when he pitched against Robinson, he would rather have Robinson hit a home run than get a base hit. He said that with Robinson on the bases, he'd get so nervous that he could hardly pitch for the rest of the inning.

The Dodgers really started to play great ball in 1947, and the player that was most responsible for the team's success was Jackie Robinson. It wasn't just his batting and his base stealing that fired up the team. It was the man. He was a fierce competitor, and he played baseball as if his life depended on it. The other Dodger players seemed to pick up this fierce way of playing. They were daring. They were confident. And you never saw anybody loafing around on that team.

Jackie Robinson played so well and became such a leader that the Dodgers won the National League pennant in 1947. Near the end of the season they had a Jackie Robinson Day at Ebbets Field. Before the game, people made speeches about Robinson and how much they admired him. When it was Jackie's turn to talk, the crowd cheered long and loud. To show their appreciation, the owners of the team gave him a gold watch and an expensive car. And you could see that every player on the Dodgers and every fan in the stands was behind him.

After winning the National League pennant, the Dodgers played the New York Yankees in the World Series. I don't want to talk much about that series, because the Yankees won it. But the Dodgers still had a great year. They won the National League pennant and they had a new star—Jackie Robinson. He finished the season at .299. He scored 125 runs. He stole twice as many bases as any other Dodger. And of course, he was named the Rookie Player of the Year.

If anybody would have said anything against Robinson at the end of the 1947 season, I'd probably have given him a piece of my mind. But I really didn't know much about Jackie Robinson at that time. I knew him only as a dazzling ball player who had the speed of lightning and the courage of a lion. But I just knew about the ball player, Jackie Robinson—not about the man.

During the winter of 1947, I did a lot of reading about Jackie Robinson. I read just about everything I could find. And the more I read, the more I realized how much courage that man had.

Lesson 67   Textbook   **259**

- Read the rest of the story to yourselves and be ready to answer some questions.

After all students have finished reading:
- Which team were the Dodgers playing when the Dodgers showed that they were on Jackie's side? **The Phillies.**
- What did one Dodger do to show that he was on Jackie's side? *Idea:* Put his arm around Jackie's shoulder.
- The narrator said that he felt about Robinson the same way you feel about your brother or sister. Is it all right for you to get mad at that person? *Response:* Student preference.
- But what happens if somebody else gets mad at them? *Idea:* You get mad at that person.
- When couldn't Jackie Robinson play well? *Idea:* When he thought everybody was against him.
- When could he play well? *Idea:* When he thought people were for him.
- What did the incident with the Phillies show Robinson? *Idea:* That his teammates were for him.
- So what happened to his playing after that game? *Idea:* He played well.
- The narrator says that Robinson was most exciting when he was on base. Why? *Idea:* He could steal bases.
- What would happen to the pitchers on the other team? *Idea:* They would get very nervous.
- Which team won the National League pennant in 1947? **The Dodgers.**
- Which player was most responsible for the Dodger's success? **Jackie Robinson.**
- How did the fans and players feel about Jackie at the end of the season? *Idea:* They loved him.
- What did they do to show their appreciation to him? *Idea:* They had a Jackie Robinson Day at Ebbets Field.
- The narrator says that he knew Jackie Robinson as a ball player at the end of the season. When did the narrator start to find out about Jackie Robinson as a man? *Idea:* That winter.
- How did the narrator find out more about Jackie Robinson? *Idea:* He read newspapers, and magazines.

Award 4 points or have the students reread to the error limit sign.

INDEPENDENT WORK

Do all the items in your skillbook and workbook for lesson 67.

ANSWER KEY FOR WORKBOOK

Story Items

1. The scoreboard shows a game between the Dodgers and the Braves.

	1	2	3	4	5	6	7	8	9
Braves	0	0	1	0	1	2	0	0	1
Dodgers	0	1	2	3	0	0	2	0	0

a. How many innings did the game last? _9_

b. Which team scored a run first? _Dodgers_

c. In which inning did that team first score? _2nd_

d. How many runs did the Dodgers score in the ninth inning? _0_

f. At the end of the game the score was Dodgers _8_, Braves _5_.

2. a. When a team is not batting, how many of its players are in the field? _9_

b. How many innings does a game last if the teams are not tied? _9_

c. How many teams bat during each inning? _2_

d. Which base must the batter cross in order to score a run? _Idea: home plate_

e. Which base does a batter try to go to after reaching first base? _second base_

f. How many outs must a team make before the other team gets a turn at batting? _3_

WORKCHECK AND AWARDING POINTS

1. *Read the questions and answers for the skillbook and workbook.*

2. *Award points for independent work as follows:*

```
0 errors . . . . . . . . . . . . . . . . . . . . .6 points
2 errors . . . . . . . . . . . . . . . . . . . . .4 points
3, 4, or 5 errors . . . . . . . . . . . . . .2 points
5 or more errors . . . . . . . . . . . . . .0 points
```

3. *Award bonus points as follows:*

```
Correcting missed items
or getting all items right . . . . . . . . .2 points
Doing the writing
assignment acceptably . . . . . . . . . .2 points
```

ANSWER KEY FOR SKILLBOOK

PART B

1. a. Branch Rickey
   b. *Idea:* He wanted blacks in the majors
   c. Jackie Robinson
   d. *Ideas:* Ignore insults; not to fight back
   e. *Idea:* It would have been more difficult for other blacks to play baseball
2. a. 1947
   b. Brooklyn Dodgers
3. a. the whole team
   b. The Phillies
   c. *Idea:* Called him names
   d. *Idea:* Ignored them
   e. *Idea:* Put his arm around Jackie's shoulder
4. a. *Idea:* Better
   b. *Idea:* They were on his side
   c. *Idea:* Very well
   d. *Idea:* Steal the next base
5. a. The National League pennant
   b. Jackie Robinson
   c. No
   d. Rookie of the Year
6. 1947

PART C

7. a. North Carolina
   b. England
   c. Canada
   d. California
8. a. Hound
   b. Airedale
   c. Collie
   d. Poodle
9. a. afford
   b. decisive
   c. determination
   d. unexpectedly
   e. sprawling
   f. intently
   g. herding

Lesson 68

WORD PRACTICE AND VOCABULARY

EXERCISE 1   Word practice

1. Everybody, find lesson 68, part A in your skillbook. *Wait.* Touch under each word in column 1 as I read it.
2. The first word is **complain.**
3. Next word. **Conference.**
4. *Repeat step 3 for each remaining word in column 1.*
5. Your turn. Read the first word. *Signal.* **Complain.**
6. Next word. *Signal.* **Conference.**
7. *Repeat step 6 for each remaining word in column 1.*
8. *Repeat the words in column 1 until firm.*

EXERCISE 2   Word practice

1. Everybody, touch under the first word in column 2. *Pause.* What word? *Signal.* **College.**
2. Next word. *Pause.* What word? *Signal.* **Dribble.**
3. *Repeat step 2 for each remaining word in column 2.*
4. *Repeat the words in column 2 until firm.*

EXERCISE 3   Vocabulary review

Task A

1. Everybody, touch column 3. *Check.* First you're going to read the words in column 3. Then we'll talk about what they mean.
2. Touch under the first word. *Pause.* What word? *Signal.* **Insult.**
3. Next word. *Pause.* What word? *Signal.* **Rookie.**
4. *Repeat step 3 for each remaining word in column 3.*
5. *Repeat the words in column 3 until firm.*

Task B

You've learned the meanings for all these words. Word 1 is **insult.** *Call on a student.* What is an **insult?** *Idea:* A name or a gesture that is supposed to make you mad.

Task C

Word 2 is **rookie.** *Call on a student.* What is a **rookie?** *Idea:* A ball player who is playing in his first year.

Task D

Word 3 is **appreciation**. *Call on a student.*
What do you do when you show **appreciation?**
Idea: You show somebody you are grateful.

Task E

1. Word 4 is **resent**. *Call on a student.*
When you **resent** something, how does that
thing make you feel? *Idea:* Angry.
2. Everybody, what's another way of saying
Her insults made him angry? *Signal.*
He resented her insults.
3. Everybody, what's another way of saying
Her dog made him angry? *Signal.*
He resented her dog.

Task F

Word 5 is **talented**. *Call on a student.*
What does **talented** mean? *Idea:* Having a lot
of skill.

EXERCISE 4 Vocabulary development

Task A

1. Everybody, touch column 4. *Check.*
First you're going to read the words in
column 4. Then we'll talk about what they
mean.
2. Touch under the first line. *Pause.*
What words? *Signal.* **Run back a punt.**
3. Next line. *Pause.*
What words? *Signal.* **Long jump.**
4. Next word. *Pause.*
What word? *Signal.* **Complain.**
5. *Repeat step 4 for each remaining word in column 4.*
6. *Repeat the words in column 4 until firm.*

Task B

Now let's talk about what those words mean.
The words in line 1 are **run back a punt.**
When you **run back a punt,** you catch a
football that has been kicked and then run until
you're tackled.

Task C

The words in line 2 are **long jump.** When
athletes compete in a **long jump,** they run up
to a line and then jump as far as they can.
Everybody, what are athletes competing in
when they run up to a line and then jump as
far as they can? *Signal.* **A long jump.**

Task D

Word 3 is **complain**. When you **complain**, you
tell about something you don't like. Here's
another way of saying **She told that she did
not like the dinner: She complained about
the dinner.** Everybody, what's another way of
saying **She told that she did not like the
car?** *Signal.* **She complained about the car.**

Task E

Word 4 is **quarterback**. *Call on a student.*
What does the **quarterback** on the football
team do? *Ideas:* He's the first one that gets the
ball; he's the one that runs the team.

Task F

Word 5 is **mechanic**. A **mechanic** is a person
who fixes automobiles and other machines.
Everybody, what do we call a person who fixes
automobiles and other machines? *Signal.*
A mechanic.

Task G

Word 6 is **fury**. When you are **full of fury,** you
are **full of anger.**
Everybody, what's another way of saying
He was full of anger? *Signal.*
He was full of fury.
Everybody, what's another way of saying
She shouted and was full of anger? *Signal.*
She shouted and was full of fury.

Task H

Word 7 is **schedule**. When you **schedule**
something, you figure out where it will be and
when it will be. Here's another way of saying
**He figured out where and when the meeting
will be: He scheduled the meeting.**
Everybody, what's another way of saying
**She figured out where and when she would
do her homework?** *Signal.*
She scheduled her homework.

Lesson 68

Jackie Robinson

PART 3

I began to read everything that I could find about Jackie Robinson, and I learned a lot. I learned that when he was one year old his mother moved the family from Georgia where he was born to California.(A) There was a lot of love in Jackie's family. There just wasn't any money. Jackie had three older brothers and an older sister. And their mother had to work so that the family would be able to eat.(B)

Even though there was a lot of love in the family, you still wonder how Jackie ever made it. His family was so poor that they sometimes did not have enough to eat.(C) If you looked at Jackie a few years later, you'd have even more doubts that he'd ever be able to climb out of the world he lived in. When he was a young teenager, he became a member of a street gang—the Pepper Street Gang. They'd throw things at cars on the street. They'd knock out street lights at night. They'd go into nearby orchards and pick fruit from the trees. And sometimes they'd get caught by the police.(D)

Jackie's mother didn't like what was happening to her son, but Jackie wanted to belong to a group. He wanted to be on the same side as the other kids in the neighborhood. Something a mechanic said to Jackie made him think about things in a different way. The mechanic worked near Jackie's house. Jackie was complaining to his mother that all the other kids were in the gang, so why shouldn't he be? The mechanic overheard what Jackie said and told Jackie, "You're behaving just like a sheep." He told Jackie that sheep are stupid animals because they all follow one sheep without even thinking. Then he told Jackie, "You've got a good head, so use it, unless you want to be like a stupid sheep."(E)

Jackie remembered what the mechanic had said, but there was something else that may have saved Jackie. He was a talented athlete, like two of his older brothers—Mack and Edgar.(F) Both Mack and Edgar were fast. To give you an idea of how talented they were, when Mack went to junior college, he set a junior college long-jump record by jumping twenty-five feet. You can't really appreciate how far that is unless you step off twenty-five feet and then try to imagine somebody taking off at one end and flying through the air for that distance.(G) Later, Mack was on the United States Olympic team. He took second place in the two hundred meter dash. And one time, Mack set a world record

in the two hundred meter dash. Let me tell you, that young man had talent.(H)
★7 ERRORS★
Edgar also had a lot of talent. And when Jackie was young, he tried to imitate everything his brothers did. He ran; he jumped; he practiced. And that may have helped Jackie to make up his mind to put his efforts into sports. In high school Jackie played football, basketball, and baseball. He was a star in all these sports.

After high school, Jackie went to a junior college—the same one his brother Mack had gone to. And Jackie went out for football, basketball, baseball, and track. By now, sports were his whole life. And he played with a fierce sense of competition. He was a quarterback on the football team. Once he ran back a punt for eighty-three yards. He was a star.

In basketball he was also a star. During one game he scored a record number of points. In baseball, he was named the most valuable player of his junior college league. As you might guess, he was also a star in track.

There was one day that showed just what a fierce competitor Jackie was. There was a baseball game scheduled in one city and a track meet in a city forty miles away. These events were scheduled at the same time, and Jackie was on both the baseball team and the track team. So the track

---

EXERCISE 5 Decoding and comprehension

1. Everybody, turn to page 260 in your textbook. *Wait. Call on a student.* What's the error limit for this lesson? **7 errors.**
2. *Call on individual students to read. Present the tasks specified for each circled letter.*

(A) Where was Jackie born? **Georgia.**
• Where did Jackie Robinson's family move when he was very young? **California.**
(B) How many children were in the family? **Five.**
• Who was the youngest? **Jackie.**
(C) Was there love in Jackie's family? **Yes.**
• Was there money? **No.**
(D) When Jackie got older, what did he join? **A gang.**
• Name some things the members of that gang would do? *Ideas:* Throw things at cars; knock out street lights; steal fruit from orchards.
• Sometimes they'd get caught. Who would catch them? **The police.**
• How do you think that made Jackie's mother feel? *Ideas:* Bad; worried.
(E) What did the mechanic compare Jackie's behavior with? **A sheep.**
• How was Jackie's behavior the same as the behavior of a sheep? *Idea:* He followed without thinking.
• What did the mechanic tell Jackie that he should use? *Idea:* His head.
(F) How was Jackie the same as two of his older brothers? *Idea:* He was a talented athlete.
• What were the names of those brothers? **Mack and Edgar.**
(G) Which brother set a long-jump record in junior college? **Mack.**
• How far did he jump? **25 feet.**
• Step off about twenty-five feet and we'll see how far that is. Think about somebody jumping that distance. *Check.*
(H) In which event did Mack compete in the Olympics? **The 200-meter dash.**
• The best people from all over the world compete in the Olympics. So he was at least the second best in the whole world. At one time, he set a world record for the 200-meter dash. What does that mean: **a world record?** *Idea:* The best in the world.
• Read the rest of the story to yourselves and be ready to answer some questions.

After all students have finished reading:
• Name the sports that Jackie competed in when he was in junior college. **Football, basketball, baseball, and track.**
• One time in junior college, Jackie had a problem because two sporting events were scheduled at the same time. Which events? **Baseball and track.**

coach asked Jackie which sporting event he wanted to compete in. Jackie said, "Both." And he did compete in both.

The track coach arranged for Jackie to compete in the long jump early, before the other events. The idea was for Jackie to compete in the long jump, get into a waiting car, be driven forty miles, and play in the baseball game, which would be already under way. So Jackie did his first long jump. It was a good jump, a little over twenty-three feet. That was enough to win the event.

But Jackie wasn't satisfied. He said, "I can do better than that." So he jumped again. The second jump was over a foot farther than the first.

The guy that was going to drive Jackie to the baseball game said, "Fantastic. Now let's get out of here."

Jackie shook his head and said, "I can do better than that." So he went for his third try. And what do you think? He jumped twenty-five feet, six-and-a-half inches—over half a foot farther than the record set by his brother, Mack.

So then Jackie darted off the field, jumped into the car, and as he was being driven to the baseball game, he changed into his baseball uniform. There were only five innings left in the game by the time they got there. But he still managed to get two hits and help his team to a victory.

Competing in all those sports and competing as hard as Jackie did requires a lot of courage, and Jackie sure showed that he had courage. He was tough. The way he acted when he entered the major leagues was not the way he acted in high school or junior college. Remember, in the majors he

262   Lesson 68   Textbook

didn't say anything when people called him names or made fun of him. But if you understand the way he was when he was younger, you know how hard that must have been for Jackie. If somebody wanted to get tough with Jackie Robinson, Jackie was pretty good at getting tough right back. During one high school basketball game, a big player on the other team began hitting Jackie with an elbow and pushing him around. Jackie warned him to stop it. He didn't, so Jackie took one swing at him and floored him.

Junior college lasts only two years, and other colleges last four years. So when Jackie finished junior college, all the major colleges were after him. Jackie considered different colleges and at last he decided to go to UCLA. (That's the University of California at Los Angeles.) He had a lot of reasons for going there, but the main reason was sort of sad. You see, when he was younger, one of his brothers worked with him on running and dribbling a basketball and playing football. That was his brother, Frank. Frank wasn't like Edgar and Mack because Frank wasn't a star athlete. But he could sure coach, and he spent a lot of time working with Jackie, particularly when Jackie was getting started in high school and junior college. So when Jackie was making up his mind about the college that he would go to, he chose UCLA because it was close to home. He told reporters, "Frank likes to watch me play and he couldn't do that if I went to school far from home."

But there is a sad ending to that part of Jackie's story. While Jackie was at UCLA, Frank was killed in an accident. That made Jackie feel terrible, but he turned his sadness into fury and he played football, basketball, baseball, and track like a fireball. In football, he set a college record for returning punts. He gained more yards carrying the ball than any other ball carrier on the team. He also led the team in scoring. In basketball, he was the top scorer in UCLA's league, and he won that honor even though he didn't get to play in all the games. He couldn't play the first games because the basketball season started while the football season was still going on. In track, he was the best long jumper from any school in UCLA's league. But strangely enough, the sport that he did the worst in was baseball. He was great when he got on base, but he didn't bat well.

Anyhow, he was the first athlete in the history of UCLA to play on four teams—football, basketball, baseball, and track. He was considered the best all-round athlete in the United States. He could do anything. And if any person ever deserved a chance to play professional baseball with the best players in the world, it was Jackie Robinson, because he was among the best in the world.

Jackie set all those records in 1941, but for black athletes back in 1941, there was no real chance of playing in the major leagues. There were Negro leagues for black professional players, but there was no hope of playing in the major leagues.

Lesson 68   Textbook   **263**

- Which did Jackie choose to participate in? *Idea:* **Both.**
- Which event did Jackie compete in at the track meet? **The long jump.**
- In the track meet, was his first jump good enough to win the long jump? **Yes.**
- Was Jackie satisfied with that jump? **No.**
- How many times did he jump in all? **Three.**
- How good was his last jump? *Idea:* He broke the record.
- When Jackie got to the baseball game, how many innings were left? **Five.**
- So how many innings had been played already? **Four.**
- How many hits did he get in that game? **Two.**
- When Jackie was in the major leagues, he didn't argue or fight. Was that the way he was in high school and junior college? **No.**
- What happened one time when a player on the other team hit him with an elbow and pushed him around? *Idea:* Jackie hit him.
- What regular college did Jackie go to after finishing junior college? **UCLA.**
- Which sports did he participate in at UCLA? **Football, basketball, baseball, and track.**
- Which one of Jackie's brothers helped coach him when he was young? **Frank.**
- What happened to Frank while Jackie was at UCLA? *Idea:* He died.
- What was Jackie's poorest sport at UCLA? **Baseball.**

Award 4 points or have the students reread to the error limit sign.

INDEPENDENT WORK

Do all the items in your skillbook and workbook for lesson 68.

ANSWER KEY FOR WORKBOOK

Review Items

1. **a.** How many innings does a game last if there is not a tie? __9__
   b. When a team is not batting, how many of its players are in the field? __9__
   c. During each inning, how many teams get a turn at bat? __2__
   d. Which player stands between second base and third base? __*shortstop*__

2. **a.** Which major league team did Jackie Robinson play for? __*Dodgers*__

   b. Is Brooklyn on the west coast or the east coast? __*east*__
   c. What city did Jackie Robinson's team move to in 1958? __*Los Angeles*__

3. What did Jackie Robinson like to do when he got on base? __*Idea: steal*__

4. **a.** What did the Dodgers win in 1947? __*Idea: the pennant*__
   b. Who won the World Series that year? __*Yankees*__
   c. In 1947, Jackie won the __*rookie*__ of the year award.
   • rookie   • batter   • pitcher

WORKCHECK AND AWARDING POINTS

1. *Read the questions and answers for the skillbook and workbook.*
2. *Award points for independent work as follows:*

   > 0 errors . . . . .6 points
   > 2 errors . . . . .4 points
   > 3, 4, or 5 errors . . . . .2 points
   > 5 or more errors . . . . .0 points

3. *Award bonus points as follows:*

   > Correcting missed items
   > or getting all items right . . . . .2 points
   > Doing the writing
   > assignment acceptably . . . . .2 points

ANSWER KEY FOR SKILLBOOK

PART B

1. **a.** 1947
   b. Brooklyn Dodgers
   c. California
2. **a.** *Idea:* A street gang
   b. *Any one:* Knock out lights; steal fruit; throw things at cars
   c. *Idea:* She didn't like it
3. A sheep
4. Long jump
5. *Idea:* Sports
6. **a.** Two years
   b. Four years
   c. Junior college
7. **a.** *Idea:* Football, basketball, baseball, and track
   b. *Idea:* Very well
8. **a.** Track
   b. *Idea:* His brother's
   c. *Idea:* The baseball game
9. **a.** UCLA
   b. *Ideas:* So he could be close to home; so his brother, Frank could watch him play
   c. *Idea:* He died
10. **a.** *Idea:* Football, basketball, baseball, and track
    b. Baseball
    c. No

PART C

11. **a.** food
    b. hunting
    c. carrying things
    d. hunting
    e. carrying things
12. **a.** intense
    b. sensitive
    c. hoarse
    d. fumbled
    e. feeling
    f. herded
    g. athlete
    h. daring

Lesson 69

Lesson 69

PART A	Word Lists		PART B

PART B
Vocabulary Sentences

1	2	3
decent	strict	**Vocabulary words**
promote	restrict	1. fury
accuse	Japanese	2. complain
graduated	practice	3. schedule
career	sizzle	4. mechanic
Monarchs	organize	
Rae	organization	

1. The hotels <u>were restricted to white people</u>, so no black people could go in them.
2. Jobs were so hard to find that he couldn't find a <u>decent</u> job.
3. He was so interested in working as a coach that he decided to make coaching his <u>career</u>.
4. The pitcher became so <u>rattled</u> that he couldn't even hold the ball.

4	5
Vocabulary words	**Vocabulary words**
1. accused of	1. restricted to
2. promoted	2. decent
3. officer	3. career
4. graduate	4. rattled
5. scout	
6. organization	

WORD PRACTICE AND VOCABULARY

EXERCISE 1   Word practice

1. Everybody, find lesson 69, part A in your skillbook. *Wait.* Touch under each word in column 1 as I read it.
2. The first word is **decent.**
3. Next word. **Promote.**
4. *Repeat step 3 for each remaining word in column 1.*
5. Your turn. Read the first word. *Signal.* **Decent.**
6. Next word. *Signal.* **Promote.**
7. *Repeat step 6 for each remaining word in column 1.*
8. *Repeat the words in column 1 until firm.*

EXERCISE 2   Word practice

1. Everybody, touch under the first word in column 2. *Pause.* What word? *Signal.* **Strict.**
2. Next word. *Pause.* What word? *Signal.* **Restrict.**
3. *Repeat step 2 for each remaining word in column 2.*
4. *Repeat the words in column 2 until firm.*

EXERCISE 3   Vocabulary review

Task A

1. Everybody, touch column 3. *Check.*
   First you're going to read the words in column 3. Then we'll talk about what they mean.
2. Touch under the first word. *Pause.*
   What word? *Signal.* **Fury.**
3. Next word. *Pause.*
   What word? *Signal.* **Complain.**
4. *Repeat step 3 for each remaining word in column 3.*
5. *Repeat the words in column 3 until firm.*

Task B

1. You've learned the meanings for all these words. Word 1 is **fury.** *Call on a student.*
   What is **fury?** *Idea:* Anger.
2. Everybody, what's another way of saying **He felt full of anger?** *Signal.*
   He felt full of fury.

Task C

1. Word 2 is **complain.** *Call on a student.*
   What does **complain** mean? *Idea:* You say you don't like something.
2. Everybody, what's another way of saying **She told that she did not like the dinner?** *Signal.* **She complained about the dinner.**
3. Everybody, what's another way of saying **She told that she did not like the car?** *Signal.* **She complained about the car.**

Task D

1. Word 3 is **schedule.** *Call on a student.*
   What does **schedule** mean? *Idea:* You figure out where and when you will do something.
2. Everybody, what's another way of saying **She figured out where and when she would do her homework?** *Signal.*
   She scheduled her homework.

Task E

Word 4 is **mechanic.** *Call on a student.*
What is a **mechanic?** *Idea:* Someone who fixes automobiles and other machines.

EXERCISE 4   Vocabulary development

Task A

1. Everybody, touch column 4. *Check.*
   First you're going to read the words in column 4. Then we'll talk about what they mean.
2. Touch under the first line. *Pause.*
   What words? *Signal.* **Accused of.**
3. Next word. *Pause.*
   What word? *Signal.* **Promoted.**
4. *Repeat step 3 for each remaining word in column 4.*
5. *Repeat the words in column 4 until firm.*

Lesson 69

PART A Word Lists

1	2	3
decent	strict	**Vocabulary words**
promote	restrict	1. fury
accuse	Japanese	2. complain
graduated	practice	3. schedule
career	sizzle	4. mechanic
Monarchs	organize	
Rae	organization	

4
Vocabulary words
1. accused of
2. promoted
3. officer
4. graduate
5. scout
6. organization

5
Vocabulary words
1. restricted to
2. decent
3. career
4. rattled

PART B
Vocabulary Sentences

1. The hotels <u>were restricted to white people</u>, so no black people could go in them.
2. Jobs were so hard to find that he couldn't find a <u>decent</u> job.
3. He was so interested in working as a coach that he decided to make coaching his <u>career</u>.
4. The pitcher became so <u>rattled</u> that he couldn't even hold the ball.

Task B

Now let's talk about what those words mean. The words in line 1 are **accused of.** When you are **accused of** doing something, you are told that you are guilty of doing that thing. If somebody tells you that you threw papers in the hall, that person accuses you of throwing papers in the hall. Everybody, what is somebody doing if that person tells you that you came in late? *Signal.*
Accusing you of coming in late.

Task C

Word 2 is **promoted.** When you are **promoted,** you get a more important job. Everybody, what happens to you when you get a more important job? *Signal.*
You are promoted.

Task D

Word 3 is **officer.** An **officer** in an army is a person who is in charge. When you're an officer, you may be a lieutenant, a captain, a major, or a general. Everybody, what do we call captains, majors, lieutenants, or generals? *Signal.* **Officers.**

Task E

Word 4 is **graduate.** When you **graduate** from school, you successfully complete your work in that school. Everybody, what happens after you successfully complete your work in a school? *Signal.* **You graduate.**

Task F

Word 5 is **scout.** A **scout** for a baseball team looks around at players in college and other places to find players that the team might hire.

Task G

Word 6 is **organization.** Another name for a **business** is an **organization.** Everybody, what's another name for a business? *Signal.*
An organization.

EXERCISE 5 Vocabulary from context

Task A

1. Everybody, touch column 5. *Check.*
   First you're going to read the words in column 5. Then we'll talk about what they mean.
2. Touch under the first line. *Pause.*
   What words? *Signal.* **Restricted to.**
3. Next word. *Pause.*
   What word? *Signal.* **Decent.**
4. *Repeat step 3 for each remaining word in column 5.*
5. *Repeat the words in column 5 until firm.*

Task B

1. Everybody, find part B in your skillbook. *Check.*
   I'll read those sentences. You figure out what the underlined part in each sentence means.
2. Sentence one. The hotels were <u>restricted to white people</u>, so no black people could go in them. *Call on a student.* What could **restricted to white people** mean? *Idea:* Only white people were let in.
3. *Repeat step 2 for each remaining sentence.*
   Answer Key: **2.** *Idea:* Good
   3. *Idea:* Main job
   4. *Idea:* Nervous

STORY READING

EXERCISE 6 Comprehension passage

1. Everybody, turn to page 264 in your textbook.
2. *Call on individual students to read. Present the tasks specified for the circled letter.*

Lesson 69

The Brooklyn Baseball Organization

The chart below shows how the Brooklyn baseball organization worked.

Players start with the minor league team. If they are very good, they go up to the major league team. The general manager is in charge of all the teams. Ⓐ

Jackie Robinson

PART 4

In 1941, a lot of sports fans wanted to know why Jackie Robinson quit college before he graduated. He had been an excellent student with very good grades but he quit school mysteriously. People asked why, but he didn't answer. He was angry with the whole system. Here he was, a big college star, and his mother still had to work for very little money. And Jackie saw his brother, Mack, trying to find odd jobs like cleaning up somebody's yard. A couple of years before, Mack had been the pride of the United States, winner of a medal in the Olympics. But now he couldn't even get a decent job. Why? Because he was black and there weren't many good jobs for black people. Ⓐ

So Jackie looked at his brother, Mack, and looked at his mother, and said to himself, "There is no point in continuing with

this sports career." What would he get for the hours that he put in practicing? What difference did it make that he had more sports talent than just about anybody in the world? He was black, and black players didn't play major league baseball, major league football, or any other major league sport. They could play in the Negro leagues, but the players in these leagues didn't earn very much money, and had to lead a very tough life.

So Jackie quit school and took a job, and then another job. In 1941, he ended up in Hawaii. During the week he worked on a construction job. On the weekends, he played professional football with a team named the Honolulu Bears. Then on one Sunday in December, something terrible happened. The Japanese attacked Pearl Harbor, which is in Hawaii. On the same day, the United States declared war against Japan and Germany. The United States was now a part of World War Two. Ⓑ

The day that we entered World War Two was a sad day. I remember sitting by the radio all day long, listening to the news. At first, we figured that the war would be over in a couple of months. But the war lasted until 1945. Ⓒ

Within a couple of months after the war began, Jackie Robinson was in the Army. He was such a strong leader that he was promoted to an officer within two years. He was in charge of a whole outfit.

The Army was divided into black outfits and white outfits. Jackie was in charge of a black outfit. The black soldiers had separate places where they had to sit in snack bars. Some of the men in Jackie's outfit complained that there were only a few seats for black soldiers in one snack bar and that the men sometimes had to wait a long time to get a seat. Jackie went to the officer who was in charge of the camp and complained. But some of the officers complained that Jackie was trying to stir up trouble. Ⓓ

Later, the Army wanted Jackie to play for the camp football team. The first team they were to play refused to play against any team with a black player. When Jackie found out what was happening he said, "If that is the way it is, I don't want to wear the uniform of the Army football team." Some people thought he was trying to stir up trouble again. Ⓔ   ★9 ERRORS★

Jackie got out of the Army in 1944. He was all ready to marry a young woman named Rae. She was studying to be a nurse, and she had known Jackie since he'd been at UCLA.

Rae lived in California, and Jackie wanted to be near her, but he still couldn't get sports out of his blood. So he went to Kansas City and took a job with the most famous professional black baseball team in the business—the Kansas City Monarchs. This was the first time that Jackie earned good money—$400 a month. That was more money than Jackie had ever seen.

But when the Monarchs went from city to city, it was the same old story. Black people could not stay in the same hotels that white people stayed in. Often the team had to sleep in the team bus. In some cities,

Ⓐ What is the name of the minor league team in the Brooklyn organization?
The Montreal Royals.

● What's the name of the major league team that the best players from Montreal go to?
The Brooklyn Dodgers.

● What is the name of the general manager over the whole Brooklyn organization?
Branch Rickey.
Remember the facts that this chart presents.

EXERCISE 7   Decoding and comprehension

1. Everybody, look at part 4. *Call on a student.* What's the error limit for this lesson? **9 errors.**

2. *Call on individual students to read. Present the tasks specified for each circled letter.*

Ⓐ What college had Jackie Robinson attended? **UCLA.**

● What sports did he participate in? **Basketball, baseball, track, and football.**

● Did he tell people why he had quit college? **No.**

● What kind of student was Jackie in college? *Idea:* Excellent.

● How do you think he felt seeing his mother have to work all the time? *Idea:* Bad.

● Which of his brothers had trouble getting a decent job? **Mack.**

● What had Mack done earlier in the Olympics? *Idea:* Won a medal.

● What were the only kind of jobs that Mack could get? *Idea:* Odd jobs.

● But now everybody seemed to forget about that medal he won. If you were Jackie Robinson and saw all those things happen, how do you think you'd feel about continuing in college? *Response:* Student preference.

Ⓑ Where was Jackie working when the United States entered World War Two? *Idea:* In Hawaii.

● In what year did that happen? **1941.**

● What kind of job did Jackie have during the week? *Idea:* A construction job.

● What kind of job did Jackie have during the weekends? *Idea:* He played professional football.

Ⓒ When did the United States enter the war? **1941.**

● When did the war end? **1945.**

Ⓓ Jackie was an officer in the army. Why was he made an officer? *Idea:* He was a strong leader.

● Why did some officers say that he was trying to stir up trouble? *Idea:* Because he tried to get more seats for black men in the snack bar.

Ⓔ Why didn't the first team want to play against Jackie's team? *Idea:* Because Jackie was on the team.

the team couldn't even eat in restaurants, because the restaurants were restricted to white people. So the players ate sandwiches on the bus.

After a while, Jackie got tired of traveling with the Monarchs. He didn't get to see Rae very often. He was on the road all the time. So he finally decided to quit the Monarchs, go back to California, and try to get a job there. In the back of his mind, he had a great desire to play in the major leagues. But that didn't seem possible. To Jackie, it seemed that as long as he stayed in baseball, he would go from city to city in the Monarch's bus, and feel like somebody who didn't really belong to those cities.

But just when Jackie had made up his mind to quit the Monarchs, something happened that changed his whole life. The Monarchs were playing in Chicago. One of the scouts from the Brooklyn Dodgers told Jackie that the general manager of the Dodgers—Branch Rickey—was thinking of starting up a new league for black players. The scout told Robinson that this league would pay the players more money and offer better living conditions. Jackie was interested, so he agreed to meet with Branch Rickey.

This part of the story is really interesting. Branch Rickey had told all his scouts to find good black players. He'd told the scouts that he was thinking of forming a new league. But he wasn't. He wanted his scouts to find one black man. This man had to have enough courage to stand up against the trouble that he would experience as the first black player in the major

leagues. He wanted a man who could thrill the crowd with his skill. He wanted a man who would be a strong team player, a leader, and a player who didn't know what it meant to quit. Branch Rickey had been looking at a lot of black players but when he met with Jackie Robinson, he knew that he had found the right man. He knew a lot about Robinson from the reports that he had on him. He knew that Robinson was very intelligent, that he was a fighter, and that the coaches he had in the past said nothing but good things about him.

Imagine how Jackie Robinson felt on that day in Brooklyn when he walked into Branch Rickey's office. Jackie had almost accepted the idea that he would never be able to play in the majors, but he was looking forward to the idea of being in a league that offered a better life than he had with the Monarchs. Imagine how he felt when he heard Rickey say, "I'll tell you the *real* reason you're here. You were brought here to play for the Brooklyn organization with our Montreal team—the Montreal Royals."

Jackie sat there shocked, trying to make sense out of what Rickey had told him. The Montreal Royal's team was one of the minor league baseball teams in the Brooklyn organization. You know how that works. The Brooklyn Dodgers pick the best players for their minor league teams. Those players move up and play for the Dodgers. So the Montreal Royals are actually part of the Dodger organization. And of course, there were no black players on that team—before Jackie Robinson.

Then Rickey told Jackie Robinson just how hard it would be for him to be the first black player. Rickey said, "I need someone who is strong enough to take insults without fighting back." He told Jackie that everybody would be looking at him and if he got in the slightest trouble, people would blame him, regardless of whose fault it really was. He told Robin-

son, "I know you've always battled for your own rights and for the rights of your people. I admire you for it."

Then Rickey went on to tell Robinson that he could do more to fight for black athletes by playing the kind of baseball that he could play. "But it's not going to be easy," Rickey warned him. And it sure wasn't.

- So what did Jackie refuse to do? *Idea:* Wear the uniform of the army football team.
- Did it sound like he was stirring up trouble or trying to deal with a real problem? **Trying to deal with a real problem.**
- Read the rest of the story to yourselves and be ready to answer some questions.

After all students have finished reading:

- What was the name of the Negro baseball team that Jackie Robinson played for? **The Monarchs.**
- How much money did he earn at first? **400 dollars a month.**
- Where did the person who Jackie wanted to marry live? **California.**
- What was her name? **Rae.**
- Tell me about some of the problems that the Monarchs had when they went from city to city. *Ideas:* They couldn't sleep in hotels; they couldn't eat in restaurants.
- When Jackie was in Chicago, a scout approached him. What does a scout do? *Idea:* Tries to find talented players.
- What organization was that scout with? **The Dodgers.**
- What did he say the manager of the Brooklyn Dodgers was thinking of doing? *Idea:* Starting a new Negro league.
- What advantages would there be for a player in that new league? *Ideas:* He'd get more money; he'd have better living conditions.
- What was the name of the general manager of the Brooklyn Dodgers? **Branch Rickey.**
- Was Branch Rickey really thinking of forming a new Negro league? **No.**
- Why was he interested in looking for outstanding black players? *Idea:* Because he wanted blacks to play major league baseball.
- Which team in the Brooklyn organization did Jackie start playing for? **The Montreal Royals.**
- Rickey told Jackie that Jackie could do more for blacks by being on the team than he could in any other way. Why? *Idea:* He could lead the way for other blacks to enter the major leagues.

Award 4 points or have the students reread to the error limit sign.

INDEPENDENT WORK

Do all the items in your skillbook and workbook for lesson 69.

ANSWER KEY FOR WORKBOOK

Review Items

1. Here are some events from Jackie Robinson's life:
   - Jackie signs up for the army
   - Jackie first plays for the Dodgers
   - Jackie leaves the army

   Write the correct event after each date on the time line.

   1947 *Jackie plays for the Royals*

   1944 *Jackie leaves the army*

   1941 *Jackie signs up for the army*

2. People have developed many breeds of dogs.
   a. Which breed is very fast?
      greyhound
   b. Which breed is very brave?
      airedale
   c. Which breed has a sensitive nose?
      hound
   d. Which breed may be the smartest?
      poodle
   e. Which breed is good at herding sheep?
      collies

WORKCHECK AND AWARDING POINTS

1. *Read the questions and answers for the skillbook and workbook.*
2. *Award points for independent work as follows:*

0 errors	6 points
2 errors	4 points
3,4, or 5 errors	2 points
5 or more errors	0 points

3. *Award bonus points as follows:*

Correcting missed items or getting all items right	2 points
Doing the writing assignment acceptably	2 points

ANSWER KEY FOR SKILLBOOK

PART C
1. *Idea:* The jewels were very valuable.
2. *Idea:* Joe brushed his teeth.
3. *Idea:* Buck could pull any sled.
4. *Idea:* Wild animals live in the jungle.

PART D
5. a. Mack
   b. *Idea:* Odd jobs
   c. *Idea:* Work
6. *Idea:* Negro League
7. a. Hawaii
   b. *Idea:* Worked on a construction job
   c. *Idea:* Played professional football
8. a. World War Two
   b. The army
   c. an officer
9. a. *Idea:* snack bar
   b. *Idea:* causing trouble
10. a. *Idea:* Because Jackie was on the team
    b. *Idea:* Play for the army team
11. a. The Kansas City Monarchs
    b. $400 a month
    c. *Idea:* In the bus
    d. *Idea:* Because they were black
    e. On the bus
    f. *Idea:* Because the restaurants were for white people
12. a. *Idea:* A Negro League
    b. Branch Rickey
    c. No
13. a. The Montreal Royals
    b. A minor league team
14. *Idea:* That Robinson would not fight back

PART E
15. a. reluctant
    b. unexpectedly
    c. athlete
    d. resented
    e. talented
    f. insulted
    g. appreciation

Lesson 70

WORD PRACTICE AND VOCABULARY

EXERCISE 1   Word practice

*Pronunciation Guide: Poseidon—Po **sigh** dun*
Zeus—Zoose
*Hermes—**Her** meez*

1. Everybody, find lesson 70, part A in your skillbook. *Wait.* Touch under each word in column 1 as I read it.
2. The first word is **Poseidon.**
3. Next word. **Zeus.**
4. Next word. **Hermes.**
5. *Repeat step 4 for each remaining word in column 1.*
6. Your turn. Read the first word. *Signal.* **Poseidon.**
7. Next word. *Signal.* **Zeus.**
8. *Repeat step 7 for each remaining word in column 1.*
9. *Repeat the words in column 1 until firm.*

EXERCISE 2   Word practice

1. Everybody, touch under the first word in column 2. *Pause.* What word? *Signal.* **Lease.**
2. Next word. *Pause.* What word? *Signal.* **Release.**
3. *Repeat step 2 for each remaining word in column 2.*
4. *Repeat the words in column 2 until firm.*

EXERCISE 3   Vocabulary review

Task A
1. Everybody, touch column 3. *Check.* First you're going to read the words in column 3. Then we'll talk about what they mean.
2. Touch under the first line. *Pause.* What words? *Signal.* **Accused of.**
3. Next line. *Pause.* What words? *Signal.* **Restricted to.**
4. Next word. *Pause.* What word? *Signal.* **Organization.**
5. *Repeat step 4 for each remaining word in column 3.*
6. *Repeat the words in column 3 until firm.*

Task B
You've learned the meanings for all these words. The words in line 1 are **accused of.** *Call on a student.* What does **accused of** mean? *Idea:* You are told that you are guilty of doing something.

Task C
The words in line 2 are **restricted to.** *Call on a student.* What does it mean when a restaurant is **restricted to** adults? *Idea:* Only adults are allowed inside the restaurant.

Task D
Word 3 is **organization.** *Call on a student.* What is an **organization?** *Idea:* A business.

Task E
Word 4 is **graduate.** *Call on a student.* What does **graduate** mean? *Idea:* You successfully complete your work in a school.

Task F
Word 5 is **promoted.** *Call on a student.* What does **promoted** mean? *Idea:* You get a more important job.

Task G
Word 6 is **officer.** *Call on a student.* What is an **officer?** *Ideas:* Captains, lieutenants, majors and generals.

Task H
Word 7 is **rattled.** *Call on a student.* How do you feel when you become **rattled?** *Idea:* Nervous.

Task I
Word 8 is **decent.** *Call on a student.* What does **decent** mean? *Idea:* Good.

Task J
Word 9 is **career.** *Call on a student.* What is a person's **career?** *Idea:* The person's main job.

EXERCISE 4   Vocabulary development

Task A
1. Everybody, touch column 4. *Check.* First you're going to read the words in column 4. Then we'll talk about what they mean.
2. Touch under the first word. *Pause.* What word? *Signal.* **Contract.**
3. Next word. *Pause.* What word? *Signal.* **Cousin.**
4. *Repeat step 3 for **balk.***
5. *Repeat the words in column 4 until firm.*

Task B

Now let's talk about what those words mean. Word 1 is **contract**. A paper that tells about the things you agree to do is a **contract**. Everybody, what is a paper that tells about the things you agree to do? *Signal.* **A contract.**

Task C

Word 2 is **cousin**. The child of your aunt or uncle is your **cousin**.

Task D

Word 3 is **balk**. In baseball, the word **balk** has a special meaning. After the pitcher winds up, the only thing he can do is throw the ball to the catcher. If he does anything else, he balks, and all players who are on base can advance one base.

Lesson 70

Jackie Robinson

PART 5 Ⓐ

CANADA
Montreal

Brooklyn

Eastern
UNITED STATES

Branch Rickey made it very plain to Jackie Robinson that Jackie would have a tough time playing for Montreal. He said that Jackie would be all alone and that the other players would resent him. The last thing he said was that Jackie should marry Rae. Then he added, "You're going to need her with you from now on."Ⓑ

When word got out that Jackie had signed a contract with Montreal, all the papers carried the stories. In March of 1946, Jackie joined the Montreal Royals for spring practice. They were in Florida.

Jackie asked Rae to come to Florida so they could be married. For a while, Rae was just about the only friend he had.Ⓒ

The first time Jackie walked into the locker room with the other Montreal players, he tried to be friendly, but they didn't talk to him. The coaches and trainers talked to him, but not the other players.

Each day Jackie got dressed in his new uniform and went out on the field. He saw the wives of the players sitting in the stands and watching the practice. He saw Rae sitting all by herself with nothing surrounding her but empty stands. Jackie was hurt and angry. There she was, the person that he loved more than anybody in the world,

and the other wives wouldn't even talk to her.Ⓓ

Rae would smile at Jackie and wave. He would smile and wave back. Jackie knew that he wasn't the only one who had to be brave. One day Jackie told Rae that he hated to see her treated that way. But she smiled, shook her head, and said, "Don't worry. Things will soon be better for us. And thanks to you, they'll soon be better for all black athletes."Ⓔ

★ 6 ERRORS ★

That is what Jackie had to keep reminding himself—that he would make things better for other black athletes. Every time he wanted to fight, and every time

---

EXERCISE 5   Decoding and comprehension

1. Everybody, turn to page 268 in your textbook. *Wait. Call on a student.* What's the error limit for this lesson? **6 errors.**

2. *Call on individual students to read. Present the tasks specified for each circled letter.*

Ⓐ What was the name of the man who hired Jackie Robinson to play professional baseball? **Branch Rickey.**

● What organization was Branch Rickey with? **The Brooklyn Dodgers.**

● Was Jackie Robinson going to start playing with the Dodgers or with one of the minor league teams in the Brooklyn Dodger organization? **With one of the minor league teams.**

● What was the name of the team he was going to play with? **The Montreal Royals.**

● The city of Montreal is in Canada. The Montreal Royals played all their home games in Montreal. Everybody, touch Montreal on the map. *Check.*

● The Brooklyn Dodgers were in Brooklyn, New York. Brooklyn is part of New York City. Everybody, touch Brooklyn on the map. *Check.*

● In which country is Brooklyn? **The United States.**

● In which country is Montreal? **Canada.**

Ⓑ Why will he need her? *Idea:* Because he will be lonely.

Ⓒ Spring practice takes place before the regular season opens. Where did the Montreal Royals go for spring practice? **Florida.**

Ⓓ Who did Rae sit with in the stands? *Idea:* Nobody.

● Did the wives of the other players talk to her or sit with her? **No.**

● How did that make Jackie feel? *Idea:* Bad.

Ⓔ What would Jackie have to do to make things better for other black players? *Idea:* Not fight back.

● Read the rest of the story to yourselves and be ready to answer some questions.

he didn't think he could take it any more, he tried to remember that he was doing something important. He told himself that even though he had to suffer, he was doing something that could help other black players. So he worked and worked, and he worked even harder.

Then one day on the field something happened that showed Jackie that maybe things would get better. A coach had Jackie playing second base. Jackie made a lot of mistakes, because he had never played second base before. He was having a lot of trouble getting in position and throwing the ball fast enough. Just after he made another error, a player came up to him and showed Jackie how to stand and how to turn so that he could make the play. The player was right, but more important than that, Jackie knew that the player wanted to play second base, yet here he was helping Jackie.

You know how Jackie was. As long as he felt that everybody was against him, he didn't play the way he could play. But once he had the feeling that there were some players on his side, he was a different kind of player. When that second baseman helped him out, Jackie was starting to get the feeling that there was somebody else on his side. Up until that day, Jackie had been playing poorly, both on the field and at bat. But now, he started to play like Jackie Robinson.

The fans got a look at his kind of play on the day that the Royals played a spring practice game with the Dodgers. At first, the fans yelled at Jackie. Jackie was scared, but he was also very determined. Early in the game, the Royals were on the field. A Dodger batter smashed a fast ground ball that looked like a hit. Jackie raced for the ball, scooped it up, and in one quick motion, fired it to the first baseman. The bat-

ter was out, and people in the stands were starting to say things like, "Did you see that man move?" and "What speed!" Jackie made a lot of dazzling plays in that game, and the fans were impressed.

The first game that Montreal played after spring training in Florida was held across the river from New York City. The place was crowded with people who had come to see Jackie. The first time that Jackie was up to bat, these people didn't have much to cheer about. Jackie tapped a little ground ball that dribbled out to the shortstop. Out.

But the next time Jackie was up, he brought all the fans to their feet. Two Montreal players were on base. The pitcher threw Jackie a sizzling fast ball. Crack. By the sound of it, the fans knew that it was gone. There it went, like a shot over the left field fence. A home run, with three players scoring. And when Jackie crossed home plate, both the players who had just scored shook his hand and slapped him on the back.

The next time up, Jackie got on first base with a hit. Before the pitcher knew what happened, Jackie had stolen second base. By now, the crowd was going wild, and the pitcher was going crazy. Before the pitcher pitched two balls to the next batter—zip, Jackie had stolen third base. Then the pitcher got so shook up with Jackie on third base—dancing around, making like he was going to steal home—that the pitcher threw the ball to third base after he had wound up for the pitch. That's a balk, which meant that Jackie could walk

to home plate and score.

The crowd was cheering and shouting. That game was the first time that baseball fans had seen the kind of baseball that Jackie Robinson could play. He was daring, ready to take a chance. But he was so fast that even when he took chances stealing bases, the other team couldn't throw the ball fast enough to get him out.

When Jackie returned to the city of Montreal after the Royals had won three games on the road, the fans loved him, and he loved the city.

There were still rough times ahead for Jackie. One time, Montreal was playing another team, when one of the players on the other team threw a black cat out of the dugout on to the field. One of the players yelled, "Hey, Jackie, there's your cousin!"

Jackie looked over at the cat and didn't say a thing. But a few moments later, he was at bat, and he made his bat do all his talking for him. He smashed the ball and ran like a streak to second base. When one of the Montreal players hit a single, Jackie scored. As he went past the dugout of the other team, he said in a very pleasant tone, "Well, I guess my cousin is pretty happy now." The players on the other team didn't say anything.

By the end of the season, Jackie had answered every player on the other teams who insulted him. He answered in a language they all understood. The Montreal Royals won the league pennant, and Jackie Robinson was the top batter in the whole league.

After all students have finished reading:

- When Jackie was first trying to play second base for Montreal, something happened that made Jackie think that things might be getting better with his teammates. What happened? *Idea:* A Montreal player helped him learn how to play second base.
- Do you think it was hard for that player to help Jackie out? **Yes.**
- Why? *Idea:* The Montreal player wanted to play second base.
- When that second baseman helped him out, what did that show Jackie? *Idea:* That somebody was on his side.
- How had Jackie been playing before the second baseman helped him? *Idea:* Poorly.
- How did he start to play after that player helped him? *Idea:* Well.
- When the Royals played across the river from New York City, a lot of people came to see the game. Why? *Idea:* Because they wanted to see Jackie play.
- Did Jackie give the fans anything to cheer about? **Yes.**
- Name some great things that he did in that game. *Idea:* He hit a home run; he stole bases; he confused the pitcher.
- How did the people in Montreal feel about Jackie? *Idea:* They liked him.
- One time, when Montreal played another team, one of the players on the other team did something that was very mean. What did the player do? *Idea:* Told Jackie that a black cat was his cousin.
- Explain what Jackie did and what he said afterward. *Idea:* He scored a run and told the player that he'd make his cousin happy.
- Jackie answered all the players who insulted him during that season. What did he use to answer them? *Idea:* His skill.
- What honors did he and his team receive at the end of the season?
  Call on individual students. Ideas: Jackie was the top batter in the league; Montreal won the league pennant.

Award 4 points or have the students reread to the error limit sign.

INDEPENDENT WORK

Do all the items in your skillbook and workbook for lesson 70.

ANSWER KEY FOR WORKBOOK

Map Skills

1. Look at the map below.

a. Which letter shows the city where Jackie Robinson played in the

minor leagues? ____M____

b. Which letter shows the city where Jackie Robinson played in the

major leagues? ____B____

c. Which letters shows where Jackie Robinson went for spring training?

____F____

d. In which country is the city of

Montreal? *Canada*

e. In which country is the city of

Brooklyn? *United States*

Review Items

2. Here are some events from Jackie Robinson's life:
   • Jackie leaves the army
   • Jackie plays for the Royals
   • Jackie signs up for the army

Write the correct event after each date on the time line.

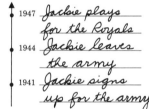

1947 *Jackie plays for the Royals*

1944 *Jackie leaves the army*

1941 *Jackie signs up for the army*

WORKCHECK AND AWARDING POINTS

1. *Read the questions and answers for the skillbook and workbook.*

2. *Award points for independent work as follows:*

> *0 errors . . . . 6 points*
> *2 errors . . . . 4 points*
> *3, 4, or 5 errors . . . . 2 points*
> *5 or more errors . . . . 0 points*

3. *Award bonus points as follows:*

> *Correcting missed items*
> *or getting all items right . . . . 2 points*
> *Doing the writing*
> *assignment acceptably . . . . 2 points*

ANSWER KEY FOR SKILLBOOK

PART B

1. **a.** No
   b. *Idea:* Badly
2. **a.** Rae
   b. Get married
3. No
4. **a.** Second base
   b. Second base
5. **a.** Scored a home run
   b. Two
6. **a.** A black cat
   b. *Idea:* His bat
   c. *Idea:* His cousin was happy now
7. **a.** The league pennant
   b. Top batter

PART C

8. **a.** Gold
   b. Canada
   c. Yukon
   d. Buck
   e. Buck
9. **a.** false
   b. false
   c. true
   d. true
   e. false
10. **a.** fact
    b. fiction
    c. fact
    d. fiction
    e. fact
11. **a.** intently
    b. emotions
    c. daring
    d. resent
    e. rookie
    f. mechanic
    g. complained

Lesson 71

PART A   **Word Lists**

1	2	3	4
miraculous	Hermes	**Vocabulary words**	**Vocabulary words**
hospitality	Poseidon	1. balk	1. oppose
honey	Apollo	2. contract	2. honor
olive	Zeus	3. cousin	3. bunt
			4. retire
			5. defeat

WORD PRACTICE AND VOCABULARY

EXERCISE 1   Word practice

1. Everybody, find lesson 71, part A in your skillbook. *Wait.* Touch under each word in column 1 as I read it.
2. The first word is **miraculous.**
3. Next word. **Hospitality.**
4. *Repeat step 3 for each remaining word in column 1.*
5. Your turn. Read the first word. *Signal.* **Miraculous.**
6. Next word. *Signal.* **Hospitality.**
7. *Repeat step 6 for each remaining word in column 1.*
8. *Repeat the words in column 1 until firm.*

EXERCISE 2   Word family

1. Everybody, touch column 2. *Check.* All those words are the names of Greek gods. Touch under the first word. *Pause.* What word? *Signal.* **Hermes.**
2. Next word. *Pause.* What word? *Signal.* **Poseidon.**
3. *Repeat step 2 for each remaining word in column 2.*
4. *Repeat the words in column 2 until firm.*

EXERCISE 3   Vocabulary review

Task A

1. Everybody, touch column 3. *Check.* First you're going to read the words in column 3. Then we'll talk about what they mean.
2. Touch under the first word. *Pause.* What word? *Signal.* **Balk.**
3. Next word. *Pause.* What word? *Signal.* **Contract.**
4. *Repeat step 3 for* **cousin.**
5. *Repeat the words in column 3 until firm.*

Task B

You've learned the meanings for all these words. Word 1 is **balk.** *Call on a student.* In baseball, what does **balk** mean? *Idea:* After the pitcher winds up, the only thing he can do is throw the ball to the catcher. If he does anything else, he balks, and all the players who are on base can advance one base.

Task C

Word 2 is **contract.** *Call on a student.* What is a **contract?** *Idea:* A paper that tells about the things you agree to do.

Task D

Word 3 is **cousin.** *Call on a student.* What is a **cousin?** *Idea:* The child of a brother or sister of your parents.

EXERCISE 4   Vocabulary development

Task A

1. Everybody, touch column 4. *Check.* First you're going to read the words in column 4. Then we'll talk about what they mean.
2. Touch under the first word. *Pause.* What word? *Signal.* **Oppose.**
3. Next word. *Pause.* What word? *Signal.* **Honor.**
4. *Repeat step 3 for each remaining word in column 4.*
5. *Repeat the words in column 4 until firm.*

Task B

1. Now let's talk about what those words mean. Word 1 is **oppose.** When you're against an idea, you **oppose** that idea. Your turn. When you're against a plan, you *Pause. Signal.* **oppose that plan.**
2. When you are against a baseball team, you *Pause. Signal.* **oppose that baseball team.**

Task C

Word 2 is **honor.** An **honor** is an award that you receive for your good work. Everybody, what is an award that you receive for your good work? *Signal.* **An honor.**

Task D

Word 3 is **bunt.** *Call on a student.* How do you **bunt** in baseball? *Idea:* Hold the bat with your hands apart and hit the ball gently.

Task E

Word 4 is **retire.** When you have worked a long time and then stop working, you **retire** from your job. Everybody, what do you do when you have worked a long time and then stop working? *Signal.* **You retire from your job.**

Task F

Word 5 is **defeat.** When you **defeat** somebody, you beat or win over that person. Here's another way of saying **She beat him at checkers: She defeated him at checkers.** Everybody, what's another way of saying **He beat his opponent?** *Signal.* **He defeated his opponent.**

Lesson 71

Jackie Robinson

PART 6 (A)

After Montreal won the league pennant, they played a team from Kentucky. The Kentucky team was the pennant winner from another league. The first team to win four games would win the series. The first three games of the series were played in Kentucky. And suddenly, Jackie felt all alone again. In those three games, he got only one hit. Montreal lost two of the games played in Kentucky. Jackie was worried about how the fans in Montreal would respond to him, now that the Royals were behind in the series two games to one. (B)

Jackie remembered how the Kentucky fans booed the Montreal team, but he was in for a pleasant surprise when the Kentucky team came to Montreal. The Montreal fans gave the team from Kentucky a taste of their own medicine. (C)

Lesson 71 Textbook **271**

EXERCISE 5 Decoding and comprehension

1. Everybody, turn to page 271 in your textbook. *Wait. Call on a student.* What's the error limit for this lesson? **8 errors.**

2. *Call on individual students to read. Present the tasks specified for each circled letter.*

(A) What was the name of the city Jackie Robinson played for in the minor leagues? **Montreal.**

● Everybody, touch Montreal on the map? *Check.* What country is that city in? **Canada.**

● What was the name of the city that the Dodgers were from? **Brooklyn.**

● Everybody, touch Brooklyn on the map. *Check.*

● In today's story, you'll read about some things that took place in Kentucky. Everybody, touch Kentucky on the map. *Check.*

● In which country is Kentucky? **The United States.** Remember where all those places are.

(B) Montreal won their league pennant. In what state was the team from that won the other league pennant? **Kentucky.**

● Were Montreal and the team from Kentucky minor league teams or major league teams? **Minor league teams.**

● Where were the first three games held, in Montreal or Kentucky? **Kentucky.**

● How well did Jackie do in those games? *Idea:* Not very well.

● How many games did a team have to win to win the series? **Four.**

● How many of those games did Montreal win? **One.**

● How many games did the team from Kentucky win? **Two.**

(C) What does that mean: **A taste of their own medicine?** *Idea:* They were rude to the Kentucky players.

Montreal fans booed the Kentucky team and cheered for Jackie. You know how he played when he got that kind of support. Jackie's team won three games in Montreal and won the series. And I'll bet you can figure out who scored the winning run of the last game. (D)

Jackie had changed the minds of many people in Montreal. The manager of the Royals had been strongly opposed to having a black man on the team. That was before the beginning of the season. At the end of the season, he told Jackie, "You're a great ball player and a fine gentleman. It's been wonderful having you on the team."

You better believe it was wonderful. Having one Jackie Robinson on the team was like having four or five excellent players.

The next year was 1947. (E) That's the year I began watching Jackie Robinson. For me it was all new. Sure, I had read some of the reports about Robinson before I saw him play. But he was just so many numbers on a piece of paper. The numbers told me that the man could bat and could steal bases. He could play the field without making errors, and he could win. But still, when I saw him for the first time, I had my doubts. (F)

By the end of the first season, after the Dodgers had won the National League pennant, the Brooklyn fans were singing a different tune. (G) We were behind Jackie all the way. And we stayed behind him for ten years. I remember how proud I was of him each time he earned a new honor. And

he earned lots of them in 1949. The Dodgers won the National League pennant again. And a Dodger was the National League batting champion—Jackie Robinson. He was also named the league's most valuable player. (H)

During the 1949 season, other teams were bringing black players into the major leagues, and that made Jackie feel good. Also during that year, Rickey released Jackie from his promise not to fight back. Rickey told him, "You've proved that you're a ball player. So it's time you stood up for yourself." And Jackie did just that. (I) ★8 ERRORS★

During the years that followed, Jackie received honor after honor. And he earned every one of them. In 1951, Jackie played first base. He made only seven fielding errors all season long.

He was named to the All Star Team year after year, and during most of those years the Dodgers won the National League pennant. But after winning it, they'd play the Yankees in the World Series and lose. By 1955, people were saying that Jackie was getting too old for the game. He didn't play much during that year, and for the fifth time since Jackie had been with the Dodgers, the Dodgers met the Yankees in the World Series.

The Yankees took the first two games. In the third game, Jackie played for the Dodgers. Most fans cheered encouragement to him. When the score was tied two to two, Jackie came to bat. A few fans were saying, "What's Old Man Robinson doing out there?"

They found out. He hit a single. Now he was on base and now the old Jackie Robinson magic started. He got the pitcher so shook up that the pitcher hit the next batter with a pitch.

Now Jackie was on second base. The next batter got a hit and Jackie shot to third. The bases were now loaded. When he was on third, Jackie kept running toward home plate and stopping. The pitcher became so rattled that he walked the next batter.

Jackie walked home, and the crowd went wild.

The next time Jackie got up to bat, he slugged a clean double, but he stretched it into a three-base hit. He scored when the next batter got a hit. The Dodgers won that game and won the next two games. Finally, in the seventh and last game of the Series, Brooklyn won. I couldn't believe it. I never thought I'd see Brooklyn win the World Series, but they did.

People were celebrating all over Brooklyn. I'm telling you, for a week, every time I'd look at one of the guys at work, we'd smile at each other. We didn't have to say anything. Brooklyn won the World Series. And Jackie Robinson won that series.

The year 1956 was the last year that Jackie played baseball. He was thirty-seven years old, and he had slowed down a lot. I wrote him a letter after he retired. I told him that I thought he was the greatest and that I'd miss him. He wrote back and thanked me for my letter. I still have that letter. And I have a lot of pictures of

Jackie, and a lot of books about him. But, most of all, I have memories. I've got happy memories, like the memory of Jackie being elected to the Baseball Hall of Fame. I've got sad memories, like the memory of his son, who was killed in an auto accident in 1971. But the saddest memory of all was of Jackie's death in 1972, just a few days after the Dodgers had retired the number that he wore on his uniform—42. He was only fifty-three years old when he died. I was retired then, and one of the men I used to work with came over that day. I remember he said, "A great man is dead."

I tried not to cry. I said, "No, a great giant is dead."

That's what he was, a giant who could teach all of us about the meaning of the word courage. You can search the world over for a person who has more strength, courage, and talent than Jackie Robinson. You're not going to find one. One sports writer did a good job of telling about Jackie in one sentence. Here's what that man wrote: "He would not be defeated, not by the other team and not by life."

(D) Who was that player? **Jackie Robinson.**

(E) So what year was it that Montreal won the minor league championship? **1946.**

● And what happened to Jackie in 1947? *Idea:* He joined the Brooklyn Dodgers.

(F) Was the narrator a big fan of Jackie Robinson at that time? **No.**

(G) What does that mean: **They were singing a different tune?** *Idea:* They had changed their minds.

● Why were they singing a different tune? *Idea:* Because Jackie Robinson was a good ball player.

(H) Which league was Jackie in now, the minors or the majors? **The majors.**
The name of that major league is the National League.

● What honors did Jackie win in 1949? *Ideas:* Most Valuable Player; National League Batting Champion.

(I) If Jackie was released from his promise to Branch Rickey, what kinds of things could Jackie do now that he wouldn't have done before? *Ideas:* Argue; fight.

● Read the rest of the story to yourselves and be ready to answer some questions.

After all students have finished reading:

● The Dodgers won the National League pennant year after year. Which team would they usually play after winning the pennant? **The Yankees.**

● What would usually happen in that series? *Idea:* The Yankees would win.

● In 1955, which team won the World Series, the Dodgers or the Yankees? **The Dodgers.**

● Tell me some things that Jackie did in that series. *Ideas:* Hit a single; made the pitcher nervous; walked in a run; hit a double, but stretched it into a three-base hit.

● In the story it said that Jackie slugged a clean double? What does **clean double** mean? *Idea:* A two-base hit.

● What was the last year that Jackie Robinson played baseball? **1956.**

● In what year did Jackie Robinson die? **1972.**

● What big lesson did the narrator think Jackie Robinson could teach everybody? *Ideas:* The definition of courage; that he would not be defeated.

Award 4 points or have the students reread to the error limit sign.

EXERCISE 6   Individual reading checkout

1. *For the individual reading checkout, each student will read 140 words. The passage to be read is the shaded area on the reproduced textbook page for lesson 71 in this presentation book.*

2. Today is a reading checkout day. While you're doing your independent work, I'll call on each student to read part of yesterday's chapter.

3. When I call on you, come up to my desk and bring your textbook with you. After you have read, I'll tell you how many points you can write in the checkout box that's at the top of your workbook page.

4. *If the student finishes the passage in one minute or less, award points as follows:*

0 errors	.....................3 points
1 or 2 errors	.... 1 point
More than 2 errors	............0 points

5. *If a student takes more than one minute to read the passage, the student does not earn any points, but have the student reread the passage until he or she is able to read it in no more than one minute with no more than two errors.*

INDEPENDENT WORK

Do all the items in your skillbook and workbook for lesson 71.

ANSWER KEY FOR WORKBOOK

Review Items

1. Write where each story took place. Choose from **Kenya, England, Canada, California,** or **North Carolina.**

a. Brown Wolf *California*
b. A Horse to Remember *England*
c. The Secret Cave *Kenya*
d. Adventure on the Rocky Ridge *North Carolina*
e. Dick Whittington *England*
f. Buck *Canada*

2. Here are some events from Jackie Robinson's life:
- Jackie helps win the World Series
- Jackie first plays for the Dodgers
- Jackie dies
- Jackie stops playing baseball

Write the correct event after each date on the time line.

1972 *Jackie dies*
1956 *Jackie stops playing baseball*
1955 *Jackie helps win the World Series*
1947 *Jackie first plays for the Dodgers*

WORKCHECK AND AWARDING POINTS

1. *Read the questions and answers for the skillbook and workbook.*

2. *Award points for independent work as follows:*

0 errors	.....................6 points
2 errors	.....................4 points
3, 4, or 5 errors	..............2 points
5 or more errors	..............0 points

3. *Award bonus points as follows:*

Correcting missed items or getting all items right	.........2 points
Doing the writing assignment acceptably	..........2 points

4. *Remind the students to put the points they earned for their reading checkout, in the box labeled* **CO**.

ANSWER KEY FOR SKILLBOOK

PART B
1. *Idea:* Vehicles use the freeway.
2. *Idea:* Hubert put on his clothes.
3. *Idea:* Francesca rode her bike.
4. *Idea:* People love to watch sports.

PART C
5. **a.** Kentucky
   b. *Idea:* Not well
   c. One
   d. Montreal
   e. *Idea:* Very well
   f. Montreal
   g. Jackie Robinson
6. The Dodgers
7. *Any two:* Rookie of the Year; Batting Champion, All Star Team, Hall of Fame
8. *Idea:* That he was getting old
9. **a.** The Yankees
   b. The Dodgers
   c. Jackie Robinson
10. 1956
11. life

PART D
12. **a.** Brains
    b. Courage
    c. *Idea:* A trip back to Kansas
    d. A heart
13. **a.** unexpectedly   **f.** scheduled
    b. feeling   **g.** accused of
    c. mechanic   **h.** business
    d. talented   **i.** graduate
    e. fury   **j.** promoted

Lesson 72

Lesson 72

PART A   Word Lists

1	2	3	4	5
Philemon	beehive	lodge	**Vocabulary words**	**Vocabulary words**
Baucis	grapevine	lodging	1. honor	1. miraculous
cultivate	neighborhood	vegetable	2. retire	2. hospitality
fertile	nightfall	disagreeable	3. defeat	3. cultivate
	mudball	lightfooted	4. oppose	4. fertile
		youth		5. staff
		fragrant		6. toiled

PART B   Main Idea Paragraphs

Read each paragraph below. For each paragraph, figure out who the main character is and what main thing that character did. Then write a sentence that tells the main idea. Start by naming the main character, then tell **what** the character did. You can write **when** the character did it, **where** the character did it, or **why** or **how** the character did it.

1.   It was a week before Christmas, and Clara had purchased presents for everyone in her family except for her brother, Tony. She knew some of the things that Tony wanted, but most of them were far too expensive for Clara to buy. So, Clara went to the department store without knowing exactly what she would buy. She looked at clothing. She looked at sporting equipment. Then, as she was walking by the tool department, she recalled that her brother spent a lot of time fixing his bike. But he never seemed to have the right tool. So, Clara inquired about a tool kit for fixing bikes. The clerk showed her a nice bike-repair tool kit that was not too expensive. Clara said, "I'll take it."

2.   It was time for lunch. Sidney followed the other students into the lunchroom. But Sidney was not hungry, so he sat at one of the tables. Then he took a paper and pencil and began to write. He stopped and thought for a moment. Then he wrote some more. Soon, Sidney was finished. Here is what he wrote:
   > The lunchroom has a lot to eat;
   > Milk, and bread, and cheese, and meat.
   > But on this day I would rather think,
   > Than get some things to eat and drink.

WORD PRACTICE AND VOCABULARY

EXERCISE 1   Word practice

Pronunciation Guide: Philemon—Fillamon
Baucis—Bawkiss

1. Everybody, find lesson 72, part A in your skillbook. *Wait.* Touch under each word in column 1 as I read it.
2. The first word is **Philemon.**
3. Next word. **Baucis.**
4. *Repeat step 3 for each remaining word in column 1.*
5. Your turn. Read the first word. *Signal.* **Philemon.**
6. Next word. *Signal.* **Baucis.**
7. *Repeat the words in column 1 until firm.*

EXERCISE 2   Word family

1. Everybody, touch column 2. *Check.*
   All those words are made up of two shorter words.
   Touch under the first word. *Pause.*
   What word? *Signal.* **Beehive.**
2. Next word. *Pause.*
   What word? *Signal.* **Grapevine.**
3. *Repeat step 2 for each remaining word in column 2.*
4. *Repeat the words in column 2 until firm.*

EXERCISE 3   Word practice

1. Everybody, touch under the first word in column 3. *Pause.* What word? *Signal.* **Lodge.**
2. Next word. *Pause.* What word? *Signal.* **Lodging.**
3. *Repeat step 2 for each remaining word in column 3.*
4. *Repeat the words in column 3 until firm.*

EXERCISE 4   Vocabulary review

Task A
1. Everybody, touch column 4. *Check.*
   First you're going to read the words in column 4. Then we'll talk about what they mean.
2. Touch under the first word. *Pause.*
   What word? *Signal.* **Honor.**
3. Next word. *Pause.*
   What word? *Signal.* **Retire.**
4. *Repeat step 3 for each remaining word in column 4.*
5. *Repeat the words in column 4 until firm.*

Task B
You've learned the meanings for all these words. Word 1 is **honor.** *Call on a student.* What is an **honor?** *Idea:* An award that you receive for good work.

Task C
Word 2 is **retire.** *Call on a student.* What does **retire** mean? *Idea:* You have worked a long time, and then stop working.

Task D

1. Word 3 is **defeat.** *Call on a student.*
   What does **defeat** mean? *Ideas:* beat; win over.
2. Everybody, what's another way of saying
   He beat his opponent? *Signal.*
   He defeated his opponent.

Task E

Word 4 is **oppose.** *Call on a student.*
What does **oppose** mean? *Ideas:* Against; don't approve of.

EXERCISE 5   Vocabulary development

Task A

1. Everybody, touch column 5. *Check.*
   First you're going to read the words in column 5. Then we'll talk about what they mean.
2. Touch under the first word. *Pause.*
   What word? *Signal.* **Miraculous.**
3. Next word. *Pause.*
   What word? *Signal.* **Hospitality.**
4. *Repeat step 3 for each remaining word in column 5.*
5. *Repeat the words in column 5 until firm.*

Task B

1. Now let's talk about what those words mean.
   Word 1 is **miraculous.** Something is **miraculous** if it is like a miracle. If the sunshine was like a miracle, the sunshine was miraculous. Everybody, what would you call a job that was like a miracle? *Signal.*
   A miraculous job.
2. What would you call a ball player that was like a miracle? *Signal.* **A miraculous ball player.**

Task C

1. Word 2 is **hospitality.** When you show **hospitality** to somebody, you are very kind to that person. Everybody, what are you showing when you are kind to a person? *Signal.*
   Hospitality.
2. *Call on a student.* How could you show hospitality to a stranger? *Idea:* By being kind to that stranger.

Task D

Word 3 is **cultivate.** When you **cultivate** a field, you get rid of the weeds and fix up the ground so that you can plant crops. Everybody, what do you do to a field when you get rid of the weeds and fix up the ground? *Signal.*
Cultivate the field.

Task E

Word 4 is **fertile. Fertile** land is land that is capable of growing very good crops. Everybody, what kind of land is capable of growing very good crops? *Signal.* **Fertile land.**

Task F

Word 5 is **staff.** A **staff** is a long stick that you carry. Some staffs are used to help people walk. Some staffs show that the person carrying it is very important.

Task G

Word 6 is **toiled.** When you **toil,** you work very hard. Everybody, what's another way of saying
He worked very hard in the fields? *Signal.*
He toiled in the fields.
Everybody, what's another way of saying
She worked very hard everyday? *Signal.*
She toiled everyday.

EXERCISE 6   Main idea paragraphs

1. Everybody, find part B. Read the instructions and the first paragraph to yourselves. Then we'll work together and make up a main-idea sentence. Raise your hand when you've finished reading the paragraph.
● *After all students have raised their hands:*
● Who was the main character in that paragraph? **Clara.**
   So, I write **Clara** as the first part of the sentence. *Write **Clara** on the chalkboard.*
● Now tell me the main thing that Clara did. Don't tell where or when, just tell what she did.
   Call on individual students. Responses: Bought a bike-repair tool kit. So, I write bought a bike-repair tool kit as the next part of the sentence.
   *After **Clara** write:* **bought a bike-repair tool kit**
● That's a good main idea sentence. But we can add more information to this sentence if we wish. We can tell **why** she bought it or **who** it is for. We can tell **when** she bought it or **where** she bought it.
● When did she buy the kit? *Idea:* A week before Christmas. *At the beginning of the sentence, write:* **A week before Christmas,**
● Who did she buy it for? *Ideas:* Tony; her brother. *At the end of the sentence, write:* **for her brother, Tony.**
● Everybody, read the new main-idea sentence. *Signal.* **A week before Christmas, Clara bought a bike-repair tool kit for her brother, Tony.**
2. Later you'll write main-idea sentences for both paragraphs in part B.
3. Remember, start out by naming the character and the main thing that character did. Then tell more. You can tell **when,** tell **why,** tell **where,** or tell **how.** But add these other things after you've made up the sentence that tells who did something and the main thing that character did.

Lesson 72

Greek Gods

This passage tells about four Greek Gods. Today, you will start reading a story that tells about two of those gods.

The Greeks who lived three thousand years ago believed that there were many gods. They thought that some of these gods lived on a mountain named Mount Olympus.Ⓐ

Zeus was the chief god.Ⓑ Zeus commanded the winds, the clouds, lightning, and thunder. He was so wise that he saw everything and knew everything. He rewarded things that were good and punished things that were evil. He punished evil with storms or tornados or floods.Ⓒ

Apollo was the god of many things. But he was most important as the god of light and the god of music.Ⓓ

Poseidon was the god of the sea. Poseidon was a brother of Zeus. Poseidon could make earthquakes and great storms at sea. He lived in an underwater palace.Ⓔ

Hermes was the god of travelers.Ⓕ Hermes protected travelers and guided them. Hermes was the messenger of Zeus, and he was an extremely fast runner. He was incredibly fast. He is sometimes known as Quicksilver.Ⓖ Hermes wore a helmet with wings on it. He carried a staff that had wings and snakes on it. Hermes was also famous for playing jokes on people.Ⓗ

274   Lesson 72   Textbook

STORY READING

EXERCISE 7   Comprehension passage

1. Everybody, turn to page 274 in your textbook. *Wait.*
2. *Call on individual students to read. Present the tasks specified for each circled letter.*

Ⓐ Where did they think the gods lived? *Idea:* On Mount Olympus; on a mountain.

Ⓑ What was the name of the chief god? **Zeus.**

Ⓒ What are some of the things that Zeus commanded? *Ideas:* The winds; the clouds; lightning; thunder.

● How wise was he? *Idea:* He knew everything.

● What did he do to punish evil? *Idea:* He created storms.

Ⓓ What was the name of the god of light? **Apollo.**

● What else was he the god of? **Music.**

Ⓔ What was the name of the Greek god of the sea? **Poseidon.**

● What did Poseidon rule? **The sea.**

● Where did he live? **In an underwater palace.**

Ⓕ Who was the god of travelers? **Hermes.**

Ⓖ What was another name for Hermes? **Quicksilver.**

Ⓗ What did Hermes wear on his head? *Idea:* A helmet with wings.

● What was unusual about the staff that Hermes carried? *Idea:* It had wings and snakes on it.
Remember the names of these gods and what they did.

● Which god was the chief god? **Zeus.**

● Which god was the god of light and music? **Apollo.**

● Which god was the god of the sea? **Poseidon.**

● Which god was the god of travelers? **Hermes.**
Look at the pictures of those gods and remember what they look like. You will be reading about them.

The Miraculous Pitcher

by Nathaniel HawthorneⒶ

PART 1

One evening, in times long ago, old Philemon and his old wife Baucis sat on a bench next to their cottage door enjoying the calm and beautiful sunset. They had already eaten their supper, and intended now to spend a quiet hour or two before bedtime. So they talked together about their garden, and their cow, and their bees, and their grapevine. But the rude shouts of children and the fierce barking of dogs in the nearby village grew louder and louder, until at last it was hardly possible for Baucis and Philemon to hear each other speak.

"Ah, wife," cried Philemon, "I fear some poor traveler is seeking hospitality in the village. But instead of giving him food and shelter, the people in the village have set their dogs on him."Ⓑ

"I do wish the people in the village felt a little more kindness for their fellow human beings," Baucis said. "They bring up their children in this evil way, and pat them on the head when they fling stones at strangers."Ⓒ

"Those children will never come to any good," said Philemon, shaking his white head. "To tell you the truth, wife, I would not be surprised if some terrible thing were to happen to all the people in the village, unless they mend their ways."Ⓓ Philemon continued, "But as for you and me, so long as we have a crust of bread, let us be ready to give half to any poor homeless stranger that may come along and need it."

"That's right, husband," said Baucis. "So we will."Ⓔ

Philemon and Baucis were quite poor, and had to work hard for a living. Philemon toiled extremely hard in his garden, while Baucis was always making a little butter and cheese with their cow's milk, or doing something around the cottage. Their food was seldom anything but bread, milk, and vegetables, with sometimes a bit of honey from their beehive. But they were two of the kindest people in the world. They would cheerfully have gone without their dinners any day rather than refuse food to a weary traveler who might come to their door. They felt that they should treat

Lesson 72 Textbook **275**

---

guests better and more thoughtfully than they treated themselves.Ⓕ

Their cottage stood on a hill a short distance from the village, which lay in a valley that was about half a mile wide. This valley, in past ages, when the world was new, had probably been the bed of a lake. There, fishes had glided back and forth in the water, and weeds had grown along the shore, and trees and hills had made reflections in the broad and peaceful water. But as the lake had dried up, men had cultivated the soil, and built houses on it, so

that it was now a fertile spot.Ⓖ

The valley bore no traces of the ancient lake, except for a very small brook which flowed through the village, and supplied the villagers with water.Ⓗ The valley had been dry land so long that oaks had sprung up, and grown great and high, and died with old age, and been followed by other oaks as tall and stately as the first. Never was there a prettier or more fertile valley. The very sight of the rich surroundings around them should have made the villagers kind and gentle.Ⓘ

276 Lesson 72 Textbook

EXERCISE 8 Decoding and comprehension

1. Everybody, look at page 275. *Wait. Call on a student.* What's the error limit for this lesson? **11 errors.**

2. *Call on individual students to read. Present the tasks specified for each circled letter.*

Ⓐ The story that you will read today is <u>The Miraculous Pitcher</u>. It was written by a great writer named Nathaniel Hawthorne, and it is based on a very old Greek story.

● What's the title of the story? **The Miraculous Pitcher.**

● Who is the author? **Nathaniel Hawthorne.**

Ⓑ At what time of day does this story take place? **Evening.**

● Is it a story that took place recently or a long time ago? **A long time ago.**

● What's the name of the old man in this story? **Philemon.**

● What's the name of the woman? **Baucis.**

● Do they live inside the village? **No.**

● What made it difficult for them to carry on a conversation? *Idea:* Children shouting and dogs barking.

● Philemon had an idea of what was causing all the commotion in the village. What did he think had happened? *Idea:* The villagers had set their dogs on a traveler.

Ⓒ What do the people in the village raise their children to do? *Idea:* Throw stones at strangers.

Ⓓ What does that mean: **Unless they mend their ways?** *Idea:* Unless they change for the better.

Ⓔ Do Philemon and Baucis treat strangers the same way that the people in the village do? **No.**

Ⓕ Are they very kindhearted people? **Yes.**

● Were Philemon and Baucis rich? **No.**

● What sorts of things did they eat?
Call on individual students. Responses: Butter, cheese, bread, milk, vegetables, honey.

● How did they feel about sharing what they had with travelers? *Idea:* They felt they should treat their guest better than themselves.

Ⓖ What used to be where the village now stands? **A lake.**

● What had happened to that lake? *Idea:* It had dried up.

● What does that mean? **A fertile spot?** *Idea:* The soil was good for planting things.

● Do you know why the place where the village stood was very fertile? *Idea:* The lake had made the soil rich.

Ⓗ What was the only trace of the ancient lake? **A small brook.**

Ⓘ Everybody, touch the stately oaks. *Check.* Is that a beautiful valley. *Response:* Student preference.
The very sight of that valley should make the people kind and gentle.

Lesson 72 **53**

But the people of this lovely village were not worthy to dwell in such a beautiful place. They were very selfish and hard-hearted people, and had neither pity for the poor, nor sympathy for the homeless. They would only laugh if anybody told them that human beings should love one another. These people taught their children to be like themselves. They used to clap their hands when they saw the boys and girls run after strangers, shout at them and pelt them with stones. They kept large and fierce dogs, and whenever a traveler came into the village, this pack of disagreeable dogs scampered to meet the traveler, barking, snarling, and showing their teeth. Then they would seize the traveler by the leg, or by its clothes. This was a very terrible thing to do to poor travelers, especially when they were sick, or feeble, or crippled, or old. Some travelers would go miles and miles out of their way rather than try to pass through the village. (J)

★11 ERRORS★

So now you can understand why Philemon spoke so sorrowfully when he heard the shouts of the children and the barking of the dogs. The noise lasted a long time, and seemed to echo all the way through the valley.

"I never heard the dogs so loud," observed the good old man.

"Nor the children so rude," answered the good old wife.

They sat shaking their heads one to another, while the noise came nearer and nearer. At last, they saw two men approaching on foot. Close behind them came the fierce dogs, snarling at their heels. A little farther behind was a crowd of children, who sent up shrill cries, and flung stones at the two strangers with all their might. From time to time the younger of the two men turned around and drove back the dogs with a staff which he carried in his hand. His companion, who was a very tall person, walked calmly along, as if he didn't notice the fierce children or the pack of dogs.

Both of the travelers were very poorly dressed, and looked as if they might not have enough money in their pockets to pay for a meal.

"Come, wife," said Philemon to Baucis, "go and meet these poor travelers."

"You go and meet them," answered Baucis, "while I see whether we can get them anything for supper. A bowl of bread and milk would raise their spirits."

Baucis hurried into the cottage. Meanwhile, Philemon went forward, extended his hand, and said, in a hearty tone, "Welcome, strangers, welcome."

"Thank you," replied the younger of the two men. "This is quite a different greeting than we received in the village. Why do you live in such a bad neighborhood?"

"Ah," observed Old Philemon with a quiet smile, "I live here so that I may make up for the rudeness of my neighbors."

"Well said, old father!" cried the traveler, laughing. "My companion and I need some amends. Those children have splattered us with their mudballs and one of the dogs has torn my cloak."

Philemon was glad to see the younger man in such good spirits. Indeed, the traveler did not seem weary from his long journey, nor upset by the rough treatment he had received. He was dressed in an odd way. The edge of the round cap he wore stuck out over both ears. Although it was a summer evening, he wore a cloak, which he kept wrapped closely around him. Philemon also saw that he had an unusual pair of shoes. But because it was growing dark, Philemon could not tell exactly what was strange about the shoes. One thing certainly seemed odd—the traveler was so wonderfully lightfooted and active that it appeared as if his feet sometimes rose from the ground.

"I used to be lightfooted in my youth," said Philemon to the traveler, "but my feet always became heavier toward nightfall."

"There is nothing like a good staff to help one along," answered the stranger, "and I happen to have an excellent one, as you can see."

The traveler's staff was the oddest-looking staff that Philemon had ever seen. It was made of olive-wood, and had something like a little pair of wings near the top. Two snakes, carved in the wood, curled themselves around the staff. The snakes were so very skillfully carved that old Philemon almost thought they were alive, and that he could see them wriggling and twisting.

"A curious piece of work!" said Philemon. "I have never seen a staff with wings!"

(J) What would the children do to strangers? *Call on individual students. Responses:* Throw rocks, shout at them, set the dogs on them.

- What would the dogs do? *Call on individual students. Ideas:* Bark, snarl, show their teeth, grab the stranger's clothes.
- How did strangers feel about going through that village? *Idea:* They didn't want to.
- Read the rest of the story to yourselves and be ready to answer some questions.

After all students have finished reading.

- The sounds of dogs and children came closer to the old people's cottage. How many strangers were the dogs and children chasing? **Two.**
- What were the children doing? *Ideas:* Shouting at them; throwing stones.
- What would the younger traveler do from time to time? *Idea:* Drive the dogs back with his staff.
- Who greeted the travelers first? **Philemon.**
- What did Baucis do while Philemon greeted them? *Idea:* Looked for something to feed them.
- Which of the men seemed to be in good spirits? **The younger man.**
- What did the younger traveler wear on his head? **A cap.**
- Why couldn't Philemon tell exactly what was strange about the younger traveler's shoes? *Idea:* Because it was getting dark.
- How did this stranger move around? *Idea:* Quickly.
- What was he carrying? **A staff.**
- What was odd about that staff? *Idea:* It had a pair of wings on top and two snakes around it.
- Who do you think the younger traveler really is? *Response:* Student preference.

Award 4 points or have the students reread to the error limit sign.

INDEPENDENT WORK

Do all the items in your skillbook and workbook for lesson 72.

ANSWER KEY FOR WORKBOOK

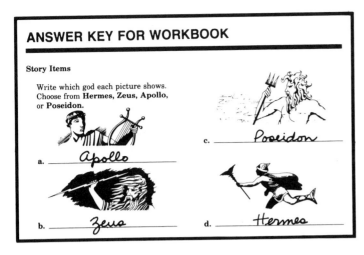

Story Items

Write which god each picture shows. Choose from **Hermes, Zeus, Apollo,** or **Poseidon.**

a. _Apollo_

b. _Zeus_

c. _Poseidon_

d. _Hermes_

WORKCHECK AND AWARDING POINTS

1. *Read the questions and answers for the skillbook and workbook.*

2. *Award points for independent work as follows:*

0 errors	*6 points*
2 errors	*4 points*
3, 4, or 5 errors	*2 points*
5 or more errors	*0 points*

3. *Award bonus points as follows:*

Correcting missed items or getting all items right	*2 points*
Doing the writing assignment acceptably	*2 points*

ANSWER KEY FOR SKILLBOOK

PART B

1. *Idea:* A week before Christmas, Clara bought a bike-repair tool kit for her brother, Tony.
2. *Idea:* During lunch, Sidney wrote a poem in the school lunchroom.

PART C

3. a. Old
   b. Poor
   c. Small
   d. Their guests
4. a. *Idea:* A lake
   b. *Idea:* A village
   c. Attractive
5. a. mean
   b. *Idea:* Attack them
   c. Their dogs
6. a. the villagers made noise
   b. *Idea:* strangers
   c. cottage
7. a. Two
   b. Poor
   c. *Idea:* To fix dinner
   d. *Idea:* Greeted the strangers
8. a. A staff
   b. *Ideas:* Snakes; wings
9. a. younger traveler
   b. Philemon
   c. village child
   d. village child
   e. Philemon
   f. younger traveler
   g. Philemon
   h. younger traveler
   i. village child

PART D

10. a. appreciation
    b. scheduled
    c. accuse
    d. intently
    e. resented
    f. talent
    g. insulting
    h. contract
    i. restricted to
    j. career

Lesson 73

WORD PRACTICE AND VOCABULARY

EXERCISE 1   Word practice

1. Everybody, find lesson 73, part A in your skillbook. *Wait.* Touch under each word in column 1 as I read it.
2. The first word is **sympathy.**
3. Next word. **Disguise.**
4. *Repeat step 3 for each remaining word in column 1.*
5. Your turn. Read the first word. *Signal.* **Sympathy.**
6. Next word. *Signal.* **Disguise.**
7. *Repeat step 6 for each remaining word in column 1.*
8. *Repeat the words in column 1 until firm.*

EXERCISE 2   Word family

1. Everybody, touch column 2. *Check.*
   All those words end with the letters **l-y.**
   Touch under the first word. *Pause.*
   What word? *Signal.* **Carelessly.**
2. Next word. *Pause.* What word? *Signal.*
   Suddenly.
3. *Repeat step 2 for each remaining word in column 2.*
4. *Repeat the words in column 2 until firm.*

EXERCISE 3   Vocabulary review

Task A

1. Everybody, touch column 3. *Check.*
   First you're going to read the words in column 3. Then we'll talk about what they mean.
2. Touch under the first word. *Pause.*
   What word? *Signal.* **Fertile.**
3. Next word. *Pause.*
   What word? *Signal.* **Miraculous.**
4. *Repeat step 3 for each remaining word in column 3.*
5. *Repeat the words in column 3 until firm.*

Task B

You've learned the meanings for all these words. Word 1 is **fertile.** *Call on a student.*
What is **fertile** land? *Idea:* Land that can grow very good crops.

Task C

Word 2 is **miraculous.** *Call on a student.*
What does **miraculous** mean? *Idea:* Like a miracle.

Task D

Word 3 is **staff.** *Call on a student.*
What is a **staff**? *Idea:* A long stick that you carry.

Task E

Word 4 is **hospitality.** *Call on a student.*
How would you show **hospitality** to somebody? *Idea:* By being kind to that person.

Task F

Word 5 is **cultivate.** *Call on a student.*
What does **cultivate** mean? *Idea:* You get rid of weeds and fix up the ground, so that you can plant crops.

Task G

Word 6 is **toiled.** *Call on a student.* What does **toiled** mean? *Idea:* Worked very hard.

EXERCISE 4   Vocabulary development

Task A

1. Everybody, touch column 4. *Check.*
   First you're going to read the words in column 4. Then we'll talk about what they mean.
2. Touch under the first line. *Pause.*
   What words? *Signal.* **Shrewd and witty.**
3. Next line. *Pause.*
   What words? *Signal.* **In disguise.**
4. Next word. *Pause.*
   What word? *Signal.* **Sympathy.**
5. *Repeat step 4 for **nimble.***
6. *Repeat the words in column 4 until firm.*

Task B

Now let's talk about what those words mean. The words in line 1 are **shrewd and witty.** Things that are **shrewd and witty** are smart and funny. *Call on a student.* What would you call remarks that are smart and funny? *Idea:* Shrewd and witty remarks.

Task C

The words in line 2 are **in disguise.** When you are **in disguise,** you are dressed so that nobody would recognize you. You might disguise yourself as a farmer or a witch.

Task D

Word 3 is **sympathy.** When you show **sympathy** toward somebody, you let the person know that you feel the things that person feels. *Call on a student.* How would you show sympathy to somebody who just lost their dog? *Idea:* Tell the person you're sorry that they lost their dog.

Task E

1. Word 4 is **nimble. Nimble** is the opposite of **awkward.** Everybody, what's the opposite of **an awkward dancer?** *Signal.* **A nimble dancer.**
2. What's the opposite of **an awkward quarterback.** *Signal.* **A nimble quarterback.**

EXERCISE 5   Vocabulary review

Task A

1. Everybody, touch column 5. *Check.* First you're going to read the words in column 5. Then we'll talk about what they mean.
2. Touch under the first word. *Pause.* What word? *Signal.* **Poseidon.**
3. Next word. *Pause.* What word? *Signal.* **Hermes.**
4. *Repeat step 3 for each remaining word in column 5.*
5. *Repeat the words in column 5 until firm.*

Task B

You've learned the meanings for all these words. Word 1 is **Poseidon.** *Call on a student.* Which Greek god was **Poseidon?** *Idea:* God of the sea.

Task C

Word 2 is **Hermes.** *Call on a student.* Which Greek god was **Hermes?** *Idea:* God of travelers.

Task D

Word 3 is **Zeus.** *Call on a student.* Which Greek god was **Zeus?** *Ideas:* The chief god; he commanded the winds, the clouds, lightning and thunder.

Task E

Word 4 is **Apollo.** *Call on a student.* Which Greek god was **Apollo?** *Idea:* God of music and light.

EXERCISE 6   Main idea paragraphs

1. Everybody, find part B in your skillbook. *Wait.* Read the instructions and the first paragraph to yourselves. Then we'll work together and make up a main-idea sentence. Raise your hand when you've finished reading the paragraph.
   - *After all students have raised their hands.*
   - Who was the main character in this paragraph? **Rochelle.**
   - So, I write Rochelle as the first part of the sentence. *Write **Rochelle** on the chalkboard.*
   - Now tell me the main thing that Rochelle did. Don't tell where or when, just tell what she did. *Call on individual students. Responses:* Flew her kite.
   - So, I write **flew her kite** as the next part of the sentence. *After **Rochelle** write: **flew her kite***
   - That's a good main-idea sentence. But we can add more information to this sentence if we wish. We can tell **when** she did it or **where** she did it.
   - When did she fly the kite? *Idea:* In March. *At the beginning of the sentence, write **In March,***
   - Where did she fly it? **In the park.** *At the end of the sentence, write: **in the park.***
   - Everybody, read the new main-idea sentence. *Signal.*
   In March, Rochelle flew her kite in the park.
2. Later you'll write main-idea sentences for both paragraphs in part B.
3. Remember, start out the sentences by naming the characters and the main things those characters did. Then tell more. You can tell **when,** tell **where,** tell **why,** or tell **how.** But tell these other things after you made up the sentences that tell who did something and the main thing those characters did.

The Miraculous Pitcher
PART 2Ⓐ

Philemon and his two guests reached the cottage door.

"Friends," said the old man, "sit down and rest yourselves here on our bench. My good wife, Baucis has gone to see what you can have for supper. We are poor folks, but you are welcome to whatever we have in the cupboard."

The young stranger sat down carelessly on the bench, and his staff fell to the ground. And then something marvelous happened. The staff seemed to get up from the ground by itself. It spread its little pair of wings, and flew up to the wall of the cottage. Then it leaned against the wall and stood quite still, except that the snakes continued to wriggle.Ⓑ

Before Philemon could ask any questions, the older stranger drew Philemon's attention from the wonderful staff by speaking to him.

The stranger spoke in a remarkably deep tone of voice. He asked, "In ancient times, wasn't there a lake covering the spot where the village now stands?"

"Not in my day, friend," answered Philemon, "and yet I am an old man, as you see. There were always the fields and meadows, just as they are now, and the old trees, and the little stream, murmuring through the valley. My father, and his father before him, never saw it otherwise, so far as I know. It will probably still be that way when old Philemon is gone and forgotten."Ⓒ

The older stranger observed, "Don't be too sure that the valley will always be as it is now." There was something very stern in his deep voice. He shook his head, too, so that his dark and heavy curls shook with the movement. He continued, "Since the people of the village have forgotten affection and sympathy, it would be better if the lake rippled over their dwellings again!"Ⓓ

The older traveler looked so stern that Philemon was frightened. But that was not all, for when the traveler frowned, the twilight seemed suddenly to grow darker; and when he shook his head there was a roll of

thunder in the air.Ⓔ

But suddenly the older stranger's face became so kindly and mild that the old man quite forgot his terror. Still, he could not help feeling that this old traveler must be no ordinary person, even though he was poorly clothed and journeying on foot. Philemon did not think he was a prince in disguise, but rather some very wise man, who went around the world in these poor clothes, seeking to add to his wisdom.Ⓕ

When Philemon raised his eyes to the stranger's face, he seemed to see more thought there than he could have observed in a lifetime.Ⓖ ★8 ERRORS★

While Baucis was getting the supper, the travelers both began to talk very sociably with Philemon. The younger traveler was extremely talkative, and made such shrewd and witty remarks that the good old man continually burst out laughing. Philemon thought that the younger man was the merriest fellow he had ever seen.

"What is your name?" asked Philemon.

"Why, I am very nimble, as you see," answered the traveler. "So, if you call me Quicksilver, the name will fit well."

"Quicksilver? Quicksilver?" repeated Philemon, looking in the traveler's face to see if he was making fun of him. "It is a very odd name. And your companion there, has he as strange a name?"

"You must ask the thunder to tell you his name," replied Quicksilver, putting on a mysterious look. "No other voice is loud enough."

Philemon turned to look at the older

traveler. He was probably the grandest figure that ever sat so humbly beside a cottage door. The older stranger talked in such a grave way that Philemon wanted to tell the stranger everything he knew. This is always the feeling that people have when they meet with anyone wise enough to comprehend all their good and evil.

Simple and kindhearted Philemon did not have many secrets to tell. He talked about the events of his past life. He had never been more than ten miles from the very spot where he lived. Baucis and he had dwelt in the cottage since their youth, and earned their bread by honest labor. They had always been poor, but contented. Philemon told what excellent butter and cheese Baucis made, and how nice the vegetables were that he raised in his garden. He said, too, that because he and his wife loved one another so very much, they both hoped that death might not separate them. They wanted to die together, just as they had lived together.

As the older stranger listened, a smile beamed over his face and made his face look as sweet as it was grand.

"You are a good old man," he said to Philemon, "and you have a good old wife. Your wish will be granted."

And it seemed to Philemon just then as if the sunset clouds threw up a bright flash from the west, and made a sudden light in the sky.

Baucis now had supper ready. She came to the door and began to make apologies for the poor meal which she was forced to set before her guests.

STORY READING

EXERCISE 7 Decoding and comprehension

1. Everybody, turn to page 279 in your textbook. *Wait. Call on a student.* What's the error limit for this lesson? **8 errors.**

2. *Call on individual students to read. Present the tasks specified for each circled letter.*

Ⓐ What's the title of the story you're reading? **The Miraculous Pitcher.**

● Who is the author? **Nathaniel Hawthorne.**

● What are the names of the old couple in this story? **Philemon and Baucis.**

● Where did they live? *Idea:* Near a village; in a cottage.

● How many travelers came to their cottage? **Two.**

● What followed the travelers to the cottage? *Idea:* Dogs and children.

● How was the young traveler dressed? *Call on individual students. Responses:* Round cap, cloak, strange shoes, staff.

● Who do you think that traveler was? *Idea:* Hermes.

Ⓑ Where did the younger man sit? *Idea:* On a bench.

● What very strange thing happened then? *Idea:* The staff fell and got up by itself.

Ⓒ What did the older stranger ask about? *Idea:* If a lake used to cover the village.

● What did Philemon tell him? *Idea:* He had never seen a lake there.

● What kind of voice did the older stranger have? *Idea:* A deep voice.

Ⓓ What does that mean: **It would be better if the lake rippled over their dwellings again?** *Idea:* The people deserve to be at the bottom of the lake.

Ⓔ Listen to that part again. *Read from* Ⓓ *to* Ⓔ.

● What happened when he shook his head? *Idea:* There was thunder.

● Who could this stranger be? *Idea:* Zeus.

Ⓕ What kind of man did Philemon think the older stranger was? *Idea:* A wise man.

● What does that mean: **He was seeking to add to his wisdom?** *Idea:* He wanted to become smarter.

Ⓖ Listen to that sentence again. *Read from* Ⓕ *to* Ⓖ.

● How much thought could Philemon observe in the stranger's face? *Idea:* A lot.

● Read the rest of the story to yourselves and be ready to answer some questions.

After all students have finished reading:

● What did the younger traveler say that his name was? **Quicksilver.**

● Who did the younger traveler say that Philemon should ask to find out the name of the older traveler? **The thunder.**

"Had we known you were coming," she said, "my husband and I would have gone without a bite. But I took most of today's milk to make cheese; and our last loaf of bread is already half-eaten. Ah me! I never feel the sorrow of being poor except when a poor traveler knocks at our door."

"All will be very well; do not trouble yourself, my good woman," replied the older stranger kindly. "An honest, hearty welcome to a guest works miracles with any meal."

"A welcome you shall have," cried Baucis, "and likewise a little honey that we happen to have left, and also a bunch of purple grapes."

"Why, Mother Baucis, it is a feast!" exclaimed Quicksilver, laughing, "an absolute feast! And you shall see how eagerly I will feast on it. I think I never felt hungrier in my life."

"Mercy on us!" whispered Baucis to her husband. "If the young man has such a terrible appetite, I am afraid there will not be half enough supper."

They all went into the cottage.

Quicksilver's staff, you will remember, had set itself up against the wall of the cottage. When Quicksilver entered the door, leaving his wonderful staff behind, it immediately spread its little wings, and went hopping and fluttering up the doorsteps. Tap, tap went the staff on the kitchen floor. It did not rest until it had leaned itself against Quicksilver's chair. Baucis and Philemon, however, were attending so closely to their guests that they did not notice the staff.

As Baucis had said, the supper was quite small. In the middle of the table were the remains of a loaf of brown bread, with a piece of cheese on one side of it and a dish of honey on the other. There was a pretty good bunch of grapes for each of the guests. A medium-sized clay pitcher, nearly full of milk, stood at a corner of the table. But when Baucis had filled two cups, and set them before the strangers, only a little milk remained in the bottom of the pitcher. Poor Baucis kept wishing that she could provide these hungry folks with a hearty supper.

And, since the supper was so very small, she could not help wishing that their appetites were smaller. But, right after they sat down, the travelers both drank all the milk in their cups in one gulp.

"A little more milk, kind Mother Baucis, if you please," said Quicksilver. "The day has been hot, and I am very thirsty."

"Now, my dear people," answered Baucis slowly, "I am so sorry and ashamed. But the truth is, there is hardly a drop more milk in the pitcher."

Quicksilver got up from the table and took the pitcher by the handle. Then he exclaimed, "Why, it appears to me that matters are not quite so bad as you think. There is much more milk in the pitcher."

And he proceeded to fill both cups from the pitcher that was supposed to be almost empty.

- How much had Philemon traveled during his lifetime? *Idea:* Very little.
- Why did Philemon want to tell the older stranger everything he knew? *Idea:* Because the stranger seemed so wise.
- Philemon told the older stranger about the wish that he and Baucis had for their death. What was their wish? *Idea:* To die together.
- What did the older stranger say when he heard about their wish? *Idea:* That they would have their wish.
- Why did Baucis apologize about the meal that she had for the strangers? *Idea:* Because there wasn't very much food.
- What would she have done if she had known they were coming? *Idea:* She and Philemon wouldn't have eaten.
- Which guest had a great appetite? **Quicksilver.**
- What does that mean: **He had a great appetite?** *Idea:* He was very hungry.
- What very strange thing happened when the younger stranger went inside the cottage? *Idea:* The staff followed him.
- Name some of the things that Baucis had prepared for the guests' supper. *Call on individual students. Responses:* Loaf of bread, cheese, honey, grapes, milk.
- What was in the pitcher? **Milk.**
- What did the travelers do with the milk they had been served? *Idea:* Drank it quickly.
- What did Quicksilver then say? *Idea:* That he wanted more milk.
- What did Baucis try to tell him? *Idea:* That there wasn't any more.
- Then what happened? *Idea:* Quicksilver filled the cups with milk from the pitcher.

Award 4 points or have the students reread to the error limit sign.

INDEPENDENT WORK

Do all the items in your skillbook and workbook for lesson 73.

ANSWER KEY FOR WORKBOOK

Review Items

- Write which character each statement describes. Choose from **Baucis, Quicksilver,** or the **older stranger.**

  a. This character made butter and cheese. _Baucis_

  b. This character looked very wise. _older stranger_

  c. This character had a very deep voice. _older stranger_

  d. This character was lightfooted. _Quicksilver_

  e. This character was always smiling. _Quicksilver_

  f. This character was worried about the amount of food. _Baucis_

  g. This character had a staff. _Quicksilver_

  h. This character wanted to die at the same time as someone else. _Baucis_

  i. When this character frowned, the twilight grew darker. _older stranger_

ANSWER KEY FOR SKILLBOOK
PART B

1. *Idea:* In March, Rochelle flew her kite in the park.
2. *Idea:* Last weekend, Veronica built a birdhouse.

PART C

3. **a.** A lake
   b. *Idea:* It got darker
   c. Wise
4. **a.** No
   b. Ten miles
   c. *Idea:* Vegetables
   d. Baucis
5. **a.** *Idea:* There wasn't enough to eat
   b. Milk
   c. *Any two:* bread, cheese, honey, grapes
6. **a.** *Idea:* It moved by itself
   b. The wings
   c. No
7. **a.** *Idea:* Just a little
   b. Two
   c. smiling

PART D

8. **a.** resented
   b. talented
   c. complained
   d. graduated
   e. business
   f. contract
   g. careers
   h. oppose
   i. defeated

Lesson 74

WORD PRACTICE AND VOCABULARY

EXERCISE 1   Word practice

1. Everybody, find lesson 74, part A in your skillbook. *Wait.* Touch under each word in column 1 as I read it.
2. The first word is **fragrance.**
3. Next word. **Century.**
4. *Repeat step 3 for each remaining word in column 1.*
5. Your turn. Read the first word. *Signal.* **Fragrance.**
6. Next word. *Signal.* **Century.**
7. *Repeat step 6 for each remaining word in column 1.*
8. *Repeat the words in column 1 until firm.*

EXERCISE 2   Vocabulary review

Task A

1. Everybody, touch column 2. *Check.* First you're going to read the words in column 2. Then we'll talk about what they mean.
2. Touch under the first line. *Pause.* What words? *Signal.* **In disguise.**
3. Next line. *Pause.* What words? *Signal.* **Shrewd and witty.**
4. Next word. *Pause.* What word? *Signal.* **Nimble.**
5. *Repeat step 4 for* **sympathy.**
6. *Repeat the words in column 2 until firm.*

Task B

You've learned the meanings for all these words. The words in line 1 are **in disguise.** *Call on a student.* What does **in disguise** mean? *Idea:* You dress so that nobody recognizes you.

Task C

The words in line 2 are **shrewd and witty.** *Call on a student.* What does **shrewd and witty** mean? *Idea:* Smart and funny.

Task D

1. Word 3 is **nimble.** *Call on a student.* What does **nimble** mean? *Ideas:* The opposite of awkward; agile.
2. Everybody, what's the opposite of **an awkward dancer?** *Signal.* **A nimble dancer.**
3. What's the opposite of **an awkward quarterback?** *Signal.* **A nimble quarterback.**

Task E

Word 4 is **sympathy.** *Call on a student.* How would you show **sympathy** to somebody who just lost a dog? *Accept a reasonable response.*

EXERCISE 3   Vocabulary development

Task A

1. Everybody, touch column 3. *Check.* First you're going to read the words in column 3. Then we'll talk about what they mean.
2. Touch under the first word. *Pause.* What word? *Signal.* **Astonishment.**
3. Next word. *Pause.* What word? *Signal.* **Inhabitant.**
4. *Repeat step 3 for each remaining word in column 3.*
5. *Repeat the words in column 3 until firm.*

Task B

1. Now let's talk about what those words mean. Word 1 is **astonishment.** Another word for **amazement** is **astonishment.** Everybody, what's another way of saying **She felt great amazement?** *Signal.* **She felt great astonishment.**
2. Everybody, what's another way of saying **They looked at the sky with amazement?** *Signal.* **They looked at the sky with astonishment.**

Lesson 74

PART A Word Lists

1
fragrance
century
abundant
spacious
inhabitant

2
Vocabulary words
1. in disguise
2. shrewd and witty
3. nimble
4. sympathy

3
Vocabulary words
1. astonishment
2. inhabitant
3. disagreeable
4. spacious
5. abundant
6. century
7. fragrance

PART B Main Idea Paragraphs

Read each paragraph below. For each paragraph, figure out who the main characters are and what main thing those characters did. Then write a sentence that tells the main idea. Start by naming the main characters, then tell **what** the characters did. You can write **when** the characters did it, **where** the characters did it, or **why** or **how** the characters did it.

1. It was the Fourth of July. Mr. and Mrs. Dunbar woke up early and began to prepare for the day's big event. Mr. Dunbar made chicken sandwiches and a big potato salad. He put the sandwiches and salad in a large basket, then went to his children's bedrooms to wake them up. Meanwhile, Mrs. Dunbar put gas in the car and checked the oil and tires. Then she picked up the family and the food and drove to Red Rock State Park. When they got to the park, the Dunbars got out of the car and put some blankets on the ground. Then they ate all the food, played volleyball, and went on a hike. They stayed at Red Rock State Park until sunset.

2. The Comets were one of the best softball teams in Springfield. There were five girls and five boys on the team, and they won almost all their games. By September, the Comets had won so many games that they ended up playing in the City Championship game. The Comets were certain that they would win. At the end of three innings, they had a five run lead. But the other team started to come back. By the last inning, the Comets were one run behind the other team. The Comets had only one more chance to bat. But the Comets did not score a run in that inning. The Comets were brokenhearted, but they went over to congratulate the other team.

Task C

1. Word 2 is **inhabitant.** Somebody who lives in a place is an **inhabitant** of that place. A person who lives in the United States is an inhabitant of the United States. Everybody, what's a person who lives in a cave? *Signal.*
An inhabitant of that cave.
2. What's a person who lives in a village? *Signal.*
An inhabitant of that village.

Task D

1. Word 3 is **disagreeable.** The opposite of **agreeable** is **disagreeable.** Everybody, what's the opposite of **an agreeable person?** *Signal.*
A disagreeable person.
2. What's the opposite of **an agreeable meal?** *Signal.* **A disagreeable meal.**

Task E

1. Word 4 is **spacious.** Something that has a lot of space in it is **spacious.** A house with a lot of space in it is a spacious house. Everybody, what's a house with a lot of space in it? *Signal.*
A spacious house.
2. What's a valley with a lot of space in it? *Signal.*
A spacious valley.

Task F

1. Word 5 is **abundant.** If there is a lot of something, that thing is **abundant.** A lot of milk is abundant milk. Everybody, what's a lot of grain? *Signal.* **Abundant grain.**
2. Everybody, what's a lot of kindness? *Signal.*
Abundant kindness.

Task G

Word 6 is **century.** A **century** is one hundred years. Everybody, how many years are in a century? *Signal.* **One hundred.**

Task H

Word 7 is **fragrance.** A pleasant smell is a **fragrance.**

EXERCISE 4 Main idea paragraphs

1. Everybody, find part B in your skillbook. Read the instructions and the first paragraph to yourselves. Then we'll work together and make up a main-idea sentence. Raise your hand when you've finished reading the paragraph.
- *After all students have raised their hands:*
- Who were the main characters in this paragraph? **The Dunbars.**
- So, I write the Dunbars as the first part of the sentence. *Write:* **The Dunbars** *on the chalkboard.*
- Now tell me the main thing that the Dunbars did. Don't tell where or when, just tell what they did. *Call on individual students. Response:* Went on a picnic. So, I write went on a picnic as the next part of the sentence. *After the Dunbars write:* **went on a picnic**
- That's a good main-idea sentence. But we can add more information to this sentence if we wish. We can tell **when** they did it or **where** they did it.
- When did they go on a picnic? *Idea:* On the Fourth of July. *At the beginning of the sentence, write:* **On the Fourth of July,**
- Where did they go for the picnic? *Idea:* To Red Rock State Park. *At the end of the sentence, write:* at **Red Rock State Park.**
- Everybody, read the new main-idea sentence. *Signal.* **On the Fourth of July, the Dunbars went on a picnic at Red Rock State Park.**
2. Later you'll write a main-idea sentence for both paragraphs in part B.
3. Remember, start out by naming the characters and the main thing those characters did. Then tell more. You can tell **when,** tell **where,** tell **why,** or tell **how.** But add these other things after you've made up the sentence that tells who did something, and the main thing those characters did.

Lesson 74

The Miraculous Pitcher
PART 3 Ⓐ

Baucis could scarcely believe her eyes. She had certainly poured out nearly all the milk, and had seen the bottom of the pitcher as she set it down upon the table.

"But I am old," thought Baucis to herself, "and may be forgetful. I suppose I must have made a mistake. In any case, the pitcher must be empty now, after filling the cups twice."

Baucis had seen that Quicksilver had turned the pitcher upside down, and had poured out every drop of milk in filling the last cup.

"What excellent milk!" observed Quicksilver, after finishing his second cup. "Excuse me, my kind hostess, but I must really ask you for a little more." Ⓑ

Of course there could not possibly be any milk left. Baucis lifted the pitcher anyway. To be polite, she went through the motion of pouring milk into Quicksilver's cup, but without the slightest idea that any milk would come from the pitcher. She was very surprised, therefore, when so much milk fell bubbling into the cup that it was immediately filled to the brim and overflowed upon the table!

And she noticed what a delicious fragrance the milk had! It seemed as if Philemon's only cow must have eaten the richest grass that could be found anywhere in the world. Ⓒ

"And now, a slice of your brown bread, Mother Baucis," said Quicksilver, "and a little of that honey."

Baucis cut him a slice. The bread, when she and her husband had eaten it, had been rather dry and crusty. But now, it was light and moist. Baucis tasted a crumb which had fallen on the table, and found it more delicious than her bread ever was before. She could hardly believe that it was a loaf of her own. Yet, what other loaf could it possibly be?

Lesson 74 Textbook **283**

Baucis began to think that something very unusual was going on. So, after helping the guests to bread and honey, she sat down by Philemon, and whispered what she had seen.

"Did you ever hear of anything like it?" she asked Philemon.

"No, I never did," answered Philemon with a smile. "And I think, my dear old wife, that you have been walking about in a sort of dream. There happened to be a little more milk in the pitcher than you thought, my dear wife—that is the only possible explanation." Ⓓ ★6 ERRORS★

"Ah, husband," said Baucis, "say what you will, but these are very unusual guests."

"Well, well," replied Philemon, still smiling, "perhaps they are. They certainly do look as if they had seen better days; and I am glad to see them having such a good supper."

Each of the guests had now taken a bunch of grapes. Baucis, who rubbed her eyes to see more clearly, thought that the grapes had grown larger and richer, and that each grape seemed to be at the point of bursting with ripe juice. It was entirely a mystery to her how such grapes could ever have been produced from the old vine that climbed against the cottage wall.

"These are marvelous grapes," observed Quicksilver, as he swallowed one after another. "Where did you gather them?"

"From my own vine," answered Philemon. "You may see one of its branches twisting across the window. But my wife and I never thought the grapes were very fine ones."

"I never tasted better," said Quicksilver. "Another cup of that delicious milk, if you please, and I shall then have eaten better than a prince."

This time old Philemon got up himself, and picked up the pitcher; for he was curious to discover whether there was any truth in what Baucis had whispered to him. He knew that his good old wife never lied, and that she was seldom mistaken. But this case was so unusual that he wanted to see into the pitcher with his own eyes. As he picked up the pitcher, he slyly glanced into it. He saw that it didn't contain a single drop. All at once, however, he saw a little white fountain, which gushed up from the bottom of the pitcher, and rapidly filled it to the brim with deliciously fragrant milk. It was lucky that Philemon, in his surprise, did not drop the miraculous pitcher from his hand.

"Who are you, you wonder-working strangers?" he cried, even more confused

284 Lesson 74 Textbook

STORY READING

EXERCISE 5 Decoding and comprehension

1. Everybody, turn to page 283 in your textbook. *Wait. Call on a student.* What's the error limit for this lesson? **6 errors.**

2. *Call on individual students to read. Present the tasks specified for each circled letter.*

Ⓐ What had just happened at the end of the last lesson? *Idea:* Quicksilver had poured more milk from the empty pitcher.

Ⓑ How many cups had Quicksilver already had? **Two.**

● What do you think is going to happen? *Idea:* The pitcher will have more milk in it.

Ⓒ What does that mean: **The milk had a delicious fragrance?** *Idea:* It smelled good.

● Why did Baucis think that Philemon's cow must have eaten the richest grass in the world? *Idea:* Because the milk smelled so good.

Ⓓ Did Philemon think that Baucis had observed what really happened? **No.**

● What did Philemon think really happened? *Idea:* There was more milk in the pitcher.

● What do you think really happened? *Idea:* Quicksilver somehow put more milk in the pitcher.

● Read the rest of the story to yourselves and be ready to answer some questions.

After all students have finished reading:

● What happened to the grapes when the guests took them? *Idea:* They got better.

● Why did Baucis think that these grapes couldn't be hers? *Idea:* Because they had never looked that good.

● After the guests had eaten the grapes, what did Quicksilver ask for? *Idea:* More milk.

● Who served him this time? **Philemon.**

● Why did Philemon want to serve the milk? *Idea:* To see if Baucis had told the truth.

● How much milk was in the pitcher when he first looked into it? *Idea:* None.

● Then what happened? *Idea:* He saw milk come up from the bottom of the pitcher.

Lesson 74 **63**

than his wife had been.

"We are your guests and your friends," replied the older traveler in his mild, deep voice, that was both sweet and amazing. Then he added, "I would also like another cup of milk."

The older traveler seemed so solemn that Philemon did not ask him any questions. And when Philemon drew Quicksilver aside, and asked how a fountain of milk could get into an old clay pitcher, Quicksilver pointed to his staff.

"There is the answer," said Quicksilver. "And if you can figure it out, please tell me. I can't understand my staff. It is always playing such odd tricks as this—sometimes getting me a supper, and quite as often stealing my supper. If I had any faith in such nonsense, I should say the stick was charmed!"

He said no more, but looked so slyly at Baucis and Philemon that they almost thought he was laughing at them.

The supper was now over, and Baucis begged the travelers to stay for the night. They accepted her offer cheerfully. The good woman showed them to the sleeping room. The magic staff went hopping at Quicksilver's heels as he left the room.

Later that night, the good old couple spent some time talking about the events of the evening, and then lay down on the floor and fell fast asleep. They had given up their sleeping room to the guests, and had no other bed for themselves except the floor.

Philemon and Baucis arose with the sun, and the strangers made their prepara- tions to depart. Philemon asked them to remain a little longer, until Baucis could milk the cow and bake some bread. The guests, however, seemed to think it better to set out before the day got hot. They therefore set out immediately, but asked Philemon and Baucis to walk with them a short distance and show them which road to take.

"Ah me!" exclaimed Philemon, when they had walked a little way from their door. "If our neighbors only knew what great rewards there are for being kind to strangers, they would tie up all their dogs and never allow their children to fling another stone."

Baucis explained, "It is a sin and a shame for them to behave the way they do! And I'm going to go and tell some of them what nasty people they are."

With a cunning smile, Quicksilver replied, "I fear that you will find none of them at home."

Just then, the older traveler's face took on such a solemn expression that neither Baucis nor Philemon dared to speak another word. They gazed into his face, as if they had been gazing at the sky.

The older traveler spoke. "When men do not treat the humblest stranger as if he were a brother, they are unworthy to exist on earth." He spoke in tones so deep that they sounded like thunder.

"And anyway, my dear old people," cried Quicksilver, with a look of fun and mischief in his eyes, "where is this village that you talk about? On which side of us does it lie? I do not see it."

Lesson 74   Textbook   **285**

- When Philemon asked who the strangers really were, did they tell him? **No.**
- Who did Philemon ask about the fountain of milk? **Quicksilver.**
- What was Quicksilver's answer? *Idea:* He said the staff had done it.
- Where did the strangers sleep that night? *Idea:* In Philemon and Baucis's bed.
- Where did Philemon and Baucis sleep? *Idea:* On the floor.
- The story says that Baucis and Philemon arose with the sun. What does that mean? *Idea:* They got up very early.
- What did Philemon want the strangers to do in the morning? *Idea:* Stay longer.
- What did the strangers decide to do? *Idea:* Leave.
- As they walked with the strangers, what did Baucis say that she was going to do after the strangers left? *Idea:* Tell the villagers they were mean.
- At the end of this part of the story, Quicksilver said something that was very strange. What did he say? *Idea:* That none of the villagers would be at home.
- Why do you think they wouldn't be at home? *Idea:* Something has happened to them.

Award 4 points or have the students reread to the error limit sign.

INDEPENDENT WORK

Do all the items in your skillbook and workbook for lesson 74.

ANSWER KEY FOR WORKBOOK

Review Items

1. Here are some events that could happen. Write whether the **villagers** or **Baucis** would do each thing.
   a. Throw stones at a stranger.
   villagers
   b. Greet a stranger kindly.
   Baucis
   c. Try to make a weary traveler comfortable. _Baucis_
   d. Make sure the door was always open. _Baucis_
   e. Refuse to give a traveler a glass of water. _villagers_
   f. Give a poor person bread only if the person pays for it.
   villagers
   g. Give a poor person something to eat for free. _Baucis_

2. Write the main use for each animal. Choose from **hunting, food,** or **carrying.**
   a. cat _hunting_
   b. donkey _carrying_
   c. goat _food_
   d. llama _carrying_
   e. chicken _food_

3. Here are some events from Jackie Robinson's life.
   - Jackie helps win the World Series
   - Jackie dies
   - Jackie first plays for the Dodgers
   - Jackie leaves UCLA

   Write the correct event after each date on the time line.

   1972 _Jackie dies_

   1955 _Jackie helps win the World Series_

   1947 _Jackie first plays for the Dodgers_

   1941 _Jackie leaves UCLA_

WORKCHECK AND AWARDING POINTS

1. *Read the questions and answers for the skillbook and workbook.*
2. *Award points for independent work as follows:*

> *0 errors . . . . .6 points*
> *2 errors . . . . .4 points*
> *3, 4, or 5 errors . . . . .2 points*
> *5 or more errors . . . . .0 points*

3. *Award bonus points as follows:*

> *Correcting missed items*
> *or getting all items right . . . . .2 points*
> *Doing the writing*
> *assignment acceptably . . . . .2 points*

ANSWER KEY FOR SKILLBOOK
PART B
1. *Idea:* On the Fourth of July, the Dunbars went on a picnic at Red Rock State Park.
2. *Idea:* In September, the Comets lost the City Championship softball game.

PART C
3. **a.** *Idea:* Hermes
   b. *Idea:* Zeus
4. **a.** No
   b. *Idea:* Because milk poured out
   c. *Ideas:* larger, juicier, richer
5. **a.** No
   b. *Idea:* A fountain of milk
   c. His staff
6. **a.** *Idea:* On the floor
   b. *Idea:* The strangers
7. **a.** *Idea:* To tell the people how mean they were
   b. *Idea:* The village

PART D
8. **a.** appreciation
   b. great anger
   c. accused
   d. promoted
   e. restricted to
   f. oppose
   g. miraculous
   h. hospitality
   i. fertile
   j. cultivated

Lesson 75

WORD PRACTICE AND VOCABULARY

EXERCISE 1 Word practice

1. Everybody, find lesson 75, part A in your skillbook. *Wait.* Touch under each word in column 1 as I read it.
2. The first word is **sour.**
3. Next word. **Calculate.**
4. *Repeat step 3 for* **inhale.**
5. Your turn. Read the first word. *Signal.* **Sour.**
6. Next word. *Signal.* **Calculate.**
7. *Repeat step 6 for* **inhale.**
8. *Repeat the words in column 1 until firm.*

EXERCISE 2 Word practice

1. Everybody, touch under the first word in column 2. *Pause.* What word? *Signal.* **Fertile.**
2. Next word. *Pause.* What word? *Signal.* **Hospitality.**
3. *Repeat step 2 for each remaining word in column 2.*
4. *Repeat the words in column 2 until firm.*

EXERCISE 3 Vocabulary review

Task A

1. Everybody, touch column 3. *Check.* First you're going to read the words in column 3. Then we'll talk about what they mean.
2. Touch under the first word. *Pause.* What word? *Signal.* **Inhabitant.**
3. Next word. *Pause.* What word? *Signal.* **Spacious.**
4. *Repeat step 3 for each remaining word in column 3.*
5. *Repeat the words in column 3 until firm.*

Task B

You've learned the meanings for all these words. Word 1 is **inhabitant.** *Call on a student.* What is an **inhabitant?** *Idea:* A person who lives in a place.

Task C

Word 2 is **spacious.** *Call on a student.* What does **spacious** mean? *Idea:* Having a lot of space.

Task D

Word 3 is **abundant.** *Call on a student.* What does **abundant** mean? *Idea:* A lot of something.

Task E

Word 4 is **disagreeable.** *Call on a student.* What does **disagreeable** mean? *Idea:* Not agreeable.

Task F

Word 5 is **century.** *Call on a student.* What is a **century?** *Idea:* One hundred years.

Task G

1. Word 6 is **astonishment.** *Call on a student.* What does **astonishment** mean? *Idea:* Amazement.
2. Everybody, what's another way of saying **They looked at the sky with amazement?** *Signal.* **They looked at the sky with astonishment.**
3. Everybody, what's another way of saying **She felt great amazement?** *Signal.* **She felt great astonishment.**

EXERCISE 4 Vocabulary from context

Task A

1. Everybody, touch column 4. *Check.* First you're going to read the words in column 4. Then we'll talk about what they mean.
2. Touch under the first word. *Pause.* What word? *Signal.* **Inhale.**
3. Next word. *Pause.* What word? *Signal.* **Calculate.**
4. *Repeat step 3 for each remaining word in column 4.*
5. *Repeat the words in column 4 until firm.*

Task B

1. Everybody, find part B in your skillbook. *Check.* I'll read those sentences. You figure out what the underlined part in each sentence means.
2. Sentence one. He was out of breath and was breathing very hard—first breathing out, then <u>inhaling</u>. *Call on a student.* What could **inhaling** mean? *Idea:* Breathing in.
3. *Repeat step 2 for each remaining sentence.*
   Answer Key: **2.** *Idea:* Figured out.
   3. *Idea:* Fall through.
   4. *Idea:* Shined.

Lesson 75

The Miraculous Pitcher

PART 4

Philemon and his wife turned toward the valley, where at sunset the day before, they had seen the meadows, the houses, the gardens, the clumps of trees, the wide street, and the children.(A) But to their astonishment, there was no longer any village! Even the fertile valley had ceased to exist. In its place they saw the broad, blue surface of a lake, which filled the great valley from brim to brim. The lake reflected the surrounding hills in its still waters. For an instant the lake remained perfectly smooth. Then a little breeze sprang up, and caused the water to dance, glitter, and sparkle in the early morning sun.

The lake seemed so strangely familiar that the two old people were greatly puzzled. They felt as if they could only have been dreaming about a village ever having been there. But the next moment they remembered the dwellings, and the faces of the inhabitants. It had not been a dream. The village had been there yesterday, and now was gone.

"Alas!" cried these kindhearted old people. "What has become of our poor neighbors?"(B)

"The villagers exist no longer as men and women," said the older traveler in his grand and deep voice, while a roll of thunder seemed to echo in the distance.

Quicksilver said with his mischievous smile, "Those foolish people are all changed to fish. It was only a small change, for they were already the coldest-blooded human beings on earth."(C)

The older traveler continued, "As for you, good Philemon, and you, kind Baucis, you have shown us much hospitality and kindness. You have done well, my dear old friends; therefore, request whatever favor you have most at heart, and it is

granted."

Philemon and Baucis looked at one another, and then seemed to answer with one voice.(D) ★6 ERRORS★

They said, "Let us live together while we live, and leave the world at the same instant when we die, for we have always loved one another!"

"It will be so," replied the older stranger, in a deep, kind voice. "Now look toward your cottage."

They did so. But to their surprise, they saw a tall palace of white marble standing where their humble cottage had been.

"There is your home," said the older stranger, smiling on them both. "Show your hospitality in that palace as freely as you did in the humble cottage."

The old folks fell on their knees to thank him, but when they looked up, they were amazed to discover that neither he nor Quicksilver were there.

So Philemon and Baucis lived in the marble palace, and they spent much of their time making travelers comfortable.

The milk pitcher was never empty. Whenever friendly guests took a drink from that pitcher, they always found it to be the sweetest milk that ever ran down their throats. But if angry and disagreeable travelers took a sip, they were certain to twist their faces, and say that it was a pitcher of sour milk!

Thus, the old couple lived in their palace a long, long time, and grew older and older. At last, however, there came a summer morning when Philemon and Baucis failed to appear. Their guests searched everywhere, from the top to the bottom of the spacious palace, but they could not find the old couple. Finally, they saw two great trees in front of the palace. Nobody could remember ever seeing the two trees before. Yet there the trees stood, with their roots fastened deep into the soil. Their leaves cast a shadow on the front of the palace. Their branches were wound together, and embraced one another, so that each tree seemed to live in the other.

These trees must have required at least a century to grow, and the guest wondered how they could have become so tall in a single night. Just then, a breeze sprang up and made the branches move. And then there was a deep, broad murmur in the air, as if the two mysterious trees were speaking.

"I am old Philemon," murmured one tree.

"I am old Baucis," murmured the other.

But as the breeze grew stronger, the trees both spoke at once: "Philemon, Baucis, Baucis, Philemon"—as if one were both and both were one, and talking together with a common heart. It was plain enough that the good old couple had been reborn, and were now to spend a quiet and delightful hundred years or so as trees. And oh, what a wonderful shade they gave! Whenever travelers paused beneath the trees, they heard a pleasant whisper of the leaves above their head, and marveled because the sounds seemed to say: "Welcome, welcome, dear traveler, welcome!"

STORY READING

EXERCISE 5   Decoding and comprehension

1. Everybody, turn to page 286 in your textbook. *Wait. Call on a student.* What's the error limit for this lesson? **6 errors.**

2. *Call on individual students to read. Present the tasks specified for each circled letter.*

(A) Do you think they'll see all those things now? **No.**

(B) Who do you think is responsible for the village not being there any more? *Idea:* The older traveler.

● Why did he do that? *Idea:* To punish the villagers.

● Would he have done that if the villagers had been kind? **No.**
Remember, Zeus rewards kindness and punishes evil.

(C) What are the villagers now? **Fish.**

(D) What does that mean: **Answer with one voice?** *Idea:* They both answered at the same time.

● Read the rest of the story to yourselves and be ready to answer some questions.

After all students have finished reading:

● What had their cottage changed into when Philemon and Baucis looked at it? *Idea:* A palace.

● How did they use this palace? *Idea:* They let strangers stay there.

● What would friendly guests find out after drinking milk from the pitcher? *Idea:* That the milk was sweet.

● What would disagreeable guests do after taking a sip of the milk? *Ideas:* Twist their faces; say that the milk was sour.

● When Philemon and Baucis did not show up one morning, what did the guests discover in the front yard? *Idea:* Trees.
The Greeks believed that people took another form after they died. They believed that some people turned into animals; other people turned into trees.

● The story says that the trees must have required at least a century to grow. How many years would that be? **One hundred.**

● What kind of sound did the trees make when the breeze came up? *Ideas:* Talking; murmuring.

And some kind soul, who knew what would have pleased old Baucis and old Philemon best, built a circular seat around both their trunks, where, for many years, the weary and the hungry and the thirsty used to sit and drink milk abundantly out of the miraculous pitcher.

- Look at the picture and see if you can find Baucis and Philemon in the tree.

Award 4 points or have the students reread to the error limit sign.

INDEPENDENT WORK

Do all the items in your skillbook and workbook for lesson 75.

ANSWER KEY FOR WORKBOOK

Crossword Puzzle

To work the puzzle, read an item and figure out which word the item describes. Then write the word in the puzzle.
Complete the entire puzzle.

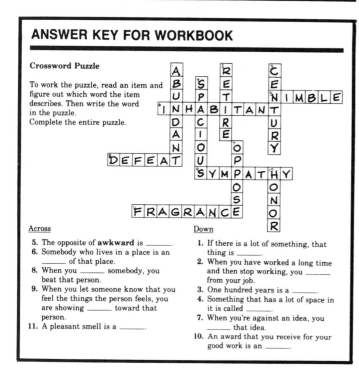

Across

5. The opposite of **awkward** is _____.
6. Somebody who lives in a place is an _____ of that place.
8. When you _____ somebody, you beat that person.
9. When you let someone know that you feel the things the person feels, you are showing _____ toward that person.
11. A pleasant smell is a _____.

Down

1. If there is a lot of something, that thing is _____.
2. When you have worked a long time and then stop working, you _____ from your job.
3. One hundred years is a _____.
4. Something that has a lot of space in it is called _____.
7. When you're against an idea, you _____ that idea.
10. An award that you receive for your good work is an _____.

WORKCHECK AND AWARDING POINTS

1. *Read the questions and answers for the skillbook and workbook.*
2. *Award points for independent work as follows:*

> *0 errors .6 points*
> *2 errors .4 points*
> *3, 4, or 5 errors . . . . .2 points*
> *5 or more errors . . . . .0 points*

3. *Award bonus points as follows:*

> *Correcting missed items*
> *or getting all items right . . . . .2 points*
> *Doing the writing*
> *assignment acceptably . . . . .2 points*

ANSWER KEY FOR SKILLBOOK

PART C
1. *Idea:* Last summer, the Chavez family took a train from Los Angeles to New York City.
2. *Idea:* In the springtime, Chico won the Steeplechase in Liverpool.

PART D
3. a. *Idea:* It turned into a lake
   b. *Ideas:* Zeus; the older stranger
   c. Baucis and Philemon
   d. Fish
   e. *Idea:* They were coldblooded
4. a. *Idea:* To live and die together
   b. *Idea:* It turned into a palace
5. a. *Idea:* They disappeared
   b. *Idea:* Took care of travelers
   c. *Idea:* Sweet
   d. *Idea:* Sour
6. a. Trees
   b. *Idea:* In front of the palace
   c. *Idea:* Baucis and Philemon
   d. *Idea:* A bench
   e. Travelers
   f. Milk
   g. *Idea:* The miraculous pitcher

PART E
7. a. False
   b. False
   c. True
   d. False
   e. True
   f. False
8. a. accused
   b. appreciation
   c. career
   d. beat
   e. cultivate
   f. miraculous
   g. sympathy
   h. shrewd and witty
   i. nimble

Lesson 76

WORD PRACTICE AND VOCABULARY

EXERCISE 1   Word practice

1. Everybody, find lesson 76, part A in your skillbook. *Wait.* Touch under each word in column 1 as I read it.
2. The first word is **Midas.**
3. Next word. **Pooh.**
4. *Repeat step 3 for* **chink.**
5. Your turn. Read the first word. *Signal.* **Midas.**
6. Next word. *Signal.* **Pooh.**
7. *Repeat step 6 for* **chink.**
8. *Repeat the words in column 1 until firm.*

EXERCISE 2   Word family

1. Everybody, touch column 2. *Check.*
   All those words are made up of two shorter words. Touch under the first word. *Pause.*
   What word? *Signal.* **Marygold.**
2. Next word. *Pause.* What word? *Signal.*
   Buttercup.
3. *Repeat step 2 for each remaining word in column 2.*
4. *Repeat the words in column 2 until firm.*

EXERCISE 3   Word practice

1. Everybody, touch under the first word in column 3. *Pause.* What word? *Signal.* **Petal.**
2. Next word. *Pause.* What word? *Signal.*
   Fragrant.
3. *Repeat step 2 for each remaining word in column 3.*
4. *Repeat the words in column 3 until firm.*

EXERCISE 4   Vocabulary review

Task A

1. Everybody, touch column 4. *Check.*
   First you're going to read the words in column 4. Then we'll talk about what they mean.
2. Touch under the first word. *Pause.*
   What word? *Signal.* **Calculate.**
3. Next word. *Pause.*
   What word? *Signal.* **Gleam.**
4. *Repeat step 3 for each remaining word in column 4.*
5. *Repeat the words in column 4 until firm.*

Task B
You've learned the meanings for all these words. Word 1 is **calculate.** *Call on a student.*
What does **calculate** mean? *Idea:* Figure out.

Task C
Word 2 is **gleam.** *Call on a student.*
What does **gleam** mean? *Idea:* Shine.

Task D
Word 3 is **sift.** *Call on a student.*
What does **sift** mean? *Idea:* Fall through.

Task E
Word 4 is **inhale.** *Call on a student.*
What does **inhale** mean? *Idea:* Breathe in.

STORY READING

EXERCISE 5   Comprehension passage

1. Everybody, turn to page 289 in your textbook.
2. *Call on individual students to read. Present the tasks specified for each circled letter.*

Lesson 76

Roman Gods Ⓐ

The people who lived in Rome had gods that were very similar to the Greek gods. But the Roman gods had different names. Ⓑ

The names of the Roman gods are not hard to remember because they are the names of many of the planets in the solar system.

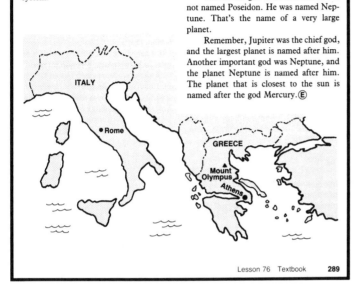

The chief Roman god was not named Zeus. He was named Jupiter. That's the name of the largest planet. Ⓒ

The Roman god who was Jupiter's messenger was not named Hermes. He was named Mercury. That's the name of the planet that is closest to the sun. Ⓓ

The Roman god who ruled the sea was not named Poseidon. He was named Neptune. That's the name of a very large planet.

Remember, Jupiter was the chief god, and the largest planet is named after him. Another important god was Neptune, and the planet Neptune is named after him. The planet that is closest to the sun is named after the god Mercury. Ⓔ

The Golden Touch
by Nathaniel Hawthorne Ⓐ

PART 1

Once upon a time there lived a very rich king named Midas, who had a daughter named Marygold.

King Midas was very fond of gold. The only thing he loved more was his daughter. Ⓑ But the more Midas loved his daughter, the more he desired gold. He thought that the best thing he could possibly do for his child would be to give her the largest pile of yellow, glistening coins that had ever been heaped together since the world began. Ⓒ So, Midas gave all his thoughts and all his time to collecting gold. When he gazed at the gold-tinted clouds of sunset, he wished that they were real gold, and that they could be herded into his strong box. When little Marygold ran to meet him with a bunch of buttercups and dandelions, he used to say, "Pooh, pooh, child. If these flowers were as golden as they look, they would be worth picking." Ⓓ

And yet, in his earlier days, before he had this insane desire for gold, King Midas had shown a great love for flowers. He had planted a garden where there were the biggest and sweetest roses that any person ever saw or smelled. These roses were still growing in the garden, as large, as lovely, and as fragrant as they were when Midas used to pass whole hours looking at them, and inhaling their perfume. Ⓔ But now, if he looked at the flowers at all, it was only to calculate how much the garden would be worth if each of the rose petals were a thin plate of gold. And though he once was fond of music, the only music for poor Midas now was the chink of one coin against another. Ⓕ ★6 ERRORS★

After a while, Midas became so unreasonable that he could scarcely bear to see or touch any object that was not gold. Therefore, he passed a large part of everyday in a dark and dreary room underground, in the basement of his palace. It was here that he kept his wealth. Midas went to this dismal hole whenever he wanted to be particularly happy. After carefully locking the door, he would take a bag of gold coins, or a golden bowl as big as a hat, or a heavy golden bar, or a bag of gold dust. He would bring his precious gold objects from the corners of the room into the one bright and narrow sunbeam that came from the window. He only liked the sunbeam because it made his treasure shine.

Midas would then count the coins in the bag, or toss up the bar and catch it as it came down, or sift the gold dust through his fingers. He would often look at the

---

Ⓐ This passage tells about the gods the Romans used to have.

Ⓑ Look at the map. It shows the countries Greece and Italy. Rome is a big city in the country of Italy. Athens is a big city in the country of Greece. The map also shows Mt. Olympus.

• Touch Italy. *Check.*
• Touch Rome. *Check.*
• Touch Greece. *Check.*
• Touch Athens. *Check.*
• What was the main way that the Roman gods were different from the Greek gods? *Idea:* They had different names.

Ⓒ Which Roman god was the chief god? **Jupiter.**

• Which is the largest planet in our solar system? **Jupiter.**
So, it's easy to remember Jupiter.

Ⓓ Which Roman god did the same things that Hermes did? **Mercury.**

Ⓔ Who was the Roman god of the sea? **Neptune.**
The planet Neptune is very large.

EXERCISE 6   Decoding and comprehension

1. Everybody, turn to page 290 in your textbook. *Wait. Call on a student.* What's the error limit for this lesson? **6 errors.**

2. *Call on individual students to read. Present the tasks specified for each circled letter.*

Ⓐ The last story that you read was written by a writer named Nathaniel Hawthorne. He also wrote the story that you will start today. Like "The Miraculous Pitcher," the story is also based on an old Greek story. Nathaniel Hawthorne was famous for taking these old stories and writing them in a new and exciting way.

Ⓑ What did he love more than anything? **His daughter.**

• What was the thing he loved next best? **Gold.**

Ⓒ Listen to that part again. *Read from* Ⓑ *to* Ⓒ.

• What happened to his love for gold when his love for his daughter increased? *Idea:* It increased.

• The more he loved her, the more he loved gold. Why did he want so much gold? *Idea:* So he could give it to his daughter.

Ⓓ What color are buttercups and dandelions? **Yellow.**

• Did Midas think they were worth picking? **No.**

• Why not? *Idea:* Because they weren't made out of gold.

Ⓔ What would Midas do in his garden? *Ideas:* Look at the flowers; smell the flowers.

• Everybody, show me how you would inhale the perfume of a flower. *Check.*

Ⓕ Did Midas still spend his time looking at his flowers and smelling them? **No.**

funny reflection of his own face in the polished surface of a golden bowl. At those times, he would whisper to himself, "Oh Midas, rich King Midas, what a happy man you are."

But it was strange to see how the reflection of his face kept grinning at him out of the polished surface of the bowl. It seemed to be aware of his foolish behavior, and to make fun of him.

Midas called himself a happy man, but he felt that he was not as happy as he might be. His peak of enjoyment would never be reached unless the whole world was to become his treasure room, filled with his own gold.

Midas was enjoying himself in his treasure room one day as usual, when he saw a shadow fall over the heaps of gold. He looked up and saw a stranger standing in the bright and narrow sunbeam. It was a young man with a cheerful face. King Midas thought that the smile on the stranger's face had a kind of golden glow. And even though the stranger blocked the sunshine, the gleam upon all the piled up treasures was brighter than before. Even the corners were lit up when the stranger smiled.

Midas knew that he had carefully turned the key in the lock, and that no human being could possibly break into his treasure room. So, Midas concluded that his visitor must be a god. In those days, gods interested themselves in the joys and sorrows of men, women, and children. Midas had met gods before now, and was not sorry to meet one of them again. The stranger's face was so kind that it seemed as if he had come to do Midas a favor.

Lesson 76   Textbook   **291**

- Why not? *Idea:* He was more interested in his gold.
- What was the only kind of music that Midas enjoyed? *Idea:* The sound of coins chinking against each other.
- Is that sound really music? **No.**
- Read the rest of the story to yourselves and be ready to answer some questions.

After all students have finished reading:

- Where did Midas like to spend most of his time? *Idea:* In the basement of the palace.
- What was in that place? *Idea:* All his gold.
- Why did he like the sunbeam that came into his basement room? *Idea:* Because it made the gold shine.
- When Midas looked at his reflection in the golden bowl, what would the reflection seem to do? *Idea:* Make fun of him.
- What would have made Midas even happier than he was? *Idea:* To have all the gold in the world.
- One day, who did Midas notice in his treasure room? *Idea:* A stranger.
- Why was Midas surprised to see anybody inside that room? *Idea:* Because the door was locked.
  So, Midas concluded that the stranger must be someone special.
- What did Midas think the stranger was? *Idea:* A god.
- Had Midas ever met a god before? **Yes.**
- What did Midas think the stranger would do for him? *Idea:* A favor.
- What kind of favor do you think Midas is going to ask for? *Response:* Student preference.

Award 4 points or have the students reread to the error limit sign.

EXERCISE 7   Special projects

1. Everybody, turn to page 121 in your skillbook. *Wait.* Find part F. We're going to do these projects.
2. Read that section to yourselves. Read it carefully so that you have the information you need to decide what you want to do. After you have read the section, we'll discuss it.
3. *After all students have finished reading:* Every student should work on at least one project. I'll name the projects, and you raise your hand if the project I name is the one you want to work on.
- Project 1. Making a list of all the Greek gods. Who wants to work on that project? *List the students who volunteer.*
- Project 2. Making a play based on "The Miraculous Pitcher." Who wants to work on that project? *List the students who volunteer.*
4. *Allow the students extra time to carry out their projects.*

Story Items

1. Look at the map.

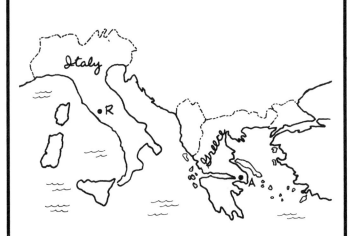

a. Write **A** next to the dot that shows Athens.
b. Write **R** next to the dot that shows Rome.
c. Write **Greece** on the country of Greece.
d. Write **Italy** on the country of Italy.

2. Write the name of the Roman god who might make each statement. Choose from **Jupiter, Mercury** or **Neptune.**
a. "I live under the ocean."

Neptune

b. "I am faster than any other god."

Mercury

c. "I can make thunder and lightning."

Jupiter

d. "I have wings on my sandals."

Mercury

INDEPENDENT WORK

Do all the items in your skillbook and workbook for lesson 76.

WORKCHECK AND AWARDING POINTS

1. *Read the questions and answers for the skillbook and workbook.*
2. *Award points for independent work as follows:*

0 errors	.6 points
2 errors	.4 points
3, 4, or 5 errors	.2 points
5 or more errors	.0 points

3. *Award bonus points as follows:*

Correcting missed items or getting all items right	.2 points
Doing the writing assignment acceptably	.2 points

ANSWER KEY FOR SKILLBOOK

PART B
1. *Idea:* On Saturday, Janet took a picture of her friends.
2. *Idea:* In 1975, William rowed a boat across Swan Lake.

PART C
3. a. *Ideas:* His daughter; Marygold
   b. Gold
   c. Marygold / gold
4. a. Roses
   b. *Ideas:* Look at them; smell them
   c. *Idea:* The sound of coins
5. a. *Idea:* In the basement
   b. *Idea:* A lot
   c. *Idea:* Happy
6. *Idea:* It made his gold shine
7. a. *Ideas:* A stranger; a god
   b. *Idea:* Golden
   c. *Idea:* It glittered
   d. A god
   e. *Idea:* Because the door was locked
   f. *Idea:* Grant him a favor

PART D
8. a. hospitality
   b. restricted to
   c. sympathy
   d. fertile
   e. in disguise

Lesson 77

Lesson 77

PART A	**Word Lists**		**PART B**

Vocabulary Sentences

1	**2**	**3**
linen	precious	flexible
frenzy	delicious	convenient
appetite	anxious	inconvenient
credit	spacious	accompany
woven		accompanied
dispair		
pity		
secure		

4	**5**
Vocabulary words	**Vocabulary words**
1. deserve credit	1. discontent
2. linen	2. appetite
3. frenzy	3. secure
4. occupied	4. pity
5. envy	
6. despair	

1. She was very unhappy about a lot of things, but she was most <u>discontented</u> about the mess that was in the basement.
2. When he started eating he had a huge <u>appetite</u>, but when he finished the main part of the meal, he had no room for dessert.
3. He didn't want anybody to steal his treasure, so he looked for a <u>secure</u> place.
4. The little boy was so poor, sad, and cold that I felt great <u>pity</u> for him.

WORD PRACTICE AND VOCABULARY

EXERCISE 1   Word practice

1. Everybody, find lesson 77, part A in your skillbook. *Wait.* Touch under each word in column 1 as I read it.
2. The first word is **linen.**
3. Next word. **Frenzy.**
4. *Repeat step 3 for each remaining word in column 1.*
5. Your turn. Read the first word. *Signal.* **Linen.**
6. Next word. *Signal.* **Frenzy.**
7. *Repeat step 6 for each remaining word in column 1.*
8. *Repeat the words in column 1 until firm.*

EXERCISE 2   Word family

1. Everybody, touch column 2. *Check.*
   All those words end with the letters **i-o-u-s.**
   Touch under the first word. *Pause.*
   What word? *Signal.* **Precious.**
2. Next word. *Pause.* What word? *Signal.*
   Delicious.
3. *Repeat step 2 for each remaining word in column 2.*
4. *Repeat the words in column 2 until firm.*

EXERCISE 3   Word practice

1. Everybody, touch under the first word in column 3. *Pause.* What word? *Signal.* **Flexible.**
2. Next word. *Pause.* What word? *Signal.*
   Convenient.
3. *Repeat step 2 for each remaining word in column 3.*
4. *Repeat the words in column 3 until firm.*

EXERCISE 4   Vocabulary development

Task A

1. Everybody, touch column 4. *Check.*
   First you're going to read the words in column 4. Then we'll talk about what they mean.

2. Touch under the first line. *Pause.*
   What words? *Signal.* **Deserve credit.**
3. Next word. *Pause.*
   What word? *Signal.* **Linen.**
4. *Repeat step 3 for each remaining word in column 4.*
5. *Repeat the words in column 4 until firm.*

Task B

1. Now let's talk about what those words mean. The words in line 1 are **deserve credit.** When you succeed in doing something, you **deserved credit** for doing that thing. Here's another way of saying **She succeeded at solving the problem: She deserved credit for solving the problem.**
   Everybody, what's another way of saying **She succeeded at solving the problem?** *Signal.* **She deserved credit for solving the problem.**
2. Everybody, what's another way of saying **She succeeded at having good manners?** *Signal.* **She deserved credit for having good manners.**

Task C

Word 2 is **linen. Linen** is an expensive cloth that some sheets and dresses are made of. Everybody, what's an expensive cloth that some sheets and dresses are made of? *Signal.* **Linen.**

Task D

1. Word 3 is **frenzy.** When you do things in a very hurried and excited way, you do them in a **frenzy.** Here's another way of saying **She ran around in excitement: She ran around in a frenzy?** Everybody, what's another way of saying **She ran around in excitement?** *Signal.* **She ran around in a frenzy.**
2. Everybody, what's another way of saying **They cooked the dinner in a hurry?** *Signal.* **They cooked the dinner in a frenzy.**

Task E

1. Word 4 is **occupied.** When you are **occupied** with something, you are busy with that thing. Here's another way of saying **You are busy with your thoughts: You are occupied with your thoughts.**
2. Everybody, what's another way of saying **She was busy with the customer?** *Signal.* **She was occupied with the customer.**
3. Everybody, what's another way of saying **They were busy with the details of the problem?** *Signal.* **They were occupied with the details of the problem.**

Task F

Word 5 is **envy.** When you **envy** people, you wish you could do something that they can do. If you wish you had somebody's wealth, you envy that person for his wealth. If you wish you had a person's skill, you envy that person for her skill.

Task G

Word 6 is **despair.** When you feel no hope, you feel **despair.**

EXERCISE 5   Vocabulary from context

Task A

1. Everybody, touch column 5. *Check.* First you're going to read the words in column 5. Then we'll talk about what they mean.
2. Touch under the first word. *Pause.* What word? *Signal.* **Discontent.**
3. Next word. *Pause.* What word? *Signal.* **Appetite.**
4. *Repeat step 3 for each remaining word in column 5.*
5. *Repeat the words in column 5 until firm.*

Lesson 77

The Golden Touch

PART 2Ⓐ

The stranger gazed about the room, and when his glowing smile had shone upon all the golden objects that were there, he turned again to Midas.

"You are a wealthy man, friend Midas," he observed. "I doubt whether any other four walls on earth contain so much gold as this room contains."

"I have done pretty well—pretty well," answered Midas in a discontented tone. "But, after all, it is a very small amount, when you consider that it has taken me my whole life to get it together."Ⓑ Midas continued, "If one could live a thousand years, he might have time to grow rich."

"What?" exclaimed the stranger. "Then you are not satisfied?"

Midas shook his head.

"And what would satisfy you?" asked the stranger. "I would like to know."

Midas paused. He felt that this stranger had the power to grant any wish. He had only to speak and obtain whatever he might want. So he thought, and thought, and thought. His imagination heaped up one golden mountain after another. But he was unable to imagine mountains that were big enough. At last, a bright idea occurred to King Midas. It seemed really as bright as the glistening metal which he loved so much.

Raising his head, he looked the stranger in the face.

The visitor observed, "Well, Midas, I see that you have at last hit upon something that will satisfy you. Tell me your wish."Ⓒ

"It is only this," replied Midas. "I am weary of collecting my treasures with so much trouble, and seeing the heap so small after I have done my best. I wish everything that I touch could be changed to gold!"

"The Golden Touch!" exclaimed the stranger. "You certainly deserve credit, friend Midas, for having such a brilliant idea. But are you quite sure that this will satisfy you?"

"How could it fail?" said Midas.

"And you will never regret having it?"

"What could make me regret it?" asked Midas. "I need nothing else to make me perfectly happy."Ⓓ ★6 ERRORS★

"You shall have your wish," replied the stranger, waving his hand in farewell. "Tomorrow, at sunrise, you will find yourself gifted with the Golden Touch."

The stranger then became so terribly

292   Lesson 77   Textbook

Task B

1. Everybody, find part B in your skillbook. *Check.* I'll read those sentences. You figure out what the underlined part in each sentence means.
2. Sentence one. She was very unhappy about a lot of things, but she was most discontented about the mess that was in the basement. *Call on a student.* What could **discontented** mean? *Idea:* Dissatisfied.
3. *Repeat step 2 for each remaining sentence. Answer Key:* **2.** *Idea:* Desire for food.
   3. *Idea:* Safe.
   4. *Idea:* Sorrow.

STORY READING

EXERCISE 6   Decoding and comprehension

1. Everybody, turn to page 292 in your textbook. *Wait. Call on a student.* What's the error limit for this lesson? **6 errors.**
2. *Call on individual students to read. Present the tasks specified for each circled letter.*

Ⓐ Where was Midas at the end of the last part? *Idea:* In his treasure room.
● Who was with him? **A stranger.**
● What did Midas think this stranger was? **A god.**
● Why did Midas think this god had paid him a visit? *Idea:* To grant him a favor.

Ⓑ Did Midas think that he had enough gold? **No.**

Ⓒ If you think about the title of this story, you'll know what Midas will wish for. What is that? *Idea:* The golden touch.
● How would a golden touch work? *Idea:* Everything you touch turns into gold.

Ⓓ Is Midas thinking clearly? **No.**
● Name some problems that you might have if everything you touched turned into gold. *Response:* Student preference.
● Read the rest of the story to yourselves and be ready to answer some questions.

After all students have finished reading:
● When did the stranger say that Midas would have the golden touch? *Idea:* At sunrise the next morning.

bright that Midas closed his eyes. When he opened them again he saw only one yellow sunbeam in the room. All around him was the glistening of the precious metal which he had spent his life collecting.

Midas did not sleep well that night. His mind was like the mind of a child who had been promised a new plaything in the morning. Day had hardly peeped over the hills when King Midas was wide awake. He stretched his arms out of bed and began to touch objects that were within reach. He was anxious to prove whether the Golden Touch had really come, according to the stranger's promise.

Midas laid his finger on a chair by the bedside, and on other things, but he was very disappointed to find that they remained exactly the same as before. He was afraid that he had only dreamed about the stranger, or else that the stranger had been making fun of him. And how miserable it would be if Midas had to be content with the little gold he could scrape together by ordinary means, instead of creating gold by a touch.

All this happened while it was only the gray of the morning, with only a streak of brightness along the edge of the sky. Midas was in a very bad mood. He kept growing sadder and sadder, until the earliest sunbeam shone through the window and lit up the ceiling over his head. It seemed to Midas that this bright yellow sunbeam reflected in an unusual way on the white covering of the bed. Looking more closely, he was astonished and delighted to find that this linen cloth had been changed into

woven gold, the purest and brightest he had ever seen! The Golden Touch had come to him with the first sunbeam!

Midas started up in a kind of joyful frenzy, and ran about the room grasping at everything that happened to be in his way. He seized one of the bedposts, and it immediately became a golden pillar. He pulled open a window curtain, and the cord grew heavy in his hand—a mass of gold. Midas took up a book from the table. At his first touch, the cover became solid gold. And when he ran his fingers through the pages, the book became a bundle of thin, gold plates, and all the wise words in the book disappeared.

Midas quickly put on his clothes, and was overjoyed to see himself in a magnificent suit of gold cloth, which was flexible and soft, although it was very, very heavy. He drew out his handkerchief, which little Marygold had made for him. That was also gold.

Somehow or other this last change did not quite please King Midas. He would have rather had his little daughter's handkerchief remain just as it was when she climbed upon his knee and put it into his hand.

But it was not worthwhile to worry about a handkerchief. Midas now took his spectacles from his pocket and put them on his nose to see more clearly. But he discovered that he could not possibly see through them, for the glass had turned into a plate of yellow metal. They were worthless as spectacles, but valuable as gold. It seemed rather inconvenient to Midas that, with all

Lesson 77 Textbook **293**

his wealth, he could never again be rich enough to own a pair of usable spectacles.

"It is no great problem," he said to himself. "Every great good is accompanied by some small inconvenience. The Golden Touch is worth the loss of a pair of spectacles. My own eyes will serve for ordinary purposes, and little Marygold will soon be old enough to read to me."

Wise King Midas was so excited by his good fortune that the palace did not seem large enough for him. He therefore went downstairs, and smiled when he observed that the handrail of the staircase became a bar of gold as his hand passed over it. He lifted the door latch. It was

brass only a moment ago, but it became golden when his fingers left it. He went into the garden, where he found a great number of beautiful roses in full bloom, and others in all the stages of lovely bud and blossom. Their fragrance was very delicious in the morning breeze.

But Midas knew a way to make them far more precious, to his way of thinking. So he went from bush to bush, and used his magic touch until every flower and bud was changed to gold. By the time this work was completed, King Midas was called to breakfast. The morning air had given him an excellent appetite, and he quickly returned to the palace.

- How well did Midas sleep that night? *Idea:* Not very well.
- Did Midas get up in the morning **before** sunrise or **after** sunrise? **Before sunrise.**
- When did Midas notice that he had the golden touch? *Idea:* When the first sunbeam came into his room.
- What was the first thing that had been changed into gold? *Idea:* The bed covering.
- What happened to the book that he touched? *Idea:* It turned into gold.
- What was lost when the book changed into gold? *Idea:* All the wise words.
- When Midas's clothes changed into gold, what else was different about them? *Idea:* They were heavier.
  Gold is very, very heavy.
- What was the first thing that Midas regretted turning into gold? *Idea:* His handkerchief.
- What was the problem with his spectacles? *Idea:* He couldn't see through them.
- How did Midas plan to solve the problem of not being able to see clearly? *Idea:* Have Marygold help him.
- What did he do in the garden? *Idea:* Turned all the roses into gold.
- Why did he return to the palace at the end of this part? *Idea:* He was called for breakfast.
- What do you think is going to happen when he tries to eat breakfast? *Response:* Student preference.

Award 4 points or have the students reread to the error limit sign.

INDEPENDENT WORK

Do all the items in your skillbook and workbook for lesson 77.

ANSWER KEY FOR WORKBOOK

Story Items

1. Put the following events in the right order by numbering them from 1 through 4.

3 Midas turned a book to gold.

4 Midas turned a rose to gold.

1 Midas asked the stranger for a favor.

2 Midas had a hard time sleeping.

Review Items

2. Write which god each picture shows. Choose from **Apollo, Hermes, Poseidon** or **Zeus**.

a. _Hermes_

b. _Poseidon_

c. _Apollo_

d. _Zeus_

3. Here are some events from Jackie Robinson's life.
   - Jackie leaves UCLA
   - Jackie dies
   - Jackie helps win the World Series
   - Jackie first plays for the Dodgers

Write the correct event after each date on the time line.

1972 _Jackie dies_

1955 _Jackie helps win the World Series_

1947 _Jackie first plays for the Dodgers_

1941 _Jackie leaves UCLA_

WORKCHECK AND AWARDING POINTS

1. *Read the questions and answers for the skillbook and workbook.*

2. *Award points for independent work as follows:*

0 errors	6 points
2 errors	4 points
3, 4, or 5 errors	2 points
5 or more errors	0 points

3. *Award bonus points as follows:*

Correcting missed items or getting all items right	2 points
Doing the writing assignment acceptably	2 points

ANSWER KEY FOR SKILLBOOK

PART C

1. *Idea:* Baucis and Philemon were kind to strangers.

PART D

2. **a.** No
   b. *Idea:* It wouldn't have been enough
   c. *Idea:* The golden touch
   d. No

3. **a.** No
   b. *Idea:* At sunrise
   c. *Idea:* The bed covering
   d. *Idea:* Read it

4. **a.** *Idea:* They were heavier
   b. His handkerchief
   c. *Ideas:* Marygold; his daughter

5. **a.** Roses
   b. *Idea:* Good
   c. *Idea:* They had no smell

PART E

6. **a.** Greyhound
   b. Collie
   c. Hound
   d. Poodle
   e. Airedale

7. **a.** Lion
   b. Cat that Walked
   c. Lion
   d. Ugly Duckling
   e. Cat that Walked

8. **a.** disagreeable
   b. main job
   c. contract
   d. in disguise
   e. astonishment
   f. inhabitants
   g. spacious
   h. a lot of

Lesson 78

Lesson 78

PART A   **Word Lists**

1	2	3
occupy	coffee	**Vocabulary words**
ornaments	experiment	1. deserve credit
terrify	breakfast	2. pity
	potato	3. secure
	appearance	4. discontented
	woven	5. envy
		6. appetite
		7. occupied
		8. linen
		9. frenzy
		10. despair

WORD PRACTICE AND VOCABULARY

EXERCISE 1   Word practice

1. Everybody, find lesson 78, part A in your skillbook. *Wait.* Touch under each word in column 1 as I read it.
2. The first word is **occupy**.
3. Next word. **Ornaments**.
4. *Repeat step 3 for* **terrify**.
5. Your turn. Read the first word. *Signal.* **Occupy**.
6. Next word. *Signal.* **Ornaments**.
7. *Repeat step 6 for* **terrify**.
8. *Repeat the words in column 1 until firm.*

EXERCISE 2   Word practice

1. Everybody, touch under the first word in column 2. *Pause.* What word? *Signal.* **Coffee**.
2. Next word. *Pause.* What word? *Signal.* **Experiment**.
3. *Repeat step 2 for each remaining word in column 2.*
4. *Repeat the words in column 2 until firm.*

EXERCISE 3   Vocabulary review

Task A

1. Everybody, touch column 3. *Check.* First you're going to read the words in column 3. Then we'll talk about what they mean.
2. Touch under the first line. *Pause.* What words? *Signal.* **Deserve credit**.
3. Next word. *Pause.* What word? *Signal.* **Pity**.
4. *Repeat step 3 for each remaining word in column 3.*
5. *Repeat the words in column 3 until firm.*

Task B

1. You've learned the meanings for all these words. The words in line are **deserve credit**. *Call on a student.* When do you **deserve credit** for something? *Idea:* When you succeed in doing something.

2. Everybody, what's another way of saying **She succeeded at solving the problem?** *Signal.* **She deserved credit for solving the problem.**

Task C

Word 2 is **pity**. *Call on a student.* What does **pity** mean? *Idea:* Sorrow.

Task D

Word 3 is **secure**. *Call on a student.* What does **secure** mean? *Idea:* Safe.

Task E

Word 4 is **discontented**. *Call on a student.* What does **discontented** mean? *Idea:* Dissatisfied.

Task F

Word 5 is **envy**. *Call on a student.* What does **envy** mean? *Idea:* You wish you could do something that somebody else does.

Task G

Word 6 is **appetite**. *Call on a student.* What's an **appetite**? *Idea:* A desire for food.

Task H

1. Word 7 is **occupied**. *Call on a student.* What does **occupied** mean? *Idea:* You are busy with something.
2. Everybody, what's another way of saying **You are busy with your thoughts?** *Signal.* **You are occupied with your thoughts.**
3. Everybody, what's another way of saying **They were busy with the details of the problem?** *Signal.* **They were occupied with the details of the problem.**

Task I

Word 8 is **linen**. *Call on a student.* What is **linen**? *Idea:* An expensive cloth that some sheets and dresses are made of.

Task J

1. Word 9 is **frenzy**. *Call on a student.* What does it mean when you are in a **frenzy**? *Ideas:* You're excited; you're in a hurry.
2. Everybody, what's another way of saying **She ran around in excitement?** *Signal.* **She ran around in a frenzy.**
3. Everybody, what's another way of saying **They cooked the dinner in a hurry?** *Signal.* **They cooked the dinner in a frenzy.**

Task K

Word 10 is **despair**. *Call on a student.* What does **despair** mean? *Idea:* No hope.

Lesson 78

The Golden Touch
PART 3Ⓐ

On this particular morning, King Midas's breakfast consisted of hot cakes, some nice little fish, roasted potatoes, fresh boiled eggs, and coffee. There was also a bowl of bread and milk for his daughter, Marygold. This was a breakfast fit for a King!

Little Marygold had not yet made her appearance, and her father ordered her to be called.Ⓑ Then Midas seated himself at the table and waited for his daughter to come before beginning his own breakfast. Midas really loved his daughter, and loved her even more this morning because of his good fortune. It was not long before he heard her coming along the hallway, crying bitterly.Ⓒ

Her crying surprised him, because Marygold was almost always cheerful, and hardly shed a spoonful of tears in a year.Ⓓ When Midas heard her sobs, he decided to put little Marygold into better spirits by giving her a surprise. So he leaned across the table and touched her pretty bowl. The bowl was instantly changed to gleaming gold, but because Midas did not touch the bread and milk, they did not change.

Meanwhile, Marygold slowly and sadly opened the door. She held her apron at her eyes and sobbed as if her heart would break.

Midas asked, "What is the matter with you this bright morning?"

Marygold, without taking the apron from her eyes, held out her hand, and showed Midas one of the roses which had recently changed to gold.

"Beautiful!" exclaimed her father. "And what is there in that magnificent golden rose to make you cry?"

"Ah, dear Father," answered the child, through her sobs, "it is not beautiful, but the ugliest flower that ever grew.

As soon as I was dressed I ran into the garden to gather some roses for you, because I know you like them. But, oh dear, dear me. All the beautiful roses that smelled so sweetly and had so many lovely colors are spoiled. They have become quite yellow, just like this one, and no longer have any fragrance. What is the matter with them?"Ⓔ ★6 ERRORS★

Midas said, "Pooh, my dear little girl. Please don't cry about it." Midas was ashamed to admit that he had brought about the change which saddened her. "Sit down and eat your bread and milk. But don't be sad. You can easily exchange the golden rose for an ordinary one which would wither in a day."

"I don't care for such roses as this!" cried Marygold, tossing it away. "It has no smell, and the hard petals stab my nose!"

The child now sat down at the table, but was so occupied with her grief that she did not even notice the wonderful change in her bowl. Perhaps this was for the best. Marygold usually took pleasure in looking at the odd figures that were painted on the bowl, yet these ornaments were now entirely lost in the yellow metal.

Midas, meanwhile, had poured out a cup of coffee, and the coffee pot, which had been brass, was gold when he set it down. He thought to himself that it was unusual to eat off golden plates, and he began to worry about keeping his treasures safe. The cupboard and the kitchen would no longer be a secure place to keep articles so valuable as golden bowls and coffee pots.

As he was thinking these thoughts, he lifted a spoonful of coffee to his lips, and, sipping it, was astonished to notice that the instant his lips touched the liquid, the coffee became liquid gold, and the next moment it hardened into a lump.

"Ugh!" Midas exclaimed.

"What is the matter, Father?" little Marygold asked, gazing at him with the tears still in her eyes.

"Nothing, child, nothing," said Midas. "Eat your bread and milk before they get cold."

He looked at one of the nice little fish on his plate and touched it with his golden fork, and then experimented by touching its tail with his finger. To his horror it immediately changed from a fried fish into a gold fish. But it was not like a goldfish that people often keep in fish bowls. It was a metal fish that looked as if it had been made by a goldsmith. Its little bones were now golden wires; its fins and tail were thin plates of gold; and there were the marks of the fork in it. It was a very pretty piece of work, only King Midas would have rather had a real fish in his dish instead of this valuable imitation.

He thought to himself, "I don't quite see how I am to eat any breakfast."

He took one of the hot cakes, and had scarcely broken it when it turned yellow. If it had been an ordinary white hot cake, Midas would have prized it a good deal more than he now did. Almost in despair, he helped himself to a boiled egg, which immediately changed the same way the fish and hot cake had changed.

STORY READING

EXERCISE 4   Decoding and comprehension

1. Everybody, turn to page 295 in your textbook. *Wait. Call on a student.* What's the error limit for this lesson? **6 errors.**

2. *Call on individual students to read. Present the tasks specified for each circled letter.*

Ⓐ Where was Midas going at the end of the last part? *Idea:* To breakfast.

Ⓑ What does that mean? **Had not yet made her appearance?** *Idea:* She had not come in yet.

● So what did Midas do? *Idea:* Had someone call her.

● Who do you think did the calling? *Idea:* A servant.

Ⓒ Why do you think she's crying? *Response:* Student preference.

Ⓓ What does that mean: **Marygold hardly shed a spoonful of tears in a year?** *Idea:* She didn't cry very often.

Ⓔ What did Midas think of the golden flowers? *Idea:* He thought that they were magnificent.

● Why did Marygold think that these golden flowers were spoiled? *Idea:* They didn't have any smell or color.

● Read the rest of the story to yourselves and be ready to answer some questions.

After all students have finished reading:

● Did Marygold notice that her bowl had changed into gold? **No.**
Midas thought that this was a wonderful change.

● Would Marygold think that the change in the bowl was wonderful? **No.**

● Why not? *Idea:* She liked the pictures on the bowl.

● As Midas ate, he began to think of one problem that would have to be solved if he had golden plates and coffee pots. What was that problem? *Idea:* That he would have to keep them safe.

● What happened to the coffee that Midas drank? *Idea:* It turned into gold.

● What happened to the fried fish when Midas touched it? *Idea:* It turned into gold.

● What would Midas have preferred, a golden fish or a real fish? **A real fish.**

● Name some other things that changed to gold at the breakfast table. *Ideas:* Hot cake; boiled egg; potato.

"Well, this is a problem," he thought, leaning back in his chair, and looking with envy at Marygold as she ate her bread and milk with great satisfaction. Midas said to himself, "My breakfast is quite valuable, but I can not eat it."

Midas thought that he might solve his problem by moving faster. He snatched a hot potato, and attempted to cram it into his mouth, and swallow it in a hurry. But the Golden Touch was too nimble for him. He found his mouth full of solid metal, which so burnt his tongue that he roared aloud. He jumped up from the table and began to dance and stamp about the room, feeling both pain and fright.

"Father, dear Father," cried Marygold. "What is the matter? Have you burnt your mouth?"

"Ah, dear child," groaned Midas sadly. "I don't know what is to become of your poor father."

And truly Midas was a person that you should pity. Here was the richest breakfast that could be set before a king, but its rich-ness was worth absolutely nothing to Midas. The poorest farmer, sitting down to his crust of bread and cup of water, was far better off than King Midas, although the fine food that Midas had before him was worth its weight in gold. And what was he to do? Already, Midas was extremely hungry. How would he feel by dinner time? And how many days could he survive on golden food?

Midas's hunger and despair were so great that he groaned aloud, and very sadly too. Marygold could endure it no longer. She gazed at her father a moment to discover what was the matter with him. Then, with a sweet and sorrowful desire to comfort him, she started from her chair. She ran to Midas, and threw her arms about him. He bent down and kissed her. At that moment he felt that his little daughter's love was worth a thousand times more than the Golden Touch.

"My precious, precious, Marygold!" he cried.

But Marygold made no answer.

Lesson 78   Textbook   **297**

ANSWER KEY FOR WORKBOOK

Review Items

1. Write which color each land is.
   a. Land of the Munchkins
      blue
   b. Land of the Quadlings
      red
   c. Land of the Winkies
      yellow
   d. Emerald City
      green

2. Write whether each animal is **wild** or **domestic**.
   a. Mule   **domestic**
   b. Tiger   **wild**
   c. Weasel   **wild**
   d. Goat   **domestic**
   e. Llama   **domestic**
   f. House cat   **domestic**
   g. Whale   **wild**
   h. Mosquito   **wild**

3. Write when each story took place. Choose from the **1360's**, the **1890's**, or the **1940's**.
   a. Buck   **1890's**
   b. Dick Whittington   **1360's**
   c. Jackie Robinson   **1940's**

- What happened when Midas tried to jam the potato into his mouth? *Idea:* The potato turned to gold and burned his tongue.
- The story asks the question: **How long could Midas survive on golden food?** Was Midas really surviving on this food? **No.**
- What did Marygold do to comfort Midas? *Idea:* She hugged him.
- Why didn't she answer when he talked to her? *Idea:* She had turned into gold.
- Do you think Midas still likes the golden touch? *Response:* Student preference.

Award 4 points or have the students reread to the error limit sign.

INDEPENDENT WORK

Do all the items in your skillbook and workbook for lesson 78.

WORKCHECK AND AWARDING POINTS

1. *Read the questions and answers for the skillbook and workbook.*
2. *Award points for independent work as follows:*

0 errors	6 points
2 errors	4 points
3, 4, or 5 errors	2 points
5 or more errors	0 points

3. *Award bonus points as follows:*

Correcting missed items or getting all items right	2 points
Doing the writing assignment acceptably	2 points

ANSWER KEY FOR SKILLBOOK

PART B

1. In June, Frank walked from Hopkinsville to Center City.

PART C

2. **a.** *Any three:* Hot cakes, fish, potatoes, eggs, coffee
   b. *Idea:* Marygold wasn't there yet
   c. *Idea:* She hardly ever cried
   d. *Idea:* The roses had turned into gold
   e. Midas
3. **a.** *Idea:* It had turned into gold
   b. *Idea:* He couldn't eat the gold fish
   c. The potato
   d. *Idea:* Burned it
4. **a.** Yes
   b. No
   c. *Idea:* It had turned into gold
5. **a.** Marygold
   b. His daughter's love
   c. No
   d. *Idea:* She had turned into gold
6. **a.** see
   b. smell
   c. eat
   d. drink
7. A piece of bread

PART D

8. **a.** restricted to
   b. nimble
   c. sympathy
   d. century
   e. astonishment
   f. breathe in
   g. calculate
   h. gleamed

Lesson 79

PART A   Word Lists

1	2	3	4
original	deadly	teardrops	Vocabulary words
victim	faithfully	wring	1. insane
desolate	seriously	moisten	2. dimple
	sincerely	stretched	3. greedy
	immediately	outstretched	4. vanish
	instantly	terrify	5. glossy
		county	6. original
		country	7. victim
		countries	

WORD PRACTICE AND VOCABULARY

EXERCISE 1   Word practice

1. Everybody, find lesson 79, part A in your skillbook. *Wait.* Touch under each word in column 1 as I read it.
2. The first word is **original.**
3. Next word. **Victim.**
4. *Repeat step 3 for desolate.*
5. Your turn. Read the first word. *Signal.* **Original.**
6. Next word. *Signal.* **Victim.**
7. *Repeat step 6 for desolate.*
8. *Repeat the words in column 1 until firm.*

EXERCISE 2   Word family

1. Everybody, touch column 2. *Check.*
   All those words end with the letters **l-y.**
   Touch under the first word. *Pause.*
   What word? *Signal.* **Deadly.**
2. Next word. *Pause.*
   What word? *Signal.* **Faithfully.**
3. *Repeat step 2 for each remaining word in column 2.*
4. *Repeat the words in column 2 until firm.*

EXERCISE 3   Word practice

1. Everybody, touch under the first word in column 3. *Pause.*
   What word? *Signal.* **Teardrops.**
2. Next word. *Pause.*
   What word? *Signal.* **Wring.**
3. *Repeat step 2 for each remaining word in column 3.*
4. *Repeat the words in column 3 until firm.*

EXERCISE 4   Vocabulary development

Task A
1. Everybody, touch column 4. *Check.*
   First you're going to read the words in column 4. Then we'll talk about what they mean.
2. Touch under the first word. *Pause.*
   What word? *Signal.* **Insane.**
3. Next word. *Pause.*
   What word? *Signal.* **Dimple.**
4. *Repeat step 3 for each remaining word in column 4.*
5. *Repeat the words in column 4 until firm.*

Task B
1. Now let's talk about what those words mean. Word 1 is **insane.** Another word for **crazy** is **insane.** Everybody, what's another way of saying **Her thoughts were crazy?** *Signal.* **Her thoughts were insane.**
2. Everybody, what's another way of saying **He had a crazy desire for wealth?** *Signal.* **He had an insane desire for wealth.**

Task C
Word 2 is **dimple.** A **dimple** is a little dent in your cheek or chin. Everybody, what do we call a little dent in your cheek or chin? *Signal.* **A dimple.**

Task D
Word 3 is **greedy.** When you are **greedy,** you are never satisifed with how much you have. A person who is rich but is not satisfied is greedy for riches. A person who is powerful but is not satisfied is greedy for power.

Task E
1. Word 4 is **vanish.** Another word for **disappear** is **vanish.**
   Everybody, what's another way of saying **His dream disappeared?** *Signal.* **His dream vanished.**
2. Everybody, what's another way of saying **The mysterious stranger disappeared?** *Signal.* **The mysterious stranger vanished.**

Task F
Word 5 is **glossy.** Something that is very smooth and shiny is **glossy.** Everybody, what do we call hair that is very smooth and shiny? *Signal.* **Glossy hair.**

Task G
Word 6 is **original.** If something is not a copy of anything else, it is an **original.** A painting that is not a copy of any other painting is an original painting. Everybody, what do we call a story that is not a copy of any other story? *Signal.* **An original story.**

Task H
1. Word 7 is **victim.** A **victim** is somebody who is harmed unfairly. A victim of a fire is a person who was harmed by a fire. *Call on a student.* How could a person be harmed by a fire? *Idea:* The person could be burned; The person's belongings could be burned.
2. *Call on a student.* What would we call somebody who was harmed by an automobile accident? *Idea:* An automobile accident victim.
3. *Call on a student.* How could a person be harmed by an auto accident? *Idea:* Be injured or killed.

Lesson 79

The Golden Touch
PART 4 Ⓐ

What had Midas done? How deadly was the gift that the stranger had given him? The moment the lips of Midas touched Marygold's forehead, a change had taken place. Ⓑ Her sweet, rose colored face changed to a glittering yellow color, with yellow teardrops on her cheeks. Her beautiful brown hair took the same yellow color. Her soft and tender little form grew hard and rigid as she stood within her father's arms. She was the victim of her father's insane desires for wealth. Marygold was no longer a human child, but a golden statue.

Midas began to wring his hands. Ⓒ He could neither bear to look at Marygold, nor bear to look away from her. Ⓓ He could not believe that she was changed to gold. But, as he glanced at her he saw the precious little figure, with a yellow teardrop on its yellow cheek. Her expression was so warm and tender that it seemed as if that expression could soften the gold and make it become flesh again. But she remained gold. So Midas could only wring his hands, and wish that he were the poorest man in the whole world. He would gladly have exchanged all his wealth to bring back the rose color to his dear child's face.

While he was in this terrible despair, he suddenly noticed somebody standing near the door. Ⓔ Midas bent down his head without speaking, for he recognized the figure as the stranger who had appeared the day before in the treasure room. The stranger's smile seemed to shed a yellow light all around the room. It gleamed on little Marygold's image and on the other objects that had been changed by the touch of Midas.

"Well, friend Midas," said the stranger, "how do you like the Golden Touch?"

Midas shook his head. "I am very miserable," he said.

"Very miserable? Indeed!" exclaimed the stranger. "And why is that? Have I not faithfully kept my promise to you? Have you not everything that your heart desired?"

"Gold is not everything," answered Midas. "And I have lost all that my heart really cared for."

"Ah, so you have made a discovery since yesterday," observed the stranger. "Let us see, then. Which of these two things do you think is really worth the most—the gift of the Golden Touch, or one cup of clear cold water?" Ⓕ

★7 ERRORS★

"The water!" exclaimed Midas. "I would love to have it moisten my dry throat."

The stranger continued, "Tell me which is worth more, the Golden Touch or a crust of bread?"

"A piece of bread," answered Midas, "is worth all the gold on earth."

The stranger then asked, "And is the Golden Touch worth more than your own little Marygold as she was an hour ago?"

"Oh my child, my dear child is worth a thousand Golden Touches," cried poor Midas, wringing his hands. "I would not have given one small dimple in her chin for the power to change the whole earth into gold!"

"You are wiser than you were, King Midas," said the stranger, looking seriously at him. "I believe that your heart has not been entirely changed from flesh to gold. You still appear to be capable of understanding that common things are more valuable than the riches so many people struggle for. Tell me now, do you sincerely desire to rid yourself of this Golden Touch?"

"Yes, yes!" Midas exclaimed. "The Golden Touch is hateful to me!"

A fly settled on his nose, but it immediately fell to the floor, for it had become gold. Midas shuddered.

"Go, then," said the stranger, "and plunge into the river that glides past your garden. Then take a vase of the river water, and sprinkle it over any object that you want to change from gold into its original

material. If you do this sincerely, you may possibly repair the mischief your greed has caused."

King Midas bowed low, and, when he lifted his head, he observed that the stranger had vanished.

Midas lost no time in snatching up a vase (which immediately turned to gold) and running to the riverside. As he scampered along and forced his way through the bushes, the leaves turned yellow behind him, as if autumn had come to one narrow strip of bushes. On reaching the river's bank, he plunged into the water, without even pulling off his shoes.

"Poof, poof, poof," snorted King Midas as his head came out of the water. Within a second he filled the vase. As he dipped it into the water, his eyes widened as he watched the vase change from gold into the good, honest clay it had been before he had touched it. He was also aware of a change within himself. A cold, hard and heavy weight seemed to have gone out of his chest, and his clothes felt lighter, although they were soaking wet.

King Midas charged back to the palace. The servants did not know what to make of it when they saw their royal master running with a vase of water, and holding his hand over the top to prevent any water from spilling out. They didn't know all the evil that Midas had caused, and that the water was more precious to Midas than an ocean of liquid gold. The first thing he did was to sprinkle handfuls of that water over the golden figure of little Marygold.

As soon as the water fell on her, the

STORY READING

EXERCISE 5 Decoding and comprehension

1. Everybody, turn to page 298 in your textbook. *Wait. Call on a student.* What's the error limit for this lesson? **7 errors.**
2. *Call on individual students to read. Present the tasks specified for each circled letter.*

Ⓐ What was the last thing that happened in the last part? *Idea:* Marygold had changed into gold.

Ⓑ What change had taken place? *Idea:* She had turned into gold.

Ⓒ Show me how he did that.

Ⓓ Listen to that sentence again.
Read from Ⓒ *to* Ⓓ.

● Why couldn't Midas bear to look at her? *Idea:* She had changed into gold.

● Why couldn't he bear not to look at her? *Idea:* He loved her.

Ⓔ Who do you think that is? *Idea:* The stranger.

● Why do you think he's there now? *Response:* Student preference.

Ⓕ What do you think Midas is going to say? *Idea:* A cup of water.

● Read the rest of the story to yourselves and be ready to answer some questions.

After all students have finished reading:

● The stranger said that Midas was wiser than before. Name some things Midas said that showed he was wiser. *Call on individual students. Responses:* He said that gold was not everything; he said that Marygold was worth more than a thousand golden touches; he said that a piece of bread was worth all the gold on earth.

● What did Midas have to do to rid himself of the golden touch? *Idea:* Jump into the river.

● What did he have to do to change things from gold back to their original form? *Idea:* Sprinkle river water on them.

● As Midas ran to the river, a narrow strip of bushes changed as if autumn had come. In what way were they like bushes in autumn? *Idea:* They were yellow.

● The weight of Midas's clothes changed as he was in the water. How did his clothes change? *Idea:* They became lighter.

● Why? *Idea:* Because they were no longer gold.

● What was the first object that Midas sprinkled water on? **Marygold.**

color came back to the child's cheeks and she began to sneeze and sputter. She was astonished to find herself dripping wet, and to see her father throwing still more water over her.

"Please stop, dear Father," she cried. "See how you have soaked my nice outfit?"

Marygold did not know that she had been a little golden statue; nor could she remember anything that had happened since the moment she ran with outstretched arms to comfort poor King Midas.

Her father did not think it necessary to tell his beloved child how very foolish he had been. Instead, he decided to show how much wiser he was now. He led little Marygold into the garden, where he sprinkled all the remainder of the water over the rosebushes. Instantly, all the roses recovered their beautiful colors.

Two things, however, reminded King Midas of the Golden Touch for the rest of his life. One was that the sands of the river bank sparkled like gold. The other was that little Marygold's hair now had a strange, golden tint. The change of color was really an improvement, and made Marygold's hair more attractive than it had ever been.

When King Midas became an old man and sat with Marygold's children on his knees, he was fond of telling them this marvelous story. And then he would stroke their glossy hair and tell them that their hair also had a rich tint of gold, just like their mother's hair.

Then King Midas would say, "And, to tell you the truth, my dear children, ever since that morning, I have hated the very sight of gold except for your beautiful golden hair."

- Why was Marygold astonished when she discovered what her father was doing? *Idea:* She didn't know she had been changed into gold.
- What did Midas tell her about his foolish deeds? *Idea:* Nothing.
- What did he change after he had changed Marygold? *Idea:* All the rose bushes.
- What were the two things that reminded King Midas of the golden touch for the rest of his life? *Idea:* Marygold's hair and the sands of the river.
- Some of the stories that you have read have a moral. A moral is a rule that you learn from a story. The story of the miraculous pitcher has this moral: Be kind to strangers.
- What is the moral of "The Golden Touch"? *Response:* Student preference.
- Here is a good moral for "The Golden Touch": Love is better than gold.

Award 4 points or have the students reread to the error limit sign.

INDEPENDENT WORK

Do all the items in your skillbook and workbook for lesson 79.

ANSWER KEY FOR WORKBOOK

Review Items

1. Write which story each moral fits.
   a. Be kind to strangers.
   The Miraculous Pitcher
   b. Love is better than gold.
   The Golden Touch

Crossword Puzzle

To work the puzzle, read an item and figure out which word the item describes. Then write the word in the puzzle. Complete the entire puzzle.

Across

1. When you feel no hope, you feel _____.
5. When you are busy with something, you are _____ with that thing.
6. Another word for **sorrow** is _____.
7. When you _____ somebody, you wish you could do something that person can do.
8. Another word for **disappear** is _____.
9. When you are never satisfied with how much you have, you are _____.

Down

1. Another word for **dissatisfied** is _____.
2. Something that is very smooth and shiny is _____.
3. If something is not a copy of anything else, that thing is an _____.
4. Another word for **safe** is _____.

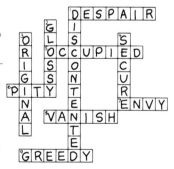

WORKCHECK AND AWARDING POINTS

1. *Read the questions and answers for the skillbook and workbook.*
2. *Award points for independent work as follows:*

> *0 errors* . . . . *6 points*
> *2 errors* . . . . *4 points*
> *3, 4, or 5 errors* . . . . *2 points*
> *5 or more errors* . . . . *0 points*

3. *Award bonus points as follows:*

> *Correcting missed items*
> *or getting all items right* . . . . *2 points*
> *Doing the writing*
> *assignment acceptably* . . . . *2 points*

ANSWER KEY FOR SKILLBOOK

PART B
1. In 1896, three men discovered gold in the Klondike River.

PART C
2. **a.** statue
   b. hard
3. **a.** *Idea:* The stranger
   b. jump into the river
   c. *Idea:* Pour water over them
4. **a.** *Idea:* Because he turned the plants into gold
   b. Clay
   c. *Idea:* Because his clothes were no longer made of gold
   d. *Ideas:* His daughter; Marygold
   e. No
   f. The roses
5. **a.** Her hair
   b. *Idea:* He hated it
   c. his grandchildren
6. **a.** The stranger
   b. Midas
   c. Midas
   d. Marygold
   e. Midas
   f. Marygold
   g. The stranger
   h. Midas
7. Love **/** gold

PART D
8. **a.** smell
   b. drink
   c. read
   d. eat
9. **a.** contract
   b. disagreeable
   c. nimble
   d. inhabitants
   e. spacious
   f. inhaled
   g. frenzy
   h. occupied
   i. envied

Lesson 80

Lesson 80

PART A	Word Lists		PART B
1	**2**	**3**	**Vocabulary Sentences**

PART A   Word Lists

1
soothe
persuade
pirates
poverty
conceal
dread
hasty

2
shipwreck
horseback
anybody
halfway
courtyard

3
ridicule
Beauty
cautious
fatigue
excuses
ridiculed
countries
furniture

4
Vocabulary words
1. vanish
2. original
3. insane
4. glossy
5. dimple
6. greedy
7. victim

5
Vocabulary words
1. desolate
2. persuade
3. terrify
4. selfish
5. soothe
6. poverty

PART B
Vocabulary Sentences

1. There was nothing within a hundred miles of this lonely, <u>desolate</u> place.
2. She was very good at talking people into doing things, but she could not <u>persuade</u> anybody to go to the beach with her.
3. The old house was very frightening, and the sounds within that house <u>terrified</u> me.
4. She seemed to be very kind, but she was really very <u>selfish</u> and thought of nobody but herself.
5. He was so upset that nothing we could do would comfort and <u>soothe</u> him.
6. At first, he was wealthy, but then he lost all his wealth and found himself in <u>poverty</u>.

WORD PRACTICE AND VOCABULARY

EXERCISE 1 Word practice

1. Everybody, find lesson 80, part A in your skillbook. *Wait.* Touch under each word in column 1 as I read it.
2. The first word is **soothe.**
3. Next word. **Persuade.**
4. *Repeat step 3 for each remaining word in column 1.*
5. Your turn. Read the first word. *Signal.* **Soothe.**
6. Next word. *Signal.* **Persuade.**
7. *Repeat step 6 for each remaining word in column 1.*
8. *Repeat the words in column 1 until firm.*

EXERCISE 2 Word family

1. Everybody, touch column 2. *Check.*
   All those words are made up of two shorter words. Touch under the first word. *Pause.* What word? *Signal.* **Shipwreck.**
2. Next word. *Pause.* What word? *Signal.* **Horseback.**
3. *Repeat step 2 for each remaining word in column 2.*
4. *Repeat the words in column 2 until firm.*

EXERCISE 3 Word practice

1. Everybody, touch under the first word in column 3. *Pause.* What word? *Signal.*
2. Next word. *Pause.* What word? *Signal.*
3. *Repeat step 2 for each remaining word in column 3.*
4. *Repeat the words in column 3 until firm.*

EXERCISE 4 Vocabulary review

Task A

1. Everybody, touch column 4. *Check.*
   First you're going to read the words in column 4. Then we'll talk about what they mean.
2. Touch under the first word. *Pause.*
   What word? *Signal.* **Vanish.**
3. Next word. *Pause.*
   What word? *Signal.* **Original.**
4. *Repeat step 3 for each remaining word in column 4.*
5. *Repeat the words in column 4 until firm.*

Task B

1. You've learned the meanings for all these words. Word 1 is **vanish.** *Call on a student.* What does **vanish** mean? *Idea:* Disappear.
2. Everybody, what's another way of saying **The mysterious stranger disappeared?** *Signal.* **The mysterious stranger vanished.**

Task C

Word 2 is **original.** *Call on a student.* What is an **original?** *Idea:* Something that is not a copy of anything else.

Task D

1. Word 3 is **insane.** *Call on a student.* What does **insane** mean? *Idea:* Crazy.
2. Everybody, what's another way of saying **He had a crazy desire for wealth?** *Signal.* **He had an insane desire for wealth.**

Task E

Word 4 is **glossy.** *Call on a student.* What does **glossy** mean? *Idea:* Smooth and shiny.

Task F

Word 5 is **dimple.** *Call on a student.* What is a **dimple?** *Idea:* A little dent in your cheek or chin.

Task G

Word 6 is **greedy.** *Call on a student.* What does **greedy** mean? *Idea:* You are never satisfied with how much you have.

Task H

Word 7 is **victim.** *Call on a student.* What is a **victim?** *Idea:* A person who is harmed unfairly.

EXERCISE 5 Vocabulary from context

Task A
1. Everybody, touch column 5. *Check.* First you're going to read the words in column 5. Then we'll talk about what they mean.
2. Touch under the first word. *Pause.* What word? *Signal.* **Desolate.**
3. Next word. *Pause.* What word? *Signal.* **Persuade.**
4. *Repeat step 3 for each remaining word in column 5.*
5. *Repeat the words in column 5 until firm.*

Task B
1. Everybody, find part B in your skillbook. *Check.* I'll read those sentences. You figure out what the underlined part in each sentence means.
2. Sentence one. There was nothing within a hundred miles of this lonely, desolate place. *Call on a student.* What could **desolate** mean? *Ideas:* Gloomy; barren; uninhabited.
3. *Repeat step 2 for each remaining sentence.*
    Answer Key: **2.** *Idea:* Convince.
    3. *Idea:* Greatly frightened.
    4. *Idea:* Concerned only with herself.
    5. *Ideas:* Relax; make him feel better.
    6. *Ideas:* Without money; a state of being poor.

Lesson 80

The Beauty and the Beast Ⓐ
by Madame d'Aulnoy

PART 1

Once upon a time there lived a merchant who was enormously rich. The merchant had six sons and six daughters, and he would let them have anything that they wanted. Ⓑ

But one day their house caught fire and burned to the ground, with all the splendid furniture, books, pictures, gold, silver, and precious goods it contained. Yet this was only the beginning of their misfortune. Shortly after the fire, the merchant lost every ship he had upon the sea, either because of pirates, shipwrecks, or fire. Then he heard that the people who worked for him in distant countries had stolen his money. At last, he fell into great poverty. Ⓒ

All that the merchant had after those misfortunes was a little cottage in a desolate place a hundred miles from the town in which he used to live. He moved into the cottage with his children. They were in despair at the idea of leading such a different life. The cottage stood in the middle of a dark forest, and it seemed to be the most dismal place on the earth.

Because they were too poor to have any servants, the girls had to work hard and the sons had to cultivate the fields to earn their living. Ⓓ The girls were poorly clothed and they missed the comforts and amusements of their earlier life. Only the youngest girl tried to be brave and cheerful. She had been as sad as anyone at first, but she soon recovered her good nature. She set to work to make the best of things. But when she tried to persuade her sisters to join her in dancing and singing, they ridiculed her and said that this miserable life was all she was fit for. But she was really far prettier and more clever than they were. She was so lovely that she was always called Beauty. Ⓔ

After two years, their father received news that one of his ships, which he had believed to be lost, had come safely into port with a rich cargo. All the sons and daughters at once thought that their poverty would be over and they wanted to set out directly for the town. But their father was more cautious. He decided to go to the town by himself. Only the youngest daughter had any doubt that they would soon be rich again. Ⓕ The other daughters gave their father requests for so many jewels and dresses that it would have taken a fortune

Lesson 80 Textbook **301**

STORY READING

EXERCISE 6 Decoding and comprehension

1. Everybody, turn to page 301 in your textbook. *Wait. Call on a student.* What's the error limit for this lesson? **8 errors.**
2. *Call on individual students to read. Present the tasks specified for each circled letter.*
Ⓐ What's the title of this story? **The Beauty and the Beast.** Here's how you say the author's name. Ma-dam doe-noy. Madame d'Aulnoy was a French woman who wrote fairy tales.
Ⓑ What do merchants do? *Idea:* Buy and sell things.
● What's another story you read that had a merchant in it? **Dick Whittington.**
● How many children did the merchant have in all? **Twelve.**
● How many daughters did he have? **Six.**
● How many sons did he have? **Six.**
● If they got everything they wanted, do you think they would be kind children or spoiled children? **Spoiled children.**
Ⓒ What was the first thing that went wrong for the merchant's family? *Idea:* Their house burned down.
● Name some other things that went wrong. *Ideas:* The merchant lost all his ships; the people who worked for him stole his money.
● How rich was the merchant after all this misfortune? *Idea:* He was very poor.
Ⓓ How do you think they liked to do this work? *Idea:* Not at all.
● Why do you think it was especially hard for these children? *Idea:* Because they were used to being rich and having servants do all the work.
Ⓔ What's the title of this story? **The Beauty and the Beast.**
● Who do you think one of the main characters will be? **Beauty.**
Ⓕ Did she believe that they would be rich again? *Idea:* Not really.
● Did the other children agree with her? **No.**

Lesson 80 **87**

to buy them. But Beauty did not ask for anything. Her father noticed her silence and said, "And what shall I bring for you, Beauty?"

"The only thing I wish for is to see you come home safely," she answered.

But this reply angered her sisters, who thought she was accusing them of asking for costly things. But her father was pleased. Still, he told her to choose something.

"Well, dear Father," she said, "since you insist upon it, I want you to bring me a rose. I have not seen one since we came here, and I love them very much." Ⓖ

★8 ERRORS★

So the merchant set out on horseback and reached the town as quickly as possible. But when he got there, he found out that his partners had taken the goods the ship had brought. So he found himself poorer than when he had left the cottage. He had only enough money to buy food on his journey home. To make matters worse, he left town during terrible weather. The weather was so bad that by the time he was halfway home he was almost exhausted with cold and fatigue. Night came on, and the deep snow and bitter frost made it impossible for his horse to carry him any further.

The merchant could see no houses or lights. The only shelter he could find was the hollow trunk of a great tree. He crouched there all night long. It was the longest night he had ever known. In spite of his weariness, the howling of the wolves kept him awake. And when the day broke,

302   Lesson 80   Textbook

he was not much better off, for falling snow had covered up every path, and he did not know which way to turn.

At last he made out some sort of path, and he started to follow it. At first, the path was so rough and slippery that he kept falling down. But the path soon became easier, and it led him to a row of trees, which ended at a splendid castle. It seemed very strange to the merchant that no snow had fallen in the row of trees. Stranger still, the trees were fruit trees, and they were covered with apples and oranges.

The merchant walked down the row of trees, and soon reached the castle. He called, but nobody answered. So he opened the door and called again. He saw a flight of steps, and went up them. He passed through several splendid rooms. The pleasant warmth of the air refreshed him, and he suddenly felt very hungry. But there seemed to be nobody in this huge palace who could give him something to eat.

The merchant wandered through the deep silence of the splendid rooms. At last, he stopped in a room smaller than the rest, where a bright fire was burning and a couch was close to it. The merchant thought that this room must be prepared for someone, so he sat down to wait. But very soon he fell into a heavy sleep.

His extreme hunger wakened him after several hours. He was still alone, but a good dinner had been set on a little table. The merchant had eaten nothing for twenty-four hours, so he lost no time in beginning his meal, which was delicious. He wondered who had brought the food,

- What did Beauty's sisters ask for? *Idea:* Jewels and dresses.
- What did Beauty ask for? **A rose.**
- Read the rest of the story to yourselves and be ready to answer some questions.

After all students have finished reading:

- What bad news did the merchant discover when he reached the town? *Idea:* His partners had taken everything off the ship.
- What was the weather like when he started back home? *Idea:* Cold and snowy.
- How much money did he have? *Idea:* Just enough to buy food on the way home.
- Where did he spend the night? *Idea:* In a hollow log.
- What kept him awake during the night? *Idea:* Wolves howling.
- Why did he have trouble finding his way in the morning? *Idea:* Snow had covered up the path.
- In the morning, he followed a path. What did that path lead to? *Idea:* A castle.
- What was unusual about the ground around the castle? *Idea:* There was no snow on it.
- What kind of trees were near the castle? **Fruit trees.**
- What was unusual about them? *Idea:* They had no snow on them; they had fruit on them.
- When the merchant called to somebody inside the castle, who answered? *Idea:* Nobody.
- Where did the merchant fall asleep? *Idea:* In a small room.
- What did he discover when he woke up? *Idea:* Food.

Lesson 80   Textbook   **303**

but no one appeared.

After dinner, the merchant went to sleep again and woke completely refreshed the next morning. There was still no sign of anybody, although a fresh meal of cakes and fruit was sitting on the little table at his elbow. The silence began to terrify the merchant, and he decided to search once more through all the rooms. But it was no use. There was no sign of life in the palace. Not even a mouse could be seen.

The merchant began to wonder what he should do. He imagined what it would be like if he owned all the treasures he saw. He considered how he would divide the riches among his children. Then he went down into the garden, and although it was winter everywhere else, the sun was shining here, the birds were singing, the flowers were blooming, and the air was soft and sweet. The merchant was so overjoyed with all he saw and heard that he said to himself, "This magic must have been put here for me." An instant later he said aloud, "If all this is meant for me, I will go and bring my children to share it with me."

He turned down a path that led to the gate. This path had roses on each side of it, and the merchant thought he had never seen or smelled such delightful flowers. They reminded him of his promise to Beauty, so he picked one to take to her. Suddenly, he heard a strange noise behind him. Turning around, he saw a frightful Beast, who seemed to be very angry. It roared in a terrible voice: "Who told you that you could pick my roses? Wasn't it enough that I allowed you to stay in my palace? Wasn't it enough that I fed you and was kind to you? This is the way you show your thanks—by stealing my flowers! But your selfishness shall not go unpunished."

The merchant was terrified by these furious words, and dropped the rose. He then threw himself on his knees and cried, "Pardon me, noble sir. I am truly grateful to you for your hospitality. I did not imagine that you would be angered if I took such a little thing as a rose."

But the Beast's anger was not soothed by that speech. "You are very ready with excuses," he cried, "but that will not save you from the death you deserve."

"Alas," thought the merchant, "if my daughter Beauty could only know what danger her rose has brought upon me."

- When the merchant searched through the palace the next day, who did he find? *Idea:* Nobody.
- What was unusual about the garden? *Ideas:* There were flowers blooming, the sun was shining, birds were singing.
- First the merchant thought: This is magic. Then what did he conclude about all the things he saw in this magnificent place? *Idea:* That it was all there for him.
- Who did the merchant decide should share in all the magic? *Idea:* His children.
- Did he carry out the plan of going to his children? **No.**
- What happened when he was about to leave? *Idea:* The Beast appeared.
- Why was the Beast angry? *Idea:* Because the merchant had picked a rose.
- What did the Beast threaten to do? *Idea:* Kill the merchant.

Award 4 points or have the students reread to the error limit sign.

ANSWER KEY FOR WORKBOOK

Review Items

1. Complete the moral for each story.
   a. The Golden Touch

   Love is better than _gold_

   b. The Miraculous Pitcher

   Be kind to _strangers_

2. Write whether each statement describes **The Miraculous Pitcher** or **The Golden Touch**.
   a. Zeus appeared in this story.

   The Miraculous Pitcher

   b. The main character was a king.

   The Golden Touch

   c. One of the characters had a magic staff.

   The Miraculous Pitcher

   d. One of the characters was changed into a statue.

   The Golden Touch

   e. The story showed how evil gold can be.

   The Golden Touch

   f. The story showed why you should be kind to strangers.

   The Miraculous Pitcher

3. Write which Greek god each statement describes. Choose from **Apollo, Hermes, Poseidon** or **Zeus**.
   a. This god was the chief god.

   Zeus

   b. This god lived in the sea.

   Poseidon

   c. This god was a messenger.

   Hermes

   d. This god was the god of light.

   Apollo

INDEPENDENT WORK

Do all the items in your skillbook and workbook for lesson 80.

WORKCHECK AND AWARDING POINTS

1. *Read the questions and answers for the skillbook and workbook.*
2. *Award points for independent work as follows:*

```
0 errors .....................6 points
2 errors .....................4 points
3, 4, or 5 errors .............2 points
5 or more errors .............0 points
```

3. *Award bonus points as follows:*

```
Correcting missed items
or getting all items right.........2 points
Doing the writing
assignment acceptably...........2 points
```

ANSWER KEY FOR SKILLBOOK

PART C

1. Last Saturday, Joanne bought a record at the record store.

PART D

2. **a.** *Idea:* Very rich
   b. Twelve
   c. *Idea:* It burned down
   d. *Idea:* They were lost at sea
   e. A cottage
   f. One hundred miles
3. **a.** *Idea:* Because the merchant let them have anything they wanted
   b. Beauty
   c. Beauty
4. **a.** *Idea:* The merchant's ship had come into port
   b. *Idea:* To the town
   c. A rose
   d. *Ideas:* Jewels; dresses
   e. *Idea:* Taken them
   f. Poorer
   g. *Idea:* Cold
   h. *Idea:* In a hollow log
5. **a.** *Idea:* There was no snow on it
   b. Fruit trees
   c. A palace
   d. *Idea:* There was nobody there
   e. Food
6. **a.** the garden
   b. *Ideas:* Warm; sunny
   c. him
   d. *Idea:* His family
   e. *Idea:* He had promised one to Beauty
   f. The Beast
   g. *Idea:* Kill him
7. **a.** The merchant's house burned down
   b. The merchant picked a rose for Beauty

PART E

8. **a.** discontented
   b. shrewd and witty
   c. century
   d. figure out
   e. desire for food
   f. safe
   g. sympathy

Lesson 81

```
Lesson 81
──────────────────────────────────────────
PART A    Word Lists      PART B
                          Vocabulary Sentences
1              2
permission     fault       1. She hated the thought of leaving town,
solution       curiosity      but she dreaded leaving her mother
condition      sensible       most of all.
possession                 2. They were in such a hurry that they ate
mention                       a hasty breakfast.
                           3. She did not want the Beast to know
3              4              that she was afraid, so she concealed her
Vocabulary words  Vocabulary words   fear.
1. selfish     1. dread
2. terrify     2. hasty
3. soothe      3. conceal
4. desolate
5. persuade
6. poverty
```

WORD PRACTICE AND VOCABULARY

EXERCISE 1 Word family

1. Everybody, find lesson 81, part A in your skillbook. *Wait.* Touch column 1. *Check.* All those words end with the sound **shun.** Touch under the first word. *Pause.* What word? *Signal.* **Permission.**
2. Next word. *Pause.* What word? *Signal.* **Solution.**
3. *Repeat step 2 for each remaining word in column 1.*
4. *Repeat the words in column 1 until firm.*

EXERCISE 2 Word practice

1. Everybody, touch under the first word in column 2. *Pause.* What word? *Signal.* **Fault.**
2. Next word. *Pause.* What word? *Signal.* **Curiosity.**
3. *Repeat step 2 for* **sensible.**
4. *Repeat the words in column 2 until firm.*

EXERCISE 3 Vocabulary review

Task A
1. Everybody, touch column 3. *Check.* First you're going to read the words in column 3. Then we'll talk about what they mean.
2. Touch under the first word. *Pause.* What word? *Signal.* **Selfish.**
3. Next word. *Pause.* What word? *Signal.* **Terrify.**
4. *Repeat step 3 for each remaining word in column 3.*
5. *Repeat the words in column 3 until firm.*

Task B
You've learned the meanings for all these words. Word 1 is **selfish.** *Call on a student.* What is a **selfish** person? *Idea:* A person only concerned about himself.

Task C
Word 2 is **terrify.** *Call on a student.* What does **terrify** mean? *Idea:* Greatly frighten.

Task D
Word 3 is **soothe.** *Call on a student.* What does **soothe** mean? *Idea:* Relax.

Task E
Word 4 is **desolate.** *Call on a student.* What does **desolate** mean? *Ideas:* Gloomy; barren; deserted.

Task F
Word 5 is **persuade.** *Call on a student.* What does **persuade** mean? *Ideas:* Win over; talk into; convince.

Task G
Word 6 is **poverty.** *Call on a student.* What is **poverty**? *Ideas:* Without money; a state of being poor.

EXERCISE 4 Vocabulary development

Task A
1. Everybody, touch column 4. *Check.* First you're going to read the words in column 4. Then we'll talk about what they mean.
2. Touch under the first word. *Pause.* What word? *Signal.* **Dread.**
3. Next word. *Pause.* What word? *Signal.* **Hasty.**
4. *Repeat step 3 for* **conceal.**
5. *Repeat the words in column 4 until firm.*

Task B
1. Everybody, find part B in your skillbook. *Check.* I'll read those sentences. You figure out what the underlined part in each sentence means.
2. Sentence one. She hated the thought of leaving town, but she dreaded leaving her mother most of all. *Call on a student.* What could **dreaded** mean? *Ideas:* Hated to; feared; didn't look forward to.
3. *Repeat step 2 for each remaining sentence.* Answer Key: **2.** *Idea:* Quick. **3.** *Idea:* Hid.

Lesson 81

The Beauty and the Beast

PART 2

The merchant feared for his life.(A) In despair, he began to tell the Beast all his misfortunes, and the reason for his journey.(B) The merchant also mentioned Beauty's request for the rose.

The merchant explained, "A king's treasure would hardly have bought all that my other daughters asked. But I thought that I might at least take Beauty her rose. I beg you to forgive me, for you see I meant no harm."

The Beast thought for a moment, and then he said, in a less furious tone, "I will forgive you on one condition—that you give me one of your daughters."(C)

"Ah!" cried the merchant. "I am not cruel enough to buy my own life at the expense of a child's life."(D) The merchant continued, "Besides, what excuse could I invent to bring one of my daughters here?"

"No excuse would be necessary," answered the Beast. "She must come willingly. See if any one of them has enough courage and loves you enough to come and save you. You seem to be an honest man, so I will trust you to go home. I will give you a month to see if any of your daughters will come back with you and stay here, so that you may go free. If none of them is willing, you must come alone, after bidding them goodbye forever, for then you will belong to me."(E) ★6 ERRORS★ The Beast continued, "And do not imagine that you can hide from me, for if you fail to keep your word, I will come and get you."

The merchant accepted this offer, although he did not really think any of his daughters would come. He promised to return a month later. Then he asked permission to set off at once. But the Beast declared that he could not go until the next day.

"Tomorrow you will find a horse ready for you," the Beast said. "Now go and eat your supper, and wait for my orders."

The poor merchant was feeling more dead than alive. He went back to his room, where a delicious supper was already served on the little table, which was near a blazing fire. But he was too terrified to eat, and he only tasted a few of the dishes. After a while, he heard a great noise in the next room, and he knew that the Beast was coming.

The Beast appeared and asked roughly if the merchant had eaten well. The merchant answered humbly that he

had, thanks to the Beast's kindness. Then the Beast warned him to remember their agreement, and to prepare his daughter for what she had to expect.

The Beast added, "Do not get up tomorrow until you see the sun and hear a golden bell ring. Then you will find your breakfast waiting for you here, and the horse you are to ride will be ready in the courtyard. It will also bring you back again when you come with your daughter a month from now. Farewell. Take a rose to Beauty and remember your promise."

The merchant was very glad when the Beast went away, and although he could not sleep, he lay down until the sun rose. He heard a bell ring. Then, after a hasty breakfast, he went to gather Beauty's rose. He mounted the horse, which carried him off so swiftly that in an instant he had lost sight of the palace. He was still occupied with gloomy thoughts when the horse stopped before the door of his cottage.

His sons and daughters rushed to meet him. When they saw the splendid horse, they thought that his journey had gone well. The merchant hid the truth from them at first. But he said to Beauty as he gave her the rose, "Here is what you asked me to bring you. You have no idea what it has cost."

This statement only excited the children's curiosity. At last, he told them his adventures from beginning to end. All the children were very unhappy. The children wept loudly over their lost hopes, and they declared that their father should not return to this terrible castle, and began to make plans for killing the Beast if it should come to get him. But he reminded them that he had promised to go back. Then the girls were very angry with Beauty, and said it was all her fault, and that if she had asked for something sensible this would never have happened.

Poor Beauty was very distressed. She said, "I have indeed caused this misfortune, but who could have guessed that a rose would cause so much misery? Because I caused this problem, it is only fair that I should suffer for it. I will go back with father to keep his promise."

At first, nobody would agree to that solution, and Beauty's father declared that nothing would make him let her go. But Beauty was firm. As the time grew near, she divided all her possessions between her sisters and said goodbye to everything she loved. And when the day came, she encouraged and cheered her father as they mounted the horse to leave.

EXERCISE 5   Decoding and comprehension

1. Everybody, turn to page 305 in your textbook. *Wait. Call on a student.* What's the error limit for this lesson? **6 errors.**

2. *Call on individual students to read. Present the tasks specified for each circled letter.*

(A) Why? *Idea:* He thought the Beast was going to kill him.

(B) What was the reason for his journey? *Idea:* To find out about his ship.

(C) The Beast said that he would forgive the merchant under one condition. What condition was that? *Idea:* That the merchant would give him one of his daughters.

(D) What does that mean: **He would not buy his own life at the expense of a child's life?** *Idea:* He would not give his child to the Beast just so he could stay alive.

(E) What does that mean: **The merchant will belong to the Beast?** *Idea:* The Beast will do what he wants with the merchant.

• Read the rest of the story to yourselves and be ready to answer some questions.

After all students have finished reading:

• When did the beast allow the merchant to leave? *Idea:* The next day.

• How much supper did the merchant eat that night? *Idea:* Not very much.

• Why didn't he eat a lot? *Idea:* He was too worried.

• What did the merchant tell the Beast when he asked if he had eaten well? *Idea:* That he had.

• In the morning, the merchant was supposed to wait for a signal before he got up. What signal was that? *Idea:* The ring of a golden bell.

• What did the Beast tell the merchant to take to Beauty? **A rose.**

• When the merchant first arrived at the cottage, his sons and daughters thought that his journey had gone well. Why did they think that? *Idea:* He was riding a fine horse.

• Who did the daughters blame when they heard what had happened to the merchant? **Beauty.**

• What did the children plan to do? *Idea:* Kill the Beast.

• Why did Beauty's sisters blame her for what had happened? *Idea:* Because her rose had caused all the trouble.

• Which daughter said that she would go back with her father to the Beast's palace? **Beauty.**

• Why did Beauty feel that she should go? *Idea:* She felt that it was all her fault.

Award 4 points or have the students reread to the error limit sign.

Lesson 81   Textbook   **307**

EXERCISE 6   Individual reading checkout

1. *For the individual reading checkout, each student will read 140 words. The passage to be read is the shaded area on the reproduced textbook page for lesson 81 in this presentation book.*

2. Today is a reading checkout day. While you're doing your independent work, I'll call on each student to read part of yesterday's chapter.

3. When I call on you, come up to my desk and bring your textbook with you. After you have read, I'll tell you how many points you can write in the checkout box that's at the top of your workbook page.

4. *If the student finishes the passage in one minute or less, award points as follows:*

> 0 errors . . . . .3 points
> 1 or 2 errors . . . . .1 point
> More than 2 errors . . . . .0 points

5. *If a student takes more than one minute to read the passage, the student does not earn any points, but have the student reread the passage until he or she is able to read it in no more than one minute with no more than two errors.*

INDEPENDENT WORK

Do all the items in your skillbook and workbook for lesson 81.

ANSWER KEY FOR WORKBOOK

Review Items

1. People have developed many breeds of dogs.
   a. Which breed has a sensitive nose?
      hound
   b. Which breed may be the smartest?
      poodle
   c. Which breed herds sheep?
      collie
   d. Which breed is very fast?
      greyhound
   e. Which breed is very brave?
      airedale

2. You read about a baseball player.
   a. What was his name?
      Jackie Robinson
   b. Which major league team did Jackie Robinson play for?
      Dodgers
   c. In which year did Jackie Robinson first play for that team?
      1947

3. Write which god each statement describes. Choose from **Apollo, Hermes, Poseidon** or **Zeus.**
   a. This god was the god of light.
      Apollo
   b. This god lived in the sea.
      Poseidon
   c. This god was the chief god.
      Zeus
   d. This god commanded the thunder and lightning. *Zeus*
   e. This god carried messages.
      Hermes

4. Write **fact** or **fiction** for each item.
   a. An article about how to bake bread.
      fact
   b. A story about a girl with super powers. *fiction*
   c. A novel about a girl from California. *fiction*
   d. A magazine article about life in California. *fact*

WORKCHECK AND AWARDING POINTS

1. *Read the questions and answers for the skillbook and workbook.*
2. Award points for independent work as follows:

> *0 errors* . . . .*6 points*
> *2 errors* . . . .*4 points*
> *3, 4, or 5 errors* . . . .*2 points*
> *5 or more errors* . . . .*0 points*

3. *Award bonus points as follows:*

> *Correcting missed items*
> *or getting all items right* . . . .*2 points*
> *Doing the writing*
> *assignment acceptably* . . . .*2 points*

4. *Remind the students to put the points they earned for their reading checkout, in the box labeled* **CO**.

ANSWER KEY FOR SKILLBOOK

PART C
1. *Idea:* Brown Wolf decided to follow Skiff Miller.

PART D
2. **a.** *Idea:* One of his daughters
   b. *Idea:* Return by himself
   c. *Idea:* Come and get him
3. **a.** A rose
   b. A rose
   c. *Idea:* A month later
   d. A horse
   e. *Idea:* He was riding a fine horse
   f. *Idea:* Kill him
   g. *Idea:* She had caused all the trouble
   h. *Idea:* She thought it was her fault
4. **a.** Beauty's sisters
   b. Beauty
   c. Merchant
   d. Beast
   e. Beauty
   f. Merchant
   g. Beast
   h. Beauty

PART E
5. **a.** astonishment
   b. inhabitants
   c. abundant
   d. gleamed
   e. dissatisfied
   f. appetite
   g. crazy
   h. greedy
   i. vanished
   j. pity

Lesson 82

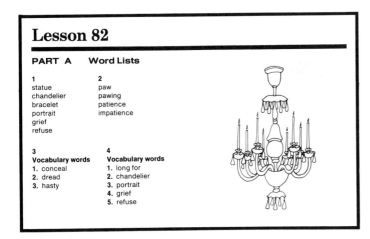
WORD PRACTICE AND VOCABULARY

EXERCISE 1   Word practice

1. Everybody, find lesson 82, part A in your skillbook. *Wait.* Touch under each word in column 1 as I read it.
2. The first word is **statue.**
3. Next word. **Chandelier.**
4. *Repeat step 3 for each remaining word in column 1.*
5. Your turn. Read the first word. *Signal.* **Statue.**
6. Next word. *Signal.* **Chandelier.**
7. *Repeat step 6 for each remaining word in column 1.*
8. *Repeat the words in column 1 until firm.*

EXERCISE 2   Word practice

1. Everybody, touch under the first word in column 2. *Pause.* What word? *Signal.* **Paw.**
2. Next word. *Pause.* What word? *Signal.* **Pawing.**
3. *Repeat step 2 for each remaining word in column 2.*
4. *Repeat the words in column 2 until firm.*

EXERCISE 3   Vocabulary review

Task A

1. Everybody, touch column 3. *Check.*
First you're going to read the words in column 3. Then we'll talk about what they mean.
2. Touch under the first word. *Pause.* What word? *Signal.* **Conceal.**
3. Next word. *Pause.* What word? *Signal.* **Dread.**
4. *Repeat step 3 for hasty.*
5. *Repeat the words in column 3 until firm.*

Task B

You've learned the meanings for all these words. Word 1 is **conceal.** *Call on a student.* What does **conceal** mean? *Idea:* Hide.

Task C

Word 2 is **dread.** *Call on a student.* What does **dread** mean? *Ideas:* hate; don't look forward to.

Task D

Word 3 is **hasty.** *Call on a student.* What does **hasty** mean? *Idea:* Quick.

EXERCISE 4   Vocabulary development

Task A

1. Everybody, touch column 4. *Check.*
First you're going to read the words in column 4. Then we'll talk about what they mean.
2. Touch under the first line. *Pause.* What words? *Signal.* **Long for.**
3. Next word. *Pause.*
What word? *Signal.* **Chandelier.**
4. *Repeat step 3 for each remaining word in column 4.*
5. *Repeat the words in column 4 until firm.*

Task B

Now let's talk about what those words mean. The words in line 1 are **long for.** When you **long for** something, you really want that thing. If you really want a vacation, you long for a vacation. Everybody, what's another way of saying **She really wanted a visit with her father?** *Signal.*
She longed for a visit with her father.

Task C

Word 2 is **chandelier.** A **chandelier** is a very fancy light with many ornaments. The picture shows a chandelier. Everybody, look at the picture. *Check.*

Task D

Word 3 is **portrait.** A painting of somebody is a **portrait** of that person. Everybody, what do we call a painting of a person? *Signal.*
A portrait of that person.

Task E

1. Word 4 is **grief.** Another word for **great sorrow** is **grief.** Everybody, what's another way of saying **She felt great sorrow?** *Signal.*
She felt grief.
2. Everybody, what's another way of saying **Her great sorrow would not go away.** *Signal.*
Her grief would not go away.

Task G

1. Word 5 is **refuse.** When you say, "no" to an offer, you **refuse** that offer. A person who says, "no" to a plan refuses that plan.
2. Everybody, what is a person doing when that person says, "no" to an invitation? *Signal.*
Refusing that invitation.

Lesson 82

The Beauty and the Beast
PART 3Ⓐ

The horse seemed to fly rather than gallop.Ⓑ But it went so smoothly that neither Beauty nor her father felt frightened. The merchant still tried to persuade Beauty to go back, but she would not listen. While they were talking the night fell, and then, to their great surprise, wonderful colored lights began to shine in all directions, and splendid fireworks blazed out before them. All the forest was lit up, and the air felt pleasantly warm, although it had been bitterly cold before.

The fireworks lasted until Beauty and her father reached the row of orange trees, where statues were holding flaming torches. When they arrived at the palace, they saw that it was lit up from the roof to the ground, and music sounded softly from the courtyard.

"The Beast must be very hungry," said Beauty, trying to laugh, "if he makes all this rejoicing over the arrival of his prey."Ⓒ

But in spite of her anxiety, Beauty could not help admiring all the wonderful things she saw.

308   Lesson 82 Textbook

The horse stopped in front of the castle. They got off the horse, and the merchant led Beauty to the little room he had been in before. They found a splendid fire burning there, and a delicious supper spread on the table.

The merchant knew that this supper was meant for them, and Beauty was quite willing to eat, for the long ride had made her very hungry. But they had hardly finished their meal when they heard the Beast approaching.Ⓓ Beauty clung to her father in terror, which became all the greater when she saw how frightened he was. But when the Beast appeared, Beauty made a great effort to hide her terror. She bowed to him respectfully, and thanked him for his hospitality.

Her behavior seemed to please the Beast. After looking at her, he said, in a tone that might have struck terror into the boldest heart, "Good evening, sir. Good evening, Beauty."

The merchant was too terrified to reply, but Beauty answered sweetly, "Good evening, Beast."

"Have you come willingly?" asked the Beast. "Will you be content to stay here when your father goes away?"

Beauty answered bravely that she was quite prepared to stay.

"I am pleased with you," said the Beast. "Because you have come of your own choice, you may stay. As for you, sir," he added, turning to the merchant, "at sunrise tomorrow you will leave. When the bell rings, get up quickly and eat your breakfast. You will find the same horse waiting to take you home. But remember that you must never expect to see my palace again."Ⓔ ★7 ERRORS★

Then the Beast turned to Beauty and said, "Take your father into the next room and help him to choose everything you think your brothers and sisters would like to have. You will find two trunks there; fill them as full as you can. It is only fair that you should send them something very precious to remember you by."

Then the Beast went away. Beauty dreaded her father's departure, but she was afraid to disobey the Beast's orders. So they went into the next room, which had shelves and cupboards all around it. They were greatly surprised at the riches the room contained. Beauty and her father went from cupboard to cupboard, selecting precious things, which they heaped into the two trunks. There were splendid dresses fit for a queen, and gorgeous jewels that were heaped on every shelf. After choosing the finest riches and filling the two trunks, Beauty opened the last cupboard. She was amazed to discover that it was completely filled with gold.

She said, "I think, Father, that the gold will be more useful to you. We should remove the other things and fill the trunks with gold."

So they removed the precious things and began heaping gold into the trunks. But the more they put in, the more room there seemed to be. They were able to put back all the jewels and dresses they had taken out, and Beauty even added many more jewels. The trunks were soon so

Lesson 82 Textbook   **309**

EXERCISE 5   Decoding and comprehension

1. Everybody, turn to page 308 in your textbook. *Wait. Call on a student.* What's the error limit for this lesson? **7 errors.**

2. *Call on individual students to read. Present the tasks specified for each circled letter.*

Ⓐ What happened at the end of the last chapter? *Idea:* Beauty decided to go to the Beast's palace.

Ⓑ Whose horse are they riding? **The Beast's.**

Ⓒ Listen to what Beauty said: **The Beast must be very hungry if he makes all this rejoicing over the arrival of his prey.** What things made Beauty think that the Beast was rejoicing? *Ideas:* The colored lights; the fireworks; the music.

● Beauty says that the Beast is rejoicing over the arrival of his prey. Who is his prey? **Beauty.**

● What does she think the Beast is going to do to her? *Idea:* Kill her.

Ⓓ What does that mean: **They had hardly finished their meal?** *Idea:* They had just finished their meal.

Ⓔ When was the merchant to leave? *Idea:* Tomorrow, at sunrise.

● What will be the signal for the merchant to eat breakfast? *Idea:* The sounding of a bell.

● What will he ride? *Idea:* The same horse he rode before.

● When would he expect to see the palace again? *Idea:* Never.

● Read the rest of the story to yourselves and be ready to answer some questions.

After all students have finished reading:

● What did the Beast tell the merchant that he should take for Beauty's brothers and sisters? *Ideas:* Things from the next room.

● Name some of the precious things that they found in the next room. *Call on individual students. Ideas:* Jewels; dresses; gold.

● Where did they put the precious things that they selected? *Idea:* Into two trunks.

● They removed things from the trunk so they could put in something that was more useful. What was that? **Gold.**

● When they put more and more gold into the trunk, they noticed something strange. What was that? *Idea:* There was more room in the trunk.

● Were they able to fit all the gold into the trunks? **Yes.**

● What else did they put into the trunks? *Ideas:* Dresses; jewels.

heavy that an elephant could not have carried them.

"The Beast was deceiving us," cried the merchant. "He must have pretended to give us all these things, knowing that I could not carry them away."

"Let us wait and see," answered Beauty. "I cannot believe that he meant to deceive us. All we can do is fasten the trunks up and leave them here."

When they arose the next morning, they found breakfast ready. The merchant ate his food with a good appetite. He secretly believed that he might come back soon and see Beauty. But she felt sure that her father was leaving her forever, so she was very sad when a bell rang. Beauty knew that the time had come for them to part.

They went down into the courtyard, where two horses were waiting. One was loaded down with the trunks, and the other was saddled for the merchant to ride. The horses were pawing the ground to show their impatience to start. The merchant was forced to bid Beauty a hasty farewell. As soon as he was mounted, he went off at such a pace that Beauty lost sight of him in an instant. Then Beauty began to cry, and wandered sadly back to her room.

Beauty soon found that she was very sleepy. She had nothing better to do, so she lay down and instantly fell asleep. She dreamed that she was walking by a brook bordered with trees. In her dream, she was very sad. Then she saw a Prince, more handsome than anyone she had ever seen. His voice went straight to her heart.

310   Lesson 82   Textbook

"Ah, Beauty," he said, "you are not so unfortunate as you think. In this palace you will be rewarded for all you have suffered. Your every wish shall be granted. I love you dearly, and in making me happy you will find your own happiness. Be as true-hearted as you are beautiful, and we shall be very happy."

Beauty asked, "What can I do, Prince, to make you happy?"

"Only be grateful," he answered, "and do not trust your eyes too much. Above all, do not desert me until you have saved me from my misery."

Beauty did not know what the Prince meant. But suddenly the Prince turned to leave. Then he said, "Dear Beauty, try not to regret all you have left behind you. Just do not let yourself be deceived by the way

things appear."

Beauty found this dream so interesting that she was in no hurry to awake. But at last the clock woke her by calling her name softly twelve times. She got up and found dinner waiting in the room next to hers. But eating dinner does not take very long when you are all by yourself, and very soon she sat down in the corner of a cozy sofa, and began to think about the charming Prince she had seen in her dream.

"He said I could make him happy," said Beauty to herself. "I think that this horrible Beast keeps him a prisoner. How can I set him free? I wonder why he told me not to be deceived by the way things appear. I don't understand it. But, after all, it was only a dream, so why should I trouble myself about it?"

- Why did Beauty's father think that the Beast had played a trick on them? *Idea:* Because the trunks weighed so much.
- Where did they find the two heavy trunks in the morning? *Idea:* Loaded on a horse.
- How many horses were in the courtyard? **Two.**
- After her father left, Beauty went to sleep. She had a strange dream. Who did Beauty see in her dream? *Idea:* A handsome Prince.
- Where was she in that dream? *Idea:* Next to a brook.
- How did the Prince feel about her? *Idea:* He loved her.
- The Prince said, "Do not trust your eyes too much." What does that mean? *Idea:* Don't believe everything you see.
- The Prince told Beauty that she should not be deceived by something. What shouldn't she be deceived by? *Idea:* By the way things appear.

Award 4 points or have the students reread to the error limit sign.

INDEPENDENT WORK

Do all the items in your skillbook and workbook for lesson 82.

ANSWER KEY FOR WORKBOOK

Review Items

1. Write which story each statement describes.
   a. The main character pulled a thousand-pound sled. *Buck*
   b. The main character turned into a swan. *The Ugly Duckling*
   c. The main character was a dog who lived in California. *Brown Wolf*
   d. The main character was a cat that could talk. *The Cat that Walked by Himself*
   e. The main character was a boy who lived in London. *Dick Whittington*

2. Write whether each statement describes **The Miraculous Pitcher** or **The Golden Touch.**
   a. Hermes appeared in the story. *The Miraculous Pitcher*
   b. Two of the characters turned into trees. *The Miraculous Pitcher*
   c. The main character had a daughter. *The Golden Touch*
   d. A village was turned into a lake. *The Miraculous Pitcher*
   e. The story showed how evil gold can be. *The Golden Touch*
   f. The story showed why you should be kind to strangers. *The Miraculous Pitcher*

3. Complete the moral for each story.
   a. The Miraculous Pitcher
      Be *kind* to strangers.
   b. The Golden Touch
      Love is better than *gold*.

ANSWER KEY FOR SKILLBOOK

PART B
1. *Idea:* Dorothy oiled the tin man.

PART C
2. a. *Idea:* Colored lights and fireworks
   b. *Idea:* It was cold before
   c. *Idea:* Food
3. a. *Idea:* Her fear
   b. *Idea:* That was the agreement
4. a. *Idea:* Things from the next room
   b. *Any two:* Jewels; dresses; gold
   c. more
   d. *Idea:* The trunks were so heavy
   e. A horse
   f. *Idea:* It carried the heavy trunks
5. a. *Idea:* In her dream
   b. Her eyes
   c. No
6. a. palace
   b. forest
   c. dream
   d. palace
   e. forest
   f. dream
   g. palace

PART D
7. a. amazement
   b. linen
   c. envy
   d. secure
   e. disappeared
   f. original
   g. victims
   h. desolate
   i. got better
   j. persuade

Lesson 83

Lesson 83

PART A	Word Lists
1	**2**
candlesticks	**Vocabulary words**
handsome	1. long for
lifetime	2. portrait
	3. chandelier

WORD PRACTICE AND VOCABULARY

EXERCISE 1   Word family

1. Everybody, find lesson 83, part A in your skillbook. *Wait.* Touch column 1. *Check.*
All those words are made up of two shorter words. Touch under the first word. *Pause.*
What word? *Signal.* **Candlesticks.**
2. Next word. *Pause.* What word? *Signal.* **Handsome.**
3. *Repeat step 2 for* **lifetime.**
4. *Repeat the words in column 1 until firm.*

EXERCISE 2   Vocabulary review

Task A
1. Everybody, touch column 2. *Check.*
First you're going to read the words in column 2. Then we'll talk about what they mean.
2. Touch under the first line. *Pause.*
What words? *Signal.* **Long for.**
3. Next word. *Pause.*
What word? *Signal.* **Portrait.**
4. *Repeat step 3 for* **chandelier.**
5. *Repeat the words in column 2 until firm.*

Task B
1. You've learned the meanings for all these words. The words in line 1 are **long for.**
Call on a student. What does **long for** mean? *Idea:* You really want something.
2. Everybody, what's another way of saying **She really wanted a visit with her father?**
Signal. **She longed for a visit with her father.**

Task C
Word 2 is **portrait.** *Call on a student.*
What is a **portrait?** *Idea:* A painting of somebody.

Task D
Word 3 is **chandelier.** *Call on a student.*
What is a **chandelier?** *Idea:* A very fancy light with many ornaments.

Lesson 83

The Beauty and the Beast
PART 4Ⓐ

Beauty began to explore some of the many rooms of the palace. The first room she entered was lined with mirrors, and Beauty saw herself reflected on every side. She thought that she had never seen such a charming room. Then a bracelet that was hanging from a chandelier caught her eye. She took it down and was greatly surprised to find that it held a portrait of the Prince that she had dreamed about. With great delight, she slipped the bracelet on her arm and went on into a large room filled with pictures. She soon found a portrait of the same handsome Prince, as large as life, and so well painted that as she studied it he seemed to smile kindly at her.Ⓑ

Beauty tore herself away from the portrait at last. She then went into a room which contained every musical instrument under the sun, and here she amused herself for a long while trying them out, and singing until she was tired. The next room was a library, and she saw everything she had ever wanted to read, as well as everything she had read. It seemed to her that there were so many books that a whole lifetime would not be long enough even to read the names of them.Ⓒ

By this time it was growing dark, and wax candles in diamond and ruby candle-sticks were beginning to light themselves in every room.

Beauty found her supper served just at the time she preferred to have it, but she did not see anyone or hear a sound. Although her father had warned her that she would be alone, she realized that her life was not dull.

After a while, Beauty heard the Beast coming. She wondered if he meant to harm her. However, the Beast did not seem at all terrifying. He said gruffly, "Good evening, Beauty."

Beauty answered cheerfully and concealed her terror. The Beast asked her how she had been amusing herself, and she told him about all the rooms she had seen.

Then the Beast asked her if she was happy in his palace, and Beauty answered that everything was so beautiful that she was very happy. And after about an hour's talk, Beauty began to think that the Beast was not nearly so terrible as she had thought at first.

At last, the Beast got up to leave, and said in a gruff voice, "Beauty, will you marry me?"

Beauty was astonished by that question. She did not know what to say, for she was afraid to make the Beast angry by

refusing.

"Say yes or no without fear," the Beast went on.

"No, Beast," said Beauty hastily.

"Since you will not marry me I will say good night, Beauty," the Beast said.

And Beauty answered, "Good night, Beast." She was very glad that her refusal had not made him angry.Ⓓ ★8 ERRORS★

After the Beast had gone, Beauty was very soon in bed and asleep, and dreaming of her unknown Prince. She dreamed that he came to her and said, "Ah, Beauty, why are you so unkind to me?"

And then Beauty's dreams changed, but the charming prince was in all of them. When morning came, her first thought was to look at the portrait and see if it was really like the Prince, and she found that it was.

That morning, Beauty decided to work in the garden. The sun was shining and all the fountains were spraying trails of sparkling water. She was astonished to find that every place was familiar to her from her dream. She came to the brook where she had first met the Prince in her dream, and that made her think more than ever that he must be the Beast's prisoner.

After supper that evening, the Beast paid her another visit, and asked the same question as before. Then with a gruff "Good night," he left, and Beauty went to bed to dream of her mysterious Prince.

The days passed swiftly. Every evening after supper, the Beast came to see her, and always before saying good night, he asked her in his terrible voice, "Beauty, will you marry me?"

Now that Beauty understood him better, it seemed to her that he went away quite sad. But her happy dreams of the

STORY READING

EXERCISE 3 Decoding and comprehension

1. Everybody, turn to page 312 in your textbook. *Wait. Call on a student.* What's the error limit for this lesson? **8 errors.**

2. *Call on individual students to read. Present the tasks specified for each circled letter.*

Ⓐ Who did Beauty dream about in the last story? **A Prince.**
   She thought the Prince was a prisoner of the Beast.

Ⓑ She went through two rooms. Name some things she saw in the first room. *Ideas:* Mirrors; a chandelier; a bracelet.

● Name some things she found in the next room. *Ideas:* Pictures; a portrait of the Prince.

Ⓒ How long did she think it would take to read just the names of these books? *Idea:* More than her lifetime.

Ⓓ How long had she talked to the Beast after dinner? *Idea:* About an hour.

● Name some things she probably told the Beast she had done that day.
   Call on individual students. Responses: Looked at herself in the mirrors; found the bracelet; sang; tried all the musical instruments; looked at the books in the library.

● What was the thing the Beast asked her before he left? *Idea:* To marry him.

● What did she reply? **No.**

● Did her answer make the Beast angry? **No.**

● Read the rest of the story to yourselves and be ready to answer some questions.

After all students have finished reading:

● Where did Beauty work the next morning? *Idea:* In the garden.

● She discovered something that she had already seen in her dream. What was that? *Idea:* The brook.

● When did the Beast return to talk with Beauty? *Idea:* After dinner.

● Each time the Beast came to see her, what would he always ask? *Idea:* To marry him.

handsome young Prince soon made her forget the poor Beast.

So the days and nights passed in the same way for a long time, until at last Beauty began to long for the sight of her father and her brothers and sisters. One night she seemed so sad that the Beast asked her what was the matter.

Beauty was no longer afraid of the Beast. She knew that he was really gentle in spite of his terrifying looks and his dreadful voice. So she explained that she wanted to see her home once more. The Beast seemed greatly distressed when he heard this, and he replied, "Ah, Beauty, do you have the heart to desert an unhappy Beast? What more do you want to make you happy? Is it because you hate me that you want to escape?"

"No, dear Beast," answered Beauty softly, "I do not hate you, and I should be very sorry never to see you any more. But I long to see my father again. Only let me go for two months, and I promise to come back to you and stay for the rest of my life."

The Beast, who had been sighing while she spoke, now replied. "I cannot refuse you anything you ask, even though it might cost me my life. Take the four boxes you will find in the room next to your own room and fill them with everything you wish to take with you. But remember your promise and come back when the two months are over. If you do not come in good time you will find your faithful Beast dead. You will not need any horse to bring you back. Only say goodbye to all your brothers and sisters the night before you leave, and when you have gone to bed, turn your ring around your finger and say, I wish to go back to the palace and see the Beast again. Good night, Beauty. Fear nothing, sleep peacefully, and before long you shall see your father once more."

As soon as Beauty was alone, she hurried to fill the boxes with all the rare and precious things she saw about her, and only when she was tired of heaping things into the boxes did they seem to be full.

Then she went to bed, but could hardly sleep for joy. And when at last she did begin to dream of her beloved Prince, she was sorry to see him stretched upon a grassy bank, sad and weary, and hardly like himself.

"What is the matter?" she cried.

He looked at her sadly, and said, "How can you ask me, cruel one? You are leaving me to my death."

"Don't be so sorrowful," said Beauty. "I am only going to show my father that I am safe and happy. I have promised the Beast faithfully that I will come back, and he would die of grief if I did not keep my word."

"What would that matter to you?" said the Prince. "Do you really care about him?"

"I should be ungrateful if I did not care for such a kind Beast," cried Beauty. "I would die to save him from pain. It is not his fault that he is so ugly."

But the Prince said nothing, and only turned his face from her.

- After a while, Beauty began to long for something. What was that? *Idea:* To see her family.
- When she told the Beast about what was making her sad, what did he tell her she could do? *Idea:* Go see her family.
- How long did Beauty want to stay with her family? **Two months.**
- Did the Beast refuse her? **No.**
- What did he say she could take with her? *Idea:* Four boxes.
- What did he say would happen if she did not return within the two months? *Idea:* He would die.
- Would she need a horse to return? **No.**
- What was she supposed to do when she wanted to return? *Idea:* Turn her ring around her finger, and say she wanted to go back to the palace.

Award 4 points or have the students reread to the error limit sign.

INDEPENDENT WORK

Do all the items in your skillbook and workbook for lesson 83.

ANSWER KEY FOR WORKBOOK

Crossword Puzzle

To work the puzzle, read an item and figure out which word the item describes. Then write the word in the puzzle. Complete the entire puzzle.

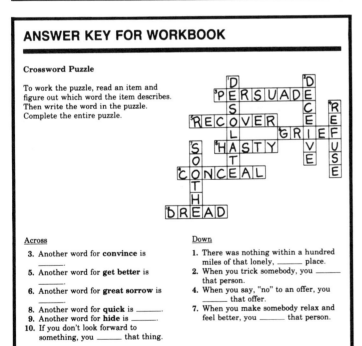

Across

3. Another word for **convince** is _____.

5. Another word for **get better** is _____.

6. Another word for **great sorrow** is _____.

8. Another word for **quick** is _____.
9. Another word for **hide** is _____.
10. If you don't look forward to something, you _____ that thing.

Down

1. There was nothing within a hundred miles of that lonely, _____ place.
2. When you trick somebody, you _____ that person.
4. When you say, "no" to an offer, you _____ that offer.
7. When you make somebody relax and feel better, you _____ that person.

WORKCHECK AND AWARDING POINTS

1. *Read the questions and answers for the skillbook and workbook.*

2. *Award points for independent work as follows:*

```
0 errors . . . . . . . . . . . . . . . . . . . . .6 points
2 errors . . . . . . . . . . . . . . . . . . . . .4 points
3, 4, or 5 errors . . . . . . . . . . . . . .2 points
5 or more errors . . . . . . . . . . . . . .0 points
```

3. *Award bonus points as follows:*

```
Correcting missed items
or getting all items right . . . . . . . .2 points
Doing the writing
assignment acceptably . . . . . . . . . .2 points
```

ANSWER KEY FOR SKILLBOOK

PART B
1. *Idea:* The Woodman built a cart.

PART C
2. a. A bracelet
   b. The Prince
   c. The Prince
   d. Musical instruments
   e. The library
3. a. The Beast
   b. Marry him
   c. No
4. a. *Idea:* To see if he was the Prince in her dream
   b. The Prince
5. a. *Idea:* To marry him
   b. No
   c. Idea: Sad
6. a. *Idea:* Back home
   b. Two months
   c. *Idea:* He would die
   d. Her ring
   e. *Idea:* "I wish to go back to the Palace and see the Beast again."
7. a. *Idea:* He would die
   b. *Idea:* The Beast

PART D
8. a. Jupiter
   b. Mercury
   c. Neptune
9. a. inhabitant
   b. frenzy
   c. pitied
   d. insane
   e. greedy
   f. greatly frightened
   g. selfish
   h. poverty
   i. hated
   j. concealed

Lesson 84

Lesson 84

PART A   Word Lists

1	2	3
produce	joyfully	**Vocabulary words**
semi	constantly	1. trust appearances
reassured	loudly	2. trace of
warehouse	dearly	3. spell
lettuce	apparently	4. despite
wad		5. warehouse

WORD PRACTICE AND VOCABULARY

EXERCISE 1   Word practice

*Pronunciation Guide: Produce—**Pro** duce*

1. Everybody, find lesson 84, part A in your skillbook. *Wait.* Touch under each word in column 1 as I read it.
2. The first word is **produce.**
3. Next word. **Semi.**
4. *Repeat step 3 for each remaining word in column 1.*
5. Your turn. Read the first word. *Signal.* **Produce.**
6. Next word. *Signal.* **Semi.**
7. *Repeat step 6 for each remaining word in column 1.*
8. *Repeat the words in column 1 until firm.*

EXERCISE 2   Word family

1. Everybody, touch column 2. *Check.*
   All those words end with the letters **l-y.**
   Touch under the first word. *Pause.*
   What word? *Signal.* **Joyfully.**
2. Next word. *Pause.* What word? *Signal.*
   Constantly.
3. *Repeat step 2 for each remaining word in column 2.*
4. *Repeat the words in column 2 until firm.*

EXERCISE 3   Vocabulary development

Task A

1. Everybody, touch column 3. *Check.*
   First you're going to read the words in column 3. Then we'll talk about what they mean.
2. Touch under the first line. *Pause.* What words? *Signal.* **Trust appearances.**
3. Next line. *Pause.* What words? *Signal.* **Trace of.**
4. Next word. *Pause.* What word? *Signal.* **Spell.**
5. *Repeat step 4 for each remaining word in column 3.*
6. *Repeat the words in column 3 until firm.*

Task B

Now let's talk about what those words mean. The words in line 1 are **trust appearances.** When you **trust appearances,** you believe in the way that things **look,** not in the way they are. Everybody, what are you doing when you believe in the way that things **look,** not in the way they are? *Signal.* **Trusting appearances.**

Task C

The words in line 2 are **trace of.** When there is no **trace of** a person, there is no clue that the person is around.

Task D

Word 3 is **spell.** A **spell** that a witch puts on somebody is a terrible charm that changes that person into something else.

Task E

1. Word 4 is **despite.** Here's another way of saying **She worked hard in spite of her sickness: She worked hard despite her sickness.**
   Everybody, what's another way of saying **She worked hard in spite of her sickness?** *Signal.* **She worked hard despite her sickness.**
2. Everybody, what's another way of saying **Julie went up the ridge in spite of her bad leg?** *Signal.* **Julie went up the ridge despite her bad leg.**

Task F

Word 5 is **warehouse.** A **warehouse** is a large building that is used to store things. Some warehouses store furniture. Some warehouses store meat or produce. Things stay in a warehouse before they go to the stores that sell these products.

Lesson 84

The Beauty and the Beast
PART 5 Ⓐ

In Beauty's dream she was about to speak to the Prince when a strange sound woke her. Someone was speaking not very far away. When Beauty opened her eyes, she found herself in a room that she had never seen before. It was nearly as splendid as the rooms in the Beast's palace. Where could she be?

She got up and dressed hastily, and then saw that the boxes she had packed the night before were all in the room. Ⓑ While she was wondering how she got to this strange place, she suddenly heard her father's voice. She rushed out and greeted him joyfully.

Her brothers and sisters were all astonished, because they had never expected to see her again, and there was no end to the questions they asked her. Ⓒ Her brothers and sisters told her much about what had happened to them while she was away. Ⓓ

When Beauty's family heard that she had only come to be with them for a short time, they sobbed loudly. Then Beauty asked her father what he thought her strange dreams could mean, and why the Prince constantly begged her not to trust appearances. Ⓔ

Her father thought for a while, then answered. "You tell me that the Beast, frightful as he is, loves you dearly. You say that the Beast deserves your love for his kindness. I think the Prince wants you to reward the Beast by marrying the Beast in spite of his ugliness." Ⓕ

Beauty thought her father's answer was right, but still, when she thought of her dear Prince who was so handsome, she did not want to marry the Beast. For two months she did not have to decide. During these months she could enjoy herself with her family. Although her family was rich now, and lived in a town again with plenty of friends, Beauty found that nothing amused her very much. She often thought of the palace, where she was so happy. Furthermore, she never once dreamed of her dear Prince, and she felt quite sad without him.

Lesson 84 Textbook **315**

Her sisters seemed to have grown quite used to being without her, and they even found her in the way. But her father begged her to stay, and seemed very sad at the thought of her leaving. So Beauty put off leaving.

On the night that Beauty was to return to the palace, she had a dismal dream. Ⓖ ★6 ERRORS★ She dreamed that she was wandering in a lonely path in the palace gardens, when she heard groans coming from a cave. She ran quickly to see what was the matter and found the Beast stretched out upon his side, apparently dying. He said that Beauty was the cause of his illness, and he moaned pitifully.

Beauty was so terrified by this dream that the next morning she announced that she was going back at once, and that very night she said goodbye to her father and all her brothers and sisters.

As soon as Beauty was in bed, she

316 Lesson 84 Textbook

EXERCISE 4 Decoding and comprehension

1. Everybody, turn to page 315 in your textbook. *Wait. Call on a student.* What's the error limit for this lesson? **6 errors.**

2. *Call on individual students to read. Present the tasks specified for each circled letter.*

Ⓐ Where was Beauty at the end of the last part? *Idea:* In the Beast's palace.

● What was her agreement with the Beast? *Idea:* That she would come back in two months.

Ⓑ Where do you think she is now? *Idea:* At home.

Ⓒ What does that mean: **There was no end to the questions they asked her?** *Idea:* They kept asking questions.

● What kind of questions do you think they asked her? *Response:* Student preference.

Ⓓ Is Beauty in a place she had been in before? **No.**

● So name one thing that must have happened while she had been away. *Idea:* Her family had moved.

Ⓔ What does that mean: **Not to trust appearances?** *Idea:* Don't believe everything you see.

Ⓕ Listen to that part again. *Read from* Ⓔ *to* Ⓕ.

● What does her father think that her dreams mean? *Idea:* That the Prince wants her to marry the Beast.

Ⓖ Did she return to the palace on the night that she was supposed to return? **No.**

● What did the Beast say would happen to him if she didn't return? *Idea:* He would die.

● Read the rest of the story to yourselves and be ready to answer some questions.

After all students have finished reading:

● What happened in the dismal dream that Beauty had? *Idea:* She found the dying Beast in a cave.

● When did she return to the palace? *Idea:* The next night.

turned her ring around her finger and said, "I wish to go back to the palace and see the Beast again."

Then she fell asleep instantly, and only woke up to hear the clock saying, "Beauty, Beauty," twelve times. She knew at once that she was in the palace again. Everything was just as before, but Beauty thought that she had never known such a long day. She was so anxious to see the Beast again that she felt as if supper time would never come.

But when it did come and no Beast appeared, she was frightened. After listening and waiting for a long time, she ran down into the garden to search for the Beast. No one answered, and she could not find a trace of him. At last, she stopped for a minute's rest, and saw that she was standing near the cave she had seen in her dreams. She entered the cave, and sure enough, there was the Beast, fast asleep. Beauty was glad to have found him. She ran up and stroked his head, but to her horror he did not move or open his eyes.

"Oh, he is dead, and it is all my fault," said Beauty, crying bitterly.

But then she looked at him again, and saw that he was still breathing. Beauty got some water from the nearest fountain and sprinkled it over his face. To her great delight, he began to wake up.

"Oh, Beast, how you frightened me," she cried. "I never knew how much I loved you until just now, when I feared I was too late to save your life."

"Can you really love such an ugly creature as I?" asked the Beast faintly.

"Ah, Beauty, you came just in time. I was dying because I thought you had forgotten your promise. But go back now and rest. I shall see you again soon."

Beauty had expected him to be angry with her, and she was reassured by his gentle voice. She went back to the palace, where supper was awaiting her. Afterwards, the Beast came in as usual, and they talked about the time she had spent with her father. The Beast asked if she had enjoyed herself, and if her family had been glad to see her.

Beauty answered politely, and quite enjoyed telling him all that had happened to her. At last, the time came for him to go, and he asked, as he had so often asked before, "Beauty, will you marry me?"

Beauty answered softly, "Yes, dear Beast."

As she spoke, a blaze of light sprang up before the windows of the palace. Beauty turned to ask the Beast what it could all mean, but found that he had disappeared. In his place stood her long-loved Prince!

"Ah, Beauty," he said. "You have rescued me at last from my terrible spell."

Beauty looked at him in amazement, and begged him to explain.

The Prince said, "When I was young, a witch put a spell on me and changed me into the Beast. She said that I would keep that form until I met a woman who had enough courage to love me despite my ugliness. You are that woman, and now we will be husband and wife."

The Prince came up to Beauty and kissed her. They were married the next day, and they lived happily ever after. And every day, the Prince would go into his garden and bring Beauty a rose.

- What things did she have to do to return? *Idea:* Turn her ring around her finger and say that she wanted to return to the palace.
- When Beauty came back to the palace did the Beast visit her before supper? **No.**
- So what did Beauty do? *Idea:* Went to look for him in the garden.
- Where did she find him? *Idea:* In the same cave she had seen in her dream.
- What condition was the Beast in? *Idea:* Unconscious.
- What did Beauty do to wake him? *Idea:* Sprinkled water on his face.
- Later, the Beast paid Beauty a visit. What did the Beast ask her? *Idea:* If she would marry him.
- What did Beauty say? **Yes.**
- Then what happened to the Beast? *Idea:* He turned into a Prince.
- Where had Beauty seen him before? *Idea:* In her dream.
- What had happened to the Prince when he was young? *Idea:* A witch had turned him into a beast.
- What did the Prince and Beauty do the next day? *Idea:* Got married.
- This story has a moral about how things look and how they really are. The Beast told that moral several times during the story. What is the moral of Beauty and the Beast? *Idea:* Do not trust appearances.
- Listen to that moral again: **Do not trust appearances.**

Award 4 points or have the students reread to the error limit sign.

INDEPENDENT WORK

Do all the items in your skillbook and workbook for lesson 84.

ANSWER KEY FOR WORKBOOK

Story Items

1. Put the following events in the right order by numbering them from 1 through 5.
   - **2** The merchant met the Beast.
   - **5** Beauty married the Beast.
   - **1** The merchant lost all his money.
   - **3** Beauty agreed to go to the Beast's palace.
   - **4** Beauty had her first dream about the Prince.

Review Items

2. Write which story each moral fits.
   a. Do not trust appearances.
   Beauty and the Beast
   b. Be kind to strangers.
   The Miraculous Pitcher
   c. Love is better than gold.
   The Golden Touch

WORKCHECK AND AWARDING POINTS

1. *Read the questions and answers for the skillbook and workbook.*
2. *Award points for independent work as follows:*

0 errors	6 points
2 errors	4 points
3, 4, or 5 errors	2 points
5 or more errors	0 points

3. *Award bonus points as follows:*

Correcting missed items or getting all items right	2 points
Doing the writing assignment acceptably	2 points

ANSWER KEY FOR SKILLBOOK

PART B

1. *Idea:* The Guardian fastened spectacles on Dorothy's eyes.

PART C

2. a. *Idea:* Her father's
   b. *Idea:* By magic
   c. *Idea:* Happy
   d. Her father
   e. *Idea:* Marry the Beast
   f. *Idea:* The Prince
3. a. Two months
   b. Her sisters
   c. a dismal dream
4. a. *Idea:* In a cave
   b. *Idea:* He was dying
   c. *Idea:* Go back to the palace
   d. *Idea:* Turned it around her finger
5. a. *Idea:* Because the Beast did not appear
   b. *Idea:* To look for the Beast
   c. *Idea:* In a cave
   d. *Idea:* In her dream
6. a. Water
   b. loved
7. a. *Idea:* Marry him
   b. Yes
   c. *Idea:* He turned into the Prince
8. a. A witch
   b. The Beast
   c. *Idea:* A woman
   d. *Idea:* She had to love him
   e. *Idea:* Because he was so ugly
   f. Beauty
   g. *Idea:* They got married

PART D

9. a. occupied
   b. vanished
   c. original
   d. persuade
   e. deserted
   f. recover
   g. selfish
   h. hasty
   i. deceived
   j. great sorrow

Lesson 85

WORD PRACTICE AND VOCABULARY

EXERCISE 1   Word practice

1. Everybody, find lesson 85, part A in your skillbook. *Wait.* Touch under each word in column 1 as I read it.
2. The words in the first line are **Carlos Hernandez.**
3. Next word. **Tomato.**
4. *Repeat step 3 for* **crayon.**
5. Your turn. Read the first line. *Signal.* **Carlos Hernandez.**
6. Next word. *Signal.* **Tomato.**
7. *Repeat step 6 for* **crayon.**
8. *Repeat the words in column 1 until firm.*

EXERCISE 2   Word family

1. Everybody, touch column 2. *Check.* All those words are made up of two shorter words. Touch under the first word. *Pause.* What word? *Signal.* **Railroad.**
2. Next word. *Pause.* What word? *Signal.* **Handcart.**
3. *Repeat step 2 for each remaining word in column 2.*
4. *Repeat the words in column 2 until firm.*

EXERCISE 3   Word practice

1. Everybody, touch under the first word in column 3. *Pause.* What word? *Signal.* **Semi.**
2. Next word. *Pause.* What word? *Signal.* **Semis.**
3. *Repeat step 2 for each remaining word in column 3.*
4. *Repeat the words in column 3 until firm.*
5. *Repeat steps 1–4 for column 4.*

EXERCISE 4   Vocabulary review

Task A
1. Everybody, touch column 5. *Check.* First you're going to read the words in column 5. Then we'll talk about what they mean.
2. Touch under the first line. *Pause.* What words? *Signal.* **Trace of.**
3. Next line. *Pause.* What words? *Signal.* **Trust appearances.**
4. Next word. *Pause.* What word? *Signal.* **Despite.**
5. *Repeat step 4 for each remaining word in column 5.*
6. *Repeat the words in column 5 until firm.*

Task B
You've learned the meanings for all these words. The words in line 1 are **trace of.** *Call on a student.* What does it mean when there is no **trace of** a crook? *Idea:* There's no clue that the crook is around.

Task C
The words in line 2 are **trust appearances.** *Call on a student.* What does **trust appearances** mean? *Idea:* Believing in the way that things look, not in the way they are.

Task D
1. Word 3 is **despite.** *Call on a student.* What does **despite** mean? *Idea:* In spite of.
2. Everybody, what's another way of saying **She worked hard in spite of her sickness?** *Signal.* **She worked hard despite her sickness.**

Task E
Word 4 is **warehouse.** *Call on a student.* What's a **warehouse?** *Idea:* A large building that is used to store things.

Task F
Word 5 is **spell.** *Call on a student.* What's a **spell?** *Idea:* A terrible charm that changes a person into something else.

Lesson 85

Carlos Hernandez
by Chuck Williams

I was working for the Olson Produce Company when I first learned how to have fun when you're working. At that time, I was nineteen years old and I had just finished my first year at the state college. I got a job with Olson Produce Company for the summer. I needed to earn money over the summer or I wouldn't be able to stay in school. (A) So, when school let out, I went job hunting. Some of the guys I went to school with got jobs that paid a lot of money. Two of them worked in an automobile factory, where the pay was really good. Another friend of mine got a job working on a railroad repair gang. He made pretty good money, and he also had a very easy job, because the gang would

spend most of its time riding around on a little train. I was unlucky because the job at Olson Produce didn't pay very well and the work was very hard.

My job was to help load and unload huge produce trucks called semis. Olson Produce had a loading dock at a giant produce warehouse. On each side of Olson's dock were docks for other produce companies. Each company had a crew of men that loaded and unloaded the trucks. A semi would back in, and the crew would go to work. Mister Olson was always yelling at us to "Work faster!" I must have heard him say a thousand times, "Come on, come on! We can't hold up this truck all day! Let's move it!"

Lesson 85 Textbook   **319**

When we unloaded a truck, we'd wheel large handcarts inside the trailer of the truck. Then we'd load the crates of produce on the handcarts and wheel them into the warehouse. (B) Some semis would be loaded with tomatoes, some with corn, and some with lettuce. (C) Semis hold an amazing amount of produce. The inside of the trailer is over ten feet high and forty feet long. And it would be piled solid with crates of produce.

The guys on the crew didn't like to work fast. The leader of the crew, Arnold Bing, kept whispering, "Slow down. Don't kill the job."

At first, I didn't know what he meant when he said that, but I soon caught on. When you finish the semi you're working on, there's always another one. So why hurry to finish the truck you're working on? You'll just have to start another job.

So there was Arnold trying to slow down the work, and there was Mister Olson saying, "Come on. We can't hold up this truck forever." And sometimes the driver of the truck would be standing next to Mister Olson, complaining and saying things like, "Hey, how long is it going to take me to get finished here? I've got to get on the road." (D) ★7 ERRORS★

Even though our crew took it as easy as we could, the work was hard. In the early morning, the work wasn't so bad, because the inside of the truck would be cool. But during the heat of the day, with the sun beating down on the truck, the inside of the truck would sometimes get over one hundred degrees. Mister Olson

would really be jumping around and shouting. "Hurry, hurry!" he'd say. Or, "That produce is going to spoil!"

When we had a break, we'd sit on the edge of the loading dock and complain a lot. "This is a lousy job," we'd say. We'd tell about our friends who had better jobs, and we'd promise that we were going to try to find better work. When I look back at it, I guess we entertained ourselves and made ourselves happy by complaining. The complaining gave us something to talk about when we weren't talking about baseball or girls.

Then one day, everything changed. That was the day that Carlos Hernandez came to work. He was a young man about twenty years old, who played football for a large college. We didn't know that he was a star football player, because he didn't talk about it at first. We just knew that he was different. I remember the first time I saw him. He was big. His sleeves were rolled up and he had arms that were very enormous. He was standing there, next to Mister Olson, towering above him. Carlos was chewing a big wad of gum and each time he chewed, you could see all the muscles in his jaw ripple. He'd chew slowly and then his face would break into a large smile. I watched him out of the corner of my eye as we were unloading a truck. Everybody on the crew was glad that Mister Olson was talking to this new man because when Olson was talking, he wasn't nagging us about working faster.

A couple of minutes later, Mister Olson walked over to us with Carlos and

---

STORY READING

EXERCISE 5   Decoding and comprehension

1. Everybody, turn to page 319 in your textbook. *Wait. Call on a student.* What's the error limit for this story? **7 errors.**
2. *Call on individual students to read. Present the tasks specified for each circled letter.*

(A) How old was the narrator when he worked for the produce company? **19.**
- Where did he go to school? **The state college.**
- Why did he have to get a summer job? *Idea:* To earn money.
- What was the name of the place where he worked? **Olson Produce Company.**

(B) Everybody, turn back to page 319 and look at the picture. *Check.*
  It shows a huge loading dock.
- Everybody, touch the part of the dock that belongs to Olson Produce. *Check.*
  The trailers of those trucks are filled with produce.
- Everybody, touch the trailer of the truck in front of Olson Produce. *Check.*
- What is that kind of truck called? **A semi.**
  Everybody, touch a handcart. *Check.*

(C) Tomatoes, corn, and lettuce are produce.
- Name some other things that are produce. *Accept appropriate response.*

(D) Why did the driver of the truck want it unloaded fast? *Idea:* So he could leave.
- What does that mean: **To get on the road?** *Idea:* To leave.
- Why do you think Mr. Olson wanted to get the trucks unloaded faster? *Ideas:* So more trucks could get unloaded.
- If you were a driver and you knew that it took forever to get a truck unloaded at Olson's, how would you feel about taking your truck there? *Idea:* Not good.
- Why did Arnold Bing always want to slow the crew down? *Idea:* So that they wouldn't have to work as hard.
- What did he mean when he said: **Don't kill the job.** *Idea:* Don't work so fast.
- Read the rest of the story to yourselves and be ready to answer some questions.

After all students have finished reading:
- At first, how did the crew entertain itself during their breaks? *Idea:* By complaining about their jobs.
- What was the name of the young man who changed the way the crew thought about work? **Carlos Hernandez.**
- Describe Carlos. *Ideas:* Large; muscular; happy; 19 years old.
- What was different about the way Carlos worked? *Idea:* He worked very fast.
- When Carlos joined the crew, who did the most work at first? **Carlos.**

introduced him. "He's replacing Hank on our crew," Olson explained. Hank had quit a couple of days before and had left the state.

As soon as Mister Olson left, Carlos clapped his hands together and said, "All right," as he peered inside the huge trailer. Then he asked, "How long does it take you guys to unload one of these things?"

Arnold told him, "About two hours if we're unlucky and a lot longer if things go well."

Everybody smiled except Carlos. He made a sour face and said. "Two hours. Well, we can do a lot better than that if we really go at it." Arnold gave Carlos a funny look but didn't say anything.

"Let's do it," Carlos said, clapping his hand together. He grabbed a handcart and flew inside the trailer. He loaded that thing up so fast I couldn't believe it. Then he pushed it on a run into the warehouse. The rest of us stood there, looking at him as if he were crazy. When he returned with the empty cart, he smiled and said, "Come on, we can beat two hours. Let's see how fast we can do this truck."

At first, Carlos was the only one who was working at high speed. The rest of us just kept plodding along at our usual pace. But it was a little embarrassing because Carlos was doing three or four times the amount of work that any of the rest of us were doing. After about ten minutes, I couldn't stand that feeling any more. I felt like I wasn't doing my part. All at once something inside of me said, "Why not? Let's surprise Mister Olson and go full speed."

The first thing you know we were all going full speed—everybody but Arnold, that is. He was still plodding along, not saying anything but looking very unhappy. As we worked, Carlos said, "See? It's a lot more fun this way. We've got some reason for working. We're going to be the best crew in the whole world."

Bugsy, one of the guys on the crew, said, "Yeah, we're the best." We unloaded the truck in one and a half hours. Everybody on the crew was wringing with sweat and Mister Olson looked as if he were going to pass out. He was just standing there on the dock watching us.

When he wasn't looking, Arnold walked up to us and said, "Look at you nuts. You're all wet with sweat."

Carlos pointed to Arnold's shirt. "You got a little sweat on you." Carlos said. "And you were trying to avoid sweating. That makes it bad, when you try to hide from work. Then it hurts when you sweat. We don't mind sweating because we are having fun. We're going to be the best."

Before Arnold could say anything, Carlos jumped down from the dock and ran over to a pile of large cardboard boxes. He split one box apart, flattened it out, got a crayon, and made a large chart that he hung on the wall just behind the dock. He wrote on it: Truck One—One and a half hours. Then he turned around and said, "Look at that. Is that the best we can do? I'll bet we can beat that record all to pieces."

And we did beat that record. The next truck we unloaded took us an hour and ten minutes. Then Carlos wrote the information on the chart, and said, "Look. We got a new record." I looked at the chart and smiled. I felt pretty good. The guys on the next dock were watching us and asked what we were doing. Carlos told them, "We're just showing that we're the best crew in the world."

The guys from the crew on the next dock came over and looked at our chart. One of them said, "Listen, if we went all out, we could beat that time."

"No way," we said. "We are lightning."

But guess what? The other crew did break our record. They unloaded a truck in an hour flat, and they made a chart twice as big as ours. Carlos smiled and said, "Well, it looks like the competition is getting tough. We're going to have to really turn it on now."

"Yeah, Arnold," I said. "Let's all work hard."

Arnold looked uncomfortable for a second. Then he said, "Let's do it. We'll show those guys how to unload trucks."

Before the day was over, we were shouting and yelling, "We're number one!" We had unloaded a truck—an entire truck—in fifty minutes. We held that record for three hours. But then one of the crews way down the line beat it—forty-eight minutes.

When Arnold heard about this, he said, "Let's set a record that nobody can beat." So when the next semi came in, we ran, we threw those crates around, we sweated, and we worked together, as a team. And we did it—forty-three minutes. We made a huge sign that showed our record time. That was the best time ever made; but by now, we could always do a truck in under an hour.

Some very interesting things happened. Mister Olson got a lot of business, because the truckers knew that we'd unload their trucks in the time it would take them to go to the diner down the street and have breakfast. Mister Olson was very proud of us. He treated us as if we were his sons and he also paid us more money. But the most interesting thing that happened was what I learned about working. I learned you can look at work like Carlos did. And work can be very satisfying if you make a game out of it.

- How did that make the narrator feel? *Idea:* Embarrassed.
- Pretty soon, everybody on the crew except one person was working at high speed. Who was the person who still plodded along? **Arnold Bing.**
- How long did it take the crew to unload that first truck? **One and a half hours.**
- How long did it take the crew to unload a truck before Carlos? **Two hours.**
- The narrator says that Mr. Olson looked as if he were going to pass out. Why was he so shocked? *Idea:* Because he had never seen them work so fast.
- Who called the other members of the crew nuts? **Arnold Bing.**
- Carlos told Arnold it's bad when you try to hide from work. What did he mean by that? *Idea:* That the work will just seem harder.
- What were Carlos and the others doing to make the work easier? *Idea:* Making a game of it.
- Carlos jumped from the dock and did something. What did he do? *Idea:* Made a chart.
- After Carlos's crew set the record of one hour and ten minutes, what did the other crew say about that record? *Idea:* That they could beat it.
- Did that crew break the record? **Yes.**
- Then what did Carlos's crew do? *Idea:* Set a new record.
- When they got a new record of fifty minutes, did anybody on the crew try to work slowly that time? **No.**
- Did the crew next to them break that record? **No.**
- Who broke it? *Idea:* A crew way down the line. That means that all the crews on the entire dock were now competing.
- What record did Olson's crew set when the other crew set a record of 48 minutes? *Idea:* Set a record of 43 minutes.
- How many people on the crew worked hard when they set that record? **All of them.**
- Why did Olson get a lot of business after the crew speeded up? *Idea:* Because his crew unloaded the trucks so fast.
- How did Mr. Olson treat the young men on the crew at the end of the story? *Idea:* As if they were his sons.
- What did the narrator learn about work? *Idea:* Work can be satisfying.

Award 4 points or have the students reread to the error limit sign.

INDEPENDENT WORK

Do all the items in your skillbook and workbook for lesson 85.

ANSWER KEY FOR WORKBOOK

Review Items

1. Write which story each statement describes.
   a. The main character was a king.

   The Golden Touch

   b. The main characters were two old people.

   The Miraculous Pitcher

   c. The main characters got married at the end of the story.

   Beauty and the Beast

   d. One of the characters had many dreams.

   Beauty and the Beast

   e. Zeus appeared in the story.

   The Miraculous Pitcher

2. Write which direction you would go from the Emerald City to find each thing.
   a. The Land of the Munchkins

   east

   b. The Land of the Quadlings

   south

   c. The Land of the Winkies

   west

   d. The river

   east

3. Write which story each moral fits.
   a. Be kind to strangers.

   The Miraculous Pitcher

   b. Love is better than gold.

   The Golden Touch

   c. Do not trust appearances.

   Beauty and the Beast

Map Skills

4. Look at the map.

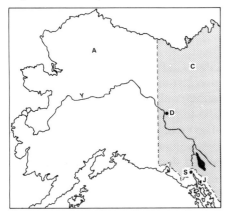

   a. What metal was discovered near town **D** in 1896? *gold*
   b. What's the name of town **D**?

   Dawson

   c. What's the name of river **Y**?

   Yukon

   d. What's the name of country **C**?

   Canada

WORKCHECK AND AWARDING POINTS

1. *Read the questions and answers for the skillbook and workbook.*
2. *Award points for independent work as follows:*

0 errors	*. . . . . .6 points*
2 errors	*. . . . . .4 points*
3, 4, or 5 errors	*. . . . . .2 points*
5 or more errors	*. . . . . .0 points*

3. *Award bonus points as follows:*

Correcting missed items or getting all items right	*. . . . . .2 points*
Doing the writing assignment acceptably	*. . . . . .2 points*

ANSWER KEY FOR SKILLBOOK

PART B

1. Beauty found the Beast.

PART C

2. **a.** Olson Produce Company
   b. Summer
   c. *Idea:* Went to college
3. **a.** Semis
   b. get on the road
4. **a.** Mr. Olson
   b. Arnold Bing
5. *Idea:* Students are to name four types of produce
6. **a.** Carlos Hernandez
   b. *Idea:* He worked fast
   c. *Idea:* Because Carlos was faster
7. **a.** Arnold Bing
   b. One and a half hours
8. **a.** *Idea:* Do it faster
   b. Yes
   c. *Idea:* Worked faster
   d. *Idea:* Down the line on the dock
   e. 43 minutes
9. *Ideas:* A box; a chart
10. **a.** more
    b. sons

PART D

11. **a.** disappeared
    b. victim
    c. persuade
    d. terrified
    e. poverty
    f. hid
    g. grief
    h. refused

Lesson 86

WORD PRACTICE AND VOCABULARY

EXERCISE 1   Word practice

1. Everybody, find lesson 86, part A in your skillbook. *Wait.* Touch under each word in column 1 as I read it.
2. The first word is **suburbs.**
3. Next word. **Mayor.**
4. *Repeat step 3 for each remaining word in column 1.*
5. Your turn. Read the first word. *Signal.* **Suburbs.**
6. Next word. *Signal.* **Mayor.**
7. *Repeat step 6 for each remaining word in column 1.*
8. *Repeat the words in column 1 until firm.*

EXERCISE 2   Word family

1. Everybody, touch column 2. *Check.*
   All those words are the names of people or places. Touch under the first line. *Pause.* What words? *Signal.* **Halsted Street.**
2. Next line. *Pause.* What words? *Signal.* **Maria Rossi.**
3. *Repeat step 2 for **Hull House.***
4. Next word. *Pause.* What word? *Signal.* **Chicago.**
5. *Repeat step 4 for **Michigan.***
6. *Repeat the words in column 2 until firm.*

EXERCISE 3   Vocabulary development

Task A

1. Everybody, touch column 3. *Check.*
   First you're going to read the words in column 3. Then we'll talk about what they mean.
2. Touch under the first word. *Pause.*
   What word? *Signal.* **Suburbs.**
3. Next word. *Pause.*
   What word? *Signal.* **Slum.**
4. *Repeat step 3 for **mayor.***
5. *Repeat the words in column 3 until firm.*

Task B

Now let's talk about what those words mean. Word 1 is **suburbs.** The **suburbs** are the small cities and towns that surround a large city. Everybody, what do we call the small cities and towns that surround a large city? *Signal.*
Suburbs.

Task C

Word 2 is **slum.** A **slum** is a crowded part of a city that has dilapidated houses. Everybody, what do we call a crowded part of a city that has dilapidated houses? *Signal.* **A slum.**

Task D

Word 3 is **mayor.** The **mayor** of a city is the chief person in charge of running that city. The person in charge of the city of New York is the Mayor of New York.
Everybody, what do we call the person who runs the city of Los Angeles? *Signal.*
The Mayor of Los Angeles.

Lesson 86

Hull House ⓐ

Chicago is a huge city, one of the largest cities in the United States. The city itself has about three million people living in it. And about another four million live in the suburbs that surround the city on the north, south, and west.ⓑ There are no suburbs on the east side of Chicago because the city is on the shore of Lake Michigan.ⓒ

Chicago is like many other modern cities. The downtown part of the city has towering buildings—one of them is one hundred and ten stories tall. The rest of the city is made up of houses and factories.

The biography that you will read begins about one hundred years ago, in 1889. The biography is about Jane Addams, who was twenty-nine years old in 1889. She worked in a very poor neighborhood in Chicago.ⓓ

It's easy to get to the neighborhood where Jane Addams worked. Just go to the

Lesson 86 Textbook **323**

middle of downtown Chicago, which is called the Loop. Then go exactly one mile to the west. You'll come to a street called Halsted Street. When Jane Addams first lived on Halsted Street the street looked greatly different from the way it· looks now.ⓔ A large university now stands right in the middle of the neighborhood where Jane Addams lived. On the edge of the university, you'll come to a big old house. Today that house is a museum. But that's the place that Jane Addams moved into back in 1889. And Jane Addams made that house into one of the most famous places in the world. It was called Hull House.ⓕ

Presidents of the United States visited Hull House. Mayors from large cities came there. Important people from all over the world came to Hull House—including kings and queens.

Hull House was very important because it changed the way that people thought about neighborhoods. Many people worked at Hull House. But Hull House might not have existed if it weren't for one person.ⓖ That person was Jane Addams.

You're going to read about the things Jane Addams did, but different narrators are going to tell you the story. One narrator will tell the first part. Another narrator will tell the second part, and a third narrator will tell the last part. The narrators are fictional. But the things the narrators tell about are facts. The first fictional narrator is Maria Rossi, who was a young girl in 1889, when Jane Addams moved into Hull House.ⓗ

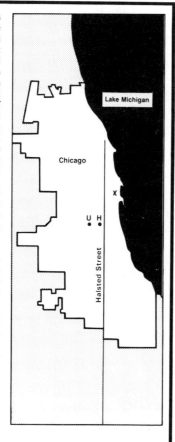

324 Lesson 86 Textbook

EXERCISE 4 Comprehension passage

1. Everybody, turn to page 323 in your textbook. *Wait.*
2. *Call on individual students to read. Present the tasks specified for each circled letter.*

ⓐ What is the title of this passage?
Chicago—Now and Then.

ⓑ About how many people live in Chicago?
Three million.

● About how many people live in the suburbs that surround the city on the north, south, and west sides? **Five million.**

ⓒ Everybody, look at the map.

● Touch the city of Chicago. *Check.*

● On which side of Chicago are there no suburbs? **The east side.**

● What's the name of the lake on that side?
Lake Michigan.

ⓓ When does the biography begin? **1889.**

● Who is the main character? **Jane Addams.**

● How old was she in 1889?
Twenty-nine years old.
The Jane Addams biography takes place in Chicago.

ⓔ Name some ways the city must have been different in 1889. *Response:* Student preference.

ⓕ Everybody, look at the map of Chicago. *Check.* Put your finger on the **X.** *Check.* That's the downtown part of the city. Now go west until you get to Halsted Street. *Check.* Now move your finger south on Halsted Street. *Check.* The **U** shows the place where a university stands today.

● The **H** shows Hull House. Today, Hull House is a museum.

ⓖ Who do you think that person is?
Jane Addams.

ⓗ Are the narrators who tell the Jane Addams story real people or fictional people?
Fictional people.

● Are the things they tell about fictional events or events that really happened?
Events that really happened.
The fictional narrators tell facts about Jane Addams.

● What's the name of the first person to tell the story of Jane Addams? **Maria Rossi.**

● In what year did Jane Addams open Hull House? **1889.**
Maria Rossi was a young girl at that time.

Jane Addams
by Camila Perez Ⓐ
PART 1

Maria Rossi tells about Jane Addams:Ⓑ
I lived a few blocks from Hull House in 1889, and **I** knew Jane Addams very well.Ⓒ You cannot appreciate the story that I have to tell unless you come back with me to 1889 and share some of the things that I saw and felt and lived with. The neighborhood around Hull House was different then. People who did not live there called it a horrible slum. And it was horrible in a lot of ways, but I lived there, and for me, it was not all bad. I lived with Mamma and Pappa on the first floor of a little building. We had three rooms, which was not much room for our family because there were eight children and Grandmother Rossi also lived with us.Ⓓ My parents did not speak English. On our street and in our house, we spoke Italian. My parents had come from Italy when I was just one year old.Ⓔ My parents had thought that it would be easy to get rich in the United States, but it was not easy. It was hard to get a good paying job, so we had to live in the neighborhood near Hull House.Ⓕ ★6 ERRORS★

Mamma did not have a job, but Pappa did, and so did all the children when they became twelve years old. I was twelve years old in 1889 and I worked in a candy factory on Halsted Street. I worked there from seven in the morning until seven at night. Pappa worked even longer hours than I did. We would not see him until nine at night, and he would come home very, very tired. Six days a week he worked these long hours, but he earned so little money that we could hardly purchase enough food.

Our neighborhood was packed with small wooden houses. We had no lawns and no playgrounds. We had no indoor toilets, and some of our houses had no inside water. The whole neighborhood had a very bad smell in the summertime. The smell came from the garbage. Sometimes city garbage collectors would not come by for weeks to pick up the garbage. We would throw the garbage in wooden boxes next to the street, and there it would stay, attracting swarms of flies and thousands of rats. There were rats in our house. We were careful about trying to catch them in traps, but there were so many rats in the neighborhood that we could not keep them out of our place.

Our neighborhood was all Italian people, and everybody spoke Italian. But you could go a few blocks away and you would

Lesson 86   Textbook   **325**

be in a Greek neighborhood, and nobody could understand Italian at all. They would speak Greek. You could go a few more blocks and you would be in a Russian neighborhood. Each neighborhood was like a small world, and I felt most comfortable in my world—my neighborhood.

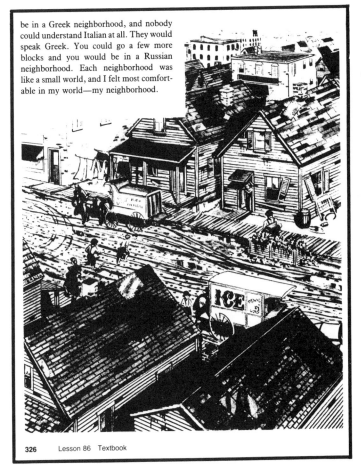

326   Lesson 86   Textbook

EXERCISE 5   Decoding and comprehension

1. Everybody, look at page 325 in your textbook. Wait. *Call on a student.* What's the error limit for this lesson? **6 errors.**

2. *Call on individual students to read. Present the tasks specified for each circled letter.*

Ⓐ Now you're going to start reading Jane Addams's biography. Who is the biography going to be about? **Jane Addams.**

● Who is the author? **Camila Perez.**

Ⓑ This is the beginning of Maria Rossi's story.

Ⓒ Who is talking now? **Maria Rossi.**

● What year is Maria telling about? **1889.**

Ⓓ What kind of place did Maria live in? *Idea:* Three rooms in a little building.

● How many people lived in that place? **Eleven.** So it must have been very crowded.

Ⓔ What language did the people in Maria's neighborhood speak? **Italian.**

● Did Maria's parents know how to speak English? **No.**

● What country had Maria's parents come from? **Italy.**

● How old was Maria when her parents came to the United States? **One year old.**

Ⓕ Did Maria's family want to move into the neighborhood near Hull House? *Response:* Student preference.

● Why did they live there, instead of another neighborhood? *Idea:* They were poor.

● Read the rest of the story to yourselves. Try to get a picture of how life was for Maria and her family.

After all students have finished reading:

● How old were the children in Maria's family when they had to go to work.

Twelve years old.

● Where did Maria work? **In a candy factory.**

● What hours did she work?

From seven in the morning until seven at night.

● Do people of today work in factories for such long hours? **No.**

● How rich was Maria's family? *Idea:* They were poor.

● Name some of the things Maria's neighborhood did not have. *Ideas:* Lawns; playgrounds.

● Why were there a lot of flies and rats? *Idea:* There was a lot of garbage.

● Were all the neighborhoods around Maria's house Italian neighborhoods? **No.**

● What were the other neighborhoods?

Greek and Russian.

● The picture at the end of this part shows the neighborhood that Maria lived in. What do you think of that place? *Response:* Student preference.

Award 4 points or have the students reread to the error limit sign.

Lesson 86   **113**

FACT GAME

1	2	3	4	5	6	7	8	9	10
11	12	13	14	15	16	17	18	19	20
21	22	23	24	25	26	27	28	29	30

2. Tell what each character wanted from Oz.
   a. Scarecrow
   b. Tin Woodman
   c. Lion
   d. Dorothy
3. a. What was the name of Tara's horse?
   b. Which country did Tara live in?
   c. Near which city did Tara win the Grand National Championship?
4. Tell whether each animal is **wild** or **domestic.**
   a. Cobra
   b. Llama
   c. Mule
   d. Tiger
5. Tell whether each statement is **fact** or **fiction.**
   a. The dog was the first animal to be domesticated.
   b. The wild Cow was domesticated in one day.
   c. The horse was domesticated after the dog.
6. a. What was the name of the boy whose cat made him rich?
   b. In which city did the boy live?

7. a. Which metal was discovered near Dawson in 1896?
   b. Which river flows through Dawson?
   c. Which story took place near Dawson?
8. a. When you climb a mountain, do the trees get larger or smaller?
   b. Is California the largest state?
   c. Which story took place in California?
9. a. Which breed of dog is very fast?
   b. Which breed of dog may be the smartest?
   c. Which breed of dog is very brave?
10. a. What was the name of the team that Jackie Robinson played for?
    b. In which city was that team located?
    c. In which year did Jackie first play for that team?
11. a. Name the chief Greek god.
    b. Name the Greek messenger god.
    c. Name the Greek god of light.
    d. Name the Greek god of the sea.
12. Tell which story each moral fits.
    a. Do not trust appearances.
    b. Be kind to strangers.
    c. Love is better than gold.

INDEPENDENT WORK

Do all the items in your skillbook and workbook for lesson 86.

WORKCHECK AND AWARDING POINTS

1. *Read the questions and answers for the skillbook and workbook.*
2. *Award points for independent work as follows:*

> *0 errors . . . . .6 points*
> *2 errors . . . . .4 points*
> *3, 4, or 5 errors . . . . .2 points*
> *5 or more errors . . . . .0 points*

3. *Award bonus points as follows:*

> *Correcting missed items or getting all items right . . . . .2 points*
> *Doing the writing assignment acceptably . . . . .2 points*

ANSWER KEY FOR FACT GAME

2. **a.** Brains
   b. A heart
   c. Courage
   d. *Idea:* A trip back to Kansas
3. **a.** Nellie
   b. England
   c. Liverpool
4. **a.** Wild
   b. Domestic
   c. Domestic
   d. Wild
5. **a.** Fact
   b. Fiction
   c. Fact
6. **a.** Dick Whittington
   b. London
7. **a.** Gold
   b. Yukon
   c. Buck
8. **a.** Smaller
   b. No
   c. Brown Wolf
9. **a.** Greyhound
   b. Poodle
   c. Airedale
10. **a.** Brooklyn Dodgers
    b. Brooklyn
    c. 1947
11. **a.** Zeus
    b. Hermes
    c. Apollo
    d. Poseidon
12. **a.** Beauty and the Beast
    b. The Miraculous Pitcher
    c. The Golden Touch

ANSWER KEY FOR SKILLBOOK

PART B
1. *Idea:* Oz can take on many forms.

PART C
2. **a.** Jane Addams
   b. Chicago
   c. Halsted Street
   d. Hull House
3. **a.** Fictional people
   b. Real events
4. **a.** Maria Rossi
   b. Eight
   c. Three
   d. Twelve
   e. *Idea:* In a candy factory
5. **a.** Poor
   b. Italian
   c. Italy
6. **a.** Seven
   b. Seven
   c. Twelve
7. **a.** *Idea:* There was a lot of garbage
   b. Rats, flies
   c. *Idea:* To catch rats

PART D
8. **a.** kind
   b. Love / gold
   c. appearances
9. **a.** hated
   b. quick
   c. trick
   d. refuse
   e. trace of

Lesson 87

WORD PRACTICE AND VOCABULARY

EXERCISE 1   Word practice

1. Everybody, find lesson 87, part A in your skillbook. *Wait.* Touch under each word in column 1 as I read it.
2. Here's how you say the words in the first line: **bwon jorno.**
3. Next word. **Sausage.**
4. *Repeat step 3 for each remaining word in column 1.*
5. Your turn. Read the first word. *Signal.* **Buon Giorno.**
6. Next word. *Signal.* **Sausage.**
7. *Repeat step 6 for each remaining word in column 1.*
8. *Repeat the words in column 1 until firm.*

EXERCISE 2   Word family

1. Everybody, touch column 2. *Check.* All those words end with the letters **l-y.** Touch under the first word. *Pause.* What word? *Signal.* **Pitifully.**
2. Next word. *Pause.* What word? *Signal.* **Instantly.**
3. *Repeat step 2 for each remaining word in column 2.*
4. *Repeat the words in column 2 until firm.*

EXERCISE 3   Vocabulary review

Task A

1. Everybody, touch column 3. *Check.* First you're going to read the words in column 3. Then we'll talk about what they mean.
2. Touch under the first word. *Pause.* What word? *Signal.* **Slum.**
3. Next word. *Pause.* What word? *Signal.* **Mayor.**
4. *Repeat step 3 for suburbs.*
5. *Repeat the words in column 3 until firm.*

Task B

You've learned the meanings for all these words. Word 1 is **slum.** *Call on a student.* What is a **slum?** *Idea:* A crowded part of a city that has dilapidated houses.

Task C

Word 2 is **mayor.** *Call on a student.* What is a **mayor?** *Idea:* A person who runs a city.

Task D

Word 3 is **suburbs.** *Call on a student.* What are **suburbs?** *Idea:* The small cities and towns that surround a large city.

EXERCISE 4   Vocabulary development

Task A

1. Everybody, touch column 4. *Check.* First you're going to read the words in column 4. Then we'll talk about what they mean.
2. Touch under the first word. *Pause.* What word? *Signal.* **Peddler.**
3. Next word. *Pause.* What word? *Signal.* **Rumor.**
4. *Repeat step 3 for each remaining word in column 4.*
5. *Repeat the words in column 4 until firm.*

Task B

Now let's talk about what those words mean. Word 1 is **peddler.** A **peddler** is a person who goes down the street with something to sell. Some peddlers sell corn. Some peddlers sell fruit. What else do peddlers sell? *Call on individual students. Ideas:* Flowers; newspapers.

Task C

Word 2 is **rumor.** A **rumor** is some news that you hear from somebody. Some rumors are true but others are not true at all. *Call on individual students.* Did you ever hear a rumor that wasn't true? *Response:* Student preference. *(If they have heard a rumor that wasn't true, have them explain the rumor.)*

Task D

Word 3 is **foreman.** A **foreman** is a boss. The foreman watches you as you work to make sure you're doing the job the right way. Everybody, what do we call a person who watches you as you work to make sure you're doing the job the right way? *Signal.* **A foreman.**

Task E

1. Word 4 is **agile.** Another word for **nimble** is **agile.** Everybody, what's another way of saying **She had nimble fingers?** *Signal.* **She had agile fingers.**
2. Everybody, what's another way of saying **He was a nimble dancer?** *Signal.* **He was an agile dancer.**

Task F

Word 5 is **flattering.** A **flattering** remark is a remark that tells you how good you are. Here's a flattering remark: **You're the best looking student in the whole school.** Everybody, what kind of remark was that? *Signal.* **A flattering remark.**

Lesson 87

Jane Addams
PART 2

Maria Rossi continues to tell about Jane Addams:Ⓐ

I have told you about the bad in my neighborhood, but you should know about the good as well.Ⓑ In the morning you would wake up to the sounds of horses clumping along the street. Most of the horses were owned by peddlers pulling carts. Some peddlers sold ice; some sold vegetables; some sold milk; some sold coal to burn in the stove. And some even bought things. The ragman would sing his song as he sat up on his cart behind an old nag that clumped down the street. "Rags for sale," he'd sing. And if people had any old things, he'd give them a penny or two for them.

And in the summertime, before I was twelve years old, we'd follow the iceman. When somebody would buy some ice, the iceman would go inside the back of his ice cart and slide out a huge block of ice. Then he'd take an ice pick and cut the ice into smaller blocks. When he did this, small chunks of ice would splinter off and fall. We would rush to pick them up. Then we would suck on them until they were all gone. It was delicious. It was wonderful—the bright sun, the yellow ice wagon with the big letters on the side, the street warm on your bare feet, and that cold, slippery ice.Ⓒ

Lesson 87 Textbook   **327**

And there were picnics. Sunday was special—always special. It was family day because it was the only day we had together. And whenever we could, we would have a picnic. We would get on the streetcar. It was pulled by horses. And we would go all the way past downtown to a beach along Lake Michigan.Ⓓ Oh, it was like going to a different world—downtown Chicago with all those rich people dressed in splendid clothes, riding in carriages that glistened. You would see those carriages pulled by horses like the ones you had seen in pictures. Then the smells of the beach— the clean water and clean air. I did not know how to swim, but I think I could have sat there forever, just watching those waves move in. I would try to remember the sound so that I could imagine it at night when it was too hot to sleep. I would think about the beach and try to ignore the mosquitos that buzzed all around.Ⓔ

On those picnic days, we would eat. To me, there is no food like Italian food and there is no Italian food like the food we would have on one of our picnics. Mamma would have some of the special sausage that came from Italy. That sausage is as hard as a brick before it is cooked. But when it is cooked and when you eat it with peppers and tomatoes, it is delicious.

We ate and we sang, and we tried to make those days last forever. But too soon they would end and we would return home on the streetcar, with the sun going down and the lamplighters lighting up the street lights. The day was over, but it wasn't really over because I had it in my memory and I would be able to think about it any time I wished. I could remember the sand on the beach and the songs, and Pappa dancing, and the food.Ⓕ

The morning after a picnic day was a work day. I would wake up to the sound of

328   Lesson 87 Textbook

EXERCISE 5   Decoding and comprehension

1. Everybody, turn to page 327 in your textbook. *Wait. Call on a student.* What's the error limit for this part? **12 errors.**

2. *Call on individual students to read. Present the tasks specified for each circled letter.*

Ⓐ In what year does this part of Maria Rossi's story start? **1889.**

● How old was Maria at that time? **Twelve.**

● In which city did she live? **Chicago.**

● Did she live in a rich neighborhood or a poor one? **A poor one.**

Ⓑ Name some things that were very bad in Maria's neighborhood. *Response:* Student preference.

Now you're going to hear about some things that she thought were good.

Ⓒ Listen to that part again and try to get the nice feeling that Maria Rossi had. *Reread the paragraph.*

● This part tells what Maria did before she had to work. How old was she when she went to work? **Twelve.**

Everybody, look at the picture. *Check.* What is the peddler selling? **Ice.**

● Why are the children standing around the ice wagon? *Idea:* To pick up the ice.

● What is the peddler doing with that sharp pick? *Idea:* Cutting the ice.

Ⓓ Remember the map of Chicago.

● In which direction would they go to reach Lake Michigan? **East.**

That trip was a big adventure for Maria, but the lake is only a couple of miles from where she lived.

Ⓔ How would Maria feel when she remembered the beach? *Idea:* Good.

● Did you ever try to go to sleep by thinking of something that you like a lot? *Response:* Student preference.

Ⓕ Everybody, look at the picture. *Check.* It shows a streetcar coming back from the beach. You can see a lamplighter lighting the streetlights. Look at the stick he uses. In those days the streetlights had gas flames, not electric lights. Each night the lamplighters would have to light gas flames.

● Maria said that when the Sunday picnic ended, the day was not really over for her. Why not? *Idea:* Because she remembered it afterwards.

Mamma calling us to get up. Oh, how I would hate to get out of the bed! The air would be cool and a gentle wind would be blowing through the open windows in the room. You would be able to hear the sounds of chickens and roosters from the house next door. The family that lived there kept chickens inside their house, but we thought they were very strange and we did not get along with them. (G) Peddlers were already calling from the street. And many people were already walking to work. Most of the people in our neighborhood walked. They did not own horses. It was silly to own a horse because if you had one, you would have to keep it inside the house with you. And we did not like to live that way. But two people on our block did have horses that they kept inside at night.(H)

I knew nearly all the people who walked past our place on their way to work. And everybody who was walking knew everybody else. So you would hear them calling greetings to each other in Italian. "Buon Giorno," they would call. And they would laugh and talk to each other. Most of the time, they did not talk about work because going to work was like going into a different world. That world was as dark and dismal as the world of downtown Chicago was bright and magnificent. So the people would joke and laugh and gesture with their hands. Just looking at them would make you want to smile and talk. (I)

★12 ERRORS★

One time I made a bad mistake at work. My job at work was to wrap pieces of hard candy with red paper. The girl who worked next to me wrapped candy in yellow paper. I got mixed up and wrapped all the hard candy in yellow paper. Oh, how I got yelled at by the foreman! Everybody in our neighborhood found out about what happened. Everybody knew about everything. So, for months people would tease me about not knowing the difference between red paper and yellow paper. Sometimes one of the men would pull a red handkerchief from his pocket and hold it up. Then he would say, "Maria, can you tell if this is red or yellow?" Everybody would laugh.

We would not argue with Mamma and Pappa. You did not want to do that. But, people in our neighborhood would argue a lot. In the morning you could hear Mamma arguing with a peddler about the prices of eggs and fresh fruit. She was so good at buying things that the people on their way to work would pause just to admire her. The peddler would tell her that the eggs were fifteen cents a dozen. Of course, that was ridiculous. Mamma would laugh and wave her arms. She would pick up one of the eggs, hold it up, and say in a very loud voice with a very large smile, "Fifteen cents!" She wasn't talking to the peddler. She was talking to the crowd of people who were on their way to work. She was putting on a show for them. "Fifteen cents! she would repeat, waving her arms. "You must be in the wrong neighborhood. There are no trees here. And there are no trees that grow money! What do you think? We pick the money from the trees so that we can

buy eggs for fifteen cents?"

The peddler would try to hush her up. "Please, please," he would say softly. "For you, twelve cents."

Mamma would shout, "Twelve cents! A penny an egg. You must think that we do not have money trees, but we have money bushes! Look around. You have eyes. Show me the money bush!"

By now the people passing by would be smiling and talking among themselves about Mamma's great performance. "Please, please," the peddler would say. "I have a family. I must earn money, too. These are good eggs and my price is fair."

"He says his price is fair," Mamma would announce. "But I ask, who is it fair to?"

Nobody paid the prices that the peddler asked. Everybody would bargain and argue. And maybe Mamma didn't get things any cheaper than the other people on the street. But she sure put on a better show.

She would come home with the things she purchased, singing and smiling. We would help her fix breakfast. Mamma would be talking all the time. Sometimes she would get mad at us, but most of the time she was very cheerful. Then we would eat breakfast, and when it was over, I would get a sad feeling because now it was time to go to work.

To get to work, I would walk on the wooden sidewalks past the old house on Halsted Street that was to become Hull House. I would walk over a mile until I came to the factory where I worked. Usually, I would walk with some of the other girls and boys who worked there. We would talk and joke with each other until we came to the factory entrance. Then we would become very serious, and we would start to speak in English. They didn't like us to speak Italian at work. I knew enough English to get by.

(G) Name some of the sounds that Maria heard in the morning? *Ideas:* Mamma calling her; chickens and roosters.

● Where were the chickens? *Idea:* Next door.

(H) How did most of the people in Maria's neighborhood get to work? *Idea:* They walked.

● What was the problem with owning a horse in Maria's neighborhood? *Idea:* You have to keep it in the house.

(I) Why didn't the people talk about their jobs as they went to work? *Idea:* Because they didn't like their jobs.

● Read the rest of the story to yourselves and be ready to answer some questions.

After all students have finished reading:

● What was Maria's job in the candy factory? **Wrapping pieces of candy.**

● One time Maria made a mistake at work. What was that mistake? *Idea:* Wrapping all the candy in yellow paper.

● Who continued to tease Maria about her mistake? *Idea:* People on the street.

● What would one of the men sometimes do to tease Maria? *Idea:* Hold up a handkerchief and ask about its color.

● Did the people in Maria's neighborhood like her? **Yes.**

● Who used to put on quite a show for the people in the morning? **Mamma.**

● Did people pay the prices the peddler asked? **No.**

● What would they do? *Idea:* Argue with the peddler.

● Why did Maria get a sad feeling after breakfast? *Idea:* She had to go to work then.

● How far did Maria have to walk to get to work in the morning? *Idea:* Over a mile.

● What street did she go up? **Halsted Street.**

● What buildings did she pass on her way to work? **The old house.**

● What language did she start to speak when she came to the factory entrance? **English.**

● Why did she start to speak English? *Idea:* Because she had to speak English in the factory.

● What language did she speak when she was in her neighborhood? **Italian.**

Award 4 points or have the students reread to the error limit sign.

INDEPENDENT WORK

Do all the items in your skillbook and workbook for lesson 87.

ANSWER KEY FOR WORKBOOK

Review Items

1. Write the main use for each animal. Choose from **hunting, food,** or **carrying.**

    a. Elephant *carrying*

    b. Hound *hunting*

    c. Donkey *carrying*

    d. Sheep *food*

    e. Dog *hunting*

    f. Chicken *food*

2. You read about the game of baseball.

    a. How many innings does a game last if there's not a tie? *9*

    b. When a team is not batting, how many of its players are on the field? *9*

    c. For each inning, how many teams get a turn at bat? *2*

    d. Which player stands between second base and third base? *shortstop*

    e. Which major league team did Jackie Robinson play for? *Dodgers*

3. Complete the moral for each story.

    a. The Golden Touch

    Love is better than *gold*

    b. Beauty and the Beast

    Do not trust *appearances*.

    c. The Miraculous Pitcher

    Be kind to *strangers*.

WORKCHECK AND AWARDING POINTS

1. *Read the questions and answers for the skillbook and workbook.*
2. *Award points for independent work as follows:*

> 0 errors . . . . .6 points
> 2 errors . . . . .4 points
> 3, 4, or 5 errors . . . . .2 points
> 5 or more errors . . . . .0 points

3. *Award bonus points as follows:*

> *Correcting missed items or getting all items right . . . . 2 points*
> *Doing the writing assignment acceptably . . . . 2 points*

ANSWER KEY FOR SKILLBOOK

PART B

1. *Idea:* The Woman tamed the Man.

PART C

2. **a.** peddlers
    b. *Any three:* Ice, vegetables, milk, coal
    c. *Idea:* The iceman
    d. Ice
3. **a.** picnics
    b. Lake Michigan
    c. downtown
    d. *Idea:* Student preference
    e. *Idea:* She would keep thinking about it
4. **a.** *Any two:* Mamma calling; roosters; peddlers; people walking
    b. Italian
5. **a.** *Idea:* Prices
    b. *Idea:* Because they liked it
    c. No
6. **a.** Halsted Street
    b. Hull House
    c. A candy factory
    d. English

PART D

7. **a.** Chicago
    b. Halsted Street
    c. Hull House
    d. poor
    e. *Any two:* Greece, Italy, Russia
8. **a.** Maria Rossi
    b. Jane Addams
9. **a.** persuade
    b. dreaded
    c. tricked
    d. trace of
    e. despite

Lesson 88

WORD PRACTICE AND VOCABULARY

EXERCISE 1   Word practice

1. Everybody, find lesson 88, part A in your skillbook. Touch under the first word in column 1. *Pause.* What word? *Signal.* **Kindergarten.**
2. Next word. *Pause.* What word? *Signal.* **Sewing.**
3. *Repeat step 2 for each remaining word in column 1.*
4. *Repeat the words in column 1 until firm.*

EXERCISE 2   Vocabulary review

Task A

1. Everybody, touch column 2. *Check.* First you're going to read the words in column 2. Then we'll talk about what they mean.
2. Touch under the first word. *Pause.* What word. *Signal.* **Flattering.**
3. Next word. *Pause.* What word. *Signal.* **Agile.**
4. *Repeat step 3 for each remaining word in column 2.*
5. *Repeat the words in column 2 until firm.*

Task B

You've learned the meanings for all these words. Word 1 is **flattering.**
Call on a student. What is a **flattering** remark? *Idea:* A remark that tells how good you are.

Task C

Word 2 is **agile.** *Call on a student.* What does **agile** mean? *Idea:* Nimble.

Task D

Word 3 is **peddler.** *Call on a student.* What is a **peddler?** *Idea:* A person who goes down the street with something to sell.

Task E

Word 4 is **foreman.** *Call on a student.* What is a **foreman?** *Idea:* A person who watches you as you work to make sure you're doing the job the right way.

Task F

Word 5 is **rumor.** *Call on a student.* What is a **rumor?** *Idea:* Some news that you hear from somebody.

Lesson 88

Jane Addams

PART 3

Maria Rossi continues to tell about Jane Addams:

If you did not get to work by seven o'clock, you would lose one hour of pay. You would lose an hour even if you were one minute late. So, I was always on time. (A)

The inside of the factory was dark, even though it had large windows in the ceiling. I didn't like the smell. It was the sweet smell of candy. When I first came to work in the factory, I loved the smell. But, we used to eat the candy when we got hungry, and after a while I grew to hate the taste of that candy and its smell. For many years after I worked in that factory, I would have a terrible feeling if I even smelled hard candy. (B)

You could not talk when you were working. A foreman walked around to make sure that you were not talking and that you were working hard. If you stopped for a moment to look at the clock, the foreman would yell at you. "Hey, what do you think we're paying you for? Get to work!" Sometimes, I would not feel well, but I just had to put it out of my mind, and try not to think about it. I would have to stand there next to the other girls near a large slide. Hundreds of pieces of candy would keep sliding down the slide. We'd wrap each piece and then toss the wrapped candy into big boxes. If the pile of candy at the bottom of the slide got too big, the foreman would yell, "Come on! Work faster!" (C)

I was very fast. My fingers were very agile and I practiced with them. I could tie my shoes in less than three seconds, which is faster than anybody I'd ever seen. And I could wrap a piece of candy in less than one second. Most of the other girls were nowhere near that fast, so they got yelled at a lot more than I did. In the morning we would stand at the line for two hours. Then we got five minutes off. We could talk during the break. Then we would go back to work and stand there until our lunch break at noon. We would get twenty minutes for lunch. We would go until six. Then we would spend the last hour cleaning up. They let us talk when we cleaned up, so that was fun. Everybody would be tired, but we were glad that the day was over. We would walk home slowly, feeling tired but happy. (D)

That's how it went everyday, summer and winter. But then, in September of 1889, we had something new to talk about. Mamma was the first to tell us about it. One morning, she came in laughing after talking to Gino, who sold milk. Mamma said, "Some rich young ladies are moving into our neighborhood." She bowed low and we all laughed.

I asked, "Why would rich young ladies want to live here?"

Mamma gave a sly smile. "To help us live better." She laughed. "Gino says that they are going to turn the old Hull place into a settlement house."

"What's a settlement house?" we asked.

"I don't know," said Mamma, with

big eyes. "But whatever it is, it will help us live better." She shook her head and added, "Crazy women." (E)

That day on the way to work, I stopped in front of the old Hull place to see if I could get a glimpse of those crazy women. And I did. There they were, standing out in front of the old place, talking to some workmen. The women were very well dressed. I had never seen women like these outside of downtown. One of them took a few steps toward the house as she said something to the workmen. I didn't know that this woman was Jane Addams and that the other one was her friend, Ellen Starr.

But before the day was over, I had heard all about them. At work, the girls passed on messages down the line. One girl would whisper the message when the foreman was not looking. Then the next girl would pass the message on. From the messages, I learned that Jane Addams and her friend were going to help the people in the neighborhoods around Hull House. Even more amazing, these women were not going to be paid for anything they did. When I heard these things, I could not understand these women, but I said to myself that if they were really going to do these things, I loved them. (F)   ★10 ERRORS★

As I stood there on the line wrapping candy, I thought about what I would do if I were a rich woman. Maybe I would do what Jane Addams was trying to do. Perhaps I would try to make things better so that the people in my neighborhood could have a better life. But in the back of my

---

EXERCISE 3   Decoding and comprehension

1. Everybody, turn to page 331 in your textbook. *Wait. Call on a student.* What's the error limit for this lesson? **10 errors.**

2. *Call on individual students to read. Present the tasks specified for each circled letter.*

(A) What does that mean: **You would lose one hour of pay?** *Idea:* You would not get paid for that hour.

That sounds pretty strict, to lose an hour's pay even if you're one minute late.

(B) How did Maria feel about the smell of candy when she first started to work in the factory? *Idea:* She loved it.

- How did she feel about that smell later? *Idea:* She hated it.

(C) Maria said that she hated candy because she used to eat a lot of it. Can you think of another reason that she learned to hate the smell of candy? *Idea:* Because of the way she was treated at work.

- Everybody, look at the picture. *Check.* It shows a line of girls working near a slide.

- Which person is standing behind the girls? **The foreman.**

- Does that look like a very nice place to work? *Response:* Student preference.

(D) How long were the breaks Maria would get? **Five minutes.**

- How long would she get off for lunch? **Twenty minutes.**

- At what time would they start to clean up? **Six.**

- Why did Maria enjoy that hour? *Idea:* Because she and her friends could talk.

- What time was work over? **Seven.**

(E) Does Maria's mother think that these women will help? **No.**

- What are these women supposed to do? *Idea:* Help the people live better.

- In what year did Maria's mother tell her the news about Hull House? **1889.**

(F) What's the name of one woman who is moving into Hull House? **Jane Addams.**

- Was she rich or poor? **Rich.**

- What did Maria find particularly amazing about Jane Addams and her friend? *Idea:* That they wouldn't get any pay for their work.

- Read the rest of the story to yourselves and be ready to answer some questions.

After all students have finished reading:

- What did Maria think that they might do if she were a rich person? *Idea:* The same things Jane Addams is doing.

mind, I couldn't really believe that Jane Addams would do this nice work. The only rich people I ever saw in my neighborhood were the rich people who came in and out of the factory. I saw the owner, Mr. Flannigan, a few times. He was a bad person. He did not care about anything but making candy. He did not care if you were sick, if you had to work until your fingers were covered with blisters, or if you did not earn enough money each day to buy the food it would take to feed you. He did not care, and I thought that all rich people did not care. I had a lot to learn about some rich people.

• • •

Two weeks after Jane Addams and her friend, Ellen Starr, moved into the old Hull place, I went inside and saw the place for myself. Before that day I almost died of curiosity. Each time I heard some news about the activities that were going on in the house, I tried to imagine what it would be like inside. The girls at work told me that there was expensive furniture inside. They told me that Jane Addams was going to start cooking classes and sewing classes. They told me that there were activities for young boys.

But the news that I found most amazing was that Hull House was going to have a kindergarten for young children. We had no kindergartens. There was a school in our neighborhood, but it was very small and nobody from the Italian neighborhood went there. But at the Hull House kindergarten, the children would play games, learn to speak English, and have a good

meal. One morning Mamma commented on the kindergarten. She shook her head and said, "This cannot be true. How could they afford to run a school? There is nothing that is free in this whole world."

But Mamma was wrong. The day after she told me about the kindergarten, I paused in front of the old house on my way to work. As I stood there, part of my mind told me that Mamma was right and that I should continue on my way to work. But another part of my mind was so curious that I decided to go inside and look around. After all, lots of other people were going in and coming out of Hull House. They were smiling and talking. I heard three different languages. There were Greek people, and Russians, and even some Italians.

I was very anxious as I walked up the front steps, following a mother who was walking with two little children. Jane Addams was at the top of the stairs, just inside the doorway, talking to an old man. When she saw the woman with the two children, she said, "I see we have two new children for our kindergarten."

The woman could not speak English, but you could see that she was apologizing because one of her children was crying.

"The child will be fine," Jane Addams said, taking the child by the hand. She led the child into the parlor. I followed them and peeked inside the parlor. The house was beautiful. And what the girls had told me about the house was correct. There was expensive furniture inside. The floors were clean and polished. I imagined

Lesson 88 Textbook **333**

---

it was just like being inside a rich person's house. I was gazing at all the things when suddenly I was aware of somebody talking to me. It was Jane Addams. She was saying, "What can I do for you?"

I wanted to apologize for coming inside. I wanted to tell her that I had a younger brother who was the right age for kindergarten. I wanted to tell her that I was curious. But before I could say anything, she said, "Welcome to Hull House."

I could not talk for a moment. Then I

managed to say, "Your house is beautiful."

She laughed and replied, "Well, thank you. But it is not beautiful yet; and it is not my house. It is our house— yours and mine and all the other neighbors."

I don't remember what I said next, but I do remember that before I left I asked if my brother could come to the kindergarten. She said, "Yes, but he's not the only one. Everybody in your family may come here. And you may come anytime."

334 Lesson 88 Textbook

- Maria knew one rich person from work. Who was that? *Idea:* Mr. Flannigan.
- What did she think of him? *Idea:* That he was a bad person.
- What was the only thing Mr. Flannigan cared about? *Idea:* Making candy.
- Name some things Mr. Flannigan didn't care about. *Accept appropriate responses.*
- What was the name of the friend of Jane Addams? **Ellen Starr.**
- How many kindergartens were in the neighborhood before the kindergarten at Hull House? **None.**
- Did Maria's mother believe that the women in Hull House really opened a kindergarten? **No.**
- When Maria finally decided to go inside Hull House, who did she follow up the stairs? *Idea:* A mother and two children.
- Why did the mother apologize about one of her children? *Idea:* Because the child was crying.
- When Maria said that Jane Addams's house was beautiful, Jane Addams told her two things about the house. What were those two things? *Idea:* That it wasn't beautiful yet; that it was for the whole neighborhood.
- Maria asked if somebody could come to the kindergarten. Who was that? **Her brother.**

Award 4 points or have the students reread to the errot limit sign.

INDEPENDENT WORK

Do all the items in your skillbook and workbook for lesson 88.

ANSWER KEY FOR WORKBOOK

Review Items

1. Write **fact** or **fiction** for each statement.
   a. There are gods who live on Mount Olympus. *fiction*
   b. The Greeks believed that gods lived on Mount Olympus. *fact*
   c. Monkeys have wings and can fly through the air. *fiction*
   d. A witch can turn a prince into a beast. *fiction*
   e. A man can have an insane desire for gold. *fact*
   f. A man can turn objects into gold by touching them. *fiction*

2. Write **true** or **false** for each statement.
   a. Redwood trees are very tall. *true*
   b. California is the largest state. *false*
   c. When you climb a mountain, the trees get taller. *false*
   d. The story Brown Wolf took place in California. *true*
   e. California is on the east coast of the United States. *false*

3. Write which story each moral fits.
   a. Be kind to strangers. *The Miraculous Pitcher*
   b. Do not trust appearances. *Beauty and the Beast*
   c. Love is better than gold. *The Golden Touch*

WORKCHECK AND AWARDING POINTS

1. *Read the questions and answers for the skillbook and workbook.*
2. *Award points for independent work as follows:*

0 errors	6 points
2 errors	4 points
3, 4, or 5 errors	2 points
5 or more errors	0 points

3. *Award bonus points as follows:*

Correcting missed items or getting all items right	2 points
Doing the writing assignment acceptably	2 points

ANSWER KEY FOR SKILLBOOK

PART B

1. a. candy
   b. *Idea:* You didn't get paid for the first hour
   c. *Idea:* She loved it
   d. *Idea:* She hated it
   e. The foreman
   f. Twelve
2. a. Jane Addams and Ellen Starr
   b. 1889
   c. settlement house
   d. A kindergarten
   e. English
   f. Sewing classes and cooking classes
3. a. *Ideas:* Mamma; Maria's mother
   b. None
4. a. *Any two:* Greek, Italian, Russian
   b. *Idea:* Expensive
   c. Jane Addams
   d. Her brother
   e. *Idea:* Come to Hull House
5. a. Maria's neighborhood
   b. Hull House
   c. Hull House
   d. factory
   e. Maria's neighborhood
   f. factory
   g. Hull House
   h. factory

PART C

6. a. suburb
   b. conceal
   c. great sorrow
   d. despite
   e. slum
   f. mayor

Lesson 89

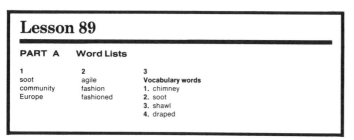

PART A   **Word Lists**

1	2	3
soot	agile	**Vocabulary words**
community	fashion	1. chimney
Europe	fashioned	2. soot
		3. shawl
		4. draped

WORD PRACTICE AND VOCABULARY

EXERCISE 1   Word practice

1. Everybody, find lesson 89, part A in your skillbook. *Wait*. Touch under each word in column 1 as I read it.
2. The first word is **soot**.
3. Next word. **Community**.
4. *Repeat step 3 for* **Europe**.
5. Your turn. Read the first word. *Signal*. **Soot**.
6. Next word. *Signal*. **Community**.
7. *Repeat step 6 for* **Europe**.
8. *Repeat the words in column 1 until firm*.

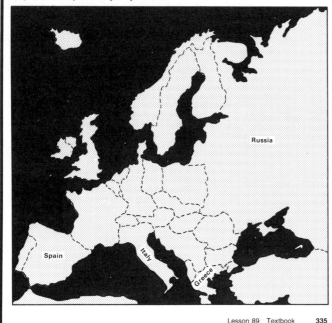

Lesson 89

Europe

Europe is a large part of the world. It is made up of many different countries. Italy is a country in Europe. Spain is a country in Europe. Russia and Greece are other countries in Europe.Ⓐ

Spain   Italy   Greece   Russia

EXERCISE 2   Word practice

1. Everybody, touch under the first word in column 2. *Pause*. What word? *Signal*. **Agile**.
2. Next word. *Pause*. What word? *Signal*. **Fashion**.
3. *Repeat step 2 for* **fashioned**.
4. *Repeat the words in column 2 until firm*.

EXERCISE 3   Vocabulary development

Task A

1. Everybody, touch column 3. *Check*. First you're going to read the words in column 3. Then we'll talk about what they mean.
2. Touch under the first word. *Pause*. What word? *Signal*. **Chimney**.
3. Next word. *Pause*. What word? *Signal*. **Soot**.
4. *Repeat step 3 for each remaining word in column 3*.
5. *Repeat the words in column 3 until firm*.

Task B

Now let's talk about what those words mean. Word 1 is **chimney**. *Call on a student*. What's a **chimney**? *Idea*: **The place where the smoke from a fireplace or wood stove goes out**.

Task C

Word 2 is **soot**. The dirt that comes out of a chimney and settles on things is called **soot**. Soot is little pieces of the material that is burned in a fireplace or a wood stove.

Task D

Word 3 is **shawl**. A **shawl** is an article of clothing that you hang over your shoulders. Everybody, what is the name of an article of clothing that you hang over your shoulders? *Signal*. **A shawl**.

Task E

Word 4 is **draped**. Something that is **draped** hangs down from something else. When you wear a shawl, you drape it over your shoulders. Everybody, what do you do with a shawl when you wear it? *Signal*. **Drape it over your shoulders**.

EXERCISE 4   Comprehension passage

1. Everybody, turn to page 335 in your textbook. *Wait*.
2. *Call on individual students to read. Present the tasks specified for the circled letter.*
Ⓐ Everybody, what do we call that large part of the world that is made up of Spain, Italy, Russia, and other countries? **Europe.**
● Look at the map of Europe. *Check*.
● Name some countries in Europe. *Accept appropriate responses*.

Jane Addams

PART 4 Ⓐ

Maria Rossi continues to tell about Jane Addams:

Every season was so different when I was a child, and every season brought some good and some bad. The season that Hull House opened was the fall, and the fall was always the most beautiful season. Not far from where I lived were streets with large trees. In the fall, they turned gold and red like a magnificent sunset.

The winter came. The good that came with winter was the way it made everything seem clean. The terrible smells of summer were gone, and just after a snowfall, everything looked like a beautiful painting. The snow covered the dirt and even made the buildings look freshly painted.

The bad that came with winter was the cold. We had one small stove in our house and we would cover the windows with old blankets so that the heat would not escape, but at night, the inside of our house would get nearly as cold as the outside. And it was dreadful getting up in the morning. Sometimes Mamma would pull back our covers and laugh. We would get dressed very, very fast. Ⓑ

By winter, Mamma no longer doubted that Jane Addams and Ellen Starr were trying to be very good neighbors. Ⓒ Mamma had been to Hull House many times. In fact, she had even helped out in one of the cooking classes for young girls. In the evening the girls would go to Hull House and learn to cook. Mamma was a teacher for a while.

Mamma talked about going to the English classes at Hull House. But she never went. Most of the people who went to these classes were people who had just come from Europe and had moved into the neighborhood around Hull House. Jane Addams and Ellen Starr taught them to speak English, and some of them soon

knew a lot more English than Mamma. Ⓓ

One December day, the factory where we worked closed down. Something went wrong with the heating system and the factory was closed for over a month until the heating system was repaired. When I found out that I would have a vacation, I jumped up and down and screamed for joy. I could not believe my good fortune. Imagine, I would have days with nothing to do. What made my vacation even more exciting was the snow. A thick blanket of fresh snow had just fallen and the air was not very cold. So, you could make snowballs or snowmen. You could make piles of snow and dive into them. You could run and chase each other and chase the dogs in the snow, and play until you were exhausted.

I would have to go inside around four in the afternoon and help Mamma with dinner. But, after dinner, I would get to go out again. What a beautiful sight—the green light from the gas street lamps, and the soft snowflakes floating down. I would stand with my mouth open and try to catch some falling snow in my mouth. The large snowflakes would land on my tongue and seem to shrink up into a little drop of cold water. Ⓔ ★8 ERRORS★

One evening, I noticed some of the girls that I worked with were all dressed up, walking toward Halsted Street. "Where are you going?" I asked.

They told me they were on their way to Hull House to practice singing songs. They told me that they were going to sing in the dining room on Sunday evening. I ran inside and asked Mamma if I could go with them. At first, she said, "No," but after I pleaded with her, she said, "Stop standing around. You certainly don't plan to go there in the clothes you are wearing." I changed clothes as quickly as I could and joined my friends.

All kinds of things were going on inside Hull House that evening. Some artists were hanging up pictures that they had painted. The parlor was filled with a group of people learning English. Jane Addams was teaching them. Ellen Starr was in another room sitting with a group of women who were reading stories aloud. And there were many other people inside. It was as if all the Greek neighbors and the Russian neighbors and the Italian neighbors were not separate neighbors. They all had come together inside Hull House to become part of one neighborhood.

Ellen Starr talked to us about the songs that we would sing on Sunday. Then we practiced for a little while. The practice did not go very well because the boys who were at a table kept looking at us and making faces. Every time we sang, they would put their hands over their ears or make sour faces. Then we would start giggling and feeling embarrassed.

Singing in front of all the people that Sunday was terrifying. I wanted to look as beautiful as I could look, and I was concerned because my dress looked a little old-fashioned. It was not really my dress. It had been my mother's dress, and it had belonged to three of my sisters before it was mine. The dress was a little small for me, but Mamma let me wear her very best

---

1. Everybody, turn to page 336 in your textbook. *Wait. Call on a student.* What's the error limit for this lesson? **8 errors.**

2. *Call on individual students to read. Present the tasks specified for each circled letter.*

Ⓐ Who is telling this part of the story about Jane Addams? **Maria Rossi.**

● In what year does the story take place? **1889.**

● Name some things people didn't have back in 1889. *Response:* Student preference.

● How old is Maria Rossi? **Twelve.**

● Where does she work? *Idea:* At a candy factory.

● What are her working hours everyday? *Idea:* From seven in the morning until seven at night.

Ⓑ What did Maria think was the most beautiful season? **Fall.**

● In which season did Hull House open? **Fall.**

● What did Maria like about winter? *Idea:* It made things look nice.

● What was the bad that came with winter? *Idea:* The cold.

● Why do you think Maria got dressed very fast after her mother pulled back the covers? *Idea:* Because she was cold.

Ⓒ Had Maria's mother doubted Jane Addams earlier? **Yes.**

Ⓓ What kind of classes did Maria's mother talk about going to? *Idea:* English classes.

● Did she ever go? **No.**

● Where had most of the people who attended these classes recently come from? **Europe.**

Ⓔ On one December day, what happened to the factory? *Idea:* The heating system broke.

● Maria particularly liked her vacation from the factory because of the weather. What was the weather like? *Idea:* Snowy.

● Name some of the things that she did in the snow. *Idea:* Played.

● Read the rest of the story to yourselves and be ready to answer some questions.

After all students have finished reading:

● One evening, who did Maria notice all dressed up? *Idea:* Some of the girls she worked with.

● Where were they going? **To Hull House.**

● What were they going to do there? *Idea:* Practice singing songs.

● Name some of the activities that were going on at Hull House when Maria and her friends went there that evening. *Call on individual students. Ideas:* Artists hanging up pictures; people learning English; people visiting.

● Describe the things that Maria wore on the Sunday that the girls were to sing at Hull House. *Ideas:* A dress and shawl from her mother; shoes that had holes in them.

shawl, and when I draped that shawl around my neck and looked at myself in the living room mirror, I thought I looked like a grown-up woman who was very rich. I just hoped that nobody would notice that my shoes had holes in them.

- How did she think she looked when she was all dressed up? *Idea:* Like a grown-up woman.
- How did Maria think that she and the others sounded when they sang to the group? *Idea:* Beautiful.
- What did Jane Addams pass around to the girls after they sang? **Candy.**
- How many of the girls wanted candy? **None.**
- Who explained to Jane Addams why the girls didn't want any candy? **Maria.**
- How long did it take Jane Addams and her friends to change the laws about children working in factories? **Four years.**
- According to the new law, how old did children have to be before they could work in factories? **Fourteen years old.**
- If the law passed four years after 1889, in which year did it pass? **1893.**
  You'll read more about that law later and how some people felt about it.

Award 4 points or have the students reread to the error limit sign.

INDEPENDENT WORK

Do all the items in your skillbook and workbook for lesson 89.

The largest downstairs room in Hull House was filled with people. Inside the room were many ladies and gentlemen dressed in splendid clothes. Ellen Starr led us into the room and introduced us. The people in the audience nodded and smiled. We sang. I think we sounded beautiful. People in the audience could not understand the words of the songs that we sang, but I could see in their eyes that they knew what the songs said. When we finished, they clapped and asked us to sing more. So we did.

At last, Jane Addams stood up and thanked us. Then she held out a large tray of hard candy and offered some to us. The first girl smiled and shook her head. "No, thank you, Miss Addams," she said. Jane looked a little puzzled and offered the candy to the next girl, who also refused. Then Jane offered the candy to me. I did not mean to be rude, but I said, "I cannot stand the sight of that candy."

She asked why I felt that way and I explained to her that we all worked in the candy factory. Her face suddenly became very serious. "You should be in school," she said. "How long do you work each day?"

We told her how many hours we worked and her expression turned from a serious one to an angry one. "How many girls work there?" she asked sharply.

"About two hundred," I replied, meekly. I felt very embarrassed about making her angry.

She turned to Ellen Starr and said, "We must change this situation." At that moment, I knew that she was strong enough to do anything she set out to do.

It took Jane Addams, Ellen Starr and their friends a great deal of work to change the situation, but four years later, in 1893, a law was passed that made it illegal for any child under fourteen to work in the factories. That law did not help me, because by then I was already sixteen and was used to hard work. But it helped three of my brothers and one sister. They had a chance to go to school, and by then our neighborhood was much nicer than it was when I was their age.

But despite the poverty and the work, I have many fond memories of my neighborhood, and a lot of these memories are of Jane Addams and the other women who lived at Hull House. They taught me what it means to be a good neighbor.

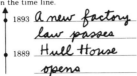

Lesson 90

WORD PRACTICE AND VOCABULARY

EXERCISE 1   Word practice

1. Everybody, find lesson 90, part A in your skillbook. *Wait.* Touch under each word in column 1 as I read it.
2. The first word is **resident.**
3. Next word. **Fascinated.**
4. *Repeat step 3 for each remaining word in column 1.*
5. Your turn. Read the first word. *Signal.* **Resident.**
6. Next word. *Signal.* **Fascinated.**
7. *Repeat step 6 for each remaining word in column 1.*
8. *Repeat the words in column 1 until firm.*

EXERCISE 2   Word practice

1. Everybody, touch under the first word in column 2. *Pause.* What word? *Signal.* **Exhibit.**
2. Next word. *Pause.* What word? *Signal.* **Nurse.**
3. *Repeat step 2 for each remaining word in column 2.*
4. *Repeat the words in column 2 until firm.*

EXERCISE 3   Vocabulary review

Task A

1. Everybody, touch column 3. *Check.*
   First you're going to read the words in column 3. Then we'll talk about what they mean.
2. Touch under the first word. *Pause.* What word? *Signal.* **Shawl.**
3. Next word. *Pause.* What word? *Signal.* **Draped.**
4. *Repeat step 3 for soot.*
5. *Repeat the words in column 3 until firm.*

Task B

You've learned the meanings for all these words. Word 1 is **shawl.** *Call on a student.* What is a **shawl?** *Idea:* An article of clothing you hang over your shoulders.

Task C

Word 2 is **draped.** *Call on a student.* What does **draped** mean? *Idea:* Hanging down from something else.

Task D

Word 3 is **soot.** *Call on a student.* What is **soot?** *Idea:* The dirt that comes out of a chimney and settles on things.

EXERCISE 4 Vocabulary development

Task A

1. Everybody, touch column 4. *Check.*
   First you're going to read the words in column 4. Then we'll talk about what they mean.
2. Touch under the first word. *Pause.*
   What word? *Signal.* **Resident.**
3. Next word. *Pause.*
   What word? *Signal.* **Fascinated.**
4. *Repeat step 3 for each remaining word in column 4.*
5. *Repeat the words in column 4 until firm.*

Task B

Now let's talk about what those words mean. Word 1 is **resident.** A **resident** is a person who lives in a place. A resident of a building is a person who lives in that building. Everybody, what would you call a person who lives in Hull House? *Signal.* **A resident of Hull House.**

Task C

1. Word 2 is **fascinated.** When you are **fascinated** with something, you are interested and delighted by that thing.
   Everybody, what's another way of saying **She was not interested and delighted by her job?** *Signal.* **She was not fascinated by her job.**
2. Everybody, what's another way of saying **She was interested and delighted by Jane Addams?** *Signal.*

   She was fascinated by Jane Addams.

Task D

Word 3 is **ward.** A **ward** is the name that is used for parts of some cities. A large city like Chicago may have many wards. Each ward is a part. Everybody, what do we call the parts of some cities? *Signal.* **Wards.**

Task E

1. Word 4 is **profit.** A **profit** is the extra money you make from a business. If you buy something for 100 dollars and you sell it for 120 dollars, you make a profit of 20 dollars. Let's say you buy something for three thousand dollars and sell it for four thousand dollars. Everybody, how much profit did you make? *Signal.* **One thousand dollars.**
2. What do we call the extra money that you made? *Signal.* **The profit.**

Task F

Word 5 is **supervisor.** Another word for a **boss** is a **supervisor.**
Everybody, what's another way of saying **Her boss was unfair?** *Signal.*
Her supervisor was unfair.

Task G

Word 6 is **infant.** A **baby** or a **very young child** is an **infant.** Everybody, what's a **baby** or a **very young child?** *Signal.* **An infant.**

Lesson 90

Jane Addams
PART 5

Rita Hansen tells about Jane Addams: (A)

I came to live in Hull House in 1893 as a resident. (B) I had read about Hull House in several magazine articles and I was fascinated by the idea of a house to help the poor and needy. But, when I heard Jane Addams talk, I knew that Hull House was more than a place. It was a new idea—the idea of trying to make the world a better place for everybody. (C) At that time, Jane was making speeches about the need for a new law that prevented young children from working in factories. (D) When I heard Jane Addams, she was talking at a club meeting in downtown Chicago. She did not talk like a speechmaker, but like a person who was concerned with others. She told about the horrible lives of the people who lived near Hull House. By now, that part of the city was well-known, thanks to the efforts of Jane and the people who worked with her. That part of the city was Ward 19, and hardly a week went by without an article in the newspaper about that ward. (E)

I had read the newspaper articles and I understood the hardships of the people in Ward 19, but it wasn't until I heard Jane talk that I actually felt their problems. Jane

talked about children who were eleven and twelve years old working in factories. She said, "Shortly after Christmas in 1889, just a few months after Hull House opened, a young boy who was in one of the clubs at Hull House was killed in an accident in a factory. The life of this fine young boy was lost because the laws permit factories to hire children who should be in school." She paused and then continued slowly. "That boy was killed in 1889, four years ago. And since that time, Hull House has been dedicated to changing laws that permit factory owners to make a profit by using young children as slaves. But the factories still hire children and some children still work twelve to fourteen hours a day." (F)

Jane then told about the school situation in Ward 19. She explained that she and the other residents at Hull House had counted the children of school age in Ward 19. There were about seven thousand children. Then she said, "But there are less than three thousand seats in the schools in Ward 19." (G)

Jane reported that she had talked with parents in Ward 19 and had explained how important it was for their children to go to school. The parents understood the need

340 Lesson 90 Textbook

---

for school, but there was no space for their children in the schools. Besides, many of the families needed the money that the children brought home from the factories.

She explained that Hull House was able to operate because people gave Hull House money or worked without pay. Finally, she said, "Hull House is a bridge bringing you and your neighbors together."

When Jane finished her speech, I introduced myself and asked her about how a person could become a resident at Hull House.

Jane smiled and explained that most of the residents had jobs in Chicago, but they lived at Hull House and they worked at Hull House in their spare time. (H)

★9 ERRORS★

I thanked Jane and told her I would think about it. And I thought a lot. In one way, I thought that the poor people in Ward 19 were a great deal like me and many other young women of that time. In 1893, women did not have the same rights that men had. Women were not able to

vote, and there were not many jobs for them. I had just finished college, and I was at the top of my class. But like other women, I was not able to get a very good job. The good jobs were for men, and I resented that. In a way, the people in Ward 19 had the same kind of problem. They had to suffer, simply because they were poor and had to live in a poor part of the city.

I worked as a clerk in a downtown bank. My supervisor was a young man who had graduated from the same college I had gone to. He had not been a very good student and he was not very intelligent. One day at work, he blamed me for a mistake that he had made. I tried to point out to the bank manager that I had not made the mistake, but he didn't believe me. When I went back to my desk, I was furious. I sat there, trying to hold my temper, and then suddenly, almost without thinking, I decided that I would become a resident at Hull House. I stood up and told my supervisor that I would like to take the rest of the day off.

Lesson 90 Textbook 341

EXERCISE 5 Decoding and comprehension

1. Everybody, turn to page 340 in your textbook. *Wait. Call on a student.* What's the error limit for this lesson? **9 errors.**

2. *Call on individual students to read. Present the tasks specified for each circled letter.*

(A) Who told the part of the Jane Addams story you just read? **Maria Rossi.**

● Who is going to tell this part? **Rita Hansen.**

(B) Who is talking? **Rita Hansen.**

● When did she come to Hull House? **1893.**

● What big event happened in that year? *Idea:* The law about children working in factories was passed.

● Rita Hansen says she **came as a resident.** What does that mean? *Idea:* She lived at Hull House.

(C) When did Rita Hansen know that Hull House was more than a place? *Idea:* When she heard Jane Addams talk.

(D) So this part of the story takes place in 1893 before the new law had been passed. Jane was talking about why that law was needed. What kinds of things do you think Jane Addams said in her speeches? *Response:* Student preference.

(E) What was the part of the city around Hull House called? **Ward 19.**

● Who had made Ward 19 famous? **Jane Addams.**

(F) Jane Addams told about what happened shortly after Christmas in 1889. What terrible thing happened? *Idea:* A young boy was killed in a factory accident.

● When Rita Hansen heard Jane talk, how long had Jane Addams and the others at Hull House been working on trying to change the law? **Four years.**

● In her speech, Jane Addams said that the old laws permitted factory owners to make a profit by using young children as slaves. What does that mean: **Make a profit?** *Idea:* Make money.

● How did factory owners use young children as slaves? *Idea:* They made them work long hours for very little money.

(G) About how many children of school age were in Ward 19? **Seven thousand.**

● How many seats were in the schools of Ward 19? **Less than three thousand.**

● Tell me about how many children in Ward 19 couldn't even go to school if they wanted to? **Four thousand.**

(H) What did Rita ask Jane Addams after Jane finished her talk? *Idea:* How to become a resident of Hull House.

Outside, I called a taxicab and told the driver to take me to Hull House. Although Hull House was not much more than a mile from the bank, I had never been there before. To get there, you had to travel through a part of the city that was very unpleasant. The odor was terrible.

Halsted Street, near Hull House, was lined with little shops. The street was so crowded with colorful peddlers that the taxi could hardly move at times. Each neighborhood the taxi passed through was different—Greek, Italian, Russian. But the people who lived there seemed to be proud. And in the middle of the neighborhood was Hull House. As soon as I saw Hull House, I understood what Jane Addams had meant when she called it a bridge that brings neighbors together. Men, women, and children from the neighborhood were walking up the steps. Many carriages that were in front of Hull House were owned by wealthy people. Hull House had attracted them to Ward 19 and had made them neighbors too.

When Hull House had first opened, it occupied only part of the old Hull place. But on the day that I first saw Hull House in 1893, Hull House was already a little community. Every inch of the house was occupied—with clubs, activities, and exhibits. Behind the house was a cottage, where Hull House operated a nursery school for infants and very young children. And next to the house was a large building that was just being completed. The upstairs would become a large gym. Downstairs would be a large lunchroom that would be open to everybody. Jane planned to send out hot lunches to the factories from this lunchroom. For five cents, factory workers would be able to buy a large bowl of soup and two rolls.

Jane was busy talking to the workmen when I arrived, so I strolled inside the house and started to look around at the activities and the art exhibits. Some of the best painters in the United States had their paintings on display here. As I was wandering through the rooms, a peppy young woman came up and asked if she could help me. I told her that I wanted to become a resident. I found out that the young woman's name was Julia Lathrop, and that she was one of the first residents.

Julia showed me to the residents' bedrooms on the top floor of the old house. And then she left. I sat on a small bed, and I had the strange feeling that I had just begun a new life, one that was completely different from anything I had ever known.

- Most of the residents in Hull House had regular jobs. Where were their jobs? **In Chicago.**
- Where did the residents live? **At Hull House.**
- When did the residents help out at Hull House? *Idea:* In their spare time.
- How much money did they earn for working at Hull House? **None.**
- Read the rest of the story to yourselves and be ready to answer some questions.

After all students have finished reading:

- Rita thought that the problems of people in Ward 19 were a lot like the problems facing many young women in 1893. Name two problems that women in 1893 had. *Ideas:* They couldn't get jobs; they couldn't vote.
- What job did Rita have downtown? *Idea:* A bank clerk.
- What is a bank clerk? *Idea:* Somebody who works in a bank.
- What incident at the bank occurred just before Rita decided to become a resident at Hull House? *Idea:* She was blamed for a mistake her supervisor had made.
- When Rita arrived at Hull House, it was different from the way it had looked when Maria told about it. Name the ways it had grown. *Ideas:* Nursery school; large building next door; very busy.
- The story said that Hull House had attracted many wealthy people and made them neighbors. These people didn't really live in Ward 19. So, in what way were they neighbors? *Idea:* They helped the neighborhood.
- There was now a nursery school for infants. What are infants? *Idea:* Babies.
- Where was this nursery? *Idea:* In a cottage behind Hull House.
  There was also a kindergarten for children who were a little older.
- What did Jane plan to send out to factory workers from the new lunchroom? *Idea:* Hot lunches.
- How much would the workers have to pay for a large bowl of soup and two rolls? **Five cents.**
- What's the name of that peppy resident who Rita Hansen met in Hull House? **Julia Lathrop.**
  Remember her. You'll read some more about her later.

Award 4 points or have the students reread to the error limit sign.

INDEPENDENT WORK

Do all the items in your skillbook and workbook for lesson 90.

ANSWER KEY FOR WORKBOOK

Review Items

1. Here are some events from the Jane Addams biography.
   ● Hull House opens
   ● A new factory law passes

Write the correct event after each date on the time line.

1893 *a new factory law passes*

1899 *Hull House opens*

2. Write which breed of dog each statement describes. Choose from **airedale, collie, greyhound, hound** or **poodle**.
   a. This breed is very fast.
      greyhound
   b. This breed is smart.
      poodle
   c. This breed has a sensitive nose.
      hound
   d. This breed is good at herding.
      collie
   e. This breed is very brave.
      airedale

Map Skills

3. Look at the map.

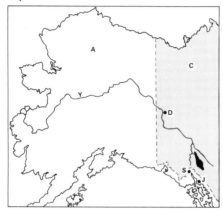

   a. What metal was discovered near town **D** in 1896? *gold*
   b. What's the name of town **D**? *Dawson*
   c. What's the name of river **Y**? *Yukon*
   d. What country is town **D** in? *Canada*

WORKCHECK AND AWARDING POINTS

1. *Read the questions and answers for the skillbook and workbook.*
2. *Award points for independent work as follows:*

0 errors	*6 points*
2 errors	*4 points*
3, 4, or 5 errors	*2 points*
5 or more errors	*0 points*

3. *Award bonus points as follows:*

Correcting missed items or getting all items right	*2 points*
Doing the writing assignment acceptably	*2 points*

ANSWER KEY FOR SKILLBOOK

PART B

1. *Idea:* Beauty and her father filled the trunks.

PART C

2. **a.** Rita Hansen
   b. 1893
   c. *Idea:* Working in factories
   d. *Idea:* He was killed in a factory
   e. *Idea:* In school
   f. Four
3. **a.** 19
   b. Jane Addams
   c. bridge
4. **a.** Rita Hansen
   b. Yes
   c. No
5. **a.** women
   b. *Idea:* Couldn't vote and couldn't get a good job
   c. important
   d. *Idea:* Her supervisor
6. **a.** To Hull House
   b. One mile
   c. Halsted Street
   d. *Idea:* It was crowded

PART D

7. **a.** Chicago
   b. Halsted Street
   c. Hull House
   d. Poor
   e. *Any two:* Greece, Italy, Russia
8. **a.** grief
   b. refused
   c. slum
   d. mayor
   e. agile

Lesson 91

WORD PRACTICE AND VOCABULARY

EXERCISE 1   Word practice

1. Everybody, find lesson 91, part A in your skillbook. *Wait.* Touch under each word in column 1 as I read it.
2. The first word is **donate.**
3. Next word. **Stubborn.**
4. *Repeat step 3 for each remaining word in column 1.*
5. Your turn. Read the first word. *Signal.* **Donate.**
6. Next word. *Signal.* **Stubborn.**
7. *Repeat step 6 for each remaining word in column 1.*
8. *Repeat the words in column 1 until firm.*

EXERCISE 2   Word practice

1. Everybody, touch under the first word in column 2. *Pause.* What word? *Signal.* **Range.**
2. Next word. *Pause.* What word? *Signal.* **Arrange.**
3. *Repeat step 2 for each remaining word in column 2.*
4. *Repeat the words in column 2 until firm.*

EXERCISE 3   Vocabulary review

Task A

1. Everybody, touch column 3. *Check.* First you're going to read the words in column 3. Then we'll talk about what they mean.
2. Touch under the first word. *Pause.* What word? *Signal.* **Ward.**
3. Next word. *Pause.* What word? *Signal.* **Supervisor.**
4. *Repeat step 3 for each remaining word in column 3.*
5. *Repeat the words in column 3 until firm.*

Task B

You've learned the meanings for all these words. Word 1 is **ward.** *Call on a student.* What is a **ward?** *Idea:* A part of some cities.

Task C

Word 2 is **supervisor.** *Call on a student.* What is a **supervisor?** *Idea:* A boss.

Task D

Word 3 is **infant.** *Call on a student.* What is an **infant?** *Idea:* A baby or a very young child.

Task E

Word 4 is **resident.** *Call on a student.* What is a **resident?** *Idea:* A person who lives in a place.

Task F

1. Word 5 is **fascinated.** *Call on a student.* What does **fascinated** mean? *Idea:* Interested and delighted.
2. Everybody, what's another way of saying **She was interested and delighted by Jane Addams?** *Signal.* **She was fascinated by Jane Addams.**
3. Everybody, what's another way of saying **She was not interested and delighted by her job?** *Signal.* **She was not fascinated by her job.**

Task G

Word 6 is **profit.** *Call on a student.* What is a **profit?** *Idea:* The extra money that you make on a business deal.

EXERCISE 4   Vocabulary development

Task A

1. Everybody, touch column 4. *Check.* First you're going to read the words in column 4. Then we'll talk about what they mean.
2. Touch under the first word. *Pause.* What word? *Signal.* **Donate.**
3. Next word. *Pause.* What word? *Signal.* **Filth.**
4. *Repeat step 3 for each remaining word in column 4.*
5. *Repeat the words in column 4 until firm.*

Task B

1. Now let's talk about what those words mean. Word 1 is **donate.** When you **donate** something, you give it away. Everybody, what are you doing when you give away money to somebody? *Signal.* **Donating money to somebody.**
2. What are you doing when you give a gift to Hull House? *Signal.* **Donating a gift to Hull House.**

Task C

Word 2 is **filth.** Another word for **garbage and dirt** is **filth.** Everybody, what's another word for **garbage and dirt?** *Signal.* **Filth.**

Task D

Word 3 is **stubborn.** When you are **stubborn,** you do not change your behavior, no matter what happens. Here's another way of saying **He would not change his behavior: He was stubborn.** Everybody, what's another way of saying **He would not change his behavior?** *Signal.* **He was stubborn.**

Lesson 91

1	2	3	4
donate	range	**Vocabulary words**	**Vocabulary words**
stubborn	arrange	1. ward	1. donate
inspector	sicken	2. supervisor	2. filth
fiery	sickening	3. infant	3. stubborn
wages		4. resident	4. fined
		5. fascinated	
		6. profit	

Lesson 91

Jane Addams

PART 6

Rita Hansen continues to tell about Jane Addams:

As a resident of Hull House, I had two jobs—my regular job at the bank and my job at Hull House. I had never worked so hard in my entire life, but I don't believe that I've ever been as happy. Ⓐ

Residents at Hull House worked around Hull House; they worked on problems in the neighborhood; and they tried to raise money for Hull House. The House depended on gifts from wealthy people, and the gifts had to keep coming in.

Jane was a marvel. She worked all day and late into the night. She made speeches, contacted wealthy people, and still had time to go into the neighborhood and work on problems. The other residents and I tried to imitate her, but it was almost impossible. She seemed to have endless energy. She had no husband, and her whole life was wrapped up in Hull House. Ⓑ

I got up early every morning and helped set up things for the activities that were scheduled at Hull House. Sometimes, I would do some work in the kitchen. Sometimes, I would go into the neighborhood in the evening and talk to families about problems, like the garbage collection

problem. The city garbage collectors were supposed to pick up garbage regularly, but sometimes weeks would go by before the collectors came by. And when they came by, they filled up their wagons so quickly that they didn't get to all parts of the neighborhood. In the meantime, the garbage would flow over the boxes that were next to the street and in some places, the streets would almost be entirely blocked by mounds of garbage. Ⓒ

When I worked in the bank, I would wonder if my work made any difference in anybody's life. I would ask myself whether it was really important. And I would usually answer, "No." But, when I worked at Hull House I had no doubt that I was working on things that were important.

Each day after work, I would go back to Hull House. I would eat with the residents and then we would plan the things that we were going to work on. Julia Lathrop was the leader of the residents. When some of the residents would complain that things weren't going well, she'd make a joke or say something like, "Now that we've heard about the bad, let's talk about the good things that we're going to do." Ⓓ

Sometimes I would talk to groups of

Task E

Word 4 is **fined.** When you are **fined** for breaking the law, you must pay a certain amount of money. A person who is caught speeding in an automobile is fined for breaking the law. Name some things a person might be fined for. *Call on individual students. Ideas:* Throwing trash out on the highway; not stopping at a stop sign; not getting tags for your dog.

STORY READING

EXERCISE 5   Decoding and comprehension

1. Everybody, turn to page 344 in your textbook. *Wait. Call on a student.* What's the error limit for this lesson? **7 errors.**
2. *Call on individual students to read. Present the tasks specified for each circled letter.*

Ⓐ How many jobs did Rita Hansen have? **Two.**
- What did she do for her regular job? *Idea:* Worked in a bank.
- What was her other job? *Idea:* Resident at Hull House.
  She would do her work as a resident and also work full time in the bank. No wonder she worked hard.
- Did the work at Hull House make her unhappy. **No.**
- Why do you think it made her happy? *Idea:* Because she felt she was doing something important.

Ⓑ Who did the residents try to imitate? **Jane Addams.**
- Why was that hard? *Idea:* Jane Addams worked so hard.
- What were the three main jobs the residents had? *Call on individual students. Ideas:* Working around Hull House; working on neighborhood problems; raising money for Hull House.
- How do you think the residents tried to raise money? *Idea:* By talking to wealthy people.
- Hull House depended on gifts from wealthy people. What was the most important kind of gift that these people gave? *Idea:* Money.
- What would happen if they stopped giving money to Hull House? *Response:* Student preference.

Ⓒ What were the problems with garbage collection? *Idea:* The garbage wasn't collected.

Ⓓ Who was the leader of the residents? **Julia Lathrop.**

women or clubs. When I talked to these groups, I would try very hard to make them understand that the people in Ward 19 were good people who wanted a better life. The people were simply victims of poverty.

Usually, the speeches I made were very successful. (E) ★7 ERRORS★ I gave several speeches that stirred up trouble. Once I told a large group of people about the conditions in Ward 19, and I pointed out that a very wealthy man named William Kent owned all the terrible buildings on one entire block in Ward 19. The houses on that block were in the worst condition of any houses in the entire ward. Old people, sick people, and babies were crowded into dwellings with chickens, pigs, and filth. There was so much filth that I would actually get sick when I went into some of the buildings. I said, "What kind of man is William Kent that he would have to become a tiny bit richer at the expense of people who are dying in pov-

erty? How important is the rent money that these people give him so they can live in such a sickening place?"

During another speech I even angered my own parents. They were fairly wealthy and they lived in one of the nicer suburbs north of Chicago. At first, they were very upset when I told them that I had become a resident of Hull House. My mother said that she was worried about my walking around in such a terrible neighborhood. My father said that I was just being a stubborn child. He said, "Is this why we sent you through college, so you could work in a slum?"

But after a while, my parents changed their minds about Hull House. So I told them that I would like to make a speech to them and some of their friends. I told them that their friends might be interested in donating some money to Hull House. So my parents arranged a large party at their house. They invited over fifty people.

On the day I was to give the speech, I found out that the city of Chicago was going to pass the law that made it illegal for children under fourteen years of age to work in factories. I also found out that one of the residents at Hull House was going to become the factory inspector for the city. Her job would be to go around to the factories. If she found children under fourteen working in a factory, she would take the factory owner to court, where the owner would be fined for breaking the law.

Lesson 91 Textbook   **345**

What was the main purpose in talking to these groups? *Idea:* To raise money.
- So what would happen if a speech was very successful? *Idea:* Hull House would get lots of money.
- Read the rest of the story to yourselves and be ready to answer some questions.

After all students have finished reading:
- What does this mean: **The people were simply victims of poverty?** *Idea:* They had no choice about being poor.
- Rita gave a speech that stirred up a lot of trouble. What was the name of the person she talked about? **William Kent.**
- What did this person own? *Idea:* A lot of buildings.
- In what kind of condition were the buildings on that block? *Idea:* Terrible.
- Rita asked what kind of man would want to become a tiny bit richer at the expense of people who were dying in poverty. How was William Kent getting richer at their expense? *Idea:* From the rent he collected.
- On the day that Rita was going to make a speech at her parents' house, the people at Hull House received some good news. What news was that? *Idea:* The factory law had been passed.
- One of the residents from Hull House was going to be made factory inspector for the city. What was that person's job going to be? *Idea:* To make sure that children under fourteen weren't working.
- Where was Rita going to give a speech that evening? *Idea:* At her parents' house.
- Were her parents rich or poor? **Rich.**
- How many people were invited to her parents' house? **Over fifty.**
- What did Rita hope that these people would do? *Idea:* Donate money to Hull House.

Award 4 points or have the students reread to the error limit sign.

EXERCISE 6   Individual reading checkout

1. *For the individual reading checkout, each student will read 150 words. The passage to be read is the shaded area on the reproduced textbook page for lesson 91 in this presentation book.*
2. Today is a reading checkout day. While you're doing your independent work, I'll call on each student to read part of yesterday's chapter.
3. When I call on you, come up to my desk and bring your textbook with you. After you have read, I'll tell you how many points you can write in the checkout box that's at the top of your workbook page.
4. *If the student finishes the passage in one minute or less, award points as follows:*

> 0 errors . . . . .3 points
> 1 or 2 errors . . . . .1 point
> More than 2 errors . . . . .0 points

5. *If a student takes more than one minute to read the passage, the student does not earn any points, but have the student reread the passage until he or she is able to read it in no more than one minute with no more than two errors.*

ANSWER KEY FOR WORKBOOK

Review Items

1. Write the name of the Greek god who might make each statement. Choose from **Apollo, Hermes, Poseidon** or **Zeus.**
   a. "I carry a strange staff."
      Hermes
   b. "I turned a village into a lake."
      Zeus
   c. "I am the god of the sea."
      Poseidon
   d. "I command the thunder and lightning."
      Zeus
   e. "I am the god of light and music."
      Apollo
   f. "I am the messenger god."
      Hermes
2. Write which **direction** you would go from the Emerald City to reach each place.
   a. Land of the Winkies   *West*
   b. Land of the Munchkins   *East*
   c. Land of the Quadlings   *South*
   d. Land of the Gillikins   *North*
3. Write whether each animal is **wild** or **domestic.**
   a. Lion   *wild*
   b. Monkey   *wild*
   c. Hound   *domestic*
   d. Goat   *domestic*
4. Complete the moral for each story.
   a. The Golden Touch
      Love is better than *gold*
   b. Beauty and the Beast
      Do not trust *appearances*
   c. The Miraculous Pitcher
      Be kind to *strangers*

INDEPENDENT WORK

Do all the items in your skillbook and workbook for lesson 91.

WORKCHECK AND AWARDING POINTS

1. *Read the questions and answers for the skillbook and workbook.*
2. *Award points for independent work as follows:*

> 0 errors .6 points
> 2 errors .4 points
> 3, 4, or 5 errors . . . . .2 points
> 5 or more errors . . . . .0 points

3. *Award bonus points as follows:*

> *Correcting missed items
> or getting all items right . . . . .2 points
> Doing the writing
> assignment acceptably . . . . .2 points*

4. *Remind the students to put the points they earned for their reading checkout, in the box labeled* **CO.**

ANSWER KEY FOR SKILLBOOK
PART B
1. *Idea:* The Parker family went to the movies.

PART C
2. a. 1893
   b. resident
   c. *Idea:* At a bank
   d. No
3. a. garbage collection
   b. *Idea:* To raise money for Hull House
4. a. William Kent
   b. *Idea:* Buildings
   c. *Idea:* Very bad
5. a. Rich
   b. *Idea:* Upset
   c. *Idea:* A speech
6. a. a factory law
   b. *Idea:* A resident
7. a. unimportant
   b. unimportant
   c. important
   d. unimportant
   e. important
   f. important

PART D
8. a. fact
   b. fiction
   c. fact
   d. fiction

Lesson 92

Lesson 92

PART A   Word Lists

1	2	3	4
investor	dilapidated	**Vocabulary words**	**Vocabulary words**
collector	wages	1. stubborn	1. abandon
inspector	sober	2. donate	2. invest
manager	vigorous	3. filth	3. wages
supervisor	abandon	4. fined	4. distressed
	spectacular		5. trance
			6. vigorous
			7. plump

WORD PRACTICE AND VOCABULARY

EXERCISE 1   Word family

1. Everybody, touch column 1. *Check.* All those words are the names of types of jobs. Touch under the first word. *Pause.*

EXERCISE 2   Word practice

1. Everybody, touch under the first word in column 2. *Pause.* What word? *Signal.* **Dilapidated.**
2. Next word. *Pause.* What word? *Signal.* **Wages.**
3. *Repeat step 2 for each remaining word in column 2.*
4. *Repeat the words in column 2 until firm.*

EXERCISE 3   Vocabulary review

Task A

1. Everybody, touch column 3. *Check.* First you're going to read the words in column 3. Then we'll talk about what they mean.
2. Touch under the first word. *Pause.* What word? *Signal.* **Stubborn.**
3. Next word. *Pause.* What word? *Signal.* **Donate.**
4. *Repeat step 3 for each remaining word in column 3.*
5. *Repeat the words in column 3 until firm.*

Task B

1. You've learned the meanings for all these words. Word 1 is **stubborn.** *Call on a student.* What does **stubborn** mean? *Idea:* You won't change your behavior.
2. Everybody, what's another way of saying **She would not change her behavior?** *Signal.* **She was stubborn.**

Task C

Word 2 is **invest.** When you **invest** in a deal, you put money into the deal and try to make a profit. If you buy some buildings that you will rent out, you invest in the buildings. Everybody, what are you doing if you buy a farm that you will rent out? *Signal.* **Investing in a farm.**

Task D

Word 3 is **wages.** The money that you earn when you work for somebody is called your **wages.** Everybody, what do you call the money I earn for my job? *Signal.* **Your wages.**

Lesson 92

PART A **Word Lists**

1	2	3	4
investor	dilapidated	**Vocabulary words**	**Vocabulary words**
collector	wages	1. stubborn	1. abandon
inspector	sober	2. donate	2. invest
manager	vigorous	2. filth	3. wages
supervisor	abandon	4. fined	4. distressed
	spectacular		5. trance
			6. vigorous
			7. plump

Task C

Word 2 is **donate.** *Call on a student.*
What does **donate** mean? *Idea:* To give
something to somebody.

Task D

Word 3 is **filth.** *Call on a student.*
What is **filth?** *Idea:* Garbage and dirt.

Task E

Word 4 is **fined.** *Call on a student.*
What must you do when you are **fined?** *Idea:*
You have to pay money.

EXERCISE 4   Vocabulary development

Task A

1. Everybody, touch column 4. *Check.* First you're
   going to read the words in column 4. Then we'll
   talk about what they mean.
2. Touch under the first word. *Pause.*
   What word? *Signal.* **Abandon.**
3. Next word? *Pause.*
   What word? *Signal.* **Invest.**
4. *Repeat step 3 for each remaining word in column 4.*
5. *Repeat the words in column 4 until firm.*

Task B

Now let's talk about what those words mean.
Word 1 is **abandon.** When you stop an activity
that you started, you **abandon** that activity.
Everybody, what are you doing when you stop
an activity that you started? *Signal.*
Abandoning that activity.

Task E

1. Word 4 is **distressed.** Another word for
   troubled is **distressed.** Everybody, what's
   another way of saying **The terrible filth
   troubled her?** *Signal.* **The terrible filth
   distressed her.**
2. Everybody, what's another way of saying
   She was troubled over her job? *Signal.*
   She was distressed over her job.

Task F

Word 5 is **trance.** A **trance** is like a dream that
you have when you are still awake.

Task G

1. Word 6 is **vigorous.** Something that is very
   strong and lively is **vigorous.**
   Everybody, what's a strong and lively dance?
   Signal. **A vigorous dance.**
2. What is strong and lively applause? *Signal.*
   Vigorous applause.

Task H

1. Word 7 is **plump.** A person who is a little fat is
   a **plump** person.
2. Everybody, what would you call a grape that is
   a little fat? *Signal.* **A plump grape.**

Lesson 92

Jane Addams
PART 7

Rita Hansen continues to tell about Jane Addams: (A)

I was delighted over the good news about the law that was going to be passed. I was in very high spirits that day at the bank. I left early so that I would arrive at my parents' home on time. When I got there, my father introduced me to all of the guests. Then everybody sat down to a wonderful dinner. After dinner my father said, "And now, my daughter is going to tell us about Hull House." (B)

I told the story of Hull House and also told about the law that would be passed. Most of the people seemed quite pleased. After it was over, a man who had a distressed expression on his face came up. In a loud voice he said, "My name is Flannigan, and I own a candy company near Hull House." (C)

Then Flannigan continued, "Our plant operates in Ward 19 so we do not have to invest a lot of money in paying high wages to adults. Candy-making is a tough business, and if we have to pay our workers high wages, we're out of business, and our workers are out of a job."

By now his face was flushed and he was yelling. Everybody in the room was

looking at him. He concluded by saying, "Jane Addams ought to be hanged from the nearest lamppost." The room became very silent. I stood there, shocked, trying to gather myself together. Then very loudly, I started to talk.

"No," I said. "Jane Addams should not be hanged from anything. She is the most noble person I have ever known. It's too bad that you are not more like Jane Addams." (D)

At this point, my father stepped between Mr. Flannigan and me. Father said, "Stop this right now." He put his arm around me and led me to a corner of the room. Then, as he looked at me with a very sober expression, his face suddenly broke into a great grin. He bent his head so that the people who were watching us couldn't see that he was smiling.

I smiled and father said, "Stop that. Look serious." Then he made his face serious again and led me back to the others. He announced to the group, "I would like to apologize for the loud voice that my daughter sometimes uses. We've had to live with that voice for twenty-four years, and her mother and I are used to it. But, despite Rita's voice, I want you to understand that she is a marvelous person and she says what she believes. She also *lives* what she believes." Almost all the people applauded loudly and cheered. (E)

Out of the corner of my eye, I saw Flannigan near the front door, grabbing his coat and hat. (F)

Camila Perez tells about Jane Addams:

In 1935, Jane Addams was seventy-four years old. That was the last year of her life. I went to Chicago that year because I was writing an article on Jane Addams, who was one of the most famous women in the world. The city had changed greatly from the time that Jane Addams first moved into the old Hull place. Although there were still a few horses pulling milk wagons or ice wagons, trucks were replacing them. The icemen didn't have as much business because the electric refrigerator could be found in most homes, even in homes of people who did not have a lot of money. The wooden sidewalks were gone, and the horse-drawn streetcars were gone. ★9 ERRORS★

The old laws had changed. In 1893, children who were fourteen years old could work in factories, but by 1935, children that young were not allowed to work in factories. Hull House had also changed. It was no longer a single house but a community of thirteen buildings.

In 1935, the United States was in a depression. There weren't enough jobs for the people who wanted to work. The worst part of the depression was over, and companies were hiring more people again, but many people still did not have jobs.

I flew from New York to Chicago on a passenger plane in May of 1935. My parents had come to this country from Mexico and they were very old-fashioned. They didn't trust airplanes, and they didn't

STORY READING

EXERCISE 6   Decoding and comprehension

1. Everybody, turn to page 346 in your textbook. *Wait. Call on a student.* What's the error limit for this lesson? **9 errors.**
2. *Call on individual students to read. Present the tasks specified for each circled letter.*

(A) What good news had Rita Hansen just received? *Idea:* About the law being passed.
- Where was Rita going to make a speech? *Idea:* At her parents' house.

(B) How many people were at her parents house? **Over fifty.**
- What did the people do before Rita talked about Hull House? *Idea:* Ate dinner.

(C) Have you read anything about this man before? **Yes.**
- What narrator told about him? **Maria Rossi.**
- Did Maria think very much of him? **No.**
- Why did Maria know Mr. Flannigan? *Idea:* She worked in his factory.

(D) Why did Mr. Flannigan hire young children instead of older people? *Idea:* He wouldn't have to pay them much.
- Who did he think was threatening his entire business? **Jane Addams.**
- What did he say should be done with her? *Idea:* She should be hanged from a lamp post.

(E) Rita's father is being very polite, but who is he sticking up for? **Rita.**
- What does he mean: **She also lives what she believes?** *Idea:* She works for what she believes in.
- Who are the other people sticking up for? **Rita.**
- How do you know that they're on Rita's side? *Idea:* Because they clapped and cheered.
- How do you think Flannigan is going to feel when he knows that Rita's father and the others are on Rita's side? *Idea:* Angry.

(F) What was Flannigan doing? *Ideas:* Grabbing his coat and hat; leaving the party.
- Read the rest of the story to yourselves and be ready to answer some questions.

After all students have finished reading:
- Who is telling the next part of the story? **Camila Perez.**
- In what year did Jane Addams die? **1935.**
- How old was she? **Seventy-four.**
- Why had Camila Perez gone to Chicago? *Idea:* She was writing a story about Jane Addams.
- Tell some ways the city had changed between 1889 and 1935. *Ideas:* Electrical street lights; trucks; refrigerators, sidewalks.

think that I should go on one. When I look back, I would have to agree with them. The strange-looking, slow-moving plane that carried me to Chicago in 1935 was a far cry from the planes of today. Today, the plane trip from Chicago to New York takes less than two hours. In 1935, the trip took nearly eight hours. The plane left New York City at five in the evening and didn't arrive in Chicago until the early morning hours. Back then only important people flew, and I felt very important to be able to fly.

I was very excited about this trip because I felt that Jane Addams was the most magnificent woman alive, and it was an honor for me to have the chance to talk to her. Jane Addams didn't do only one thing. She did many things. And as I sat there in the darkness of the plane, listening to the steady hum of the engines, I fell into a trance as I thought about her.

I first pictured Jane Addams as a young woman starting Hull House with Ellen Starr. I saw her inviting all the Italian, Greek, and Russian neighbors into the house for the first time. I saw her teaching English classes with Julia Lathrop and the other residents. And I saw her helping to pass a law that prevented children under the age of fourteen years of age from working in the factories of Chicago.

Then, in my mind, I saw Jane Addams getting older and a little bit plumper. By now, she was a famous woman, but she did not let fame pull her from her goal of helping neighbors. When she was forty years old, Hull House had both female and male residents. Twenty-five residents lived in Hull House. By the time Jane Addams was fifty, Hull House occupied thirteen buildings. At this time, hundreds of other settlement houses were springing up in different parts of the United States. But Hull

House still remained the best of them.

Many visitors to Chicago visited Hull House—hundreds of thousands of people. The president of the United States at that time, Theodore Roosevelt, also came there. A group of seventy boys in the Hull House band played several numbers that were so loud that some of the people in the audience had to hold their hands over their ears. But Theodore Roosevelt loved it and applauded vigorously.

Jane Addams was the first at doing so many things that I had trouble imagining how she had the time to do them. But I was shaken from my thoughts about Jane Addams as the plane started to go through some very rough air. A member of the flight crew told us to try to relax and that everything would be all right. After perhaps ten minutes of rough air, the plane began to move more smoothly, and I tried to return to my thoughts of Jane Addams. Where was I? My mind moved forward in time and I saw Jane Addams in 1914, which was twenty-five years after Hull House opened. Jane was now fifty-four years old and was still doing the same thing—trying to help people in need—but

now she was not simply dealing with one neighborhood. She was dealing with the world.

World War One had begun, and soon people that she loved so much were at war—the people in Germany and Italy, the French people, and the Russians. Jane Addams tried to stop this war. She traveled around Europe, trying to point out the terrible harm that the war was creating. But the war continued for a year, another, another, and still another. During this time, Jane Addams was deeply saddened; however, she did not quit and she did not abandon her goals.

In 1918, the war ended, and countries in Europe were in terrible condition. So Jane Addams again went to Europe, this time to help the people who were starving and diseased. Many people in Europe did not care about the starving people in the countries they had been at war with. But Jane Addams said, "All the people in the world are neighbors. Hull House taught me that. I must go on working for peace among my worldwide neighbors." And she did.

- The plane trip from New York to Chicago takes less than two hours today. How long did that trip take in 1935? **Almost eight hours.**
- Why did it take so much longer then? *Idea:* Planes were slower.
- What did Camila Perez do as she sat in the dark plane on her way to Chicago? *Idea:* Thought about Jane Addams.
  First she thought about Jane Addams as a young woman. Then she thought about some of the things that Jane Addams did when she was older.
- At one time a very famous visitor came to Hull House and the boys' band played for that person. Who was that person? *Idea:* Theodore Roosevelt.
- Hull House was a settlement house. Other settlement houses were started up in different parts of the United States. What kinds of things do you think went on in those places? *Response:* Student preference.
- In 1914, something happened that upset Jane Addams greatly. What was that? *Idea:* World War One began.
- The people that she loved so much were at war. So what did Jane Addams do? *Idea:* Traveled around Europe trying to stop the war.
- Did she succeed in stopping the war? **No.**
- In which year did the war end? **1918.**
- After the war, Jane Addams went back to Europe. Why? *Idea:* To help the people who were starving.
  She viewed all the people of the world as her neighbors and she tried to help all people in need.

Award 4 points or have the students reread to the error limit sign.

INDEPENDENT WORK

Do all the items in your skillbook and workbook for lesson 92.

ANSWER KEY FOR WORKBOOK

Review Items

1. Write which Roman god each statement describes. Choose from **Jupiter**, **Mercury**, or **Neptune**.
   a. He had wings on his sandals.

   Mercury

   b. He lived under the ocean.

   Neptune

   c. He commanded the thunder.

   Jupiter

2. Look at the row of pictures below.

a. Which picture shows a place that would hold an animal's scent well?

_A_

b. Which picture shows a place that would hold an animal's scent, but not very well?

_C_

c. Which picture shows a place that would not hold an animal's scent?

_B_

WORKCHECK AND AWARDING POINTS

1. *Read the questions and answers for the skillbook and workbook.*

2. *Award points for independent work as follows:*

0 errors	6 points
2 errors	4 points
3, 4, or 5 errors	2 points
5 or more errors	0 points

3. *Award bonus points as follows:*

Correcting missed items or getting all items right	2 points
Doing the writing assignment acceptably	2 points

ANSWER KEY FOR SKILLBOOK

PART B

1. *Idea:* Last week, Juan read a novel about a spider.

PART C

2. **a.** *Idea:* At her parents' house
   b. Mr. Flannigan
   c. A candy factory
   d. Maria Rossi
3. **a.** Jane Addams
   b. *Idea:* To stop them from arguing
   c. Rita's

4. **a.** 1935
   b. Seventy-four
   c. 46 years
   d. *Idea:* They were electric
   e. Thirteen
5. **a.** depression
   b. Better
6. *Idea:* By plane
7. **a.** Jane Addams
   b. Residents
8. **a.** World War One
   b. 1918
   c. *Ideas:* Went to Europe; tried to help people
   d. neighbors

PART D

9. **a.** rumor
   b. deceived
   c. agile
   d. resident
   e. fascinated
   f. profit
   g. boss
   h. infant

Lesson 93

WORD PRACTICE AND VOCABULARY

EXERCISE 1   Word family

1. Everybody, find lesson 93, part A in your skillbook. *Wait.* Touch column 1. *Check.*
   All those words have the sound **er** in them.
   Touch under the first word. *Pause.*
   What word? *Signal.* **Surround.**
2. Next word. *Pause.* What word? *Signal.* **Picture.**
3. *Repeat step 2 for each remaining word in column 1.*
4. *Repeat the words in column 1 until firm.*

EXERCISE 2   Word practice

1. Everybody, touch under the first word in column 2. *Pause.* What word? *Signal.* **Stubborn.**
2. Next word. *Pause.* What word? *Signal.* **Month.**
3. *Repeat step 2 for* **plumbing.**
4. *Repeat the words in column 2 until firm.*

EXERCISE 3   Vocabulary review

Task A
1. Everybody, touch column 3. *Check.*
   First you're going to read the words in column 3. Then we'll talk about what they mean.
2. Touch under the first word. *Pause.*
   What word? *Signal.* **Trance.**
3. Next word. *Pause.*
   What word? *Signal.* **Wages.**
4. *Repeat step 3 for each remaining word in column 3.*
5. *Repeat the words in column 3 until firm.*

Task B
You've learned the meanings for all these words. Word 1 is **trance.** *Call on a student.* What is a **trance?** *Idea:* A dream you have when you are still awake.

Task C
Word 2 is **wages.** *Call on a student.* What are **wages?** *Idea:* The money you earn for a job.

Task D
1. Word 3 is **distressed.** *Call on a student.* What does **distressed** mean? *Idea:* Troubled.
2. Everybody, what's another way of saying **She was troubled over her job?** *Signal.* **She was distressed over her job.**
3. Everybody, what's another way of saying **The terrible filth troubled him?** *Signal.* **The terrible filth distressed him.**

Task E
Word 4 is **plump.** *Call on a student.* What does **plump** mean? *Idea:* A little fat.

Task F
Word 5 is **invest.** *Call on a student.* What do you do when you **invest** in a deal? *Idea:* You put money into a deal and try to make a profit.

Task G
Word 6 is **vigorous.** *Call on a student.* What does **vigorous** mean? *Idea:* Strong and lively.

Task H
Word 7 is **abandon.** *Call on a student.* What does **abandon** mean? *Idea:* You stop doing something that you started.

EXERCISE 4   Vocabulary development

Task A
1. Everybody, touch column 4. *Check.*
   First you're going to read the words in column 4. Then we'll talk about what they mean.
2. Touch under the first word. *Pause.*
   What word? *Signal.* **Interview.**
3. Next word. *Pause.* What word? *Signal.* **Spectacular.**
4. *Repeat the words in column 4 until firm.*

Task B
Now let's talk about what those words mean.
Word 1 is **interview.** When a reporter conducts an **interview,** the reporter asks somebody questions.
Everybody, what is a reporter conducting when the reporter asks somebody questions? *Signal.* **An interview.**

Task C
1. Word 2 is **spectacular.** Something that is very impressive is **spectacular.**
   Everybody, what's another way of saying **Her jewels were very impressive?** *Signal.* **Her jewels were spectacular.**
2. Everybody, what's another way of saying **The fireworks were very impressive?** *Signal.* **The fireworks were spectacular.**

Lesson 93

Jane Addams

PART 8

Camila Perez continues to tell about Jane Addams:Ⓐ

I looked out the window of the plane and noticed that the night sky was clear, with stars that glittered brightly. Below was a city that looked like a little toy city, with tiny lights marking all the streets. I watched the city as we moved slowly over it, and I listened to the constant humming of the engines. Most of the passengers around me were sleeping. But I was too excited to sleep. So I returned to my thoughts of Jane Addams. Where did I leave her? Oh yes, after the war, working for her neighbors around the world.

My mind moved forward in time again, to the year 1931.Ⓑ During this year Jane received one of the greatest honors that a person can receive. She received the Nobel Peace Prize. That prize is awarded to only one or two people each year.Ⓒ The people selected to receive the Nobel Peace Prize have done more than anybody else to work for peace. Nobody ever deserved the Peace Prize more than Jane Addams. But by the time she received it, she was seventy-one years old, and her health was failing.Ⓓ ★6 ERRORS★

Jane Addams had never been a healthy person. Most people didn't know this fact about her, but before she opened Hull House, she had gone to college to become a doctor. She had to drop out of school because of her poor health.

The plane was now flying over Lake Michigan. I could see the lights of Chicago. Slowly, the city grew larger and brighter until we were flying right over it. The plane was now so low that I had the impression that I could almost reach out of the window and touch the cars and the buildings below. It was a spectacular sight. The passengers were going "Ooooo," and "Aaahh" over the glittering sight of Chicago at night.

After the plane landed I went to a hotel. I arose very early the next morning and phoned Hull House. I was told that I would be able to talk with Jane Addams that afternoon. That morning, however, I wanted to visit Hull House and see how it looked in the year 1935.

I stood outside Hull House for a long time, looking at the buildings and watching the activities. Then I went inside to interview some very interesting people who were working without pay at Hull House. Inside the kitchen I met a very charming woman who looked to be about sixty years old. Her name was Maria and

350   Lesson 93   Textbook

---

she told me about her experiences with Hull House when she was a young girl. Then she told me, "I now live in another part of the city, but I come down every morning to help out in the kitchen for a few hours." She smiled warmly and continued, "Some people say I'm crazy and that I could earn money by getting a job that pays. But I don't agree with them. With the work that I do, I am paying back only a small amount my family owes to Hull House."

I next talked with a splendid woman who was a retired vice-president of a large bank. Her name was Rita and she told me stories of Hull House in the early days. Then she added, "Now I work here with several of the clubs. I am no longer a resident, but Hull House is still a very important part of my life."

Later that afternoon, I talked with Jane Addams. Our talk was short but I don't think I'll ever forget it. Although her eyes looked very tired, I could tell that the spirit behind those eyes was as strong as it had ever been. She told me about the book that she was writing on Julia Lathrop. When I talked with Jane Addams, I didn't learn much more than I already knew, but the experience of talking to her was magnificent. She was everything I had imagined—kind, warm, determined, and very sincere.

After our brief talk, she said, "You'll have to excuse me now. I have to visit a sick neighbor." She had trouble standing up, and I could see that she was very weak. She visited the sick neighbor. Later that evening, however, she became extremely ill. She died a week later.

STORY READING

EXERCISE 5   Decoding and comprehension

1. Everybody, turn to page 350 in your textbook. *Wait. Call on a student.* What's the error limit for this lesson? **6 errors.**

2. *Call on individual students to read. Present the tasks specified for each circled letter.*

Ⓐ The last thing that Camila Perez was thinking about was what Jane Addams did in World War One. When did that war end? **1918.**

Ⓑ World War One ended in 1918. What year is Camila Perez skipping ahead to now? **1931.** That's thirteen years later. So, Jane Addams would be fairly old by 1931.

Ⓒ What did Jane Addams receive? **The Nobel Peace Prize.** That's a great honor. Only one or two people receive that prize each year.

Ⓓ How old was Jane Addams in 1931? **Seventy-one.**

● How was her health at that time? *Idea:* Not good.

● Read the rest of the story to yourselves and be ready to answer some questions. Read it very carefully because you'll meet some people you've met before.

After all students have finished reading:

● At what time of day did Camila Perez arrive in Chicago? **Nighttime.**

● How long had the trip taken? **Over eight hours.**

● Where did Camila Perez spend the night? *Idea:* In a hotel.

I can't describe the grief that I experienced when I received news of her death. For several days, I had to fight back the tears as I wrote my article. But then, I began to realize that she was still with us. She was still living in my mind and in the minds of people like Maria Rossi, Rita Hansen, and the thousands and thousands of people that she helped. I just hope that Jane Addams lives forever in this way.

- Where did she go the next morning?
  To Hull House.
- How many buildings did Hull House have at that time? **Thirteen.**
- When Camila Perez was inside Hull House, she interviewed some people. How do you interview somebody? *Idea:* You ask them questions.
- Who did Camila Perez interview first? **Maria Rossi.**
- How old was Maria now? *Idea:* About sixty.
- What did she do in Hull House? *Idea:* Worked in the kitchen.
- Why didn't she have a job that paid, instead of her job at Hull House? *Idea:* Because she felt she was repaying Hull House.
- Who was the splendid woman that Camila Perez interviewed next? **Rita Hansen.**
- She had retired from a very good job. What job? *Idea:* Vice-president of a bank.
- What did she do at Hull House now? *Idea:* Worked with different clubs.
- Was she still a resident? **No.**
- Why did Jane Addams have to leave after her brief talk with Camila Perez? *Idea:* To visit a sick neighbor.
- What happened later that day? *Idea:* Jane Addams got very sick.
- What happened a week later? *Idea:* Jane Addams died.
- Listen to the last part of the story again, because it says something that is really true about Jane Addams. *Read the last paragraph of the story.*

Award 4 points or have the students reread to the error limit sign.

ANSWER KEY FOR WORKBOOK

Review Items

1. You read about a baseball player.
   a. What was his name?

   Jackie Robinson

   b. What major league team did he

   play on? _Dodgers_

   c. Which city did that team play in?

   Brooklyn

   d. Who was the general manager of

   the team? _Branch Rickey_

Crossword Puzzle

To work the puzzle, read an item and
figure out which word the item describes.
Then write the word in the puzzle.
Complete the entire puzzle.

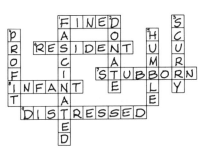

Across

1. When you are _____, you must pay
   money for breaking the law.
6. A person who lives in a place is a
   _____ of that place.
7. When you are _____, you do not
   change your behavior, no matter what
   happens.
8. A baby or a very young child
   is an _____.
9. Another word for **troubled** is _____.

Down

1. When you are interested and delighted
   by something, you are _____ by that
   thing.
2. When you give something away, you
   _____ that thing.
3. Another word for **scamper** is _____.
4. The extra money you make from a
   business is called the _____.
5. The opposite of **very proud** is _____.

WORKCHECK AND AWARDING POINTS

1. *Read the questions and answers for the skillbook
   and workbook.*
2. *Award points for independent work as follows:*

0 errors	6 points
2 errors	4 points
3, 4, or 5 errors	2 points
5 or more errors	0 points

3. *Award bonus points as follows:*

Correcting missed items or getting all items right	2 points
Doing the writing assignment acceptably	2 points

ANSWER KEY FOR SKILLBOOK

PART B

1. *Idea:* Sylvia drew a picture of some things on
   the street.

PART C

2. **a.** World War One
   b. neighbors
   c. The Nobel Peace Prize
   d. No
3. **a.** Jane Addams
   b. A sick neighbor
   c. She died
   d. 1935
4. memories

PART D

5. **a.** interested and delighted
   b. gave
   c. rumor
   d. filth
   e. stubborn

Lesson 94

Lesson 94

PART A   **Word Lists**

1	2	3
opportunity	**Vocabulary words**	**Vocabulary words**
pauper	1. spectacular	1. hardware
	2. interview	2. harbor
		3. pauper
		4. plumbing
		5. prince
		6. scurry

WORD PRACTICE AND VOCABULARY

EXERCISE 1   Word Practice

1. Everybody, find lesson 94, part A in your skillbook. *Wait.* Touch under the first word in column 1. *Pause.* What word? *Signal.* **Opportunity.**
2. Next word. *Pause.* What word? *Signal.* **Pauper.**
3. *Repeat the words in column 1 until firm.*

EXERCISE 2   Vocabulary review

Task A

1. Everybody, touch column 2. *Check.* First you're going to read the words in column 2. Then we'll talk about what they mean.
2. Touch under the first word. *Pause.* What word? *Signal.* **Spectacular.**
3. Next word. *Pause.* What word? *Signal.* **Interview.**
4. *Repeat the words in column 2 until firm.*

Task B

You've learned the meanings for all these words. Word 1 is **spectacular.** *Call on a student.* What does **spectacular** mean? *Idea:* Very impressive.

Task C

Word 2 is **interview.** *Call on a student.* What does a reporter do when conducting an **interview?** *Idea:* Asks somebody questions.

EXERCISE 3   Vocabulary development

Task A

1. Everybody, touch column 3. *Check.* First you're going to read the words in column 3. Then we'll talk about what they mean.
2. Touch under the first word. *Pause.* What word? *Signal.* **Hardware.**
3. Next word. *Pause.* What word? *Signal.* **Harbor.**
4. *Repeat step 3 for each remaining word.*
5. *Repeat the words in column 3 until firm.*

Task B

Now let's talk about what those words mean. Word 1 is **hardware.** Screws, bolts, nails, and other things that are used to build things are sold in a **hardware** store. Name some other things that are sold in a hardware store. *Call on individual students. Ideas:* Hammers; saws; locks; sandpaper.

Task C

Word 2 is **harbor.** *Call on a student.* What is a **harbor?** *Idea:* A place where ships tie up.

Task D

Word 3 is **pauper.** People who have no money are **paupers.**
Everybody, what do we call people who have no money? *Signal.* **Paupers.**

Task E

Word 4 is **plumbing.** The **plumbing** inside a building is all the pipes and fixtures that are used for the water that comes into the building. Everybody, what do we call all the fixtures and pipes that are used for water? *Signal.* **Plumbing.**

Task F

Word 5 is **prince.** *Call on a student.* What's a **prince?** *Idea:* The son of a king or a queen.

Task G

Word 6 is **scurry.** Another word for **scamper** is **scurry.**
Everybody, what's another way of saying **The rabbits scampered around the garden?** *Signal.* **The rabbits scurried around the garden.**

Lesson 94

England in the 1500's
by Steve Osborn

PART 1

In lesson 98, you will begin reading a novel titled *The Prince and the Pauper*. The novel takes place in England in the 1500's.Ⓐ It describes how a very poor young boy—the pauper—happens to meet the richest boy in all of England—the prince. The two of them have many exciting adventures.

The map shows England in the 1500's. England was just one part of a large island that contained two other countries—Wales and Scotland. Another country called Ireland was on an island to the west of England. Before the 1500's, England had conquered the countries of Wales and Ireland. Scotland, however, was still a separate country, and it had many wars with England during the 1500's.Ⓑ

London was already a large city in the 1500's. About a quarter of a million people were crammed into its narrow streets and wooden houses. The houses had no plumbing, no gas, and no electricity. They did, however, have fireplaces. People used the fireplaces to stay warm and to cook their food.Ⓒ

London had a busy harbor. Every day, dozens of sailing ships came into the

city on the Thames River. These ships brought goods from many parts of the world and carried other goods away. There was only one bridge across the Thames. It was called London Bridge. The city was so crowded that some people built houses right on the bridge. (The picture on page 387 of this book shows London Bridge.)Ⓓ

Lesson 94 Textbook **353**

The streets of London were filled with beggars and peddlers. There were very few stores, so people had to buy whatever they needed from peddlers. Many sold water, while others sold milk, bread, pots, clothes, coal, or mousetraps. Some streets were paved with stones, but most were made of dirt. Garbage was piled in the streets, and mice scurried from one pile to another.Ⓔ ★5 ERRORS★

Dirt roads connected London to other towns in England. Most travelers walked along these roads, but some rode horses, and a few used wagons. The roads were in terrible condition. They were often muddy, and they had deep ruts. If a wagon got stuck in a rut, a traveler might have to spend several hours digging it out. Travelers also had to worry about robbers who

hid along the roads and attacked people. To protect themselves, most travelers carried swords or guns.

The biggest wagons on the roads were called stage-wagons. These wagons were pulled by six to ten horses and carried goods from one town to another. The wagons moved so slowly that the driver walked along next to the horses and guided them through the ruts and the mud. On a good day, a wagon might go about three miles an hour.

Messengers went much faster. They rode fast horses along the road and shouted at everybody else to get out of the way. It took a messenger about a week to go from London to Scotland. Today, that trip takes about six hours by car and less than an hour by plane.

354 Lesson 94 Textbook

EXERCISE 4 Decoding and comprehension

1. Everybody, turn to page 353 in your textbook. *Wait. Call on a student.* What's the error limit for this lesson? **5 errors.**
2. *Call on individual students to read. Present the tasks specified for each circled letter.*

Ⓐ What's the title of the next novel you will read? **The Prince and the Pauper.**

● What's a prince? *Idea:* The son of a king or queen.

● What's a pauper? *Idea:* A poor person.

● You have read two other stories that take place in England. Which stories were those? *Idea:* Dick Whittington and A Horse to Remember.

Ⓑ Everybody, look at the map.

● Name the three parts of the island on the east side of the map. *Idea:* England, Wales, Scotland.

● That whole island is sometimes called Britain.

● What is the name of the island on the west side of the map? **Ireland.**

● Which parts did England control in the 1500's? **Wales and Ireland.**

● Which part was still a separate country? **Scotland.**

Ⓒ Why do you think the houses didn't have any electricity? *Idea:* People hadn't discovered electricity yet.

● Name some electrical machines that the houses wouldn't have. *Ideas:* Refrigerators, televisions, clocks, radios, heaters, toasters, and so on.

● How are water and gas carried into modern homes? *Idea:* Through pipes.
These houses had no pipes.

● How did the people stay warm in the 1500's? *Idea:* By using fireplaces.

Ⓓ Look at the picture on page 387. *Wait.* Now turn back to page 353.

● What kind of ships came into London on the Thames River? **Sailing ships.**

● Do you think those ships had any motors? *Idea:* No.
Ships didn't get motors until the 1800's.

● What was the bridge across the river called? **London Bridge.**

● What was unusual about that bridge? *Idea:* People lived on it.

Ⓔ Why do you think so many peddlers sold water? *Idea:* The houses didn't have running water.

● What other items did peddlers sell? *Ideas:* Milk, bread, pots, clothes, coal, mousetraps.

● Why do you think mousetraps were so popular? *Idea:* There were mice everywhere.

● What other story told about mice in London? *Idea:* Dick Whittington.

Lesson 94 **147**

The country around London was quite beautiful. There were gently rolling green hills as far as the eye could see. Small farms dotted the landscape, and sheep were everywhere. During the 1500's, rich English farmers sold a lot of wool, so they kept raising more and more sheep. There were so many sheep, in fact, that they began to create problems. The rich sheep farmers started buying up land for their sheep and even stealing land that didn't belong to them. As a result, many poor farmers lost their farms. These poor farmers tried to fight back, and they came up with a famous saying: "Sheep eat men." Sheep don't really eat men, but because of the sheep, many poor farmers were ruined.

Farther away from London, there were many forests. Loggers were busy in these forests, cutting down trees for houses, ships, and firewood. The demand for wood was so great that some forests were completely destroyed. Fortunately, people discovered that they could build fires with coal instead of firewood. During the 1500's, people began to dig coal mines to bring the coal out from under the earth. The mines were simple pits or long tunnels dug into hillsides.

People also dug pits to find rocks with iron in them. Workers hauled these rocks to factories that had very hot ovens called blast furnaces. When the rocks were put into the blast furnaces, the iron in them melted and fell to the bottom of the furnace. Workers gathered the hot iron, which was then used to make weapons, tools, and other hardware.

Today, England is very different than it was in the 1500's. But some things are still the same. London is still the biggest city. There are still plenty of sheep and forests. And there are still many coal mines and blast furnaces. But the houses now have gas, water, and electricity, and the roads are much better and safer.

- Read the rest of the article to yourselves and be ready to answer some questions. This article contains a lot of information, so read it carefully to make sure you understand all the information.

After all students have finished reading:

- What were most of the roads made of? **Dirt.**
- What problems did wagons have when they went on the roads? *Ideas:* They got stuck in the ruts; they got stuck in the mud; robbers attacked them.
- How many miles an hour could a wagon go on a good day? *Idea:* About three miles an hour.
- How many miles an hour does a truck go today? *Idea:* About fifty-five miles an hour.
- Why did travelers carry swords or guns? *Idea:* To protect themselves from robbers.
- Why did rich sheep farmers want more land? *Ideas:* To raise more sheep; to produce more wool.
- What is the meaning of the saying, "Sheep eat men"? *Ideas:* The sheep harmed the poor farmers; the sheep forced many poor farmers off their land.
- Why were some forests completely destroyed? *Ideas:* The demand was so great; people used a lot of wood for houses, ships, and firewood.
- People started using another material to heat their houses. What material was that? **Coal.**
- Describe how people used blast furnaces to make iron. *Idea:* They put rocks with iron into the blast furnaces, which were very hot. The iron would melt and fall to the bottom of the furnace.
- How is England today the same as it was in the 1500's? *Ideas:* London is still the biggest city. It still has sheep, forests, coal mines, and blast furnaces.
- How is England today different than it was in the 1500's? *Ideas:* The roads are much better. The houses have gas, water, and electricity.

Award 4 points or have the students reread to the error limit sign.

INDEPENDENT WORK

Do all the items in your skillbook and workbook for lesson 94.

ANSWER KEY FOR WORKBOOK

Story Items

1. Look at the map and answer the questions.

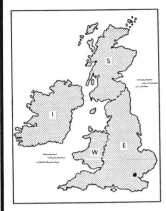

a. What is the name of area **E**?
England

b. What is the name of area **I**?
Ireland

c. What is the name of area **S**?
Scotland

d. What is the name of area **W**?
Wales

e. Which area was not controlled by England in the 1500's?
Scotland

f. Which city does the dot show?
London

g. What is the name of the river that flows through that city?
Thames River

2. The list below shows things that you find in modern houses. Write whether you would find each thing in a house in London in the 1500's. Write **yes** if you would find the thing; write **no** if you would not.

a. Fireplace _yes_

b. Electric clock _no_

c. Mousetrap _yes_

d. Cooking pots _yes_

e. Gas heater _no_

f. Shower _no_

g. Loaf of bread _yes_

h. Television set _no_

WORKCHECK AND AWARDING POINTS

1. *Read the questions and answers for the skillbook and workbook.*
2. *Award points for independent work as follows:*

0 errors . . . . .6 points
2 errors . . . . .4 points
3, 4, or 5 errors . . . . .2 points
5 or more errors . . . . .0 points

3. *Award bonus points as follows:*

Correcting missed items or getting all items right . . . . .2 points
Doing the writing assignment acceptably . . . . .2 points

ANSWER KEY FOR SKILLBOOK

PART B
1. *Idea:* Mrs. Putnam fixed her radio.

PART C
2. **a.** The Prince and the Pauper
   b. England
   c. *Idea:* The 1500's
3. **a.** *Idea:* The houses had no running water
   b. Mousetraps
4. **a.** *Ideas:* They were muddy; they had ruts
   b. *Idea:* To protect themselves from robbers
   c. Messengers
5. **a.** *Idea:* The rich farmers wanted land for their sheep
   b. Sheep eat men
6. **a.** *Idea:* Heating, houses, ships
   b. High
   c. *Idea:* They were destroyed
7. **a.** *Idea:* Heating
   b. Iron

PART D
8. **a.** agile
   b. infant
   c. residents
   d. profit
   e. abandoned
   f. donate
   g. distressed
   h. plump

Lesson 95

Lesson 95

PART A   **Word Lists**

1	2	3
opportunity	**Vocabulary words**	**Vocabulary words**
optimistic	1. scurry	1. ruler
earl	2. hardware	2. opportunity
Tudor	3. plumbing	
	4. pauper	
	5. prince	

WORD PRACTICE AND VOCABULARY

EXERCISE 1   Word Practice

1. Everybody, find lesson 95, part A in your skillbook. *Wait.* Touch under the words in column 1 as I read them.
2. The first word is **opportunity.**
3. Next word. **Optimistic.**
4. *Repeat step 3 for each remaining word in column 1.*
5. Your turn. Read the first word. *Signal.* **Opportunity.**
6. Next word. *Signal.* **Optimistic.**
7. *Repeat step 6 for each remaining word in column 1.*
8. *Repeat the words in column 1 until firm.*

EXERCISE 2   Vocabulary review

Task A

1. Everybody, touch column 2. *Check.* First you're going to read the words in column 2. Then we'll talk about what they mean.
2. Touch under the first word. *Pause.* What word? *Signal.* **Scurry.**
3. Next word. *Pause.* What word? *Signal.* **Hardware.**
4. *Repeat step 3 for each remaining word.*
5. *Repeat the words in column 2 until firm.*

Task B

You've learned the meanings for all these words. Word 1 is **scurry.** *Call on a student.* What does **scurry** mean? *Idea:* Scamper.

Task C

Word 2 is **hardware.** *Call on a student.* Name some things that are sold in a **hardware** store. *Ideas:* Screws, bolts, nails.

Task D

Word 3 is **plumbing.** *Call on a student.* What is the **plumbing** inside a building? *Idea:* All the pipes and fixtures that are used for the water coming into the building.

Task E

Word 4 is **pauper.** *Call on a student.* What is a **pauper?** *Idea:* Someone who has lost all his money.

Task F

Word 5 is **prince.** *Call on a student.* What is a **prince?** *Idea:* The son of a king or queen.

EXERCISE 3   Vocabulary development

Task A

1. Everybody, touch column 3. *Check*. First you're going to read the words in column 3. Then we'll talk about what they mean.
2. Touch under the first word. *Pause*. What word? *Signal*. **Ruler.**
3. Next word. *Pause*. What word? *Signal*. **Opportunity.**
4. *Repeat the words in column 3 until firm.*

Task B

Now let's talk about what those words mean. Word 1 is **ruler.** A **ruler** is a person who rules a country.
Everybody, what do we call a person who rules a country? *Signal*. **A ruler.**

Task C

1. Word 2 is **opportunity.** When you have a chance to do something, you have an **opportunity** to do that thing.
   Everybody, what's another way of saying **He had a chance to make a profit?** *Signal*. **He had an opportunity to make a profit.**
2. Everybody, what's another way of saying **She had a chance to go to the beach?** *Signal*. **She had an opportunity to go to the beach.**

Lesson 95

England in the 1500's

PART 2

At the beginning of the 1500's, England was ruled by a king named Henry the Seventh. The king was the richest and most powerful person in the country.Ⓐ He commanded the army and the navy and helped to make the laws. He also owned a great deal of land and earned money by collecting taxes from the people. When people talked to the king, they called him "Your Highness" or "Your Majesty."Ⓑ

The king's family was called the royal family. His sons were princes and his daughters were princesses. The firstborn son was called the Prince of Wales. As you learned in the last lesson, Wales was a country that England had conquered before the 1500's. The English king who conquered Wales decided to call his firstborn son the Prince of Wales. Ever since then, the firstborn son of the English king or queen has been called the Prince of Wales.Ⓒ

When he sat on the throne, the king wore a crown. The crown showed that he was the ruler of England. When the king died, the crown was placed on the head of the Prince of Wales, who then became the new king.Ⓓ

356   Lesson 95   Textbook

Next in power to the royal family were the lords and ladies. Some lords and ladies lived in the king's palace. Others had their own castles and controlled large areas of land. The king gave the lords and ladies different titles to show how powerful they were. The dukes and duchesses were the most powerful, followed by the earls, counts, countesses, barons, baronesses, and knights. Each one had certain powers, but they all obeyed the king.Ⓔ

Henry the Seventh ruled England from 1485 to 1509. He was the first English king to come from the Tudor family. His children and grandchildren ruled England until 1603, when the last Tudor died. The time line shows when each Tudor began to rule England.Ⓕ   ★5 ERRORS★

Henry the Seventh was a greedy king who collected many taxes and became very rich. The next Tudor king was his son, Henry the Eighth, who was one of the cruellest kings England has ever known. Henry the Eighth ruled from 1509 to 1547. He was quite handsome and intelligent, but he was also very selfish and mean. His soldiers would kill anyone who dared to criticize him, either by beheading the per-

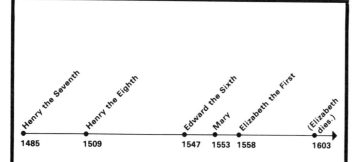

son or by burning the person alive in a huge bonfire. It was against the law to even think about harming the king.

More than anything else, Henry wanted a son. England had never been ruled by a queen, and Henry believed that only men were fit to rule the country. Henry was so eager to have a son that he married six times. His first wife gave birth to a girl named Mary, but when the wife failed to give Henry a son, he decided to divorce her. His second wife gave birth to a girl named Elizabeth. When that wife also failed to give Henry a son, he had her beheaded. His third wife finally gave birth to a boy named Edward, but she died in childbirth. Edward is the prince in the novel *The Prince and the Pauper*.

After Henry's third wife died, he mar-

ried three more times but had no more children. He divorced his fourth wife and beheaded his fifth wife. His sixth wife, however, outlived him. People became so confused about all of Henry's wives that they made up a saying to remember them by. The saying goes, "Divorced, beheaded, died; divorced, beheaded, survived." The six words in the saying tell what happened to Henry's six wives.

The next Tudor king was Edward, who became king in 1547. He was called Edward the Sixth. Edward was much kinder than his father and changed some of the harsh laws that Henry had made. But Edward soon became very ill and died in 1553 at the age of sixteen. His older sister Mary then became the queen. She was almost as cruel as her father and had many

Lesson 95   Textbook   357

EXERCISE 5   Decoding and comprehension

1. Everybody, turn to page 356 in your textbook. *Wait. Call on a student.* What's the error limit for this lesson? **5 errors.**

2. *Call on individual students to read. Present the tasks specified for each circled letter.*

Ⓐ Who was the richest man in England at the beginning of the 1500's? *Ideas:* The king; Henry the Seventh.

- Is our president the richest person in the country? **No.**
Many people are much richer than our president.

Ⓑ What military groups did the king command? **The army and the navy.**

- How did the king earn money? *Idea:* By collecting taxes.

- What did people call the king when they talked to him? *Ideas:* Your Highness; Your Majesty.

Ⓒ What is the firstborn son of the English king or queen called? **The Prince of Wales.**

Ⓓ What did the king wear on his head? **A crown.** That crown still exists today.

Ⓔ Some lords and ladies had their own castles. Where did the other lords and ladies live? *Idea:* In the king's palace.

- What do you think the difference is between a duke and a duchess? *Idea:* A duke is a man and a duchess is a woman.

- What's the difference between a count and a countess? *Idea:* A count is a man and a countess is a woman.

Ⓕ Everybody, look at the time line. The time line shows all the Tudor kings and queens.

- Who was the first Tudor king? **Henry the Seventh.**

- In what year did he begin to rule England? **1485.**

- Who was the next Tudor king? **Henry the Eighth.**

- In what year did his rule begin? **1509.**

- Who was the last Tudor queen? **Elizabeth the First.**

- During what years did she rule England? *Idea:* From 1558 to 1603.

- Read the rest of the article to yourselves. The article gives information about each Tudor king and queen. Read it carefully to make sure you understand all the information.

people burned alive. People called her "Bloody Mary." In her five years as queen, she had more than three hundred people killed.

After Mary died in 1558, her sister became Queen Elizabeth the First. Elizabeth was the last Tudor to rule England. She was one of the greatest rulers England has ever had. During her rule, life in England improved greatly. She wrote laws that protected poor people, and she helped to create many new jobs. She also encouraged English sailors to explore the world and trade with foreign countries. People had more freedom during her rule than they had ever had before. Great writers, such as William Shakespeare, were free to say whatever they wanted. During the rule of Henry the Eighth, these writers might have been killed.

Elizabeth ruled England for forty-five years. She refused to get married and have children, so when she died in 1603 there were no Tudors who could become king or queen. Another family took over the throne and a new king was crowned. Since then, England has had many kings and queens from many different families. Very few of them, however, have been as great as Elizabeth the First or as cruel as Henry the Eighth.

After all students have finished reading:

- Who was the first Tudor king? **Henry the Seventh.**
- Name two ways that Henry the Eighth's soldiers killed people. *Ideas:* By beheading them; by burning them alive.
- Why did Henry want a son more than anything else? *Idea:* He believed that England should be ruled by a man.
- The saying for Henry's wives is: Divorced, beheaded, died; divorced, beheaded, survived.
- What happened to Henry's second wife? *Idea:* She was beheaded.
- Which other wife died in the same way? *Idea:* His fifth wife.
- Who is the prince in **The Prince and the Pauper?** *Ideas:* Edward; Edward the Sixth; Henry the Eighth's son.
- Why was Mary called Bloody Mary? *Idea:* She had so many people killed.
- Name some of the good things that Elizabeth did for England. *Ideas:* She wrote laws that protected poor people; she helped to create new jobs; she encouraged sailors to explore the world and trade with foreign countries; she gave people freedom.
- Who was the Tudor ruler when William Shakespeare wrote plays and poems? *Ideas:* Elizabeth; Elizabeth the First.
- Why might Shakespeare have been killed if he wrote during Henry the Eighth's rule? *Ideas:* For saying what he believed; for criticizing the king.
- Why was Elizabeth the last Tudor? *Idea:* She had no children.
- Does England still have a king or a queen today? **Yes.**
- Who is the king or queen of England? *Accept correct answer.*

Award 4 points or have the students reread to the error limit sign.

INDEPENDENT WORK

Do all the items in your skillbook and workbook for lesson 95.

ANSWER KEY FOR WORKBOOK

Story Items

1. Here are the names of the Tudor kings and queens.
   - Edward the Sixth
   - Elizabeth the First
   - Henry the Seventh
   - Henry the Eighth
   - Mary

   The time line shows the years when each Tudor's rule began. Write the correct name next to each year.

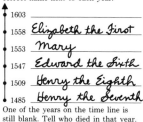

1603	
1558	*Elizabeth the First*
1553	*Mary*
1547	*Edward the Sixth*
1509	*Henry the Eighth*
1485	*Henry the Seventh*

2. One of the years on the time line is still blank. Tell who died in that year.

   Elizabeth the First

3. Write which Tudor king or queen each statement describes.
   a. This person was the first Tudor to rule England.

   Henry the Seventh

   b. This person died at the age of sixteen.

   Edward the Sixth

   c. This person wanted a son more than anything else.

   Henry the Eighth

   d. This person gave the people more freedom.

   Elizabeth the First

   e. This person had six wives.

   Henry the Eighth

   f. This person earned a nickname.

   Mary

   g. This person was the last Tudor.

   Elizabeth the First

WORKCHECK AND AWARDING POINTS

1. *Read the questions and answers for the skillbook and workbook.*
2. *Award points for independent work as follows:*

0 errors	*6 points*
2 errors	*4 points*
3, 4, or 5 errors	*2 points*
5 or more errors	*0 points*

3. *Award bonus points as follows:*

Correcting missed items or getting all items right	*2 points*
Doing the writing assignment acceptably	*2 points*

ANSWER KEY FOR SKILLBOOK

PART B

1. *Idea:* Darlene climbed Mount Whitney.

PART C

2. **a.** Seventh
   b. Henry the Seventh
   c. *Idea:* He was nis son
   d. *Idea:* Henry the Eighth
3. **a.** duchess
   b. count
   c. *Ideas:* earls, knights, barons, baronesses
4. **a.** Henry the Eighth
   b. *Idea:* They were killed
   c. 6
   d. Divorced, beheaded, died; divorced, beheaded, survived
5. **a.** Edward
   b. Elizabeth
   c. Bloody Mary
   d. *Idea:* She had many people killed
6. **a.** Elizabeth
   b. *Idea:* They had more freedom
   c. Shakespeare
   d. *Idea:* She had no children

PART D

7. **a.** rumor
   b. fascinated
   c. supervisor
   d. garbage and dirt
   e. invested
   f. wages
   g. vigorous

Lesson 96

┌─────────────────────────────────────┐
Lesson 96

PART A   **Word Lists**

1	2	3
collector	**Vocabulary words**	**Vocabulary words**
manager	1. opportunity	1. carve
investor	2. ruler	2. properly
supervisor		
inspector		
└─────────────────────────────────────┘

WORD PRACTICE AND VOCABULARY

EXERCISE 1   Word family

1. Everybody, find lesson 96, part A in your skillbook. *Wait.* Touch column 1. *Check.*
All those words are the names of types of jobs.
Touch under the first word. *Pause.*
What word? *Signal.* **Collector.**
2. Next word. *Pause.* What word? *Signal.*
Manager.
3. *Repeat step 2 for each remaining word in column 1.*
4. *Repeat the words in column 1 until firm.*

EXERCISE 2   Vocabulary development

Task A

1. Everybody, touch column 2. *Check.* First you're going to read the words in column 2. Then we'll talk about what they mean.
2. Touch under the first word. *Pause.*
What word? *Signal.* **Opportunity.**
3. Next word. *Pause.* What word? *Signal.* **Ruler.**
4. *Repeat the words in column 2 until firm.*

Task B

Word 1 is **opportunity.** *Call on a student.*
What does **opportunity** mean? *Idea:* That you have a chance to do something.

Task C

Word 2 is **ruler.** *Call on a student.* What's a **ruler?** *Idea:* Someone who rules a country.

EXERCISE 3   Vocabulary development

Task A

1. Everybody, touch column 3. *Check.* First you're going to read the words in column 3. Then we'll talk about what they mean.
2. Touch under the first word. *Pause.*
What word? *Signal.* **Carve.**
3. Next word. *Pause.* What word? *Signal.* **Properly.**
4. *Repeat the words in column 3 until firm.*

Task B

1. Now let's talk about what those words mean.
Word 1 is **carve.** When you **carve** wood, you shape it by cutting it.
Everybody, what are you doing when you shape wood by cutting it? *Signal.* **Carving.**

Task C

1. Word 2 is **properly.** When you do things the right way, you do them **properly.**
2. Everybody, what's another way of saying **She did her job the right way?** *Signal.* **She did her job properly.**
3. Everybody, what's another way of saying **He always dressed the right way?** *Signal.* **He always dressed properly.**

Lesson 96

England in the 1500's

PART 3

During the 1500's, England had two main classes of people: rich and poor. The rich people included the royal family, the lords and ladies, and some of the merchants. Most of the other people, such as the farmers, the coal miners, and the peddlers, were poor. The rich people led very easy and pleasant lives, while the poor people led lives that were full of misery and hard work. Ⓐ

Many of the rich lords and ladies had large houses in the country. These houses were made of wood, brick, or stone. They were large enough to house about fifty people, including the lord and the lady, their children, their servants, and their guests. Most of the rooms had windows, but glass was so rare and expensive that the windows were often quite small. Ⓑ Every room had a fireplace and a stone or tile floor. In the richest houses, there might be wool carpets on the floor or on the walls. Ⓒ

There was not much furniture. In those days, furniture was made of fancy carved wood. It took so long for workers to carve the wood properly that many large houses had only a few chairs, tables, and beds.

The biggest pieces of furniture were the beds for the lords and ladies, their children, and their guests. These beds had tall posts on all four corners. Curtains were strung between the posts. When people went to bed, they would pull the curtains and sleep in total darkness. It would be a comfortable sleep, because the mattress was made of feathers and the blankets were made of fine English wool. Ⓓ

Lesson 96   Textbook   **359**

The lord was the master of the house. His family and his servants had to obey him at all times, or they would be punished. His children had to call him Sir, and they had to kneel down in front of him whenever they wanted to make a request. Ⓔ The lord spent most of his time dealing with the farms and other lands that he owned. The lady, meanwhile, had the job of running the house. Because there were so few stores, many products had to be made right in the house. Some servants made clothes, while others made soap and candles. The lady had to command all these servants. She also had to make medicines and teach her children how to read. Her biggest job, however, was to supervise the kitchen servants. About a dozen servants would work in the kitchen all day long preparing food for the lord and his guests. Ⓕ ★6 ERRORS★

The food was mainly meat, which was cooked in the kitchen fireplace. Sometimes the meat would be stuck on a long rod called a spit that hung over the fire. Servant boys would spend hours slowly turning the spit so that the meat was evenly cooked. At other times, the meat would be put in a strong iron box and placed directly in the fire.

Rich people spent a lot of money on spices for their meat and sweets for dessert. They didn't eat many vegetables, however, because they thought vegetables were just for poor people. But in the 1580's, an English explorer went to America and brought back a strange new vegetable called the potato. The rich people loved this new vegetable and started growing it on their land.

Lunch was the biggest meal of the day. It would start at eleven o'clock in the morning and last for up to three hours. The lord, the lady, and their guests would sit in the huge dining room and eat course after course of beef, lamb, chicken, and pork. Their plates were made of silver, and they ate with their fingers, a knife, and a spoon. Forks were not used.

During the 1500's, the lords and ladies wore very fine clothes made of velvet, fur, and silk. The ladies' dresses often had silver threads woven into them, and the lords liked to wear belts made of gold. Hats with jewels on them were also quite popular. In the later part of the 1500's, the lords' and ladies' clothes became even more complicated. Ladies wore long dresses with fancy coats and collars. Lords wore tight vests and long stockings. They also wore strange short pants called trunks. These trunks were sometimes so padded with cloth and fur that it was difficult for the lords to sit down.

360   Lesson 96   Textbook

EXERCISE 4   Decoding and comprehension

1. Everybody, turn to page 359 in your textbook. *Wait. Call on a student.* What's the error limit for this passage? **6 errors.**

2. *Call on individual students to read. Present the tasks specified for each circled letter.*

Ⓐ What were the two main classes of people in England? **Rich and poor.**

● Name the types of people who were rich. *Ideas:* The royal family; the lords and ladies; some merchants.

● Name the types of people who were poor. *Ideas:* Farmers, coal miners, peddlers.

● Which class of people led lives that were full of misery? **The poor people.**

Ⓑ Why were the windows so small? *Idea:* Because glass was rare and expensive.

● Is glass still rare and expensive? **No.**

Ⓒ Why do you think every room had a fireplace? *Idea:* For heat.

● What material were the carpets made of? **Wool.**

● Where does that material come from? **Sheep.**

Ⓓ Why did it take so long to make each piece of furniture? *Idea:* It had to be carved from wood.

● Look at the picture.

● How is that bed different from modern beds? *Ideas:* It has posts; it has curtains; the mattress is made of feathers.

● Why does the bed have curtains? *Idea:* To make the bed dark.

Ⓔ What does that mean: **The lord was the master of the house?** *Ideas:* He was the ruler of the house; he was the chief.

● What would happen to people who didn't obey the lord? *Idea:* They would be punished.

● Pretend you are one of the lord's children. Show me how you would ask him if you could go outside and play. *Idea:* Student should kneel down and say something like, "May I go out and play, sir?"

Ⓕ Name some of the things the lady had to do to run the house. *Ideas:* Command servants who made products; make medicines; teach her children how to read; command the kitchen servants.

● Why did some products have to be made in the house? *Idea:* There were few stores.

● Name some of those products. *Ideas:* Clothes, soap, candles, medicines.

● Read the rest of the article to yourselves. The article gives information about how the rich people lived in the 1500's. Read carefully to make sure you understand all the information.

The lords and ladies entertained themselves with different sports and hobbies. They played chess, dice, and cards, and they went hunting for deer and other animals. They grew fancy gardens behind their houses, with rare fruit trees, fountains, and even mazes made from hedges. In the evening, they played musical instruments and performed complicated dances. Some of them spent the evening reading by candlelight. The printing press had just been invented, and rich people all over England had the opportunity to buy books for the first time.

Plays were the one form of entertainment that both rich people and poor people could enjoy. One of the great playwrights of all time, William Shakespeare, began writing plays during the 1500's. Groups of actors would travel around the country, putting on plays in every village they came to. The plays would be performed outside, and everyone from around the village, including the lords and ladies, would come to the performances. Of course, the lords and ladies didn't sit with the poor people. They would sit in balconies or houses overlooking the stage. When the first theaters were built in the 1500's, they always included balconies for the rich and an open area on the ground for the poor. The theaters were just like everything else in England in the 1500's: the best spots were for the rich, while everything else was for the poor.

PART E   Special Projects

1. Jane Addams solved many problems in Ward 19. She put children in school; she built a playground; she made sure the garbage was picked up; she made sure factories didn't hire children.

   Think about some of the problems that you have in your town. Get together with other students and make up a list of at least three problems. Write the list of problems on a large piece of paper. Then try to come up with a solution for each problem. When you agree on a solution, write it next to the problem. Finally, write a few sentences that explain why each solution will work. When you finish, you will have a large poster that shows several problems and solutions. Show the poster to the rest of the class and find out if they agree with your solutions.

2. "The Miraculous Pitcher," "The Golden Touch," and "Beauty and the Beast" all had morals. Write a story that has a moral. Make your story at least twenty sentences long. When you finish the story, read it to the rest of the class and ask them what they think the moral is.

   Here are some morals you might want to use:
   - It is better to give than to receive.
   - A penny saved is a penny earned.
   - Don't put all your hopes on just one thing.
   - Don't complain about what has already happened.

   You can also think up your own moral.

After all students have finished reading:

- Why didn't the rich people eat many vegetables? *Idea:* They thought vegetables were for poor people.
- What new vegetable did rich people begin eating in the 1580's? **The potato.**
- Name some of the fancy materials that were used for clothing. *Ideas:* Velvet, fur, silk.
- Name some of ornaments that were attached to the clothes. *Ideas:* Silver threads, gold belts, hat jewels.
- Why was it difficult for some of the men to sit down? *Idea:* Their trunks were so padded.
- Why did books become more popular in the 1500's? *Idea:* The printing press had just been invented. The book you are reading was made on a printing press.
- Who was one of the great playwrights of all time? **William Shakespeare.**
- Can anyone name any plays by William Shakespeare? *Ideas:* Romeo and Juliet; Hamlet; Macbeth; A Midsummer Night's Dream; Julius Caesar; and so on.
- Describe the seating arrangement in the first theaters. *Idea:* The rich people sat on balconies and the poor people sat on the ground.
- How was that seating arrangement just like everything else in England in the 1500's? *Idea:* The best spots were for the rich.

Award 4 points or have the students reread to the error limit sign.

EXERCISE 5   Special projects

1. Everybody, turn to page 152 in your skillbook. Read part E silently and decide which project you want to work on.
2. *After all students have finished reading:* Every student should work on at least one project. I'll name the projects, and you raise your hand if you want to work on that project. *List students who volunteer for each project.*
3. *Allow students extra time to complete the projects.*

ANSWER KEY FOR WORKBOOK

Story Items

1. The statements below describe people in England in the 1500's. Write whether each statement describes **rich people**, **poor people**, or **both**.
   a. They ate mainly meat.

   rich people

   b. They watched plays.

   both

   c. They followed orders in the kitchen.

   poor people

   d. Some of them lived in a lord's house.

   rich people

   e. They slept in beds with posts on all four corners.

   rich people

   f. They ate mainly vegetables.

   poor people

Review Items

2. How many wives did Henry the Eighth have?

   six

3. Look at the map and answer the questions.

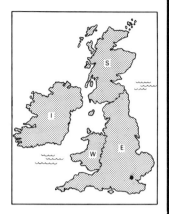

   a. What is the name of area **S**?

   Scotland

   b. What is the name of area **W**?

   Wales

   c. What is the name of area **I**?

   Ireland

   d. What is the name of area **E**?

   England

   e. Which city does the dot show?

   London

INDEPENDENT WORK

Do all the items in your skillbook and workbook for lesson 96.

WORKCHECK AND AWARDING POINTS

1. *Read the questions and answers for the skillbook and workbook.*
2. *Award points for independent work as follows:*

0 errors	6 points
2 errors	4 points
3, 4, or 5 errors	2 points
5 or more errors	0 points

3. *Award bonus points as follows:*

Correcting missed items or getting all items right	2 points
Doing the writing assignment acceptably	2 points

ANSWER KEY FOR SKILLBOOK

PART B

1. **a.** *Idea:* Rich and poor
   b. Rich
   c. Poor
2. 50
3. **a.** *Idea:* With fireplaces
   b. *Idea:* It took so long to make
   c. *Ideas:* They had posts; they had curtains; the mattresses were made of feathers
4. **a.** The lord
   b. The lady
   c. *Ideas:* Clothes; soap; candles
   d. *Idea:* There were so few stores
5. **a.** Meat
   b. The potato
6. **a.** fancy, jeweled, costly
   b. *Ideas:* Chess; dice; cards; hunting; growing gardens; playing music; performing dances; reading
   c. *Idea:* The printing press had just been invented
7. **a.** *Idea:* In the balcony
   b. Shakespeare

PART C

8. **a.** distressed
   b. spectacular
   c. stubborn
   d. investing
   e. scampered
   f. infants

Lesson 97

Lesson 97
_____

PART A   Word Lists

1
Vocabulary
1. spectacular
2. opportunity
3. properly

2
New vocabulary
1. confine
2. humble
3. optimistic

WORD PRACTICE AND VOCABULARY

EXERCISE 1   Vocabulary review

Task A

1. Everybody, find lesson 97, part A in your skillbook. _Wait._ Touch column 1. _Check._ First you're going to read the words in column 1. Then we'll talk about what they mean.
2. Touch under the first word. _Pause._ What word? _Signal._ **Spectacular.**
3. Next word. _Pause._ What word? _Signal._ **Opportunity.**
4. _Repeat step 3 for **properly**._
5. _Repeat the words in column 1 until firm._

Task B

You've learned the meanings for all these words. Word 1 is **spectacular.** _Call on a student._
What does **spectacular** mean? _Idea:_ Very impressive.

Task C

Word 2 is **opportunity.** _Call on a student._ What does **opportunity** mean? _Idea:_ That you have the chance to do something.

Task D

Word 3 is **properly.** _Call on a student._ What does **properly** mean? _Idea:_ The right way.

EXERCISE 2   Vocabulary development

Task A

1. Everybody, touch column 2. _Check._ First you're going to read the words in column 2. Then we'll talk about what they mean.
2. Touch under the first word. _Pause._ What word? _Signal._ **Confine.**
3. Next word. _Pause._ What word? _Signal._ **Humble.**
4. _Repeat step 3 for **optimistic**._
5. _Repeat the words in column 2 until firm._

Task B

1. Now let's talk about what those words mean. Word 1 is **confine.** When you are **confined** to a place, you cannot leave that place. If you can't leave an island, you are **confined** to that island.
   Everybody, what happens if you can't leave the island? _Signal._ **You are confined to the island.**
2. What happens if you can't leave your room? _Signal._ **You are confined to your room.**

Task C

1. Word 2 is **humble.** The opposite of **very proud** is **humble.**
   Everybody, what's the opposite of a very proud person? _Signal._ **A humble person.**
2. What's the opposite of a very proud house? _Signal._ **A humble house.**

Task D

Word 3 is **optimistic.** When you are **optimistic,** you look on the good side of things. Everybody, what are you being when you look on the good side of things? _Signal._ **Optimistic.**

Lesson 97

England in the 1500's

PART 4

Most of the people in England in the 1500's were poor. There were poor coal miners and poor ironworkers who earned such low wages that they were almost slaves.(A) There were also thousands of poor farmers. As you learned in lesson 94, many poor farmers lost their land to rich sheep farmers.(B) A few poor farmers were able to earn a little money by watching the sheep. Most, however, left their homes and started wandering from town to town looking for work. In the later part of the 1500's, Queen Elizabeth helped the poor farmers by telling the rich farmers to stop raising so many sheep. She asked them to raise cows and grow wheat instead.(C)

A farmhouse in the 1500's was just a one-room wooden house with a dirt floor and a roof made out of dead branches and straw. Most had a simple fireplace that was used for heating and cooking. The fireplaces were often quite smoky, and the air in the farmhouse was usually pretty bad. During the winter, the family would sit around the fireplace and try to stay warm. They would cook soup and vegetables in

pots that hung over the fire. If they were lucky, they might eat meat once a week.(D)

The farmhouse had almost no furniture. There were no beds, no tables, and no chairs. The family slept on piles of straw and ate while sitting on the ground or perhaps on stools. Some families had a simple wooden chest for their blankets and other valuable items.(E)

Poor people usually had only one set of clothes, which were made of wool or coarse cotton. A man would wear a plain shirt and a pair of pants, while a woman would wear a long dress that touched the ground. Adults wore leather shoes to protect their feet, but children often went barefoot. Poor people were forbidden to wear jewels, fancy shoes, or socks. If a lord didn't like the way a poor person was dressed, the lord could have the poor person whipped.(F) ★4 ERRORS★

Some of the farmers who lost their land became beggars, while others became robbers. The robbers would often form into groups and attack rich people on the roads and in the streets. Some robbers carried large hooks. They would stick the hooks through rich people's windows and try to pull out valuable items.

The rich people feared the robbers and carried weapons to protect themselves. When a robber was caught, he or she was taken to court and tried before a judge. If the robber was found guilty, the judge would say what kind of punishment the robber should receive. These punishments could be quite cruel. Some robbers had

their ears cut off, while others lost their hands. If the robber had killed a rich person, he might be boiled alive or burned to death.

The robbers were not the only people to receive punishment from the judges. People without homes were sometimes put into the stocks, which was a device that clamped around their hands and feet. (The picture on page 427 of this book shows the stocks.) Homeless people might also be branded with a hot iron, just like cattle. Another punishment was the ducking stool. Women who were not humble were strapped onto a stool and ducked over and over again into a river. And whenever the king or queen needed money, the judges would collect large fines from people who wore the wrong clothes or said the wrong things.

EXERCISE 3   Decoding and comprehension

1. *Everybody, turn to page 362 in your textbook. Wait. Call on a student.* What's the error limit for this passage? **4 errors.**

2. *Call on individual students to read. Present the tasks specified for each circled letter.*

(A) What does that mean: **They were almost slaves?** *Idea:* They had to work for very low wages.

(B) What material did the sheep farmers sell to get rich? **Wool.**

● Why did the rich sheep farmers need more land? *Idea:* For their sheep.

(C) What did most poor farmers do after they lost their land? *Idea:* Wandered from town to town looking for work.

● How did Queen Elizabeth help the poor farmers? *Idea:* She told the rich farmers to stop raising so many sheep.

(D) What made the air in the farmhouse bad? *Idea:* Smoke from the fireplace.

● How was the poor people's food different from the rich people's food? *Idea:* The poor people ate vegetables, but the rich people ate meat.

(E) What do you think it would be like to sleep on the ground every night? *Ideas:* Uncomfortable, cold, wet.

(F) Compare the materials used for poor people's clothes and rich people's clothes. *Idea:* The poor people's clothes were made of cotton and wool, while the rich people's clothes were made of velvet, fur, and silk.

● How would you like it if somebody told you that you couldn't wear certain things? *Accept reasonable answers.*

● How were poor people punished for wearing the wrong things? *Idea:* They were whipped.

● Read the rest of the article to yourselves. The article gives information about robbers and punishments in the 1500's. Read the article carefully to make sure you understand all the information.

The punishments were cruellest during the rule of Henry the Eighth. Poor people feared his laws and grew to hate him. When Henry died, some optimistic people hoped that his children would be kinder. Although conditions got a little bit better under his son Edward the Sixth, they soon got worse under Bloody Mary. It was not until the rule of Elizabeth the First that poor people's lives began to really improve. During her rule, the cruellest punishments were stopped and laws were passed to protect poor people. Life was still not easy for the poor, but it was not as bad as before.

• • •

When you read *The Prince and the Pauper*, it is important to know that the book is not a true story. It tells about real people, such as Henry the Eighth and Edward the Sixth, but it also tells about people that the writer made up, such as Tom Canty and Miles Hendon. It describes real events, such as the death of Henry the Eighth, but it also describes events that never happened, such as Edward's meeting with Tom. The book mixes fact and fiction to come up with a good story. But you have to remember that it's only a story: the real story was quite a bit different and much less exciting.

The original version of *The Prince and the Pauper* is very long. You will be reading a shorter version that keeps the basic story but leaves some parts out. We hope that someday you will read the entire original version.

After all students have finished reading:

- How did some robbers use hooks? *Idea:* They stuck them into rich people's houses and pulled out valuable items.
- What happened to robbers who killed rich people? *Ideas:* They were boiled alive or burned to death.
- What other punishments did robbers receive? *Ideas:* Their ears were cut off; they lost their hands.
- How did the judges help the king when he needed more money? *Idea:* They collected fines.
- What was the name of the device that clamped around the hands and feet? **The stocks.**
- Which Tudor ruler did poor people hate the most? **Henry the Eighth.**
- Which Tudor ruler improved things for poor people? *Ideas:* Elizabeth; Elizabeth the First.
- Is *The Prince and the Pauper* a true story or a fictional story? **A fictional story.**
- Name some characters in the story who are not fictional. *Ideas:* Henry the Eighth; Edward the Sixth.
- The writer mixes those true parts with parts that he made up.

Award 4 points or have the students reread to the error limit sign.

Story Items

1. The statements below describe people in England in the 1500's. Write whether each statement describes **rich people, poor people,** or **both.**

   a. They lived in houses with roofs made of straw.

   poor people

   b. They used a fireplace to stay warm.

   poor people

   c. Their clothes were made of cotton.

   poor people

   d. They wore jewels in their hats.

   rich people

   e. They could be punished for wearing socks.

   poor people

   f. They enjoyed watching plays.

   both

Review Items

2. Here are the names of the Tudor kings and queens.
   - Edward the Sixth
   - Elizabeth the First
   - Henry the Seventh
   - Henry the Eighth
   - Mary

   The time line shows the years when each Tudor's rule began. Write the correct name next to each year.

   1603 _____
   1558 _Elizabeth the First_
   1553 _Mary_
   1547 _Edward the Sixth_
   1509 _Henry the Eighth_
   1485 _Henry the Seventh_

3. One of the years on the time line is still blank. Tell who died in that year.

   Elizabeth the First

INDEPENDENT WORK

Do all the items in your skillbook and workbook for lesson 97.

WORKCHECK AND AWARDING POINTS

1. *Read the questions and answers for the skillbook and workbook.*
2. *Award points for independent work as follows:*

0 errors	*.....6 points*
2 errors	*.....4 points*
3, 4, or 5 errors	*.....2 points*
5 or more errors	*.....0 points*

3. *Award bonus points as follows:*

Correcting missed items or getting all items right	*.....2 points*
Doing the writing assignment acceptably	*.....2 points*

ANSWER KEY FOR SKILLBOOK

PART B

1. *Idea:* Andre painted his room blue.

PART C

2. **a.** *Idea:* The rich sheep farmers took it for their sheep
   b. *Idea:* Wandered around looking for work
   c. Elizabeth
3. **a.** One
   b. Dead branches and straw
   c. *Idea:* They didn't have one
   d. *Idea:* On piles of straw
4. **a.** *Ideas:* Cotton; wool
   b. *Idea:* They were forbidden to wear them
5. **a.** *Ideas:* They were killed; they were boiled alive; they were burned to death
   b. *Ideas:* They had their ears cut off; they had their hands cut off
   c. The stocks
   d. The ducking stool
6. *Idea:* She was kinder
7. **a.** fiction
   b. *Idea:* Henry the Eighth and Edward the Sixth

PART D

8. **a.** troubled
   b. wages
   c. opportunity
   d. pauper
   e. abandoned
   f. vigorous

Lesson 98

Lesson 98

PART A   Word Lists

1	2	3	4
presence	jewel	**Vocabulary review**	**New vocabulary**
gifted	ancient	1. confine	1. ignorant
abilities	beggar	2. humble	2. unleash
wisdom	jeweled		3. ability
Westminster	ate		4. gifted
	create		5. wisdom
	imitation		
	dilapidated		

WORD PRACTICE AND VOCABULARY

EXERCISE 1   Word practice

1. Everybody, find lesson 98, part A in your skillbook. *Wait.* Touch under each word in column 1 as I read it.
2. The first word is **presence.**
3. Next word. **Gifted.**
4. *Repeat step 3 for each remaining word in column 1.*
5. Your turn. Read the first word. *Signal.* **Presence.**
6. Next word. *Signal.* **Gifted.**
7. *Repeat step 6 for each remaining word in column 1.*
8. *Repeat the words in column 1 until firm.*

EXERCISE 2   Word practice

1. Column 2.
2. Your turn. Read the first word. *Signal.* **Jewel.**
3. Next word. *Signal.* **Ancient.**
4. *Repeat step 3 for each remaining word in column 2.*
5. *Repeat the words in column 2 until firm.*

EXERCISE 3   Vocabulary review

Task A
1. Everybody, touch column 3. *Check.*
   First you're going to read the words in column 3. Then we'll talk about what they mean.
2. Touch under the first word. *Pause.*
   What word? *Signal.* **Confine.**
3. Next word. *Pause.* What word? *Signal.* **Humble.**
4. *Repeat the words in column 3 until firm.*

Task B
You've learned the meanings for all these words. Word 1 is **confine.** *Call on a student.* What happens when you are **confined** to a place? *Idea:* You cannot leave that place.

Task C
Word 2 is **humble.** *Call on a student.* What does **humble** mean? *Idea:* The opposite of very proud.

EXERCISE 4   Vocabulary development

Task A
1. Column 4. New vocabulary.
   First you're going to read the words in column 4. Then you're going to read about what they mean.
2. Read the first word. *Signal.* **Ignorant.**
3. Next word. *Signal.* **Unleash.**
4. *Repeat step 3 for each remaining word in column 4.*

1. **ignorant**—If a person is **ignorant,** that person does not understand things. A person who does not understand arithmetic is **ignorant** about arithmetic.
   - A person who does not understand steeplechases is _____.
   - And a person who doesn't understand much about anything is just ignorant.

2. **unleash**—When you **unleash** something, you let it run free. If you let your feelings run free, you **unleash** your feelings.
   - If you let your imagination run free, you _____.

3. **ability**—If you have the **ability** to do something, you are able to do that thing. If you are able to write, you have the **ability** to write.
   - If you can run as fast as a dog, you _____.

4. **gifted**—Somebody who has a lot of ability is **gifted.** She had a lot of running ability, so she was a **gifted** runner.
   - He had a lot of speaking ability, so he _____.

5. **wisdom**—Great knowledge is **wisdom.**
   - If a person has great knowledge, that person has _____.

Lesson 98

CHAPTER 1

The Birth of the Prince and the Pauper

In London, during the year 1537, two boys were born on the same day. One boy was born to a poor family named Canty. This family did not want their boy. The other boy was born to a rich family named Tudor. This family did want their boy. In fact, everybody in England wanted him so much that they were nearly crazy with joy when he was born.Ⓐ People took holidays to celebrate the birth of the Tudor boy, and people hugged people they scarcely knew. People feasted and danced and sang—for days and days. And they talked and talked about the Tudor baby. For, you see, the Tudor baby was a prince—Edward Tudor, Prince of Wales, who lay wrapped in silk, with lords and ladies watching over him.Ⓑ

But there was no talk about the other baby, Tom Canty, who was wrapped in rags.Ⓒ The only people who discussed this baby were those in his family. But they weren't happy about the baby, because they were paupers, and the presence of the baby meant more work and less food for them.Ⓓ

When Tom Canty grew old enough he became a beggar.Ⓔ Tom Canty lived in a small dilapidated house on Pudding Lane.

The house was packed full of terribly poor families. Tom's family occupied a room on the third floor of this house. His mother and father slept in a bed that was in a corner of the room. But Tom, his grandmother and his two sisters, Bet and Nan, did not have beds.Ⓕ They slept on the floor in any place they chose. They covered themselves with the old remains of blankets or some bundles of ancient, dirty straw.Ⓖ

Tom was nine years old when the year 1547 began. His twin sisters, Bet and Nan, were fifteen.Ⓗ Bet and Nan were good girls, but very ignorant.Ⓘ Tom's father, John Canty, was a thief, Tom's mother was a beggar, and all the children were beggars, too. Tom grew up with a lot of yelling and fighting. He was hungry much of the time, but he was not unhappy. Although Tom never went to school, he learned how to read and write from a priest named Father Andrew. In the summer, Tom spent most of his time listening to people tell charming old stories about enchanted castles and kings and queens. At night, when he lay in the dark on his straw, tired and hungry, he would unleash his imagination and soon forget his hunger.

Task B

1. Everybody, look at part B.
   You're going to read this part out loud.

2. *For each item, call on a student to:*
   - *read one item aloud*
   - *read the meaning*
   - *read the question(s) for that item*
   - *answer each question orally*

   Answer Key:
   1. **ignorant about steeplechases**
   2. **unleash your imagination**
   3. **have the ability to run as fast as a dog**
   4. **was a gifted speaker**
   5. **wisdom**

STORY READING

EXERCISE 5   Decoding and comprehension

1. Everybody, turn to page 366 in your textbook. *Wait. Call on a student.* What's the error limit for this chapter? **9 errors.**

2. *Call on individual students to read. Present the tasks specified for each circled letter.*

Ⓐ Name the family that had a boy who wasn't wanted. **Canty.**
- Name the family that had a boy that they wanted a lot. **Tudor.**
  These boys were born on the same day.

Ⓑ What did people do to celebrate the birth of the Tudor baby? *Ideas:* Took holidays; hugged each other; had big dinners; danced; sang.
- Why were they so happy about his birth? *Idea:* Because he was a prince, son of a king.
- The chapter says that **lords and ladies watched over him.** What does that mean? *Idea:* Made sure he was properly taken care of.

Ⓒ What was the full name of the other boy born on the same day? **Tom Canty.**
- What was he wrapped in? **Rags.**
- That tells you something about how rich his family was. How rich were they? *Idea:* Not rich at all.

Ⓓ Why weren't they happy over the birth of Tom Canty? *Ideas:* He was just another mouth to feed; he meant more work for them.
- Why would the baby mean more work for them? *Response:* Student preference.
- Why would the baby mean less food for them? *Idea:* Because he would need food.

Ⓔ What does a beggar do? *Idea:* Ask people for money and food.

Ⓕ Name the people in Tom's family. *Idea:* His father, mother, grandmother, sisters Bet and Nan, and Tom.
- Where did Tom's parents sleep? *Idea:* In a bed.
- Name the people who did not sleep in beds. *Idea:* Tom, his grandmother, Bet, and Nan.

His mind would create pictures of himself as a real prince. As Tom became more fascinated with princes, he developed a strong desire to see a real prince. Tom mentioned his desire to some of his comrades, but they laughed at him and teased him so much that he decided not to share his dream with them. Ⓙ

Later Tom found some old books about princes and he read them again and again until he began to act like a prince. He amused his friends with his imitations of a prince. As the days passed, a strange thing happened. The young people who knew Tom began to show him more and more respect. They treated him as if he were a special person. Most of them couldn't read, but Tom could read and seemed to know a great deal. And he could say marvelous things, just like a real prince. Ⓚ When stories of Tom's abilities reached the parents of his comrades, they began to discuss him and to regard him as a most gifted person. Adults brought their problems to Tom and were often astonished at his wisdom in solving those problems. In fact, Tom became a hero to all who knew him, except the members of his family. They saw nothing special about him. Ⓛ

★9 ERRORS★

After a while, Tom started to play prince with some of his comrades. Tom was the prince, of course. His best friends were earls, guards, horsemen, lords or ladies. As a prince, Tom would imitate the things that a real king or prince would do. He would make laws, and send messages to his army. When the game was finished each day, Tom would go out into the streets, wearing his rags, and beg for a few pennies. He would go home at night, eat some stale bread, stretch out on his dirty straw and continue his dream of being a prince.

One January day in 1547, as he was begging, Tom tramped up and down a neighborhood that had many food shops. He was barefoot and cold. A slow rain was falling through a thick fog. The smells of the pork pies and other dishes reached Tom, and he imagined how good they would taste. He had to use his imagination, because he had never tasted any of the things that he saw in the shop windows.

When Tom came home that night, he had a lot of difficulty escaping into his dream world. The cold, the wet, and the hunger seized him so firmly that he just lay awake for a long time, listening to the arguing, singing, and yelling, and to the sound of horses on the street below. But at last his thoughts drifted away to a far away land, and he fell asleep in the company of jeweled kings and queens who lived in great palaces.

When Tom awoke in the morning and looked around, his life seemed so cruel that he got up and tried to think of his magnificent dream to keep from crying. But the dream seemed very distant from his life on Pudding Lane. On this day he wandered here and there in the city, hardly noticing where he was going or what was happening around him. People pushed him, and some talked sharply to him. But Tom ignored his surroundings.

As Tom walked aimlessly through the city, he suddenly noticed that he was approaching a beautiful road. As he moved down the road, he walked past a small palace and then continued toward a far larger one, called Westminster. Tom stared in wonder at the huge palace and the marvelous gates, with stone lions on each side. "This is the king's palace," he said to himself. "Wouldn't it be something if I saw the king or a prince?"

On both sides of the gate stood a guard dressed in armor. A small crowd of people had gathered outside the gate. From time to time, people in splendid carriages with splendid servants would be admitted through the gates.

Poor little Tom, in his rags, approached the gate, slowly and timidly. As he neared the gate, he caught sight of something that almost made him shout for joy. On the other side of the gate was a boy, dressed in lovely silk clothing. At his side was a jeweled sword. Several splendid gentlemen stood near. They were his servants. Tom said to himself, "He is a prince, a prince, a real, living prince."

Tom's eyes grew big with wonder and delight. And as he stood there, staring at the prince, he had one desire—to have a closer look at this marvelous boy. Before Tom realized what he was doing, he pressed his face against the bars of the gate. In the next instant, one of the guards grabbed him and sent him spinning among the people who were crowded near the gate.

The guard said, "Mind your manners, you young beggar."

The crowd laughed, but suddenly the young prince ran to the gate.

His eyes were flashing with anger. The prince said something to the guard that changed Tom's life.

Ⓖ Everybody, look at the picture on the next page of the room they lived in, with rags and straw and all the people crowded into it. *Check.*

Ⓗ In what year was Tom nine years old? **1547.**

● Why were Bet and Nan the same age? *Idea:* They were twins.

Ⓘ What does that mean: **Very ignorant?** *Idea:* They didn't know very much.

Ⓙ How long did Tom go to school? *Idea:* He never did.

● But what did he learn? *Idea:* How to read and write.

● Who taught him? *Ideas:* A priest; Father Andrew.

● What kind of stories did Tom like to listen to? *Idea:* Stories about castles, kings, and queens.

● What was his favorite daydream? *Idea:* Becoming a real prince.

● Do you think it made his life easier to escape into his dreams? **Yes.**

● Who else did you read about who had daydreams about nice things? *Idea:* Maria Rossi.

● What did Tom have a strong desire to do? *Idea:* See a real prince.

● Who are comrades? *Idea:* Friends.

● How did his comrades respond when he told them of his dream to see a real prince? *Idea:* They laughed at him.

Ⓚ How did the young people begin to treat Tom? *Idea:* With great respect.

● Name some ways that Tom was different from the other people he knew. *Ideas:* He could read; he knew a lot about royalty; he could write.

Ⓛ Who didn't treat Tom as if he were a special person? **Members of his family.**

● How did other adults show that they treated Tom as a special person? *Idea:* They brought their problems to him.

● Read the rest of the chapter to yourselves and be ready to answer some questions. Make sure that you really understand what is happening.

After all students have finished reading:

● One night in January, Tom had trouble going to sleep? How did he feel? *Ideas:* Cold; wet; hungry.

● What had he seen earlier that day that made his life seem very unpleasant? *Idea:* A lot of shops with good food in them.

● At last he came to a large palace. What was the name of that palace? **Westminster.**

● Who lived there? *Idea:* The king and his family.

- Who did Tom see on the other side of the gate? **A prince.**
- Describe what the prince was wearing. *Ideas:* Silk clothes; a jeweled sword.
- Why did Tom press forward against the bars of the gate? *Idea:* To get a closer look at the prince.
- What happened when he did that? *Idea:* A guard grabbed him and threw him back into the crowd.
- How did the people in the crowd react? *Idea:* They laughed.
- How did the prince react? *Idea:* He ran up to the guard.

  The prince said something that changed Tom's life. In the next chapter, we'll find out what the prince said.

Award 4 points or have the students reread to the error limit sign.

INDEPENDENT WORK

Do all the items in your skillbook and workbook for lesson 98.

WORKCHECK AND AWARDING POINTS

1. *Read the questions and answers for the skillbook and workbook.*
2. *Award points for independent work as follows:*

0 errors	6 points
2 errors	4 points
3, 4, or 5 errors	2 points
5 or more errors	0 points

3. *Award bonus points as follows:*

Correcting missed items or getting all items right	2 points
Doing the writing assignment acceptably	2 points

ANSWER KEY FOR WORKBOOK

Story Items

1. Write which character each statement describes. Choose from **Tom Canty** or **Edward Tudor.**
   a. His family did not want him.
   Tom Canty
   b. He was dressed in silk clothes.
   Edward Tudor
   c. He lived in Westminster Palace.
   Edward Tudor
   d. He pretended to be a prince.
   Tom Canty
   e. His family was very happy when he was born. *Edward Tudor*

   f. He lived on Pudding Lane.
   Tom Canty
   g. He had to beg for money.
   Tom Canty

Review Items

2. Write the correct date next to each event on the time line.

   1931 Jane Addams wins the Nobel Prize
   1914 World War One begins
   1893 A new factory law passes
   1889 Hull House opens

ANSWER KEY FOR SKILLBOOK

PART C

1. **a.** 1537
   b. 1547
   c. four hundred
   d. London
   e. England
2. **a.** Edward Tudor
   b. *Idea:* Because he was a prince
   c. Tom Canty
   d. *Idea:* Because they were so poor
3. **a.** *Idea:* Not any
   b. *Idea:* By begging
   c. Pudding Lane
   d. One
   e. *Idea:* On the floor
   f. *Ideas:* Old blankets; straw
   g. Nan and Bet
   h. hungry
   i. *Ideas:* He could read and write; he knew about royalty
   j. A real prince

4. **a.** *Idea:* Princes
   b. A prince
   c. respect
   d. *Idea:* Because they thought he was wise
   e. *Idea:* His family
5. **a.** 10
   b. 15
   c. *Idea:* By begging
   d. *Idea:* Nothing
   e. *Idea:* Never
6. **a.** No
   b. Westminster Palace
   c. Henry the Eighth
   d. *Ideas:* The prince; Edward
   e. A sword
   f. *Idea:* To get a better look
   g. A guard
   h. *Ideas:* The prince; Edward

PART D

7. **a.** interested and delighted
   b. scampered
   c. a little fat
   d. abandon
   f. confined
   g. humble

Lesson 99

Lesson 99

PART A   **Word Lists**

1	2	3	4	5
salute	gifted	entertain	**Vocabulary review**	**New vocabulary**
hustle	feasted	entertainment	1. ability	1. rude
dignity	dilapidated	wrestle	2. wisdom	2. salute
alley	enchanted	bruise	3. unleash	3. priest
	drifted	shove	4. ignorant	4. trade
	suspected	wrestling	5. gifted	5. tattered
				6. hustle

PART B   **New Vocabulary**

1. **rude**—The opposite of **polite** is **rude**. The opposite of a **polite** party is a **rude** party.
   a. What's the opposite of a **polite** student?
   b. What's the opposite of a **polite** experience?

2. **salute**—When you **salute**, you make a gesture that shows respect.
   • Show how soliders **salute** officers.

3. **priest**—A **priest** is an important man who works in a church. When you talk to a **priest**, you call him, "Father."

4. **trade**—What do you do when you **trade** with another person?

5. **tattered**—Something that is torn and shredded is called **tattered**. A torn and shredded coat is a **tattered** coat.
   • A torn and shredded shirt is _____.

6. **hustle**—When you move very fast, you **hustle**.
   • What are you doing when you move very fast?

WORD PRACTICE AND VOCABULARY

EXERCISE 1   Word practice

1. Everybody, find lesson 99, part A in your skillbook. *Wait.* Touch under each word in column 1 as I read it.
2. The first word is **salute.**
3. Next word. **Hustle.**
4. *Repeat step 3 for each remaining word in column 1.*
5. Your turn. Read the first word. *Signal.* **Salute.**
6. Next word. *Signal.* **Hustle.**
7. *Repeat step 6 for each remaining word in column 1.*
8. *Repeat the words in column 1 until firm.*

EXERCISE 2   Word family

1. Column 2. All those words end in the sound **ed.**
2. Your turn. Read the first word. *Signal.* **Gifted.**
3. Next word. *Signal.* **Feasted.**
4. *Repeat step 3 for each remaining word in column 2.*
5. *Repeat the words in column 2 until firm.*

EXERCISE 3   Word practice

1. Column 3.
2. Your turn. Read the first word. *Signal.* **Entertain.**
3. Next word. *Signal.* **Entertainment.**
4. *Repeat step 3 for each remaining word in column 3.*
5. *Repeat the words in column 3 until firm.*

EXERCISE 4   Vocabulary review

Task A
1. Everybody, touch column 4. *Check.*
   First you're going to read the words in column 4. Then we'll talk about what they mean.

2. Touch under the first word. *Pause.*
   What word? *Signal.* **Ability.**
3. Next word. *Pause.* What word? *Signal.* **Wisdom.**
4. *Repeat step 3 for each remaining word in column 4.*
5. *Repeat the words in column 4 until firm.*

Task B
You've learned the meanings for all these words. Word 1 is **ability.** *Call on a student.* What does **ability** mean? *Idea:* You are able to do things.

Task C
Word 2 is **wisdom.** *Call on a student.* What is **wisdom**? *Idea:* Great knowledge.

Task D
Word 3 is **unleash.** *Call on a student.* What do you do when you **unleash** something. *Idea:* You let it run free.

Task E
Word 4 is **ignorant.** *Call on a student.* What's an **ignorant** person? *Idea:* A person who does not understand things.

Task F
Word 5 is **gifted.** *Call on a student.* What's a **gifted** person? *Idea:* Somebody who has a lot of ability.

EXERCISE 5   Vocabulary development

Task A
1. Column 5. New vocabulary.
   First you're going to read the words in column 5. Then you're going to read about what they mean.
2. Read the first word. *Signal.* **Rude.**
3. Next word. *Signal.* **Salute.**
4. *Repeat step 3 for each remaining word in column 5.*
5. *Repeat the words in column 5 until firm.*

Task B
1. Everybody, look at part B.
   You're going to read this part out loud.
2. *For each item, call on a student to:*
   • *read one item aloud*
   • *read the meaning*
   • *read the question(s) for that item*
   • *answer each question orally*

    Answer Key: **1. a. A rude student**
                  b. A rude experience
               2. *Student should salute.*
               3. *No answer required.*
               4. *Idea:* Make a bargain.
               5. a tattered shirt
               6. Hustling

EXERCISE 6 Main idea and supporting details

1. Everybody, turn to page 101 in your workbook. You're going to read that passage out loud.

2. *Call on individual students to read. Present the tasks specified for each circled letter.*

Ⓐ Name three things Miguel did as he cleaned the house. *Ideas:* Swept all the floors, cleaned the bathroom sink; mopped the kitchen floor.

Ⓑ Tell me the main idea.
   On Saturday, Miguel cleaned up the house.

● What number is in front of the main idea? **One.**

● Tell me the first supporting detail.
   He swept the floors.

● What letter is in front of the first supporting detail? **A.**

● What letter is in front of the second supporting detail? **B.**

● What letter is in front of the third supporting detail? **C.**
   The details **a, b,** and **c** are indented. That means that the letters a, b, and c are not directly under the number 1. The letters are moved over to the right, so that you can see that they come under the main idea.

Ⓒ Everybody, copy the main idea and the supporting details now. Raise your hand if you need help.

STORY READING

EXERCISE 7 Decoding and comprehension

1. Everybody, turn to page 369 in your textbook. *Wait. Call on a student.* What's the error limit for this chapter? **7 errors.**

2. *Call on individual students to read. Present the tasks specified for each circled letter.*

Lesson 99

CHAPTER 2

Tom's Meeting with the Prince Ⓐ

The prince ran to the gate. In an instant, the people in the crowd took off their hats. In a single voice, they shouted, "Long live the Prince of Wales!"

The prince cried out to the guard, "How dare you treat anyone in this kingdom so rudely! Open the gates and let that pauper in!"

The guard quickly saluted as Tom Canty, the Prince of Poverty, passed in, with the rags of his costume fluttering behind him. Ⓑ

The Prince of Wales, Edward Tudor, said to the pauper, "You look tired and hungry. You have been treated poorly. Come with me."

Half a dozen lords who were in the courtyard sprang forward to object to the Prince allowing a beggar inside the gates, but the prince waved his hand in a gesture that told them to hold their tongues. Ⓒ The lords stopped in their tracks and stood silently, like half a dozen statues.

Edward led Tom inside the palace, past rows of guards, lords and ladies. The boys went to a small apartment that was very splendid. Edward then commanded servants to bring food for Tom. Within a few minutes, they returned with food that

Tom had only read about. Edward waved his hand for the servants to leave. He did this now so that Tom would not be embarrassed by their presence. As Tom ate, Edward sat near him and asked questions.

"What is your name, lad?"

Tom replied, with his mouth full.

"Where do you live?"

Tom explained that he lived on Pudding Lane with his parents, his grandmother, and his twin sisters, Nan and Bet.

"Is your life hard?" Edward inquired.

Tom replied, "During the winters things are bad, but during the summer my life is pretty good."

Edward asked about the room that Tom lived in and asked about how Tom spent his days.

As Edward listened a fierce look came into his eyes, and he cried out, "This is terrible!" Then he added, "Are your servants good to you and your sisters?"

Tom answered meekly, "We do not have servants."

"What?" demanded Edward. "How do your sisters dress in the morning, without the help of servants?"

"They don't need to get dressed," Tom said. "Because they have only one outfit."

Edward looked shocked.

"That is not a problem," Tom explained. "They each have only one body, so they don't need more than one outfit."

Edward laughed, then said, "Pardon me for laughing. But I shall see to it that your sisters have many changes of clothes." Ⓓ

Tom started to object, but Edward raised his hand. "Do not thank me. It is nothing." Then Edward frowned and continued. "You speak very well. Have you had a great deal of schooling?"

Tom explained that he learned to read from a priest named Father Andrew, and that he had learned about the world from the books he had read. Ⓔ ★7 ERRORS★

"Tell me, what do you do for entertainment?" Edward asked.

Tom explained the races, the games, the swimming and the other things that he did for fun. "We have the most fun in the river," Tom observed. "We play tag and dunk each other."

Edward leaned back and looked up at the ceiling. "Oh," he said slowly, "I wish I could have such pleasant experiences."

Tom continued. He told about the neighborhood dances, about being buried in the sand, about making mud pies, and about wading and wrestling in the mud.

"Don't tell me any more," Edward said, at last. "I cannot do any of those things. All my experiences must be here,

inside the walls of this palace. I can enjoy no mud pies, neighborhood dances or games in the river. I just wish that for once, I could dress as you dress and delight in the mud with nobody to scold me and tell me that a prince does not behave that way."

"I have a different dream," Tom said. "If I could dress as you are dressed, just once, and . . ."

"Would you like that?" Edward interrupted. "Then you shall have it. We'll trade outfits. Take off your rags and put on the clothes I am wearing. I'll put on the rags, and for a few minutes, we'll trade places."

A few minutes later the little Prince of Wales was wearing Tom's fluttering rags and the Prince of Poverty was wearing the splendid clothes of a real prince. The two boys stood side by side in front of a great mirror. At first they smiled, but then their expression changed to wonder. The boys could not tell that a change had taken place. Edward looked exactly like Tom and Tom looked exactly like Edward.

Edward looked at Tom with a puzzled expression and said, "What do you make of this?"

"I'm afraid to say anything," Tom replied.

"Then I will say it," Edward said. "Everything about us is the same—the same voice, the same face, the same hair. If we were both without our clothes on, nobody in the world could tell us apart."

Tom stood in amazement as Edward continued. "Now that I look like you, I should be able to experience some of the

---

Ⓐ What happened at the end of the last chapter? *Ideas:* The prince ran toward Tom and the guard.

● How old was Tom when he visited Westminster? **Ten years old.**

● In what year did that happen? **1547.**

Ⓑ Listen to that sentence again.
Read from the guard quickly . . . to Ⓑ.

● Was Tom a real prince? **No.**
So the author is making a joke by calling Tom the Prince of Poverty. He was dressed as differently from a real prince as he could possibly dress.

Ⓒ What did the lords want to object about? *Idea:* Allowing a beggar inside the gates.

● What did the prince do when they began to object? *Idea:* Waved his hand and told them to be quiet.

● Everybody, show me how he did that. *Check.* With one little motion, the prince has a lot of power.

● What does that mean: **In a gesture that told them to hold their tongues?** *Idea:* It told them to be quiet.

● The chapter says that there were half a dozen lords. How many is that? **Six.**

Ⓓ Do you think the prince had ever talked to anybody like Tom before? **No.**
So he asked a lot of questions.

● Where were they when the prince asked these questions? *Idea:* In the prince's apartment.

● What was Tom doing while the prince asked questions? *Idea:* Eating.

● Why had the prince told the servants to leave? *Idea:* So that Tom wouldn't be embarrassed.

● Everybody, show me how the prince motioned the servants to leave. *Check.*

● What are some things the prince asked Tom? *Call on individual students. Ideas:* His name; where he lived; how he was treated.

● During which season was Tom's life the worst? **Winter.**

● What did Tom say when the prince asked about Tom's servants? *Idea:* He had none.

● Why did Tom think that his sisters only needed one outfit? *Idea:* Because they each had only one body.
They slept in the same outfit they wore during the day. That outfit must have been pretty dirty.

● You read about the prince's father. What was his name? **Henry the Eighth.**

● Does Edward seem to be much like his father? **No.**
Edward seems like a very nice person.

the gate and deal with this matter."

Tom tried to object, but Edward said, "I command you to stay here." Edward picked up a strange, heavy object the size of a small shoe. Tom had no idea what this object was, but it was something that would become very important to Tom and Edward. Edward quickly hid the object, and Tom observed where he put it. A moment later, Edward was out the door and running across the palace grounds in his tattered rags. As soon as he reached the great gate, he pointed a finger at the guards on the other side and shouted, "Open these gates!"

One of the guards opened it. As Edward walked through the gate he began to scold the guard saying, "How dare you treat poor beggars . . ."

The guard gave Edward a rude shove that sent him whirling to the street. "Take that, you beggar. I ought to give you more for getting me in trouble with the prince."

The crowd roared with laughter. Edward picked himself up and shouted to the guard, "I am the Prince of Wales! You shall hang for laying your hand on me!"

The guard saluted Edward and said in a mocking voice, "I salute Your Gracious Highness." Then his voice became harsh, "Now get out of here, you filthy beggar."

Some people in the crowd grabbed Edward and hustled him down the street, laughing and shouting, "Make way for His Royal Highness! Here comes the Prince of Wales!"

things that you experience." Suddenly Edward stopped. He pointed to Tom's hand. "That bruise on your hand is the only thing that makes you look different from me. Where did you get it?"

"When the soldier at the gate pushed me back into the crowd . . ."

Edward stamped his bare foot. "That was a shameful and cruel thing," he cried. "You stay here until I return. I shall go to

E Had Tom learned to read in school? **No.**
- Who taught him? *Ideas:* A priest; Father Andrews.
- Where did Tom learn about the world? *Idea:* From books he had read.
- Read the rest of the chapter to yourselves and be ready to answer some questions. Read it over twice because it contains a lot of information. Part of what you will read describes something Edward does that will later be very important to Tom and Edward. Read that part very carefully.

After all students have finished reading:
- Tom told Edward about some things that Tom did. These things made Edward feel envious. What things did Tom describe? *Call on individual students. Ideas:* Races; games; swimming; dances; making mud pies; mud games.
- Why did Edward envy Tom? *Idea:* Because he couldn't do those things.
- Tom said that he dreamed of things that were quite different. What did Tom dream about? *Idea:* Being a prince.
- What did the boys do after Tom explained his dream? *Idea:* Exchanged clothes.
- What was unusual about the boys after they had traded clothes? *Idea:* They looked just the same.
- Edward noted one thing that made the boys look different. What was that? *Idea:* A bruise on Tom's hand.
- How had Tom received that bruise? *Idea:* When the guard at the gate pushed him.
- What did Edward do when Tom told him about the bruise? *Idea:* Went to see the guard.
- A part of the story tells about something Edward did that would later be very important to Tom and him. Edward did this just before he ran outside to scold the guard. What did Edward do? *Idea:* Hid a strange object.
- Did Edward say something to the guard at the gate? **Yes.**
- What did the guard do? *Idea:* Shoved Edward out into the street.
- Did anybody believe Edward when he tried to tell them who he was? **No.**
- What did the people in the crowd do at the end of the chapter? *Idea:* Pushed Edward and teased him.
- They were calling him the Prince of Wales. Were they serious or just mocking? **Mocking.**

Award 4 points or have students reread to the error limit sign.

INDEPENDENT WORK

Do all the items in your skillbook and workbook for lesson 99.

ANSWER KEY FOR WORKBOOK

Main Idea and Supporting Details

Here's a passage with a main idea:

It was Saturday, and Miguel had a lot of work to do. First of all, he grabbed a broom and swept all the floors. Then he cleaned the bathroom sink. Finally, he mopped the kitchen floor.

Here's the main idea of the passage: On Saturday, Miguel cleaned up the house.

The main idea tells the main thing that Miguel did. To do this main thing, Miguel had to do some other things.

The three things you named are called supporting details of the main idea.

Here's how to write a main idea and three supporting details:

1. On Saturday, Miguel cleaned up the house.
   a. He swept the floors.
   b. He cleaned the bathroom sink.
   c. He mopped the kitchen floor. Ⓑ

Copy the main idea and the supporting details. Ⓒ

1. On Saturday, Miguel cleaned up the house.
   a. He swept the floors.
   b. He cleaned the bathroom sink.
   c. He mopped the kitchen floor.

WORKCHECK AND AWARDING POINTS

1. *Read the questions and answers for the skillbook and workbook.*
2. *Award points for independent work as follows:*

0 errors	*6 points*
2 errors	*4 points*
3, 4, or 5 errors	*2 points*
5 or more errors	*0 points*

3. *Award bonus points as follows:*

Correcting missed items or getting all items right	*2 points*
Doing the writing assignment acceptably	*2 points*

ANSWER KEY FOR SKILLBOOK

PART C

1. a. *Idea:* Let Tom in
   b. *Idea:* Poorly
   c. *Idea:* They didn't think a beggar should enter the palace gates
   d. *Idea:* By a wave of his hand
2. a. envious
   b. Servants
   c. *Idea:* They had only one body
   d. Yes
   e. *Idea:* Because Tom seemed smart
   f. *Any three:* Raced; played games; swam; danced; made mud pies; wrestled
   g. No
3. a. Tom
   b. Edward
   c. *Idea:* Exchange clothes
4. a. *Idea:* They looked alike
   b. *Idea:* A bruise on Tom's hand
   c. The guard
   d. The guard
5. a. *Idea:* Hid it
   b. Tom
6. a. *Idea:* Like a begger
   b. *Idea:* Shoved him into the street
   c. *Idea:* They laughed
7. a. Tom
   b. Tom
   c. Edward
   d. Tom
   e. Edward
   f. Edward

PART D

8. a. baby
   b. distressed
   c. opportunity
   d. optimistic
   e. pauper

Lesson 100

Lesson 100

PART A   Word Lists

1	2	3	4
dirty	remodel	**Vocabulary review**	**New vocabulary**
sorry	whisk	1. salute	1. torment
poverty	remodeling	2. rude	2. sole
crazy	whisked	3. hustle	3. saucer
misery	merciful	4. tattered	4. dignity
mercy	sauce		5. alley
	saucer		6. foul
	sword		
	stricken		

PART B   New Vocabulary

1. **torment**—The crowd teased and annoyed him so much that he could hardly stand the **torment**.
   • What does **torment** mean?

2. **sole**—A **sole** is the bottom part of your foot or of your shoes.
   • Touch the sole of your shoe.

3. **saucer**—A **saucer** is a little plate that is placed under a cup.
   • What do we call a little plate that is placed under a cup?

4. **dignity**—When somebody acts with confidence and good manners, that person acts with **dignity**.
   • The queen acted with confidence and good manners, so the queen acted with _____.

5. **alley**
   • What is an **alley**?

6. **foul**—Another word for **very bad** is **foul**.
   A very bad sight is a **foul** sight.
   • A very bad smell is a _____.

WORD PRACTICE AND VOCABULARY

EXERCISE 1   Word family

1. Everybody, find lesson 100, part A in your skillbook. *Wait.*
2. Column 1. All those words end with the letter **y.**
3. Your turn. Read the first word. *Signal.* **Dirty.**
4. Next word. *Signal.* **Sorry.**
5. *Repeat step 4 for each remaining word in column 1.*
6. *Repeat the words in column 1 until firm.*

EXERCISE 2   Word practice

1. Column 2.
2. Your turn. Read the first word. *Signal.* **Remodel.**
3. Next word. *Signal.* **Whisk.**
4. *Repeat step 3 for each remaining word in column 2.*
5. *Repeat the words in column 2 until firm.*

EXERCISE 3   Vocabulary review

Task A

1. Everybody, touch column 3. *Check.*
   First you're going to read the words in column 3. Then we'll talk about what they mean.
2. Touch under the first word. *Pause.*
   What word? *Signal.* **Salute.**
3. Next word. *Pause.* What word? *Signal.* **Rude.**
4. *Repeat step 3 for each remaining word in column 3.*
5. *Repeat the words in column 3 until firm.*

Task B

You've learned the meanings for all these words. Word 1 is **salute.** *Call on a student.* Show how soldiers **salute** officers. *Idea:* The student should salute.

Task C

1. Word 2 is **rude.** *Call on a student.* What does **rude** mean? *Idea:* The opposite of polite.
2. Everybody, what's the opposite of **a polite experience?** *Signal.* **A rude experience.**
3. What's the opposite of **a polite student?** *Signal.* **A rude student.**

Task D

Word 3 is **hustle.** *Call on a student.* What are you doing when you **hustle?** *Idea:* Moving very fast.

Task E

Word 4 is **tattered.** *Call on a student.* What does **tattered** mean? *Idea:* Torn and shredded.

EXERCISE 4   Vocabulary development

Task A

1. Column 4. New vocabulary.
   First you're going to read the words in column 4. Then you're going to read about what they mean.
2. Read the first word. *Signal.* **Torment.**
3. Next word. *Signal.* **Sole.**
4. *Repeat step 3 for each remaining word in column 4.*
5. *Repeat the words in column 4 until firm.*

Task B

1. Everybody, look at part B.
   You're going to read this part out loud.
2. *For each item, call on a student to:*
   • *read one item aloud*
   • *read the meaning*
   • *read the question(s) for that item*
   • *answer each question orally*

   Answer Key: **1.** *Idea:* Suffering.
   2. *The student should touch the sole of his or her shoe.*
   3. A saucer
   4. dignity
   5. *Idea:* A narrow or back street.
   6. a foul smell

Main Idea and Supporting Details

Mr. Griffin turned on his television set at six o'clock. A television reporter told about the news. Then another reporter told about the sports. Then another reporter told about the weather. After the program was over, Mr. Griffin turned off his television set.

Here's the main idea of this passage: At six o'clock, Mr. Griffin watched the news.

Write three supporting details of the main idea. (A)
1. At six o'clock, Mr. Griffin watched the news. *Idea:*
   a. *A reporter told about the news.*
   b. *A reporter told about sports.*
   c. *A reporter told about the weather.*

Review Items

2. Write which breed of dog each statement describes. Choose from **airedale, collie, greyhound, hound,** or **poodle.**
   a. This breed is very fast.
      greyhound
   b. This breed is quite smart.
      poodle
   c. This breed has an excellent nose.
      hound
   d. This breed is extremely brave.
      airedale
   e. This breed is good at herding.
      collie

Lesson 100

CHAPTER 3

Edward's Troubles Begin(A)

The crowd teased Edward for over an hour. People in the crowd would explain to others along the sidewalk, who were watching the teasing, "This beggar went to see the Prince of Wales, and when he came out, he thought he was the Prince."

The crowd continued to make fun as long as Edward objected that he was the Prince of Wales and that all who touched him would be punished. At last he realized that the crowd would continue to torment him as long as he continued to insist that he was the prince. So he became silent, and his tormentors quickly left.(B)

Edward now looked around and could not recognize where he was. He was somewhere in the city of London, but that was all he knew. He moved aimlessly down the streets, until he came to a place where the houses were far apart and there were not many people on the street. The soles of his bare feet were not used to walking on rough stones, and they were very sore.

As Edward approached a large church, he suddenly knew where he was. His father, the king, had taken over a church and had been remodeling it so that it would be a home for poor people. Edward said to himself, "They will serve me

here and give me shelter. After all my father has done for them, they will certainly serve me."

Soon he was among a crowd of poor boys, who were running, jumping, playing ball, and making a great deal of noise. All the boys were dressed alike. Each boy wore a black cap about the size of a saucer. Each boy's haircut looked as if a bowl had been placed over his head and all the hair that stuck out beneath the bowl had been cut off. Each boy wore a blue gown that hung below the knees, a broad red belt, bright yellow stockings and low shoes that had large metal buckles. Edward thought their costumes looked ugly.

The boys stopped playing when they saw Edward and flocked around him. With great dignity he said, "Good lads, tell your schoolmaster that the Prince of Wales wants to talk to him."

Great shouts of laughter went up from the boys. Then one of them said, "What are you, the messenger for the prince?"

Edward looked at the boy with sharp anger, and without thinking, he reached for the sword at his hip. Nothing was there. Again, a storm of laughter went up from the boys, and one of them said, "Did

---

EXERCISE 5   Main idea and supporting details

1. Everybody, turn to page 102 in your workbook. *Wait.* You're going to read the passage out loud.
2. *Call on individual students to read. Present the task specified for the circled letter.*
(A) Name three supporting details. *Ideas:* A reporter told about the news, a reporter told about sports, a reporter told about the weather.
● Write those details in the blanks. Raise your hand if you need help.

STORY READING

EXERCISE 6   Decoding and comprehension

1. Everybody, turn to page 372 in your textbook. *Wait. Call on a student.* What's the error limit for this chapter? **8 errors.**
2. *Call on individual students to read. Present the tasks specified for each circled letter.*
(A) What happened at the end of the last chapter? *Idea:* The guard shoved Edward out into the street.
(B) What would have happened if Edward kept objecting? *Idea:* The crowd would have kept tormenting him.
● Why do you think the crowd stopped tormenting him? *Idea:* Because he stopped insisting that he was the real prince.
(C) What place had Edward recognized? *Idea:* A church.
● Why did Edward think that the people in that church would help him? *Idea:* Because his father had taken over the church.

you see him reach for his sword, just like a real prince?"

This comment brought more laughter. Edward stood up tall, with his chest out, and said, "I am the prince and you would do well to treat me like a prince."

The boys enjoyed the announcement. "I am serious," Edward shouted, and waved his arm angrily.

Slowly, the boys stopped laughing. One of them said, "This game has gone far enough. Let's get this loud beggar out of here."

Edward cried out as the boys pushed and shoved him until he was in the middle of the street. "And don't come back," one of the bigger boys said, in a threatening tone.© ★8 ERRORS★

As night approached, Edward found himself wandering through a very dark and poor part of the city. His feet were so sore that he could hardly walk. And as he slowly limped along, he thought of where he would find shelter for the night. He thought back to the questions he had asked Tom and how Tom had answered. He

Lesson 100   Textbook   **373**

asked himself, "What was the name of that lane where Tom lived?" In a moment, he remembered.

A plan formed in his mind. "If I can find Tom's place, I will explain the situation to his parents. They will take me back to the palace and prove that I am not Tom but that I am the Prince of Wales."

The lights began to twinkle in the houses as people lit their lamps. Now came a heavy rain, blown by a raw wind. Edward moved slowly on through the disgusting alleys where people lived in hives of poverty and misery.

Suddenly, a large man grabbed Edward by the collar and said, "Here you are, out at night again and you haven't brought a thing home for me and your poor mother, not even a crust of bread."

Edward twisted himself loose, and began to brush himself off. He said, "So you are Tom's father. I'm so glad I found you. We must go back to the palace so that you can pick him up and I can once again take up my duties as prince."

John Canty slowly shook his finger at Edward. "Don't you play those games with me, Tom Canty, or you'll be one sorry boy."

"Oh, please," Edward pleaded. "I'm not joking. I'm tired and sore. I can't take any more. Please, just take me to the king and he will make you a rich man. Please, believe me. I am not your son. I am the Prince of Wales."

John Canty stared down at Edward with a shocked expression. Then he shook his head and muttered, "This boy has gone mad." With a rude sweep of his arm, he grabbed Edward by the collar and began to walk quickly down the dirty alley, dragging Edward behind him. As John Canty pulled the struggling Edward along, he said, "I don't care if you're crazy or not, you're coming home with me right now."

John Canty dragged Edward through places that Edward could not have imagined, past the paupers who peeked out of the shadows of the buildings and shouted, "Tom's going to get it tonight." Some boys in rags followed John and Edward to the building on Pudding Lane. As they shouted and laughed at Edward, John Canty whisked him up the stairs into the disgusting room that the Canty family occupied.

"Be glad," John Canty said as he shoved Edward into the room, "Be glad that you're not getting the whipping of your life."

Edward lay on the floor without moving for a long time. He closed his eyes and tried to tell himself that he was simply having a terrible nightmare. He told himself, "When I open my eyes, all this will be gone and I will be in my own bed in my own apartment." But when Edward opened his eyes, he saw a wood floor covered with dirty foul-smelling straw. He saw the dark forms of other people huddled on the floor. He heard the sounds of snoring and of people making merry on the street below. And he felt pain, hunger and fear. As he lay there in the dark, he began to cry. A feeling of hopelessness came over him. How would he get out of this terrible place?

374   Lesson 100   Textbook

- Describe the costumes that all the boys were wearing. *Ideas:* Black caps; blue gowns; red belts; yellow socks; shoes with metal buckles.
- Look at the picture. It shows those boys talking to Edward. *Check.*
- How did the boys react when Edward told them who he was? *Idea:* They laughed at him.
- What did the boys do after they tired of listening to Edward? *Ideas:* Pushed him out into the street.
- Read the rest of the chapter to yourselves and be ready to answer some questions. Make sure that you really understand what is happening.

After all students have finished reading:
- In what kind of neighborhood was Edward that night? *Idea:* A poor neighborhood.
- What was the weather like? *Idea:* Cold.
- Who found Edward? *Ideas:* Tom's father; John Canty.
- What did Edward want John Canty to do? *Idea:* Take him back to the palace.
- How did John Canty react to that suggestion? *Idea:* He thought his son had gone mad.
- Who did John Canty think Edward really was? *Ideas:* His son; Tom.
- Where did John Canty take Edward? *Idea:* To Pudding Lane.
- What did Edward tell himself as he lay in the room? *Ideas:* That he was having a nightmare; that he would wake up and be in his own room.

Award 4 points or have the students reread to the error limit sign.

INDEPENDENT WORK

Do all the items in your skillbook and workbook for lesson 100.

ANSWER KEY FOR WORKBOOK

Main Idea and Supporting Details

Mr. Griffin turned on his television set at six o'clock. A television reporter told about the news. Then another reporter told about the sports. Then another reporter told about the weather. After the program was over, Mr. Griffin turned off his television set.

Here's the main idea of this passage: At six o'clock, Mr. Griffin watched the news.

Write three supporting details of the main idea. Ⓐ

1. At six o'clock, Mr. Griffin watched the news. *Idea:*
   a. *A reporter told about the news.*
   b. *A reporter told about sports.*
   c. *A reporter told about the weather.*

Review Items

2. Write which breed of dog each statement describes. Choose from **airedale, collie, greyhound, hound,** or **poodle.**
   a. This breed is very fast.
   greyhound
   b. This breed is quite smart.
   poodle
   c. This breed has an excellent nose.
   hound
   d. This breed is extremely brave.
   airedale
   e. This breed is good at herding.
   collie

WORKCHECK AND AWARDING POINTS

1. *Read the questions and answers for the skillbook and workbook.*
2. *Award points for independent work as follows:*

3. *Award bonus points as follows:*

ANSWER KEY FOR SKILLBOOK

PART C

1. a. *Idea:* That he was the prince
   b. *Idea:* Stopped talking
   c. *Idea:* He had spent his life in the palace
   d. *Idea:* He wasn't used to walking barefoot
   e. A church
   f. had taken over the building
2. a. saucer
   b. The schoolmaster
   c. *Idea:* They teased him
   d. *Idea:* A sword
   e. *Idea:* The sword wasn't there
   f. *Idea:* Pushed him out into the street
3. a. *Idea:* Tom's parents
   b. *Idea:* Back to the palace
   c. *Ideas:* John Canty; Tom's father
   d. *Ideas:* His son; Tom
   e. Yes
4. a. straw
   b. nightmare

PART D

5. a. vigorous
   b. confined
   c. optimistic
   d. ignorant
   e. ability
   f. scurried
   g. gifted
   h. wisdom
   i. humble

Lesson 101

Lesson 101

PART A   Word Lists

1	2	3 Vocabulary review	4 New vocabulary
poverty	pose	1. saucer	1. regain your senses
alley	magnificent	2. foul	2. pose
crazy	magnificence	3. torment	3. merciful
misery	activity	4. sole	4. stricken
dignity	activities	5. dignity	
	posing		

PART B   New Vocabulary

1. **regain your senses**—If you lose the power to think clearly, you lose your senses.
   - If you **regain** the power to think clearly, you _____.

2. **pose**—When you **pose**, you try to look very attractive. A boy who is trying to look very attractive in front of a girl is **posing** in front of a girl.
   - A boy who is trying to look very attractive in front of a mirror is _____.

3. **merciful**—The opposite of **cruel** is **merciful**.
   a. What's the opposite of a **cruel king**?
   b. What's the opposite of a **cruel act?**

4. **stricken**—When you are struck by a powerful emotion, you are **stricken** by that emotion. If you are struck by horror, you are horror-stricken.
   - If you are struck by grief, you are _____.

WORD PRACTICE AND VOCABULARY

EXERCISE 1   Word family

1. Everybody, find lesson 101, part A in your skillbook. *Wait.*
2. Column 1. All those words end with the letter **y.**
3. Your turn. Read the first word. *Signal.* **Poverty.**
4. Next word. *Signal.* **Alley.**
5. *Repeat step 4 for each remaining word in column 1.*
6. *Repeat the words in column 1 until firm.*

EXERCISE 2   Word practice

1. Column 2.
2. Your turn. Read the first word. *Signal.* **Pose.**
3. Next word. *Signal.* **Magnificent.**
4. *Repeat step 3 for each remaining word in column 2.*
5. *Repeat the words in column 2 until firm.*

EXERCISE 3   Vocabulary review

Task A

1. Everybody, touch column 3. *Check.*
   First you're going to read the words in column 3. Then we'll talk about what they mean.
2. Touch under the first word. *Pause.*
   What word? *Signal.* **Saucer.**
3. Next word. *Pause.*
   What word? *Signal.* **Foul.**
4. *Repeat step 3 for each remaining word in column 3.*
5. *Repeat the words in column 3 until firm.*

Task B

You've learned the meanings for all these words. Word 1 is **saucer.** *Call on a student.* What is a **saucer?** *Idea:* A little plate that is placed under a cup.

Task C

Word 2 is **foul.** *Call on a student.*
What does **foul** mean? *Idea:* Very bad.

Task D

Word 3 is **torment.**
She could not stand the **torment.**
Call on a student. What does **torment** mean?
Ideas: Teasing, annoyance; harrassment.

Task E

Word 4 is **sole.** *Call on a student.*
Touch the **sole** of your shoe.
Check to be sure student does not touch heel.

Task F

Word 5 is **dignity.** *Call on a student.*
When you act with **dignity,** how do you act?
Idea: With confidence and good manners.

EXERCISE 4   Vocabulary development

Task A

1. Column 4. New vocabulary.
   First you're going to read the words in column 4. Then you're going to read about what they mean.
2. Read the first line. *Signal.*
   Regain your senses.
3. Next word. *Signal.* **Pose.**
4. *Repeat step 3 for each remaining word in column 4.*
5. *Repeat the words in column 4 until firm.*

Task B

1. Everybody, look at part B.
   You're going to read this part out loud.
2. *For each item, call on a student to:*
   - *read one item aloud*
   - *read the meaning*
   - *read the question(s) for that item*
   - *answer each question orally*

   Answer Key: **1. regain your senses**
   2. posing in front of a mirror
   3. a. A merciful king
   b. A merciful act
   4. grief stricken

Lesson 101

CHAPTER 4
Prince Tom Ⓐ

As Edward was having his terrible adventure, Tom Canty was having a very different kind of experience. Left alone in Edward's apartment, he spent some time standing in front of the great mirror admiring his fine clothes. He practiced walking like a prince as he observed himself sideways in the mirror. Next, he drew the jeweled sword and bowed in the gesture of a great knight. After he became tired of posing in front of the mirror, he admired all the ornaments and decorations in the room. He sat in the grand chairs and felt the fine drapes that hung next to the windows. Ⓑ

After half an hour had passed, Tom realized that Edward had been gone a long time. Suddenly, Tom felt uneasy and strangely alone. He stopped looking at the things in the room and began to worry. What if somebody came into the room and caught him in Edward's clothes? Edward wasn't around to explain. Tom guessed that they would hang him and ask questions later. As his fears rose, he quietly opened the door to the servant's chamber. He had almost resolved to run from the palace and find Edward.

Six finely dressed gentlemen and two young boys sprang to their feet and bowed as soon as they saw Tom. Tom quickly stepped back into the room and shut the door. He said, "They're making fun of me. Now they'll tell on me and I'll be in great trouble." Ⓒ

Tom paced up and down the floor, feeling fears that he could not name. Every tiny sound made him jump. Suddenly, the door swung open and a finely dressed boy said politely, "Lady Jane Grey is here to see you, my prince." Ⓓ

A young girl in rich clothes bounded through the door. She stopped suddenly in front of Tom and said in a distressed voice, "Oh, what's wrong with you, my lord?"

Tom could hardly catch his breath, but he managed to stammer, "Be merciful. I am only poor Tom Canty. Talk to the real prince and he will explain. I didn't intend to do anything wrong."

The boy was now on his knees. The young girl seemed horror-stricken. She cried out, "I can't believe it! My lord is bowing to me!" Ⓔ

Then Jane Grey ran from the room in fright, and Tom sank down on to the floor, murmuring, "There is no hope for me now. They will come and take me away."

"The prince has gone mad!" Jane Grey announced as she left the apartment,

and that message followed her as she ran down the halls of the palace: "The prince has gone mad!" Ⓕ

Soon, groups of gentlemen and ladies formed in every marble hall. After a while, a splendid gentleman came marching by these groups, saying solemnly, "In the name of the king, nobody is to talk about this foolish matter, unless he wants to leave the palace forever." Ⓖ ★7 ERRORS★

The whisperings ceased. Then suddenly, a buzz of voices sounded through the halls. "The prince. The prince is coming."

Poor Tom came slowly walking past the bowing groups, trying to bow in return. Soon, a group of people formed around him. The king's doctors were in the group. They led him to the king's apartment and stood around him. In front of Tom was a very large and fat man with a wide face and a stern expression. His hair was very gray, and his whiskers were gray also. His clothing was made of very rich material. One of his swollen legs lay on a pillow. Everybody bowed and became very silent. The man was King Henry the Eighth. His face grew gentle as he said to Tom, "What is this, my prince? Why are you playing jokes on me?"

Tom listened as well as he could, but when he realized that he was in front of the King of England, he felt as if he had been shot. "Oh," he cried, "now I'm really in trouble!"

The king looked stunned. His eyes settled on the confused boy who stood before him. He spoke in a tone of disappointment, "I think you are sick. Come here to your father." He held out his arms.

Tom approached the king, who held Tom's face between his hands and gazed earnestly into it, as if he was looking for evidence that his son was regaining his senses. After a while, he said, "Don't you know your father, child?"

Meekly, Tom replied, "Yes, you are my father and king."

"That's right. But why are you trembling? Nobody here would hurt you. We love you."

Tom said, "I am the lowest of the people in your kingdom, a pauper. But I am too young to die. Please tell them not to kill me."

"Die?" exclaimed the king. "Rest your troubled mind. You shall not die."

For a moment Tom trembled. Then he sprang up and turned a joyful face toward the gentlemen in the room. "You heard it," he announced. "I am not to die. The king said so."

The gentlemen smiled at Tom. Tom smiled back. Then Tom turned toward the king, saying, "May I please go now?"

"Of course," the king said. Where do you want to go?"

Tom looked down and answered timidly, "I must go back to the place where my mother and sisters wait for me. I am not used to all the magnificence of this palace. I belong in the filth of Pudding Lane. Please let me go."

The king was thoughtful for a while and his face showed his uneasiness. Then he said, "Perhaps his mind is all right in

---

STORY READING

EXERCISE 5   Decoding and comprehension

1. Everybody, turn to page 375 in your textbook. *Wait. Call on a student.* What's the error limit for this chapter? **7 errors.**

2. *Call on individual students to read. Present the tasks specified for each circled letter.*

Ⓐ Where did we leave Edward? *Idea:* At Tom's house.

● Where was Tom Canty? *Idea:* At the palace.

Ⓑ Name some of the things that Tom did in Edward's apartment. *Ideas:* Looked in the mirror; practiced walking like a prince; bowed; admired the ornaments.

Ⓒ Tom opened the door that led to somebody's chamber. Whose chamber? **The servant's chamber.**

● What happened when he opened the door? *Idea:* The servants jumped up and bowed to Tom.

● What did Tom think they were doing? *Idea:* Making fun of him.

● Do you think they were mocking him? **No.**

● Why not? *Idea:* Because they thought he was the prince.

Ⓓ Who is coming to see the prince? **Lady Jane Grey.**

● Who announced Lady Jane Grey? *Idea:* A boy dressed in fine clothes.

● Does this boy realize that he is talking to Tom Canty and not the Prince of Wales? **No.**

Ⓔ What's unusual about the prince bowing to Lady Jane? *Idea:* She should be bowing to him.

Ⓕ What did Lady Jane do after Tom bowed to her? *Idea:* Ran out of the room in fright.

● What rumor spread throughout the palace? *Idea:* The prince has gone mad.

● Why did Lady Jane think the prince was mad? *Idea:* Because he had bowed to her.

Ⓖ Who came marching down the hall? *Idea:* A splendid gentleman.

● What did this gentleman order everybody to do? *Idea:* Stop talking about the prince being mad.

● Read the rest of the chapter to yourselves and be ready to answer some questions. Make sure that you really understand what's happening.

After all students have finished reading:

● Who did Tom meet in the hall? *Ideas:* A group of people; the king's doctors.

● Where did the king's doctors lead Tom? *Idea:* To the king's apartment.

● Who talked to Tom in the king's apartment? *Idea:* The king.

● Did the king know that the boy was Tom and not the prince? **No.**

● What did the king say that made Tom very happy? *Idea:* That he wouldn't be killed.

other ways. We will find out."

The king asked Tom a question about history, and Tom answered it correctly. The king was delighted. So were the lords and doctors. "At least part of him is all right," the king said.

One of the doctors bowed and replied, "I think you're right."

"Let's have another test," the king said. He turned to Tom and asked a question in French.

"I don't know that language," Tom said.

The king fell back upon his couch. Then he raised himself back up and said to Tom, "Don't worry. You'll soon be well." As he turned to the others, his gentle manner changed and it seemed as if he had lightning in his eyes. "Listen carefully," he said sternly. "My son is mad, but he will get over it. You've done this by keeping him penned up too much. He is reading too many books and listening to too many teachers. This boy needs sports and activities that will build up his health." The king continued in a sharper tone, "If any of you speak of this madness, you will be severely punished."

After more discussion, Tom was led from the king's apartment and down the hallways, which once more buzzed, "The prince. Here comes the prince."

As Tom went sadly back to Edward's apartment, he realized that he was a prisoner. He longed for the freedom of the streets, and he realized that although his dreams of being a prince were very pleasant, the life the prince led was very dreary.

- Where did Tom say that he wanted to go? *Idea:* Home.
- To test the prince, the king asked some questions. What language didn't Tom know? **French.**
- What did the king think had caused his son's madness? *Ideas:* Too much schooling; he had been penned up too long.
- What did the king think that the prince needed? *Ideas:* Activities that would improve his health.
- Where was Tom at the end of the chapter? *Idea:* In Edward's apartment.
- What was he beginning to realize about the life of a prince? *Idea:* That it was very dreary.

Award 4 points or have the students reread to the error limit sign.

EXERCISE 6   Individual reading checkout

1. *For the individual reading checkout, each student will read 150 words. The passage to be read is the shaded area on the reproduced textbook page for lesson 101 in this presentation book.*
2. Today is a reading checkout day. While you're doing your independent work, I'll call on each student to read part of yesterday's chapter.
3. When I call on you, come up to my desk and bring your textbook with you. After you have read, I'll tell you how many points you can write in the checkout box that's at the top of your workbook lesson.
4. *If the student finishes the passage in one minute or less, award points as follows:*

> 0 errors . . . . .3 points
> 1 or 2 errors . . . . .1 point
> More than 2 errors . . . . .0 points

5. *If a student takes more than one minute to read the passage, the student does not earn any points, but have the student reread the passage until he or she is able to read it in no more than one minute with no more than two errors.*

INDEPENDENT WORK

Do all the items in your skillbook and workbook for lesson 101.

ANSWER KEY FOR WORKBOOK

Main Idea and Supporting Details

Read this passage:

The cat said, "What happens if you praise me once?"

"I never shall," said the woman, "but if I praise you once, you may sit near the mouth of the cave."

"And if you praise me twice?" said the cat.

"I never shall," said the woman, "but if I praise you twice, you may sit near the back of the cave."

"And if you praise me three times?" said the cat.

"I never shall," said the woman, "but if I praise you three times, you may drink the milk."

Then the cat arched his back and said, "I accept your bargain."

Write the main idea and three supporting details. *Idea:*

1. *The cat and the woman made a bargain.*

   a. *If the woman praised him once, the cat could sit near the mouth of the cave.*

   b. *If the woman praised him twice, the cat could sit near the back of the cave.*

   c. *If the woman praised him three times, the cat could drink the milk.*

Story Items

2. Tom did some things that made people think the prince was crazy. Below is a list of things that Tom might do. Write **normal** if people would think it is normal for the prince to do. Write **crazy** if people would think it is crazy for the prince to do.

   a. Wear silk clothes. *normal*
   b. Call Henry the Eighth, "Father." *normal*
   c. Ask to go to Pudding Lane. *crazy*
   d. Bow down to a servant. *crazy*
   e. Know how to read books. *normal*
   f. Not recognize his relatives. *crazy*

WORKCHECK AND AWARDING POINTS

1. *Read the questions and answers for the skillbook and workbook.*
2. *Award points for independent work as follows:*

0 errors	6 points
2 errors	4 points
3, 4, or 5 errors	2 points
5 or more errors	0 points

3. *Award bonus points as follows:*

Correcting missed items or getting all items right	2 points
Doing the writing assignment acceptably	2 points

4. *Remind the students to put the points they earned for their reading checkout in the box labeled* **CO.**

ANSWER KEY FOR SKILLBOOK

PART C

1. a. *Ideas:* In Edward's room; in the palace
   b. *Ideas:* The prince's; Edward's
   c. *Ideas:* The prince; Edward
   d. *Ideas:* Scared; uneasy
   e. *Idea:* He would be killed
2. a. Lady Jane Grey
   b. *Ideas:* Bowed; kneeled
   c. *Idea:* Because the prince had never bowed to her
   d. *Idea:* He had gone mad
3. a. *Idea:* King Henry the Eighth
   b. *Ideas:* Fat; large; stern; gray
   c. *Ideas:* The prince; his son
   d. *Idea:* He would be killed
   e. *Idea:* Tom wouldn't be killed
   f. *Idea:* Home
4. a. not crazy
   b. *Idea:* The one about history
   c. *Idea:* He had read so many books
   d. *Idea:* The one about French
   e. *Idea:* He didn't know any French
   f. too much studying
   g. less studying
5. a. *Idea:* Back on the streets
   b. dreary

PART D

6. a. chance
   b. ability
   c. plump
   d. vigorous
   e. abandoned
   f. spectacular
   g. rude

Lesson 102

Lesson 102

PART A   Word Lists

1	2	3
identical	Elizabeth	**New vocabulary**
Hertford	hesitate	1. page
banquet	cause	2. dismiss
advantage	hesitating	3. mad
	causing	4. identical
	hesitant	

PART B   New Vocabulary

1. **page**—A **page** is a young boy who serves a member of a royal family.
   - What do we call a young boy who serves a member of a royal family?

2. **dismiss**—When you **dismiss** somebody, you tell that person to leave. If you tell a servant to leave, you **dismiss** a servant.
   - What do you do if you tell a class to leave?

3. **mad**—**Mad** is another word for **insane**.
   a. What's another way of saying **She was insane?**
   b. What's another way of saying **The king was insane?**

4. **identical**—Things that are **identical** are the same in every way. Shoes that are the same in every way are **identical** shoes.
   - What are houses that are the same in every way?

PART C   Vocabulary Review

> foul
> stricken
> pose
> ability
> regain your senses
> abandon
> merciful

1. a. The opposite of **cruel** is _____.
   b. What's the opposite of a **cruel act?** _____
   c. What's the opposite of a **cruel king?** _____

2. a. When you are struck by a powerful emotion, you are _____ by that emotion.
   b. If you are struck by horror, you are _____.
   c. If you are struck by grief, you are _____

3. If you regain the power to think clearly, you _____.

4. a. When you try to look very attractive, you _____
   b. A boy who is trying to look very attractive in front of a girl is _____
   c. A child who is trying to look very attractive in front of a mirror is _____

WORD PRACTICE AND VOCABULARY

EXERCISE 1   Word practice

1. Everybody, find lesson 102, part A in your skillbook. *Wait.* Touch under each word in column 1 as I read it.
2. The first word is **identical.**
3. Next word. **Hertford.**
4. *Repeat step 3 for each remaining word in column 1.*
5. Your turn. Read the first word. *Signal.* **Identical.**
6. Next word. *Signal.* **Hertford.**
7. *Repeat step 6 for each remaining word in column 1.*
8. *Repeat the words in column 1 until firm.*

EXERCISE 2   Word practice

1. Column 2.
2. Your turn. Read the first word. *Signal.* **Elizabeth.**
3. Next word. *Signal.* **Hesitate.**
4. *Repeat step 3 for each remaining word in column 2.*
5. *Repeat the words in column 2 until firm.*

EXERCISE 3   Vocabulary development

Task A
1. Column 3. New vocabulary. First you're going to read the words in column 3. Then you're going to read about what they mean.
2. Read the first word. *Signal.* **Page.**
3. Next word. *Signal.* **Dismiss.**
4. *Repeat step 3 for each remaining word in column 3.*
5. *Repeat the words in column 3 until firm.*

Task B
1. Everybody, look at part B. You're going to read this part out loud.
2. *For each item, call on a student to:*
   - *read one item aloud*
   - *read the meaning*
   - *read the question(s) for that item*
   - *answer each question orally*

   Answer Key: **1. A page**
            2. Dismiss a class
            3. a. She was mad.
               b. The king was mad.
            4. Identical houses

EXERCISE 4   Vocabulary review

1. Everybody, look at part C. The words in the box are words you've learned.
2. Read the first word. *Signal.* **Foul.**
3. Next. *Signal.* **Stricken.**
4. *Repeat step 3 for the remaining words in the box.*
5. *Repeat the words in the box until firm.*
6. I'll read the items. When I come to a blank, everybody say the part that goes in the blank.
7. Look at item 1a. *Pause.* Listen. The opposite of cruel is *Pause. Signal.* **merciful.**
8. *Repeat step 7 for each remaining item.*

   Answer key: **1. b. A merciful act**
               c. A merciful king
            2. a. stricken
               b. horror-stricken
               c. grief stricken
            3. regain your senses
            4. a. pose
               b. posing in front of a girl
               c. posing in front of a mirror

Lesson 102

CHAPTER 5
Tom Receives InstructionsⒶ

Tom was to have one teacher, an earl named Hertford. All of the other teachers who usually instructed the prince were ordered to leave.Ⓑ Hertford explained to Tom, "You have lost your memory. We will take things slowly and soon you'll remember everything. We will not spend time reading books. Instead, we'll entertain ourselves in other ways. After all, we don't want you to be all worn out when you go to the banquet."

Tom gave Hertford a puzzled look. Gracefully, Hertford said, "I guess you have forgotten about the banquet tomorrow evening. But don't worry about it. I was referring to the City Banquet. The king said that you would attend. Do you remember it now?"

"No," Tom said, in a hesitating voice.Ⓒ

At that moment, a page announced, "Elizabeth and Lady Jane Grey are here to see the prince."

Hertford stepped quickly toward the door. As the girls passed him, he said in a low voice, "Do not pay attention to the odd way he behaves and do not act surprised if he doesn't remember things."

Then Hertford walked over to Tom and whispered in his ear, "Act as if you remember everything. Don't let your sister or Jane Grey know that your memory is as poor as it is."Ⓓ

Jane Grey approached Tom and asked pleasantly, "Have you seen the queen today, my prince?"

Tom didn't know what to say. Hertford said, "Indeed he has and it made him feel a lot better. Isn't that right, Your Highness?"Ⓔ

Then Jane Grey said, "It's a shame that you're not continuing with your studies, my lord. I'm sure that you'll someday be as well learned as your father."

"My father," cried Tom. "That thief doesn't know anything. He's . . ."

Hertford was slowly shaking his head no.

Tom continued, "I have a problem remembering things. My mind wanders. I certainly didn't mean to call the king a thief."

"We know that," Elizabeth said, holding her brother's hand tightly.Ⓕ
★6 ERRORS★

Then Jane Grey made a comment about the shoes that Tom was wearing. Tom forgot himself again and replied, "These are not my shoes. They belong to the prince. He told me that . . ."

Hertford was shaking his head again.

As the conversation went on, Tom grew more and more at ease, seeing that the girls were very kind and were trying to be helpful. When the girls mentioned that they were to accompany him to the city's banquet, his heart jumped with delight, for he felt that he would then be with friends at the banquet.

After the girls had left, Tom discovered that he really didn't know much about how to behave like a prince. Two lords and three servants came into his apartment. He reached for a pitcher of water. The instant his fingers touched the pitcher, a servant respectfully picked it up, dropped to one knee and poured out a glass of water for Tom.

Because Tom didn't know how to dismiss his attendants with a wave of his arm, they stayed with him in the apartment, standing stiffly and waiting for their prince to command them. But Tom didn't command them. He didn't know what to do.

Tom also didn't know that he was causing serious problems in the kingdom. After Hertford left Tom, he met with a

---

STORY READING

EXERCISE 5   Decoding and Comprehension

1. Everybody, turn to page 378 in your textbook. *Wait. Call on a student.* What's the error limit for this chapter? **6 errors.**

2. *Call on individual students to read. Present the tasks specified for each circled letter.*

Ⓐ Where did we leave Tom at the end of the last chapter? *Idea:* In Edward's apartment.

● What had the king said was wrong with Tom? *Idea:* That he was crazy.

Ⓑ Tom was to have one teacher. Who was that? **Hertford.**

Ⓒ What banquet is the prince supposed to attend? **The City Banquet.**

● What is a banquet? *Idea:* A big dinner party.

● What's the name of the city where the banquet is being held? **London.**

Ⓓ Name the two girls who are visiting Tom. **Elizabeth and Lady Jane Grey.**

● Which one is the prince's sister? **Elizabeth.**

Ⓔ Had Tom seen the queen. **No.**

Ⓕ Is it really her brother's hand that she is holding? **No.**

● Read the rest of the chapter to yourselves and be ready to answer some questions. Make sure that you really understand what's happening.

After all students have finished reading:

● When Tom was back in Edward's apartment, he discovered that he really didn't know much about behaving like a prince. What was the first thing he did that was wrong? *Idea:* He started to pour a glass of water for himself.

● Why did his attendants stand around without leaving the room? *Idea:* Because he hadn't dismissed them yet.

lord named Lord Saint John. They talked about Edward's condition. Then Lord Saint John said, "I fear that the king is so sick that he will soon die. The prince is obviously mad. If the king dies, a madman will become King of England. What a horrible thought."

Hertford replied, "Do you have any doubts that the prince is . . ." His voice trailed off.

"Speak up," Lord Saint John said. "We are alone. Tell me what you are thinking."

"All right," Hertford said. "I find it very strange that the prince seems to be perfectly healthy in many ways. Yet he seems to have forgotten French. He doesn't seem to know who his parents are. And he has forgotten how to behave like a prince. Although his voice is the same, his manners are different. And I was wondering whether he is really the . . ."

"Don't say it," Lord Saint John interrupted. "Do you want us both to be hanged? If word got out that you were even thinking such thoughts, your life would not be worth a penny."

"I beg your pardon," Hertford said.

"Perhaps I was hasty in thinking such thoughts. I shall not mention the subject again."

After his meeting with Lord Saint John, Hertford went to his chambers and paced the floor. He was once more considering Edward's behavior. "He must be the prince," Hertford said to himself. "The only other explanation is that there are twin boys who are so identical in every way that it is impossible to tell them apart. But . . ." He shook his head. "But if that were true, how could it be possible for the other boy to take the place of the prince? And where is the real prince?" Again he shook his head. "No, it's not possible," he concluded. "No person could look so much like the prince that he could fool his father and all the others who have known the prince since birth."

Hertford tried to dismiss the thought that there could be a boy who looked so much like the real prince. But the thought would not leave his head. At last, he pounded his fist into his hand and said aloud, "No. He must be the real prince. But if he is, he has gone completely mad."

- After Hertford left the prince, he talked with another man. What was that man's name? **Lord Saint John.**
- What did Hertford think was really wrong with the prince? *Idea:* That he might not be the real prince.
- What made Hertford suspect that the boy wasn't really the prince? *Ideas:* He'd forgotten French; he didn't know who his parents were; his manners were different.
- What did Lord Saint John caution Hertford not to do? *Idea:* Tell anybody what he was thinking.
- Why was Lord Saint John afraid of anybody hearing about Hertford's suspicions? *Idea:* Because they could both be hanged.
- When Hertford went back to his chambers, he concluded that Tom must be the prince. He thought that the only other possible explanation was impossible. What explanation was that? *Idea:* That there could be two identical boys.
- What did Hertford finally think was wrong with the prince? *Idea:* That he was crazy.

Award 4 points or have the students reread to the error limit sign.

ANSWER KEY FOR WORKBOOK

Main Idea and Supporting Details

Read this passage:

Rodney was in the fifth grade. On most days, Rodney would walk home after school. But on Friday, Rodney did something different. After school, he went to the library. He looked at the shelves and shelves of books. He picked out several books. Then he took his books to the desk and the librarian stamped them. Rodney put the books in his bag and left the library.

Write the main idea and three supporting details.

1. *On Friday, Rodney checked books out of the library.*
   a. *He looked at the shelves of books.*
   b. *He picked out several books.*
   c. *He took his books to the librarian.*

Review Items

2. You read about the game of baseball.
   a. How many innings does a game last if there's not a tie? __*9*__
   b. When a team is not batting, how many of its players are in the field? __*9*__
   c. Which base must a runner cross to score a run? *Idea: home plate*
   d. Which person calls the balls and strikes? __*umpire*__

3. Write **true** or **false** for each statement.
   a. Silver was discovered near Dawson in 1896. __*false*__
   b. The Yukon River flows through California. __*false*__
   c. Redwoods are very tall trees. __*true*__
   d. Los Angeles is in Canada. __*false*__
   e. San Francisco is in California. __*true*__
   f. Dawson is in Canada. __*true*__

INDEPENDENT WORK

Do all the items in your skillbook and workbook for lesson 102.

WORKCHECK AND AWARDING POINTS

1. *Read the questions and answers for the skillbook and workbook.*
2. *Award points for independent work as follows:*

0 errors	6 points
2 errors	4 points
3, 4, or 5 errors	2 points
5 or more errors	0 points

3. *Award bonus points as follows:*

Correcting missed items or getting all items right	2 points
Doing the writing assignment acceptably	2 points

ANSWER KEY FOR SKILLBOOK

PART D

1. a. Hertford
   b. The City Banquet
   c. *Idea:* Tomorrow evening
2. a. Lady Jane Grey
   b. Elizabeth
   c. *Idea:* All right
3. a. *Idea:* A servant poured Tom a glass of water
   b. *Ideas:* Tom's commands; to be dismissed
4. a. Lord Saint John
   b. *Idea:* That he would die
   c. *Idea:* Tom
   d. Nervous
   e. *Any two:* The prince could not speak French; he didn't know his father; his manners were different
5. a. the prince's twin
   b. Yes
   c. No
   d. the real prince
6. a. normal
   b. normal
   c. normal
   d. crazy
   e. normal
   f. normal

PART E

7. a. optimistic
   b. confined
   c. pauper
   d. ignorant
   e. gifted
   f. torn and shredded
   g. hustled
   h. torment

Lesson 103

Lesson 103

PART A   Word Lists

1	2
sternly	**New vocabulary**
gently	1. take advantage
gracefully	2. lumbering
pleasantly	3. stout
hesitantly	4. retreat
	5. seaman

PART B   New Vocabulary

1. **take advantage**—When a person is helpless and you make that person do what you want, you **take advantage** of that person.
   - How could a boss take advantage of a very poor person?

2. **lumbering**—When you walk with very heavy steps, you are **lumbering**.
   - What are you doing when you walk with very heavy steps?

3. **stout**—Something that is very thick and sturdy is called **stout**. A thick and sturdy stick is a **stout** stick.
   - What's a thick and sturdy person?

4. **retreat**—When you **retreat**, you move backwards.
   a. What's another way of saying **He moved backwards toward the door?**
   b. What's another way of saying **She could not move backwards any farther?**

5. **seaman**—Another word for a **sailor** is a **seaman**.
   a. What's another way of saying **The sailor was stout?**
   b. What's another way of saying **Ten sailors lumbered down the street?**

PART C   Vocabulary Review

> identical
> tattered
> ignorant
> a page
> dismiss
> mad
> optimistic

1. A young boy who serves a member of the royal family is called _____.
2. a. When you tell people to leave, you _____ them.
   b. If you tell a class to leave, you _____.
   c. If you tell a servant to leave, you _____.

3. a. Things that are the same in every way are _____ things.
   b. Shoes that are the same in every way are _____.
   c. Houses that are the same in every way are _____.
4. a. Another word for **insane** is _____.
   b. What's another way of saying **She was insane?** _____
   c. What's another way of saying **The king was insane?** _____

WORD PRACTICE AND VOCABULARY

EXERCISE 1   Word family

1. Everybody, find lesson 103, part A in your skillbook. *Wait.*
2. Column 1. All those words end with the letters **l-y.**
3. Your turn. Read the first word. *Signal.* **Sternly.**
4. Next word. *Signal.* **Gently.**
5. *Repeat step 4 for each remaining word in column 1.*
6. *Repeat the words in column 1 until firm.*

EXERCISE 2   Vocabulary development

Task A

1. Column 2. New vocabulary.
   First you're going to read the words in column 2. Then you're going to read about what they mean.
2. Read the first line. *Signal.* **Take advantage.**
3. Next word. *Signal.* **Lumbering.**
4. *Repeat step 3 for each remaining word in column 2.*
5. *Repeat the words in column 2 until firm.*

Task B

1. Everybody, look at part B.
   You're going to read this part out loud.
2. *For each item, call on a student to:*
   - *read one item aloud*
   - *read the meaning*
   - *read the question(s) for that item*
   - *answer each question orally*

   Answer Key: 1. *Idea:* A boss could make the person work very hard and pay the person very little.
   2. Lumbering
   3. A stout person
   4. a. He retreated toward the door.
      b. She could not retreat any farther.
   5. a. The seaman was stout.
      b. Ten seamen lumbered down the street.

EXERCISE 3   Vocabulary review

1. Everybody, look at part C.
   The words in the box are words you've learned.
2. Read the first word. *Signal.* **Identical.**
3. Next. *Signal.* **Tattered.**
4. *Repeat step 3 for the remaining words in the box.*
5. *Repeat the words in the box until firm.*
6. I'll read the items. When I come to a blank, everybody say the part that goes in the blank.
7. Look at item 1. *Pause.* Listen.
   A young boy who serves a member of the royal family is called *Pause. Signal.* **a page.**
8. *Repeat step 7 for each remaining item.*

   Answer key: 2. a. dismiss
      b. dismiss a class
      c. dismiss a servant
   3. a. identical
      b. identical shoes
      c. identical houses
   4. a. mad
      b. She was mad.
      c. The king was mad.

Lesson 103

Outlining

The outline below shows three main ideas for <u>The Wizard of Oz.</u>

Write three supporting details for each main idea.

• The first main idea is: <u>Dorothy visited the Land of the East.</u> Tell which people lived there. Tell what color the land was. Tell what Dorothy did there. **(A)**

• The second main idea is: <u>Dorothy visited the Emerald City.</u> Tell which person lived there. Tell what color the city was. Tell what Dorothy did there. **(B)**

• The third main idea is: <u>Dorothy visited the Land of the West.</u> Tell which people lived there. Tell what color the land was. Tell what Dorothy did there. **(C)**

1. Dorothy visited the Land of the East.

a. _____
_____

b. _____
_____

c. _____
_____

2. Dorothy visited the Emerald City.

a. _____
_____

b. _____
_____

c. _____
_____

3. Dorothy visited the Land of the West.

a. _____
_____

b. _____
_____

c. _____
_____

Lesson 103

CHAPTER 6

Pudding Lane

The morning found the true Prince of Wales in a dismal place. **(A)** The room was dark and filled with the smell of burnt candles. In the corner of the room was a woman. Two girls were sprawled out on the floor, with an older woman propped up in the corner, staring with fierce eyes. Long gray hair streamed over her shoulders.

John Canty, who was standing over Edward, said, "I will not stand for any more of your games. Last night was the last night you'll go wandering around by yourself without bringing home even a penny. If you do anything like that again . . ." John Canty raised his hand in a threatening gesture.

Edward raised his eyes and looked at John Canty with a steady gaze. Then he said, "You are very ill-mannered. And I will tell you again what I told you before. I am Edward, Prince of Wales, and nobody else." **(B)**

John Canty looked stunned for a moment, then burst into laughter. But Tom's mother and his sisters responded differently. They huddled around Edward, saying, "Oh, poor Tom, poor Tom."

Tom's mother put her hands upon Edward's shoulders and looked into his face. "Oh, my poor boy," she said. "Your foolish reading has ruined your mind." **(C)**

Edward replied gently, "Your son is well and has not lost his mind. If you will take me to the palace where he is, my father the king will quickly return him to you."

"Your father the king," Tom's mother cried. "Oh, my child. Stop these horrible games. Try to remember who you really are. Don't you know who you are? I am your mother and he is your father." She pointed to John Canty. **(D)**

Edward said slowly, "I don't want to make you sad, but I have never seen you or him before."

Tom's mother sank down, covered her face with her hands and began to cry.

"Enough of this nonsense!" shouted John Canty. "Get away from him and let's start doing something about earning a living."

Nan said, "Oh please, father. Let him rest and sleep so his memory will come back."

"Yes, father," said Bet. "He's worn down. He'll be himself again tomorrow. If he rests today, I'm sure that he'll bring

---

EXERCISE 4 Outlining

1. Everybody, turn to page 104 in your workbook. You're going to read that passage out loud.

2. *Call on individual students to read. Present the tasks specified for each circled letter.*

(A) Name three supporting details for the main idea, **Dorothy visited the Land of the East.**
Ideas: The Munchkins lived there; the land was blue; Dorothy killed the Witch of the East.

(B) Name three supporting details for the main idea, **Dorothy visited the Emerald City.**
Ideas: Oz lived there; the city was green; Dorothy had a meeting with Oz.

(C) Name three supporting details for the main idea, **Dorothy visited the Land of the West.**
Ideas: The Winkies lived there; the land was yellow; Dorothy killed the Witch of the West.

• Everybody, write the supporting details now. Raise your hand if you need help.

STORY READING

EXERCISE 5 Decoding and comprehension

1. Everybody, turn to page 381 in your textbook. *Wait. Call on a student.* What's the error limit for this chapter? **7 errors.**

2. *Call on individual students to read. Present the tasks specified for each circled letter.*

(A) Where did we last see the true Prince of Wales? *Idea:* At Tom Canty's house.
Now we're going to pick up the story the next morning.

(B) Is Edward afraid of Tom's father? **No.**

• Name the people who are in the room with Edward and Tom's father. *Ideas:* Tom's mother, grandmother, and sisters.

(C) What did Tom's mother think was wrong with her son? *Idea:* That he had been reading too much.
That is the same thing that Henry the Eighth thought was wrong with the prince.

(D) What was Tom's father's name? **John Canty.**

• Does Tom's mother seem like a **mean** person or a **kind** person? **A kind person.**

• What about his sisters? **Kind.**

• What about John Canty? **Mean.**

home some money tomorrow."

John Canty turned sternly to the girls. "Let me remind you," he said, "that our rent is due tomorrow. If we do not pay two pennies for this hole, out we go." **(E)**

★7 ERRORS★ John Canty continued, "But how much money did Tom bring in?"

Edward said, "Will you please leave me alone? I told you that I am the king's son."

John Canty grabbed Edward and pulled him to his feet. The frightened girls retreated to their corner, but Tom's mother stepped forward to help her son. Edward waved her away, saying, "You shall not suffer for me. I am not afraid of this man."

John Canty pushed Edward around and yelled loudly at him. When the girls objected, John Canty held up a warning fist to let them know that they must be silent.

As John Canty pushed Edward out the door with him, Tom's mother slipped a crust of bread to Edward. Fortunately, John Canty did not observe her action.

After John Canty and Edward had left the room, Tom's mother began to think strange thoughts. Speaking aloud, she said, "I have known that boy from the time he was born, but . . ." She was bothered by some of the things the boy did. She remembered that he had awakened during the night and cried out. Her Tom had never done that before. And he had never talked the way he was now talking. "Could it be that he is not . . ." She couldn't force herself to finish the question. She realized

382 Lesson 103 Textbook

that he did not stand or move in his usual manner. She was aware of the strange things that came from his lips. But how could she believe that he was not her son?

• • •

John Canty held Edward firmly by the wrist as they walked down the alleys. "Today," John Canty said, "I'm going to keep a good eye on you."

No sooner were the words out of John Canty's mouth than another voice said, "So there you are, John Canty. I've been looking for you."

Edward turned and saw a large man lumbering toward them. The man had a determined expression on his face. He said, "When you owe me money, you pay or I'll pound it out of you."

"Run," John Canty said, and began to dodge through the swarms of people in the alley, as he hung onto Edward's arm. They slowed down after they had gone a few blocks, but then a lumbering form could be seen behind them, over the heads of the other people. "He won't give up," John Canty said. "If we get separated, go to the far end of London Bridge and wait there. Remember that."

John Canty shook a warning fist at Edward. Then, he began to plow rudely through the crowd, still holding onto Edward. As they tried to push past a stout seaman, the seaman grabbed John Canty and said, "What's the hurry? Slow down and stop shoving people around."

When John Canty turned to answer the seaman, he let go of Edward. Edward

wasted no time in scampering off through the crowd. He ran until he was a safe distance from John Canty. Then he slowed to a walk and began to form a plan.

People were talking about the great City Banquet that would take place that evening. They mentioned that it would be a fine affair with the Prince of Wales present. Edward concluded that the pauper, Tom Canty, had taken advantage of

him and was pretending to be the real prince. Edward's plan was simple. He would go to that banquet. He would make himself known to the people and he would declare that Tom Canty was a pretender, a humbug. Then after the people realized that he was the real prince, he would deal harshly with Tom. Edward would see to it that Tom was severely punished for taking advantage of him.

Lesson 103 Textbook **383**

(E) How much rent did they have to pay for their room? **Two pennies.**

- What will happen to them if they don't come up with the two pennies? *Idea:* They will have to move out.
- Read the rest of the chapter to yourselves and be ready to answer some questions.

After all students have finished reading:

- Who pushed Edward around? **John Canty.**
- What did Tom's mother slip to Edward? *Idea:* A crust of bread.
- Did John Canty see this? **No.**
- What do you think would have happened if he had seen it? *Idea:* He would have taken the bread away.
- What did Tom's mother begin to think after John Canty and Edward left the room? *Idea:* Maybe Edward was not her real son.
- What made her question whether Edward was really her son? *Ideas:* He had cried out during the night; he talked differently; his manners were different.
- Who stopped John Canty and Edward in the alley? *Idea:* A large man.
- Who was that man angry with? **John Canty.**
- Why? *Idea:* Because John Canty owed him money.
- What did John Canty and Edward do? *Idea:* They ran.
- Where did John Canty tell Edward that he should go if the two got separated? *Idea:* To the far end of London Bridge.
- What happened that made it possible for Edward to escape from John Canty? *Idea:* A seaman grabbed John Canty.
- Edward formed a plan. Where would he go that evening? *Idea:* To the City Banquet.
- What would Edward do when he got there? *Idea:* He would show everybody that he was the real prince.
- How did Edward think that Tom had taken advantage of him. *Idea:* By pretending to be the real prince.
- What did Edward plan to do to Tom? *Idea:* Punish him severely.

Award 4 points or have the students reread to the error limit sign.

INDEPENDENT WORK

Do all the items in your skillbook and workbook for lesson 103.

ANSWER KEY FOR WORKBOOK

Outlining

The outline below shows three main ideas for The Wizard of Oz.

Write three supporting details for each main idea.

- The first main idea is: Dorothy visited the Land of the East. Tell which people lived there. Tell what color the land was. Tell what Dorothy did there. Ⓐ
- The second main idea is: Dorothy visited the Emerald City. Tell which person lived there. Tell what color the city was. Tell what Dorothy did there. Ⓑ
- The third main idea is: Dorothy visited the Land of the West. Tell which people lived there. Tell what color the land was. Tell what Dorothy did there. Ⓒ

1. Dorothy visited the Land of the East. **Idea:**

  a. *The Munchkins lived there.*

  b. *The land was blue.*

  c. *Dorothy killed the Witch of the East.*

2. Dorothy visited the Emerald City.

  a. *Oz lived there.*

  b. *The city was green.*

  c. *Dorothy had a meeting with Oz.*

3. Dorothy visited the Land of the West.

  a. *The Winkies lived there.*

  b. *The land was yellow.*

  c. *Dorothy killed the Witch of the West.*

WORKCHECK AND AWARDING POINTS

1. Read the questions and answers for the skillbook and workbook.
2. Award points for independent work as follows:

0 errors	6 points
2 errors	4 points
3, 4, or 5 errors	2 points
5 or more errors	0 points

3. Award bonus points as follows:

Correcting missed items or getting all items right	2 points
Doing the writing assignment acceptably	2 points

ANSWER KEY FOR SKILLBOOK

PART D

1. a. *Idea:* In Tom's room
   b. *Idea:* Money
   c. *Idea:* Tom's mother and sisters
   d. *Idea:* Too much reading
   e. *Idea:* Rest
   f. *Idea:* rent
2. *Idea:* Cried out
3. a. A large man
   b. *Idea:* Because John Canty owed the man money
   c. Ran
   d. *Idea:* London Bridge
   e. A seaman
   f. *Idea:* Ran off by himself
4. a. The City Banquet
   b. Yes
   c. Tell everyone he was the real prince
   d. No
5. a. both
   b. only Edward
   c. both
   d. both
   e. only Edward
   f. only Edward

PART E

6. a. confine
   b. spectacular
   c. ignorant
   d. foul
   e. rude
   f. dignity
   g. tried to look very attractive

Lesson 104

Lesson 104

PART A   Word Lists

1	2	3
Thames River	merry	**New vocabulary**
wand	merriment	1. vast
cushion	hurl	2. barge
ragged	shield	3. file
suspicious	hurled	4. wand
ruffian		

PART B   New Vocabulary

1. **vast**—Something that is **very large** is **vast.**
   a. What's a **very large** room?
   b. What's a **very large** river?

2. **barge**—A **barge** is a large, flat boat that can carry cargoes on rivers. State barges are **barges** that are owned by the state.
   a. What do we call flat boats that can carry cargoes on rivers?
   b. What do we call those boats when they are owned by the state?

3. **file**—A **file** is a line. A line of people is a **file** of people.
   ● What is a line of barges?

4. **wand**—A **wand** is a small staff that is decorated.
   ● What do we call a small staff that is decorated?

PART C   Vocabulary Review

rude
lumbering
seaman
dignity
take advantage
retreat
ignorant
stout

1. When someone is helpless and you make that person do what you want, you _____ of that person.
2. a. Another word for a **sailor** is a _____.
   b. What's another way of saying **Ten sailors ran down the street?** _____
   c. What's another way of saying **The sailor was tall?** _____

3. a. Something that is very thick and sturdy is called _____.
   b. A thick and sturdy stick is a _____.
   c. A thick and sturdy person is a _____.

4. a. When you move backwards, you _____.
   b. What's another way of saying **He moved backwards toward the door?** _____
   c. What's another way of saying **She could not move backwards any farther?** _____

5. When you walk with very heavy steps, you are _____.

WORD PRACTICE AND VOCABULARY

EXERCISE 1   Word practice

Pronunciation Guide: Thames River—Tems River

1. Everybody, find lesson 104, part A in your skillbook. *Wait.* Touch under each word in column 1 as I read it.
2. The first line is **Thames River.**
3. Next word. **Wand.**
4. *Repeat step 3 for each remaining word in column 1.*
5. Your turn. Read the first line. *Signal.*
   Thames River.
6. Next word. *Signal.* **Wand.**
7. *Repeat step 6 for each remaining word in column 1.*
8. *Repeat the words in column 1 until firm.*

EXERCISE 2   Word practice

1. Column 2.
2. Your turn. Read the first word. *Signal.* **Merry.**
3. Next word. *Signal.* **Merriment.**
4. *Repeat step 3 for each remaining word in column 2.*
5. *Repeat the words in column 2 until firm.*

EXERCISE 3   Vocabulary development

Task A

1. Column 3. New vocabulary.
   First you're going to read the words in column 3. Then you're going to read about what they mean.
2. Read the first word. *Signal.* **Vast.**
3. Next word. *Signal.* **Barge.**
4. *Repeat step 3 for each remaining word in column 3.*
5. *Repeat the words in column 3 until firm.*

Task B

1. Everybody, look at part B.
   You're going to read this part out loud.
2. *For each item, call on a student to:*
   ● *read one item aloud*
   ● *read the meaning*
   ● *read the question(s) for that item*
   ● *answer each question orally*

   Answer Key: **1. a. A vast room**
   b. A vast river
   2. a. Barges
   b. State barges
   3. A file of barges
   4. A wand

EXERCISE 4   Vocabulary review

1. Everybody, look at part C.
   The words in the box are words you've learned.
2. Read the first word. *Signal.* **Rude.**
3. Next. *Signal.* **Lumbering.**
4. *Repeat step 3 for the remaining words in the box.*
5. *Repeat the words in the box until firm.*
6. I'll read the items. When I come to a blank, everybody say the part that goes in the blank.
7. Look at item 1. *Pause.* Listen.
   When someone is helpless and you make that person do what you want, you *Pause. Signal.* **take advantage** of that person.
8. *Repeat step 7 for each remaining item.*

   Answer Key: **2. a. seaman**
   b. Ten seaman ran down the street.
   c. The seaman was tall.
   3. a. stout
   b. stout stick
   c. stout person
   4. a. retreat
   b. He retreated toward the door.
   c. She could not retreat any further.
   5. lumbering

Lesson 104

Outlining

The outline below shows three main ideas for <u>The Cat that Walked by Himself.</u>

Write three supporting details for each main idea.
- The first main idea is: <u>Three animals visited the cave.</u> Name those three animals. Ⓐ
- The second main idea is: <u>The cat and the woman made a bargain.</u> Tell what would happen if the woman praised the cat once, if she praised hime twice, and if she praised him three times. Ⓑ
- The third main idea is: <u>The cat did three things to win the bargain.</u> Tell what it did with the baby outside the cave. Tell what it did with the baby inside the cave. Tell what it caught for the woman. Ⓒ

1. Three animals visited the cave.

    a. _____

    _____

    b. _____

    _____

    c. _____

    _____

2. The cat and the woman made a bargain.

    a. _____

    _____

    b. _____

    _____

c. _____

_____

_____

3. The cat did three things to win the bargain.

    a. _____

    _____

    b. _____

    _____

    c. _____

    _____

Story Items

4. Put the following events in the right order by numbering them from 1 through 4.

    _____ Tom became King of England.

    _____ Tom stepped onto the royal barge.
    _____ Edward tried to get into the banquet.
    _____ A messenger entered the banquet.

WORKBOOK LESSON 104 **105**

Lesson 104

CHAPTER 7

The City Banquet

At nine in the evening, the whole vast riverfront of the royal palace was blazing with lights. Ⓐ The river itself was crowded with boats and barges as far as you could see. These boats were fitted with colored lanterns that cast glorious reflections on the water. A file of fifty state barges drew up in front of the palace. Some barges were decorated with banners and streamers, some with gold cloth and silk flags, some with hundreds of tiny silver bells that danced and sent out showers of joyous sounds. The barge that Tom would occupy was decorated with large shields and silk streamers.

Attendants rolled out a thick carpet from the palace to the river. And as a large band began to play, two pages holding white wands walked slowly from the palace, along the carpet. They were followed by a group of lords and ladies. A loud blast from the horns announced that the members of the royal family would appear next. Lord Saint John appeared, wearing a scarlet robe. Princess Elizabeth was next, wearing a magnificent yellow gown. Then a roar went up from the crowd that could be heard for miles down the river as Tom Canty, dressed as the Prince of Wales, stepped from the palace and started down

the carpet. He was dressed in purple and white, and wore a long white diamond-studded cape. Ⓑ

Tom stepped into the royal barge. Slowly, the line of barges moved down the Thames River, through the crowds of decorated riverboats. The banks of the river were lighted with torches and bonfires that sent many slim towers of flame into the sky. The line of barges was met with a roar of cheers as it moved along.

Tom was half-buried in his silk cushions. This incredible sight left him in silent wonder. Soon the barges reached the center of London. Tom and the others stepped from the barge and walked slowly past huge crowds to a large hall.

Inside, the Mayor of London bowed and greeted the royal party. After the party was seated at a huge table in the front of the hall, hundreds of finely dressed men and women filed into the hall and took their seats. When everybody was seated, Princess Elizabeth reminded Tom that he should stand up. He did, and everybody else in the hall stood up at the same time. Tom drank from a large golden loving cup. Then, Princess Elizabeth drank from it also. This drinking signaled that the banquet had begun. Ⓒ ★7 ERRORS★

384 Lesson 104 Textbook

EXERCISE 5 Outlining

1. Everybody, turn to page 105 in your workbook. You're going to read that passage out loud.

2. *Call on individual students to read. Present the tasks specified for each circled letter.*

Ⓐ Name three supporting details for the main idea, **Three animals visited the cave.** *Ideas:* Wild Dog visited the cave; Wild Cow visited the cave; Wild Horse visited the cave.

Ⓑ Name three supporting details for the main idea, **The cat and the woman made a bargain.** *Ideas:* If the woman praised the cat once, he could sit in the front of the cave; if the woman praised the cat twice, he could sit in the back of the cave; if the woman praised the cat three times, he could drink the milk.

Ⓒ Name three supporting details for the main idea. **The cat did three things to win the bargain.** *Ideas:* The cat made the baby laugh. The cat made the baby go to sleep. The cat caught a mouse.

- Everybody, write the supporting details now. Raise your hand if you need help.

STORY READING

EXERCISE 6 Decoding and comprehension

1. Everybody, turn to page 384 in your textbook. *Wait. Call on a student.* What's the error limit for this chapter? **7 errors.**

2. *Call on individual students to read. Present the tasks specified for each circled letter.*

Ⓐ What event was taking place that evening? *Idea:* The City Banquet.

Ⓑ Get a picture of this splendid event. How many barges drew up in front of the palace? **Fifty.**

- Describe how some of those barges were decorated. *Ideas:* With banners; streamers; gold cloths; silk flags; silver bells.

- How was the prince's barge decorated? *Idea:* With large shields and silk streamers.

- Name the people from the royal family who came down the carpet to the royal barge. **Lord Saint John, Princess Elizabeth, and the Prince of Wales.**

- Who received the greatest cheer from the crowd? **Tom Canty.**

- What was he wearing? *Ideas:* Purple and white clothes, a diamond studded cape.

Ⓒ Where did the barges stop? **The center of London.**

- Who greeted Tom and the others inside? **The Mayor of London.**

- Where did the royal family sit? *Idea:* At a huge table in the front of the hall.

- Then who came into the great hall? *Idea:* Hundreds of ladies and gentlemen.

By midnight, the banquet was at its height of merriment. A group of dancers with torches was performing inside, and Tom was dazzled by their skill. But outside the great hall, the scene was quite different. The real Prince of Wales was at the gates of the hall, shouting, "I am the real Prince of Wales. Let me pass and I will prove that the other prince is a humbug."

The crowd outside enjoyed this show nearly as much as the people inside enjoyed the dancers. They started to tease Edward, saying such things as, "I can see from the way you dress that you are the real prince." These comments brought howls of laughter from the crowd.

Another person shouted, "Where is your diamond-studded cape, prince?" and another howl went up from the crowd.

Edward stood tall and announced, "I'm not moving from this spot until I am recognized as the real prince."

As the crowd laughed and hurled insults at Edward, a tall, strong gentleman wearing a long sword pushed forward and stood in front of Edward. He said, "My name is Miles Hendon. I don't know if you really are the prince, but I do know that you are a very brave lad. So I will stand by your side and be your comrade." Then Miles Hendon continued, "But don't waste your voice on these alley rats."

Another roar of laughter went up from the crowd. "Look here," somebody shouted, "we have another prince. The city is full of them tonight."

Somebody else shouted, "Let's take the little prince and throw him in the river!"

A ragged seaman grabbed Edward. In an instant Miles Hendon drew his sword and held it high. "Remove your hand or else," Miles threatened. The seaman let go and backed away.

People in the crowd began to shout, "Get them! Get them!" and slowly the crowd advanced. Edward and Miles backed against the wall of the great hall, and just as the crowd seemed ready to pounce on them, everyone was stunned motionless by the blast of a loud horn and the thundering of a horse's hooves.

"Make way for the king's messenger!" one of the horsemen shouted.

Instantly, Miles grabbed Edward and ran from the crowd. As they ran away, a solemn scene took place inside the hall. The king's messenger entered the great hall, bowed, and began to read a long announcement as the lords and ladies listened. The last words of the announcement were these: "The king is dead."

A moment of silence was followed with some quiet sobbing, as the people bowed their heads. Then the people sank to their knees and held their hands toward Tom. They let out one mighty shout that seemed to shake the building—"Long live the king."

Poor Tom's eyes wandered over this kneeling crowd, then rested on Princess Elizabeth and Hertford, who were kneeling next to him. Slowly he began to realize that everybody thought he was the King of England. Tom bent over and quietly asked Hertford, "Am I really the king?"

"Yes, Your Royal Highness. You are the King of England. Your word is the law."

The news was soon carried to the mob of people outside the great hall. A shout burst from the crowd, "Long live Edward, King of England!"

- What did Princess Elizabeth remind Tom to do? **Stand up.**
- What happened when he stood up? *Idea:* Everyone else stood up.
- Then what did Tom and Elizabeth do? *Idea:* Drank from a gold cup.
- What did that signal? *Idea:* That the banquet had started.
- Read the rest of the chapter to yourselves and be ready to answer some questions.

After all students have finished reading:

- By midnight, what kind of entertainment was going on inside the hall? *Idea:* Dancers with torches were performing.
- What kind of entertainment was going on outside? *Idea:* Edward was shouting and people were teasing him.
- What was Edward trying to tell the crowd? *Idea:* That he was the real prince.
- What was their response? *Idea:* They laughed at him.
- Someone in the crowd stepped forward to stand with Edward. Who was that? **Miles Hendon.**
- What happened when the seaman grabbed the prince? *Idea:* Miles told the man to let go.
- Then what did the crowd start to do? *Idea:* Started walking toward Edward and Miles.
- What prevented the crowd from pouncing on Edward and Miles? *Idea:* A king's messenger rode up.
- What did Edward and Hendon do when the messenger rode up? *Idea:* They ran off.
- What message did the messenger bring to the people inside the hall? *Idea:* The king was dead.
- The people shouted something that shook the building. What did they shout? **Long live the king.**
- Who were they calling their king now? **Tom Canty.**

Award 4 points or have the students reread to the error limit sign.

INDEPENDENT WORK

Do all the items in your skillbook and workbook for lesson 104.

ANSWER KEY FOR WORKBOOK

Outlining

The outline below shows three main ideas for <u>The Cat that Walked by Himself</u>.

Write three supporting details for each main idea.

- The first main idea is: <u>Three animals visited the cave.</u> Name those three animals. Ⓐ
- The second main idea is: <u>The cat and the woman made a bargain.</u> Tell what would happen if the woman praised the cat once, if she praised hime twice, and if she praised him three times. Ⓑ
- The third main idea is: <u>The cat did three things to win the bargain.</u> Tell what it did with the baby outside the cave. Tell what it did with the baby inside the cave. Tell what it caught for the woman. Ⓒ

1. Three animals visited the cave. *Idea:*
   a. *Wild Dog visited the cave.*
   b. *Wild Cow visited the cave.*
   c. *Wild Horse visited the cave.*

2. The cat and the woman made a bargain.
   a. *If the woman praised the cat once, he could sit in front of the cave.*
   b. *If the woman praised the cat twice, he could sit in the back of the cave.*
   c. *If the woman praised the cat three times, he could drink the milk.*

3. The cat did three things to win the bargain.
   a. *The cat made the baby laugh.*
   b. *The cat made the baby go to sleep.*
   c. *The cat caught a mouse.*

Story Items

4. Put the following events in the right order by numbering them from 1 through 4.

   _4_ Tom became King of England.
   _1_ Tom stepped onto the royal barge.
   _2_ Edward tried to get into the banquet.
   _3_ A messenger entered the banquet.

WORKCHECK AND AWARDING POINTS

1. *Read the questions and answers for the skillbook and workbook.*
2. *Award points for independent work as follows:*

0 errors	*.6 points*
2 errors	*.4 points*
3, 4, or 5 errors	*.2 points*
5 or more errors	*.0 points*

3. *Award bonus points as follows:*

Correcting missed items or getting all items right	*.2 points*
Doing the writing assignment acceptably	*.2 points*

ANSWER KEY FOR SKILLBOOK

PART D

1. a. *Idea:* Nine in the evening
   b. Thames River
   c. Bright
   d. *Ideas:* Boats and barges; people
   e. *Any three:* Colored lanterns; banners; streamers; flags; bells; shields
   f. *Idea:* To the banquet
2. a. London
   b. In the front
   c. *Idea:* They stood up
   d. *Idea:* Drank from a cup
3. a. Edward
   b. *Idea:* The real prince
   c. *Idea:* They laughed at him
   d. Miles Hendon
   e. His sword
   f. Miles and Edward
   g. the king's messenger
   h. *Idea:* Ran away
4. a. *Idea:* The king was dead
   b. Long live the king
   c. Tom
   d. Edward

PART E

5. a. abandoned
   b. wisdom
   c. foul
   d. rude
   e. tattered
   f. torment
   g. merciful

Lesson 105

Lesson 105

PART A   Word Lists

1	2	3
blurred	swallow	**New vocabulary**
curse	basin	1. shudder
injury	faults	2. blurred
return	swallowed	3. inn
		4. regret
		5. belongings
		6. convince

PART B   New Vocabulary

1. **shudder**—Another word for **shiver** is **shudder.**
   a. Show how you shudder.
   b. What did you just do?

2. **blurred**—Things that do not look clear are **blurred.** A picture that does not look clear is a blurred picture.
   ● What is an image that does not look clear?

3. **inn**—An **inn** is a small hotel that serves meals and has rooms for people to stay.
   ● What's another word for a small hotel?

4. **regret**—When you are very sorry about something that happened, you **regret** that thing.
   a. What's another way of saying **She was sorry about what she had done?**

   b. What's another way of saying **She would not be sorry about what she did?**

5. **belongings**—The things that you own are your **belongings.**
   ● What do we call the things that we own?

6. **convince**—When you make somebody believe something, you convince that person it is true.
   a. What's another way of saying **She made her mother believe that she worked hard?**
   b. What's another way of saying **He will try to make me believe that it is true?**

PART C   Vocabulary Review

> barge
> wisdom
> wand
> merciful
> foul
> vast
> file

1. a. Something that is very large is _____.
   b. A very large room is a _____.
   c. A very large river is a _____.

2. A large, flat boat that can carry cargoes on rivers is called a _____.
3. a. A line is a _____.
   b. A line of people is a _____.
   c. A line of barges is a _____.
4. A small staff that is decorated is called a _____.

WORD PRACTICE AND VOCABULARY

EXERCISE 1   Word family

1. Everybody, find lesson 105, part A in your skillbook. *Wait.*
2. Column 1. All those words have the sound **er** in them.
3. Your turn. Read the first word. *Signal.* **Blurred.**
4. Next word. *Signal.* **Curse.**
5. *Repeat step 4 for each remaining word in column 1.*
6. *Repeat the words in column 1 until firm.*

EXERCISE 2   Word practice

1. Column 2.
2. Your turn. Read the first word. *Signal.* **Swallow.**
3. Next word. *Signal.* **Basin.**
4. *Repeat step 3 for each remaining word in column 2.*
5. *Repeat the words in column 2 until firm.*

EXERCISE 3   Vocabulary development

Task A
1. Column 3. New vocabulary.
   First you're going to read the words in column 3. Then you're going to read about what they mean.
2. Read the first word. *Signal.* **Shudder.**
3. Next word. *Signal.* **Blurred.**
4. *Repeat step 3 for each remaining word in column 3.*
5. *Repeat the words in column 3 until firm.*

Task B
1. Everybody, look at part B.
   You're going to read this part out loud.
2. *For each item, call on a student to:*
   ● *read one item aloud*
   ● *read the meaning*
   ● *read the question(s) for that item*
   ● *answer each question orally*

   Answer Key: **1. a.** *Student should shudder.*
   b. Shuddered
   2. A blurred image
   3. An inn
   4. a. She regretted what she had done.
   b. She would not regret what she did.
   5. Belongings
   6. a. She convinced her mother that she worked hard.
   b. He will try to convince me that it is true.

EXERCISE 4   Vocabulary review

1. Everybody, look at part C.
   The words in the box are words you've learned.
2. Read the first word. *Signal.* **Barge.**
3. Next. *Signal.* **Wisdom.**
4. *Repeat step 3 for the remaining words in the box.*
5. *Repeat the words in the box until firm.*
6. I'll read the items. When I come to a blank, everybody say the part that goes in the blank.
7. Look at item la. *Pause.* Listen.
   Something that is very large is *Pause. Signal.* **vast.**
8. *Repeat step 7 for each remaining item.*

   Answer Key: **1. b. vast room**
   c. vast river
   2. barge
   3. a. file
   b. file of people
   c. file of barges
   4. wand

Lesson 105

CHAPTER 8
The King and his Knight Ⓐ

As soon as Miles Hendon and Edward ran from the mob, they made their way through the alleys toward the river. When they approached London Bridge, they met a huge crowd of people. Edward, who was now really the king, learned from a thousand voices that the king was dead. This news sent a shudder through Edward's body. He began to cry as he and Miles slowly made their way through the crowd. He wasn't paying attention to the things around him. Everything seemed blurred through the tears in his eyes. Then suddenly, he heard a shout that thrilled him in his sadness. "Long live King Edward!"

He thought, "How strange. I am actually the King of England."

• • •

London Bridge was like a little town. It had stood over the river for six hundred years. Along the bridge were inns and shops of all kinds, with family dwellings above them. Children were born in dwellings that were on the bridge. They grew up there, and they died of old age there. Ⓑ

Miles lived in a little inn on the bridge. As he and Edward neared the door of the inn, a harsh voice said, "So there you are. You kept me waiting here for hours, and now you're going to pay for it." Ⓒ

John Canty reached out to seize Edward.

Miles stepped between them and said, "Not so fast. What is this boy to you?"

"It's none of your business," John Canty replied. "But if you must know, he is my son."

"That's not true," cried Edward.

Miles turned toward Edward and said, "I believe you."

"I don't know this man!" Edward exclaimed. "And I hate him. I would rather die than go with him."

Miles replied, "Then it is settled. You will stay with me."

John Canty pushed forward. "We'll see about that!" he shouted.

"If you touch him, you'll regret it," Miles said in a low voice, as he moved in front of John Canty and began to reach for his sword.

John Canty backed away and Miles continued, "I didn't save this lad from a mob so that I could turn him over to somebody like you. So be on your way. And do it quickly."

John Canty moved off, muttering threats. Soon the crowd swallowed up the sight of him. Miles and Edward entered the inn and ordered a meal to be delivered to Miles's room.

The room was small and a little shabby. Edward went to the bed and dropped down on it. His mind was blurred with sadness, hunger, and exhaustion. It was now three o'clock in the morning. "Call me when the food arrives," he said, and immediately went to sleep. Ⓓ

★7 ERRORS★

As Miles studied the sleeping king, he began to wonder about the boy. How could such a friendless little pauper think that he was the Prince of Wales, and now the King of England? Yet, the way he behaved was like a noble soldier. He had faced the crowd with the bravery of a king. "I like him," Miles said aloud. "And, although he has no other friends, I will become like a big brother to him."

A servant entered the room with a hot, steaming meal, which he placed on the table. The door slammed as the servant left the room. Edward awoke and sprang to a sitting position. For an instant, his eyes flashed around the room as he tried to remember where he was. Then he saw the meal on the table. He said to Miles, "You are kind to me. Thank you."

Edward got up, walked to the empty wash basin in the corner of the room, and stood there, waiting. Miles asked, "What's wrong?"

Edward replied, "Pour the water for me and bring me a towel." Miles laughed, took a towel that was right in front of Edward, and handed it to him without a comment. Then he poured water from a large pitcher into the basin. After Edward washed his face, he sat down at the table. He did not wait for Miles to sit down but began to eat immediately. Then he stopped

STORY READING

EXERCISE 5 Decoding and comprehension

1. Everybody, turn to page 387 in your textbook. *Wait. Call on a student.* What's the error limit for this chapter? **7 errors.**

2. *Call on individual students to read. Present the tasks specified for each circled letter.*

Ⓐ Where did we leave Edward at the end of the last chapter? *Idea:* Running from the crowd.

● What was the name of the man who was with Edward? **Miles Hendon.**

Ⓑ What news saddened Edward as he made his way through the crowd? *Idea:* That the king had died.

● What news gave him a thrill? *Idea:* That he was now king.

● Everybody, look at the picture. *Check.* It shows London Bridge as it looked in 1549. It's like a little community with shops and family dwellings.

Ⓒ Where did Miles live? *Idea:* In an inn on London Bridge.

● Where were Miles and Edward? *Idea:* By an inn on London Bridge.

● Somebody stopped them near the door of the inn. Who do you think that person is? *Ideas:* Tom's father; John Canty.

Ⓓ What did Miles tell John Canty? *Idea:* Not to touch Edward.

● What did John Canty do when Miles reached for his sword? *Idea:* Backed off.

● The chapter says: **The crowd swallowed up the sight of John Canty.** What does that mean? *Idea:* He disappeared in the crowd.

● Where did Miles and Edward go? *Idea:* Into the inn.

● What time was it? **Three o'clock in the morning.**

● What did Edward do? *Idea:* He went to sleep.

● Read the rest of the chapter to yourselves and be ready to answer some questions.

After all students have finished reading:

● Was Miles convinced that Edward was the King of England? **No.**

● Why did he decide to protect Edward? *Ideas:* Because he liked him; he thought he was brave.

● When the food arrived Edward woke up and went to the wash basin. Then he waited for something. What was he waiting for? *Idea:* For Miles to pour the water and bring him a towel.

● Did Edward wait for Miles to sit down before he ate? **No.**

in the middle of his meal, looked suddenly at Miles, and said, "You behave like a nobleman. Are you one?"

"In a way," Miles replied. "My father is one of the least important lords of England, Sir Richard Hendon."

"Tell me more," Edward said as he continued to eat.

"There's not much more to tell," Miles said. "I was full of mischief when I was a lad. My brother, Hugh, wanted all my father's belongings when my father died. So Hugh turned all my faults into great crimes. He convinced my father that I was worthless. So my father threw me out and told me never to return. For the last seven years I have been in France. As soon as I could, I came back to England. I've been back for only a few weeks. And, as you can see, I'm not very rich. That's my story."

"You have had terrible experiences," Edward said with flashing eyes. "But I will set things right."

Then Edward told Miles his own story. He described all the misfortunes that he had experienced during the past two days.

Miles was astonished. To himself, he said, "What an imagination this boy has. He does not have an ordinary mind, but a very strange one that can make up amazing stories." As Miles listened to Edward he resolved that he would take care of the boy until his mind was cured.

Edward said, "You have saved me from injury and maybe from death. Name anything you want and if it is within my royal power to give it to you, you shall have it."

For a moment, Miles stared at Edward, not knowing what to say. At last he said, "Would it be possible for me and my children, if I have any, to sit in the palace in the presence of the king?"

"Kneel," Edward commanded. And before Miles realized what he was doing, he kneeled before the young king.

"I declare that from this day on, you are Sir Miles Hendon. You are a knight. You and your children will live in the palace with me and you may sit in my presence." The little king bowed his head and then said to the astonished knight, "You may rise now, Sir Miles."

Miles said to himself, "I will not laugh, but here I am—a knight in the kingdom of dreams."

- Edward asked Miles if he was a nobleman. What did Miles reply? *Idea:* That he was noble in a way.
- Miles told his story. Why did his father throw him out of the house? *Idea:* Because Hugh had turned their father against him.
- Where had Miles been for the last seven years? **In France.**
- How long had he been back in England? *Idea:* Just a few weeks.
- Was Miles rich? **No.**
- When Miles listened to Edward's story, did he believe it? **No.**
- What did Miles resolve to do? *Idea:* Take care of Edward.
- Edward told Miles that he would grant any wish. What did Miles want? *Idea:* To be able to sit in the presence of the king.
- So Edward made Miles a very important person. What did he make Miles? *Idea:* A knight.
- What special privilege would Sir Miles have as a knight? *Idea:* He could sit in front of the king.
- Did Miles believe that he had really become a knight? **No.**

Award 4 points or have the students reread to the error limit.

INDEPENDENT WORK

Do all the items in your skillbook and workbook for lesson 105.

ANSWER KEY FOR WORKBOOK

Outlining

The outline below shows three main ideas for The Ugly Duckling.
Write three supporting details for each main idea.
- The first main idea is: When he lived with the other ducks, the duckling was unhappy. Tell what the duckling looked like. Tell how the other ducks treated him. Tell how many friends he had.
- The second main idea is: The duckling had several adventures. Tell which birds he stayed with. Tell what happened to him one cold night. Tell which people saved him.

The third main idea is: The duckling turned into a swan. Tell what he did with his wings. Tell which animals greeted him. Tell where he saw himself.

1. When he lived with the other ducks, the duckling was unhappy. *Idea:*

   a. *He was ugly.*

   b. *The other ducks were mean to him.*

   c. *He had no friends.*

2. The duckling had several adventures.

   a. *He stayed with geese.*

   b. *He almost froze to death.*

   c. *A man saved his life.*

3. The duckling turned into a swan.

   a. *He flew with his wings.*

   b. *The swans greeted him.*

   c. *He saw himself in the water.*

Story Items

4. Below is a list of statements.
   Write **king** after each statement that tells about a king.
   Write **pauper** after each statement that does not tell about a king.

   a. He wears rags. *pauper*
   b. He expects to be obeyed. *king*
   c. He makes somebody a knight. *king*
   d. He wanders around the streets. *pauper*
   e. He eats before anybody else. *king*

WORKCHECK AND AWARDING POINTS

1. *Read the questions and answers for the skillbook and workbook.*
2. *Award points for independent work as follows:*

0 errors	*6 points*
2 errors	*4 points*
3, 4, or 5 errors	*2 points*
5 or more errors	*0 points*

3. *Award bonus points as follows:*

Correcting missed items or getting all items right.	*2 points*
Doing the writing assignment acceptably	*2 points*

ANSWER KEY FOR SKILLBOOK

PART D

1. **a.** To London Bridge
   b. *Idea:* The king was dead
   c. King of England
2. **a.** an inn
   b. *Idea:* On London Bridge
   c. John Canty
   d. *Idea:* Take him away
3. **a.** No
   b. *Ideas:* Because Edward was brave; because Edward had a great imagination
   c. *Idea:* Hand it to him
   d. *Idea:* Because he was the king
4. **a.** Yes
   b. *Ideas:* His brother; Hugh
   c. In France
   d. No
5. **a.** No
   b. *Idea:* Was cured
   c. knight
   d. Sir Miles
   e. *Idea:* Sit in the presence of the king

PART E

6. **a.** retreat
   b. take advantage
   c. lanterns
   d. file
   e. vast
   f. confidence and good manners
   g. move very fast
   h. rude
   i. very impressive
   j. barge
   k. wand
   l. lumbering
   m. stout

Lesson 106

Lesson 106

PART A   Word Lists

1	2	3
innkeeper	plunge	1. ruffian
hardship	worm	2. suspicious
madman	busy	3. drowsy
grandmother	busied	
	wormed	
	yawn	
	plunged	

PART B   New Vocabulary

1. **ruffian**—A **ruffian** is a rude and rough person.
   - What's another word for a **rude and rough person?**

2. **suspicious**—When you are **suspicious** about something, you don't really believe that it is true. If you don't really believe a statement, you are **suspicious** about that statement.
   - If you don't really believe a person,
   _____.

3. **drowsy**—It was very late at night and she was so **drowsy** she could hardly keep her eyes open.
   - What could **drowsy** mean?

PART C   Vocabulary Review

> lantern
> inn
> shudder
> donate
> belongings
> convince
> regret
> hustle
> blurred

1. The things that you own are your _____.

2. a. Things that do not look clear are _____.
   b. A picture that does not look clear is a _____.
   c. An image that does not look clear is a _____.

3. Another word for a **small hotel** that serves meals and has rooms for people to stay in is an _____.

4. a. When you are very sorry about something that happened, you _____ that thing.
   b. What's another way of saying **She was sorry about what she had done?**
   c. What's another way of saying **She would not be sorry about what she did?** _____
5. Another word for **shiver** is _____.
6. a. When you make somebody believe something, you _____ that person it is true.
   b. What's another way of saying **He will try to make me believe that it is true?** _____
   c. What's another way of saying **She made her mother believe that she worked hard?** _____

WORD PRACTICE AND VOCABULARY

EXERCISE 1   Word family

1. Everybody, find lesson 106, part A in your skillbook. *Wait.*
2. Column 1. All those words are made up of two shorter words.
3. Your turn. Read the first word. *Signal.* **Innkeeper.**
4. Next word. *Signal.* **Hardship.**
5. *Repeat step 4 for each remaining word in column 1.*
6. *Repeat the words in column 1 until firm.*

EXERCISE 2   Word practice

1. Column 2.
2. Your turn. Read the first word. *Signal.* **Plunge.**
3. Next word. *Signal.* **Worm.**
4. *Repeat step 3 for each remaining word in column 2.*
5. *Repeat the words in column 2 until firm.*

EXERCISE 3   Vocabulary development

Task A

1. Column 3. New vocabulary.
   First you're going to read the words in column 3. Then you're going to read about what they mean.
2. Read the first word. *Signal.* **Ruffian.**
3. Next word. *Signal.* **Suspicious.**
4. *Repeat step 3 for* **drowsy.**
5. *Repeat the words in column 3 until firm.*

Task B

1. Everybody, look at part B.
   You're going to read this part out loud.
2. *For each item, call on a student to:*
   - *read one item aloud*
   - *read the meaning*
   - *read the question(s) for that item*
   - *answer each question orally*

   Answer Key: **1. A ruffian**
   2. you are suspicious about that person
   3. *Idea:* Sleepy.

EXERCISE 4   Vocabulary review

1. Everybody, look at part C.
   The words in the box are words you've learned.
2. Read the first word. *Signal.* **Lantern.**
3. Next. *Signal.* **Inn.**
4. *Repeat step 3 for the remaining words in the box.*
5. *Repeat the words in the box until firm.*
6. I'll read the items. When I come to a blank, everybody say the part that goes in the blank.
7. Look at item 1. *Pause.* Listen.
   The things that you own are your *Pause. Signal.* **belongings.**
8. *Repeat step 7 for each remaining item.*

   Answer Key: **2. a. blurred**
   b. blurred picture
   c. blurred image
   3. inn
   4. a. regret
   b. She regretted what she had done.
   c. She would not regret what she did.
   5. shudder
   6. a. convince
   b. He will try to convince me that it is true.
   c. She convinced her mother that she worked hard.

Lesson 106

CHAPTER 9
The Disappearance of the King Ⓐ

After the little king had eaten, he stood up and yawned. He took off his rags and plunged into Miles's bed, saying to the man he had just knighted, "I will sleep here. You sleep in front of the door and guard it against anybody who tries to enter." Ⓑ

Sir Miles was going to object, but then he thought to himself, "I have slept in worse places for the last seven years. And the lad needs a good sleep. So it will be no great hardship for me to sleep in front of the door." And he did.

Miles awoke early the next morning. He sat up and glanced at the bed, where Edward was stirring. "I will let him sleep a while more," Miles said to himself. "The way the lad acts, he should have been born a real king, not a pauper."

Miles busied himself around the room for a few moments. Then he decided that this would be a good time to mend some of his socks. He searched for a needle and thread but found none. Again he glanced at the sleeping king and decided to run out and buy a needle and thread. He said to himself, "This task will take me only a few minutes and I'll certainly be back before the boy wakes up."

Miles went down the stairs and out on to the bridge, which was already crowded with people. He went to a tiny shop that repaired shoes and sold needles and thread. After making his purchase, Miles returned to the room and glanced at the bed. The bulging form under the covers seemed to be resting silently, as if the boy was in a deep sleep.

Miles sat in the corner and sang softly to himself as he tried to mend his socks. He was not good at sewing, and he soon drove the needle into the end of his finger. "Ouch!" he cried out. Afraid that this noise would awaken the sleeping king, he glanced over at the bed. The form under the covers did not stir, and Miles continued sewing.

After mending all the socks that he possessed, Miles decided that it was time to awaken Edward, so he said, "My lord, it is time to get up. Arise and we will have a hearty breakfast."

The form in the bed did not stir. Miles stared at the form for a moment. Then he rushed to the bed and threw back the covers. The bed was empty, except for some blankets and pillows under the cover, rolled up to look like the form of a sleeping person.

"What!" Miles shouted. He flew to

the door and shouted for the innkeeper. "Get up here!" he demanded. Ⓒ
★7 ERRORS★

The innkeeper waddled up the stairs as fast as he could, huffing and puffing for breath. "What is wrong?" he asked, timidly.

"The boy!" Miles shouted. "Where is the boy?"

"Well . . . Well . . ."

"Well, what?" Miles demanded.

"A minute after you left the inn, a young boy came here and said that he had a message from you. I let him into the room."

"Go on," Miles said impatiently. "Go on."

"Well, the boy who came in woke up the lad who was sleeping in your bed and told him that he was to go along with him. So the lad in your bed put on his rags. He said that it was very rude of you to send a

STORY READING

EXERCISE 5   Decoding and comprehension

1. *Everybody, turn to page 390 in your textbook. Wait. Call on a student.* What's the error limit for this chapter? **7 errors.**
2. *Call on individual students to read. Present the tasks specified for each circled letter.*

Ⓐ Where did we leave Edward and Miles? *Idea:* In Miles's room at the inn.

● What time was it now? *Idea:* Sometime after three o'clock in the morning.

Ⓑ Edward is giving orders as if he is a king. Does Miles think Edward is really a king? **No.**

● Does Miles believe that he is really a knight? **No.**

Ⓒ Was Edward in bed when Miles went out? **Yes.**

● Why had Miles gone out? *Idea:* To buy a needle and thread.

● Where did Miles get the needle and thread? *Idea:* At a shop.

● What did Miles discover when he pulled back the covers on the bed? *Idea:* That Edward was gone.

● What do you think had happened? *Response:* Student preference.

● Who did Miles call for to find out what happened? **The innkeeper.**

● Read the rest of the chapter to yourselves and be ready to answer some questions.

After all students have finished reading:

● The innkeeper told what had happened to Edward. Who came for him while Miles was out? *Idea:* A boy.

● What message did that boy bring? *Ideas:* That Edward was to go with him.

● Why was Edward a little upset by this message? *Idea:* Because he thought it was rude of Miles not to deliver the message himself.

● Who stuffed the blanket in the bed so that it would look like a sleeping form? *Idea:* The messenger boy.

● When the boys left, somebody followed them on the bridge. Who was that? **John Canty.**

● When Miles heard about what had happened where did he go? *Idea:* To look for Edward.

● What did he resolve to do? *Idea:* To set things right.

Award 4 points or have the students reread to the error limit sign.

messenger when you should have come yourself. Then he said . . ."

"What happened, man? Just tell me what happened."

"They went down the stairs together and then they went outside. That's all."

"That's all?" Miles exclaimed. "That can't be all. Tell me, was the boy who came with the message alone?"

"Yes, quite alone," the innkeeper replied. Suddenly, the innkeeper's expression became thoughtful. "Now that I think about it . . ."

"Tell me, man. Tell me," Miles said earnestly.

"Now that I think about it, I remember that the two lads walked on to the bridge. And then it seemed that a large ruffian dressed in rags stepped from the crowd and followed the boys."

Miles knew instantly who that ruffian was. "So, that man who claimed to be the lad's father tricked me," Miles said and paced across the room. Then he whirled around and demanded, "Tell me what happened then."

"That's all sir. That's all. There was a large crowd on the bridge, as you know, and soon the crowd swallowed up all sight of them."

"This is horrible!" Miles shouted. Then he pointed to the bed and said, "Who fixed the bed so that it would look as if somebody was still sleeping there?"

"The boy who said he was your messenger," the innkeeper replied. "I have no idea why he did that. I thought that you had ordered him to do it. I . . ."

"Get out of here," Miles said in an angry voice.

"Yes, sir," the innkeeper said, and backed toward the door. Then he paused and said, "But you must not think that it was my fault. I had no way of knowing that you did not send the message. The boy told me that you had and . . ."

"Out!" Miles shouted. Then Miles grabbed his coat, threw it over his shoulders, and dashed down the stairs, two at a time. He passed the innkeeper before he reached the second floor and almost knocked him over.

As Miles plunged into the crowd on the bridge, his eyes flashed this way and that way for signs of Edward and John Cantry. Miles pushed through the crowds of people who were walking or standing in front of the shops. He said to himself, "I have lost that poor little mad boy. But I swear that he will not stay lost. If I have to turn over every stone in this land, I will find him again."

For an instant Miles thought about the breakfast that he had planned to have with Edward. "But I am no longer hungry," he thought. He had only one goal now, to find that boy. As he wormed his way through the crowd, he kept thinking about the cruel trick. If anybody else had sent a messenger, Edward would have been suspicious and would not have gone. But he went because he thought the message had come from Miles. "I will make this up to the brave lad," Miles resolved. "I will make it up."

INDEPENDENT WORK

Do all the items in your skillbook and workbook for lesson 106.

WORKCHECK AND AWARDING POINTS

1. *Read the questions and answers for the skillbook and workbook.*
2. *Award points for independent work as follows:*

> *0 errors . . . . .6 points*
> *2 errors . . . . .4 points*
> *3, 4, or 5 errors . . . . .2 points*
> *5 or more errors . . . . .0 points*

3. *Award bonus points as follows:*

> *Correcting missed items*
> *or getting all items right . . . . .2 points*
> *Doing the writing*
> *assignment acceptably . . . . .2 points*

ANSWER KEY FOR SKILLBOOK

PART D
1. a. *Idea:* In front of the door
   b. *Idea:* To protect him
2. a. His socks
   b. *Idea:* To buy a needle and thread
   c. *Idea:* Just a few minutes
   d. Edward
   e. *Idea:* Pillows and blankets
3. a. The innkeeper
   b. a boy
   c. message
   d. John Canty
4. a. Edward
   b. No
   c. *Ideas:* Because he liked Edward; because he wanted to help him
5. a. Edward went to sleep
   b. Miles left the inn to find Edward

PART E
6. a. ignorant
   b. posed
   c. merciful
   d. convince
   e. shudder
   f. belongings
   g. inn
   h. regret
   i. blurred
   j. vast

ANSWER KEY FOR WORKBOOK

Main Idea and Supporting Details

Read this passage:

John Thornton raised his voice and yelled. "Gee!" Buck followed the command. He swung to the right, and a crisp crackling arose from under the frozen sled runners.

"Haw!" Thornton commanded.

Buck made the same move, this time to the left. The crackling turned into a snapping. The sled was broken out.

"Now, MUSH!"

Buck threw himself forward, tightening the harness with a jarring lunge. His whole body was gathered together in the tremendous effort. The sled swayed, trembled, and started forward.

Write the main idea and three supporting details. *Idea:*

1. *Buck pulled the sled.*

a. *He swung to the right.*

b. *He swung to the left.*

c. *He threw himself forward.*

FACT GAME

FACT GAME SCORECARD

1	2	3	4	5	6	7	8	9	10
11	12	13	14	15	16	17	18	19	20
21	22	23	24	25	26	27	28	29	30

Fact Game

2. Tell which **people** lived in each Land.
   a. Land of the West.
   b. Land of the East.
   c. Land of the South.
3. Tell the **title** of the story for each main character.
   a. A cat that could talk.
   b. A bird that turned into a swan.
   c. A dog that pulled a thousand-pound sled.
   d. A dog that followed his old master to the north.
4. Tell which **country** each story took place in.
   a. A Horse to Remember
   b. Buck
   c. Dick Whittington
   d. Adventure on the Rocky Ridge
5. Tell whether each animal is used for **hunting, carrying,** or **food.**
   a. goat
   b. donkey
   c. chicken
   d. hound
6. Tell whether each statement is **true** or **false.**
   a. Dawson is in California.
   b. Gold was discovered near Dawson.
   c. Redwoods are short trees.
   d. San Francisco is in Canada.

7. Tell which **breed** of dog each statement describes.
   a. This breed is very fast.
   b. This breed herds sheep.
   c. This breed has a sensitive nose.
   d. This breed is very brave.
8. a. What game did Jackie Robinson play?
   b. Which team did he play for?
   c. Which city was that team located in?
9. Tell which **story** each moral fits.
   a. Be kind to strangers.
   b. Do not trust appearances.
   c. Love is better than gold.
10. a. What was the name of the house that Jane Addams started?
    b. Which city was that house located in?
    c. Did Jane Addams help poor people or rich people?
    d. Which war did Jane Addams try to stop?
11. Tell which **Greek god** each statement describes.
    a. He was the chief god.
    b. He was the god of the sea.
    c. He was the messenger god.
    d. He was the god of music and light.
12. Tell whether each statement describes **Tom Canty** or **Edward Tudor.**
    a. He was born on Pudding Lane.
    b. He was born in Westminster Palace.
    c. He was the real Prince of Wales.
    d. He was made the new King of England.

FACT GAME ANSWER KEY

2. a. Winkies
   b. Munchkins
   c. Quadlings
3. a. The Cat that Walked by Himself
   b. The Ugly Duckling
   c. Buck
   d. Brown Wolf
4. a. England
   b. Canada
   c. England
   d. United States
5. a. Food
   b. Carrying
   c. Food
   d. Hunting
6. a. False
   b. True
   c. False
   d. False
7. a. Greyhound
   b. Collie
   c. Hound
   d. Airedale
8. a. Baseball
   b. Dodgers
   c. Brooklyn
9. a. The Miraculous Pitcher
   b. Beauty and the Beast
   c. The Golden Touch
10. a. Hull House
    b. Chicago
    c. Poor people
    d. World War One
11. a. Zeus
    b. Poseidon
    c. Hermes
    d. Apollo
12. a. Tom Canty
    b. Edward Tudor
    c. Edward Tudor
    d. Tom Canty

Lesson 107

Lesson 107

PART A   Word Lists

1	2	3
mourn	background	**New vocabulary**
secretary	daylight	1. article of clothing
Humphry	hairdresser	2. garment
parlor	fingernails	3. ordeal
	withdrawn	4. mourn
	ordeal	5. shattered
		6. withdraw
		7. assist
		8. parlor

PART B   New Vocabulary

1. **article of clothing**—An **article of clothing** is a piece of clothing.

2. **garment**—Another word for an **article of clothing** is a **garment.**

3. **ordeal**—An extremely difficult experience is an **ordeal.**
   - What's another way of saying **She suffered through an extremely difficult experience?**

4. **mourn**—When you **mourn** the death of a person, you show that you are very sad about that person's death.

5. **shattered**—When something is broken into many pieces, it is **shattered.** A window that is broken into many pieces is a **shattered** window.
   - What is a hope that is broken into many pieces?

6. **withdraw**—When you take something back, you **withdraw** that thing. When you take back your hand, you **withdraw** your hand.
   - When you take back a suggestion, you

7. **assist**—When you help somebody, you **assist** that person.

8. **parlor**–A **living room** or a **small sitting room** is a **parlor.**
   - What's a living room or a small sitting room?

PART C   Vocabulary Review

> merciful
> regret
> ruffian
> drowsy
> shudder
> suspicious

1. It was very late at night and she was so _____ she could hardly keep her eyes open.

2. A person who is rude and rough is called a _____.

3. a. When you don't really believe that something is true, you are _____ about that thing.
   b. If you don't really believe a statement, you are _____.
   c. If you don't really believe a person

WORD PRACTICE AND VOCABULARY

EXERCISE 1   Word practice

1. Everybody, find lesson 107, part A in your skillbook. *Wait.* Touch under each word in column 1 as I read it.
2. The first word is **mourn.**
3. Next word. **Secretary.**
4. *Repeat step 3 for each remaining word in column 1.*
5. Your turn. Read the first word. *Signal.* **Mourn.**
6. Next word. *Signal.* **Secretary.**
7. *Repeat step 6 for each remaining word in column 1.*
8. *Repeat the words in column 1 until firm.*

EXERCISE 2   Word family

1. Column 2. All those words are made up of two shorter words.
2. Your turn. Read the first word. *Signal.* **Background.**
3. Next word. *Signal.* **Daylight.**
4. *Repeat step 3 for each remaining word in column 2.*
5. *Repeat the words in column 2 until firm.*

EXERCISE 3   Vocabulary development

Task A

1. Column 3. New vocabulary. First you're going to read the words in column 3. Then you're going to read about what they mean.
2. Read the first line. *Signal.* **Article of clothing.**
3. Next word. *Signal.* **Garment.**
4. *Repeat step 3 for each remaining word in column 3.*
5. *Repeat the words in column 3 until firm.*

Task B

1. Everybody, look at part B. You're going to read this part out loud.
2. *For each item, call on a student to:*
   - *read one item aloud*
   - *read the meaning*
   - *read the question(s) for that item*
   - *answer each question orally*

Answer Key: **1.** *No answer required.*
            2. *No answer required.*
            3. **She suffered through an ordeal.**
            4. *No answer required.*
            5. **A shattered hope**
            6. **withdraw that suggestion**
            7. *No answer required.*
            8. **A parlor**

EXERCISE 4   Vocabulary review

1. Everybody, look at part C. The words in the box are words you've learned.
2. Read the first word. *Signal.* **Merciful.**
3. Next. *Signal.* **Regret.**
4. *Repeat step 3 for each remaining word in the box.*
5. *Repeat the words in the box until firm.*
6. I'll read the items. When I come to a blank, everybody say the part that goes in the blank.
7. Look at item 1. *Pause.* Listen. It was very late at night and she was so *Pause.* *Signal.* **drowsy** she could hardly keep her eyes open.
8. *Repeat step 7 for each remaining item.*

Answer Key: **2.** **ruffian**
            3. **a.** **suspicious**
                b. **suspicious about that statement**
                c. **you are suspicious about that person**

STORY READING

EXERCISE 5   Narrative poem

1. Everybody, turn to page 442 in your textbook. *Wait.* We're going to read this poem over the next few days.
- What's the title of the poem?
  The Spider and the Fly.
- Who wrote the poem? **Mary Howitt.**
  Mary Howitt was a poet who lived in England.
2. The parts of a poem are called stanzas.
- What are they called? **Stanzas.**
3. In the first stanza of this poem, the spider is trying to convince the fly to come into his web. The spider is trying to make the web seem very attractive.
4. I'll read the first stanza. *Read the first stanza.*

5. Listen to the first line again.
   "Will you walk into my parlor?" said the Spider to the Fly.
- Everybody, say that line with me.
  Read aloud with the students.
- What is a real parlor? *Idea:* A living room.
- What is the spider referring to as his parlor? *Idea:* His web.
6. Listen to the next line.
   "Tis the prettiest little parlor that ever you did spy."
- Everybody, say that line with me.
  Read aloud with the students.
- The word **tis** is another way of saying **it is.**
- The spider says that the parlor is the prettiest one that every you did spy. What does that mean: **ever you did spy?** *Idea:* Ever saw.
7. Listen to the next line.
   "The way into my parlor is up a winding stair."
- Everybody say that line with me.
  Read aloud with the students.
- What do you think the winding stair refers to? *Idea:* The spider web.
8. Listen to the next line.
   "And I've many curious things to show when you are there."
- Everybody, say that line with me.
  Read aloud with the students.
9. Listen to the next line.
   "Oh, no, no, said the little Fly, to ask me is in vain."
- Everybody, say that line with me.
  Read aloud with the students.
- **To ask me is in vain** means **it's no use to ask me.** What does **to ask me is in vain** mean? **It's no use to ask me.**
10. The fly is still talking in the next line. Listen.
    "For who goes up your winding stair can ne'er come down again."
- Everybody, say that line with me.
  Read aloud with the students.
- **Ne'er** means **never.** The fly says that it's no use to ask her into the web because anybody who goes into it never comes out again.
11. Let's read the whole first stanza together.
    Read aloud with the students.
12. We'll read the next stanza in the next lesson.

Lesson 107

CHAPTER 10
The Whipping Boy Ⓐ

Toward daylight of the same morning that Edward disappeared, Tom woke up suddenly and didn't know where he was.Ⓑ For a moment, he was tempted to call out to Bet and Nan and tell them about his incredible dream. He reached out to feel the straw around him, but his hand touched nothing but the silk of his bed. He was still not ready to believe that the whole thing had not been a crazy dream, when he saw a dark form moving toward him. A voice spoke. "What is your command?" the voice said.

"Tell me," Tom said earnestly. "Who am I?"

There was a pause. Then the voice repeated, "Who are you?" The voice continued, "Why, until last night, you were the Prince of Wales. But now, gracious ruler, you are Edward, King of England."

Tom buried his head among his pillows, murmuring, "It was not a dream." He looked for a moment and ordered the servant to go back to sleep.

Tom also went back to sleep, and after a time, he had a pleasant dream. In his dream, it was summer and he was playing in a meadow. He was digging a cave. As he dug he found twelve bright new pennies.

He felt wonderfully rich. Twelve pennies! In his dream, Tom ran to Pudding Lane and decided to give one penny to his mother every night. In that way, he wouldn't have to come home in fright every evening if he did not get anything from begging. He gave his mother one of the pennies when he got home. She was so pleased that she hugged him.

Then a voice said, "It is getting late, Your Majesty. Do you wish to get up?"Ⓒ

Tom's dream was shattered. He opened his eyes and looked around the apartment, which was not quite light. The voice had come from a lord, who was kneeling next to Tom's bed. Other lords were standing in the room. Everybody was wearing purple cloaks. From the books that Tom had read, he knew that these were the outfits that were worn to mourn the death of an important person.Ⓓ

It took some time to dress Tom. Of course, Tom didn't do any of the dressing. Four gentlemen assisted him. One gentleman selected each article of clothing the young king was to wear. Then he passed the article to another gentleman. Then two more gentlemen put the clothes on Tom. They put a shirt on him, and each of his

other garments. When they were about to put on one of his long socks, one of the gentlemen stopped and quickly withdrew the sock. He handed the pair of socks back to the gentleman who had selected it and said in a soft voice, "One sock has a snag in it."

One tiny piece of thread was out of place in the sock, causing a tiny ripple in the silk.Ⓔ ★8 ERRORS★ Quickly, the gentleman selected another pair and handed it to the gentlemen who dressed the king. In the background, one gentleman said to another, "The head keeper of the king's socks shall go to prison for this."

When Tom overheard the gentleman's remarks, he said, "No, it really doesn't make any difference, and he shall not suffer for it."

All the gentlemen looked astonished by Tom's statement. They all bowed and one of them said, "As you wish, Your Gracious Majesty."

By the time Tom was fully dressed, he wondered how anybody could waste so much time on nonsense. But his ordeal was not over. He now went to the palace hairdresser. As he walked down the halls, soldiers stood like statues, while lords and ladies fell to their knees. The royal hairdresser curled Tom's hair, trimmed his fingernails, and oiled his hands, so that his hands would look attractive.

Next, Tom went to the breakfast hall, where lords and ladies again fell to their knees when he entered. After breakfast, he was led to the throne room. He sat on the throne. Standing next to him on one side

was Hertford. In front of him was a male secretary who wrote down the decisions that the young king made.

The first decision Tom made was about the burial of King Henry the Eighth. Several lords suggested that he should be buried two weeks from that day. Tom had seen people die, and he had seen them buried on the same day. He started to say that Henry should be buried at once, but Hertford whispered to him, "Their plan for Henry's burial is all right."

The next business had to do with the amount of money the palace was spending. This business shocked Tom so severely that he could hardly talk. The rent that his family paid for the room on Pudding Lane was two pennies for six months. You can imagine how he felt when he heard the secretary say that the palace had cost twenty-five thousand pounds for the last six months. Tom said, "We can't spend that kind of money. We'll have to let some of the servants go and move into a smaller palace." Then he added, "I know of a nice house just off Pudding Lane that we could . . ."

Hertford was shaking his head no, and Tom stopped talking.

The business of the court went on and on. Tom, who didn't understand most of what the lords were talking about, finally became drowsy and fell asleep—right in the middle of a long speech by one of the most important lords in the kingdom. The speech stopped suddenly, and everybody stood in silence as Tom snored. After a few moments, Hertford dismissed everybody

EXERCISE 6   Decoding and comprehension

1. Everybody, turn to page 393 in your textbook. *Wait. Call on a student.* What's the error limit for this chapter? **8 errors.**

2. *Call on individual students to read. Present the tasks specified for each circled letter.*

Ⓐ Where did we leave Edward at the end of the last chapter? *Idea:* With a messenger boy.

Ⓑ Who are you going to read about on the same morning that the king disappeared? **Tom Canty.**

● Where was Tom? *Idea:* In the palace.

Ⓒ What did Tom dream that he found in a cave? **Twelve pennies.**

● What was his plan for the pennies? *Idea:* To give them to his mother.

● Why wouldn't he just give them to his mother all at the same time? *Idea:* So he could make them last longer.

Ⓓ What important person were they mourning? **King Henry the Eighth.**

● What color were they wearing to show that they were in mourning? **Purple.**

Ⓔ What's wrong with his sock? *Idea:* It has a snag in it.

● What is a snag? *Idea:* A thread that is out of place.
That's ridiculous. He can't wear the sock because it has one snag in it.

● Read the rest of the chapter to yourselves and be ready to answer some questions.

After all students have finished reading:

● When one of the the gentlemen discovered that there was a snag in one of the socks, another gentleman observed that somebody would be punished for this. Who would be punished? *Idea:* The head keeper of the king's socks.

● What did the gentleman think the punishment would be? *Idea:* Imprisonment.

● What did Tom say? *Ideas:* That the man would not go to prison.

● How did the gentlemen react to Tom's announcement? *Idea:* With surprise.

● Where did Tom go after he was dressed? *Idea:* To the royal hairdresser.

● After breakfast, where did Tom go? *Idea:* To the throne room.

● Tom made some decisions. The first was about the burial of somebody. Who was that? *Idea:* King Henry the Eighth.

● When did the lords suggest burying the king? *Idea:* In two weeks.

● Tom started to suggest that the king should be buried at a different time. When? *Idea:* At once.

● Why didn't Tom finish the suggestion? *Idea:* Hertford stopped him.

from the throne room. "The king needs his rest," he said.

After lunch, a young lad who was about twelve years old was admitted to Tom's chamber. Tom asked what the boy wanted, and the boy replied, "Your memory fails you. I am Humphry, your whipping boy."

"What's a whipping boy?" Tom asked.

"When you do poorly in your studies," Humphry replied, "I get whipped."

"That's insane," Tom said. "I'll take my own whippings if I do a bad job."

The boy giggled, then covered his mouth. "Pardon me, Your Grace. But you cannot be beaten."

"You shall not be beaten either," Tom replied.

"But," the boy said hesitantly, "if I am not beaten, I do not earn any money and I will be returned to the streets of London."

Suddenly Tom had a brilliant idea. He led the boy into a closet of his chambers where nobody could hear him. Then he told Humphry, "From now on, you come here everyday. But not for any whippings. We shall just pretend that you get whipped so nobody else will know. When you come here, tell me everything you hear from the people in the palace. Tell me what they're saying, and what's going on. In that way, you will help my memory return. And you will still have a job."

"Oh, thank you! I will keep this secret and tell nobody. But I will tell you everything I learn."

Lesson 107   Textbook   **395**

- The next business that was discussed shocked Tom. What business was that? *Idea:* How much money the palace cost.
- How much rent did Tom's family pay for six month's rent on Pudding Lane? **Two pennies.**
- How much had the royal palace spent during the last six months? **Twenty-five thousand pounds.**
- What did Tom suggest doing? *Ideas:* Lay off some servants; move to a smaller palace.
- During court, somebody would give Tom clues about what to say and what not to say. Who was that? **Hertford.**
- Why did the business in the throne room suddenly stop? *Idea:* Because Tom had fallen asleep.
- After lunch somebody came to Tom's apartment. Who was that? *Ideas:* Humphry; the king's whipping boy.
- What was Humphry's job? *Idea:* To get whipped if the king did poorly in his studies.
- Why did Humphry get beaten if the king did poorly? *Idea:* Because the king couldn't be hit.
- What problem would Humphry have if he didn't get beaten? *Idea:* He wouldn't get paid.
- Tom had a plan for Humphry. What was that plan? *Ideas:* Tom would pretend he was whipping Humphry; Humphry would tell Tom everything he heard in the palace.

Award 4 points or have the students reread to the error limit sign.

INDEPENDENT WORK

Do all the items in your skillbook and workbook for lesson 107.

Outlining

The outline below shows three main ideas for <u>Buck</u>.

Write three supporting details for each main entry.

- The first main idea is: <u>John Thornton saved Buck's life</u>. Tell what Thornton did to Buck's driver. Tell what happened to Buck's sled. Tell how Buck changed over the next few months.
- The second main idea is: <u>Buck saved Thornton's life in the river</u>. Tell what the men tied around Buck. Tell how Buck reached Thornton. Tell how they reached the shore.
- The third main idea is: <u>Buck pulled the sled</u>. Tell what Buck did first. Tell what he did next. Tell the last thing he did.

1. John Thornton saved Buck's life. *Idea:*
   a. *Thornton fought with Buck's driver.*
   b. *Buck's sled fell in the river.*
   c. *Buck became healthy again.*

2. Buck saved Thornton's life in the river.
   a. *The men tied a rope around Buck.*
   b. *Buck swam to Thornton.*
   c. *Buck and Thornton were pulled to shore.*

3. Buck pulled the sled.
   a. *Buck swung to the right.*
   b. *Buck swung to the left.*
   c. *Buck started forward.*

WORKCHECK AND AWARDING POINTS

1. *Read the questions and answers for the skillbook and workbook.*

2. *Award points for independent work as follows:*

0 errors	.6 points
2 errors	.4 points
3, 4, or 5 errors	.2 points
5 or more errors	.0 points

3. *Award bonus points as follows:*

Correcting missed items or getting all items right	.2 points
Doing the writing assignment acceptably	.2 points

PART D

1. a. *Ideas:* In Edward's apartment; in the palace
   b. *Ideas:* Bet and Nan; his sisters
   c. Straw
   d. Silk
2. a. 12 pennies
   b. *Idea:* Give one penny to his mother every night
   c. *Idea:* Because she was happy he had brought a penny
   d. *Idea:* home
   e. A lord
3. a. Four
   b. *Idea:* A thread was out of place
   c. To prison
   d. No
4. a. The throne room
   b. Hertford
   c. *Idea:* To save money
   d. *Idea:* A place near Pudding Lane
   e. Hertford
   f. *Idea:* Because Tom fell asleep
5. a. Humphry
   b. *Idea:* He would be whipped
   c. *Idea:* He didn't like it
   d. *Idea:* News of the palace
6. a. Henry the Eighth
   b. Tom
   c. Henry the Eighth
   d. Tom
   e. Henry the Eighth

PART E

7. a. mend
   b. dismiss
   c. identical
   d. convince
   e. shudder
   f. belongings
   g. suspicious
   h. blurred
   i. regret
   j. inn
   k. ruffian

Lesson 108

Lesson 108

PART A   Word Lists

1	2
official	**New vocabulary**
lawyer	1. conduct business
Hugo	2. official
charred	3. seal
	4. evidence
	5. misplaced

PART B   New Vocabulary

1. **conduct business**—When you do business, you **conduct business**.

2. **official**—Rules are **official** if they come from an office that can make the rules.
   - A rule coming from the office of the President is an **official** rule. A rule coming from a court of law is an **official** rule.

3. **seal**—A **seal** is a tool that puts a special design on a piece of paper. The official papers that a king wrote always had a special design on them. That design was made by the royal **seal**. Unless a paper had that design, it was not official.

4. **evidence**—Facts that make you conclude something are **evidence**.
   - What **evidence** would make you conclude that somebody had walked through fresh snow?

5. **misplaced**—If you don't remember where you put something, you have **misplaced** that thing.
   - If you don't remember where you put your shoes, you have **misplaced** your shoes.
   - If you don't remember where you put your keys, you have _____.

PART C   Vocabulary Review

ordeal	mourn
parlor	identical
mend	shattered
garment	withdraw
assist	article of clothing
convince	

1. When you show that you are very sad about a person's death, you _____ the death of that person.
2. When you help somebody, you _____ that person.
3. a. An extremely difficult experience is an _____.
   b. What's another way of saying **She suffered through an extremely difficult experience?**
4. Another word for an **article of clothing** is a _____.
5. Another word for a **living room** or a **small sitting room** is a _____.
6. A piece of clothing is an _____.
7. a. When you take something back, you _____ that thing.
   b. When you take back your hand you _____ your hand.
   c. When you take back a suggestion, you _____.
8. a. When something is broken into many pieces, it is _____.
   b. A window that is broken into many pieces is a _____.
   c. A hope that is broken into many pieces is a _____.

WORD PRACTICE AND VOCABULARY

EXERCISE 1   Word practice

1. Everybody, find lesson 108, part A in your skillbook. *Wait.* Touch under each word in column 1 as I read it.
2. The first word is **official.**
3. Next word. **Lawyer.**
4. *Repeat step 3 for each remaining word in column 1.*
5. Your turn. Read the first word. *Signal.* **Official.**
6. Next word. *Signal.* **Lawyer.**
7. *Repeat step 6 for each remaining word in column 1.*
8. *Repeat the words in column 1 until firm.*

EXERCISE 2   Vocabulary development

Task A

1. Column 2. New vocabulary.
   First you're going to read the words in column 2. Then you're going to read about what they mean.
2. Read the first line. *Signal.*
   Conduct business.
3. Next word. *Signal.* **Official.**
4. *Repeat step 3 for each remaining word in column 2.*
5. *Repeat the words in column 2 until firm.*

Task B

1. Everybody, look at part B.
   You're going to read this part out loud.
2. *For each item, call on a student to:*
   - *read one item aloud*
   - *read the meaning*
   - *read the question(s) for that item*
   - *answer each question orally*

   Answer Key: **1.** *No answer required.*
   2. *No answer required.*
   3. *No answer required.*
   4. *Ideas:* Snow on boots, snow or water on floor.
   5. misplaced your keys

EXERCISE 3   Vocabulary review

1. Everybody, look at part C. The words in the box are words you've learned.
2. Read the first word. *Signal.* **Ordeal.**
3. Next. *Signal.* **Parlor.**
4. *Repeat step 3 for the remaining words in the box.*
5. *Repeat the words in the box until firm.*
6. I'll read the items. When I come to a blank, everybody say the part that goes in the blank.
7. Look at item 1. *Pause.* Listen.
   When you show that you are very sad about a person's death, you *Pause. Signal.* **mourn** the death of that person.
8. *Repeat step 7 for each remaining item.*

   Answer Key: **2. assist**
   3. a. ordeal
   b. She suffered through an ordeal.
   4. garment
   5. parlor
   6. article of clothing
   7. a. withdraw
   b. withdraw
   c. withdraw that suggestion
   8. a. shattered
   b. shattered window
   c. shattered hope

STORY READING

EXERCISE 4   Narrative poem

1. Everybody, turn to page 442 in your textbook.
2. What are the parts of poems called? **Stanzas.**
   You have already read the first stanza. Let's read it again.
   Read the first stanza aloud with the students.
3. Listen to the first line of the second stanza.
   "I'm sure you must be weary, dear, with soaring up so high."
   - Everybody, say that line with me.
   Read aloud with the students.
   - Who is telling in this line? **The spider.**
   - What does **weary** mean? *Idea: Tired.*
   - What does that mean: **from soaring up so high?** *Idea: From flying so high.*
4. The spider is still talking in the next line. Listen.
   "Will you rest upon my little bed?" said the Spider to the Fly.
   - Everybody, say that line with me.
   Read aloud with the students.
   - What little bed is the spider talking about? *Idea: His nest.*
5. Listen to the next line and figure out who is talking.
   "There are pretty curtains drawn around; the sheets are fine and thin."
   - Who is talking in that line? **The spider.**
   - Everybody, say that line with me. *Read aloud with the students.*
   - What are the curtains and the sheets? *Idea: The web.*
6. Listen to the next line.
   "And if you like to rest a while, I'll snugly tuck you in."
   - Everybody, say that line with me.
   Read aloud with the students.
   - How do you tuck somebody in? *Idea:* Put the person in bed.
   - Is that what the spider actually plans to do? **No.**
7. Listen to the next two lines.
   **"Oh, no, no," said the little Fly, "for I've often heard it said,
   They never, never wake again, who sleep upon your bed."**
   - Everybody, say those lines with me.
   Read aloud with the students.
   - What does the fly mean when she says, **They never, never wake again?** *Idea:* They die.
8. Let's read the whole second stanza together.
   Read aloud with the students.
9. We'll read the next stanza in the next lesson.

Lesson 108

CHAPTER 11
Tom as King

Shortly before King Henry the Eighth had died, he had misplaced the royal seal. That seal was· very important because it was used to put a special mark on all official papers that were sent out. A paper could not be official without the royal seal. The king had told Hertford that he thought he had given the seal to the prince. So, on Tom's third day in the palace, Hertford, in the company of two other lords, asked about the royal seal.

"The royal seal," Tom said thoughtfully. He tried to remember if Humphry the whipping boy had mentioned anything about the seal, but of course, the lad would know nothing about such matters. At last, Tom replied, "What does the seal look like?"

One of the lords groaned and said, "Oh, his memory is still damaged."

Hertford quickly said, "Well, don't worry about the seal. It will turn up." Ⓐ

By now, Tom was getting used to seeing people drop to their knees in his presence, but he found the business of being king very boring. One day, he was getting ready to conduct the business when loud noises outside the palace attracted his attention. Tom looked out the window and saw a large, noisy mob approaching the palace gates. Three people were being pushed along in front of the mob: a man, a woman, and a young girl.

"Go find out what's happening out there," Tom said to his page. The page bowed and quickly disappeared from the throne room. Tom watched him go quickly to the palace gates and return. "My king," he said, as he kneeled before Tom. "The mob is bringing in three people for you to deal with. These people are accused of committing great crimes. The mob is demanding their death."

"Bring the three of them to me," Tom said. His simple command caused a great deal of activity. Within a few moments, a long line of guards marched across the palace grounds to the gate. Judges and lords entered the throne room so that they would be present as the king conducted official business. Each lord and judge who entered kneeled. Almost without thinking, Tom waved his hand so that they could rise again. Ⓑ

The guards and the sheriff brought three people into the room. Tom studied the man and observed something very familiar about this pauper, but he could not place him at first. Then suddenly, he remembered. On New Year's Day, a boy had

fallen into the Thames River near Pudding Lane. Tom remembered that this man had jumped into the icy river and saved the boy from drowning. Ⓒ

"What crime is this man charged with?" Tom asked.

"He poisoned another man," the sheriff said.

"That is a serious crime," Tom said. "And if it is true, he deserves to die. But what evidence is there that he committed this crime?"

The sheriff replied, "He went to the house of a sick old man. Shortly after he left, the man died. And he died in a way that showed he had been poisoned."

Tom asked, "Did anyone see this man poison the other man?"

"No, Your Highness," the sheriff said.

"Then you don't have very good evidence against this man."

"There is more evidence," the sheriff said. "A witch said that the man would die of poison and that he would be poisoned by a stranger who wore a brown coat."

Tom said, "I suppose that this is the only man in England who has a brown coat."

The judges and lords smiled at Tom's comments. Hertford turned to the lord standing next to him and whispered, "This lad has not lost his wits. His questions are brilliant." Ⓓ ★10 ERRORS★

Tom continued, "Do you have evidence that this is the kind of man who would take the life of another?"

The sheriff stammered, "Well, not exactly, Your Highness, but we don't have evidence that he wouldn't take the life of another."

Tom turned to the man, who was trembling and kneeling, with his head bowed. Tom asked, "Is that true? Can you give us any evidence that you would not take a life?"

"My king," he said without looking up. "On New Year's Day I saved the life of a youth that had fallen into the river. And I . . ."

"You are free," Tom announced. Tom was surprised that his announcement was followed by loud applause from the lords and judges in the room.

One of the judges said, "The king is brilliant."

Next, the woman was brought before Tom. The sheriff explained that she was charged with being a witch. She was accused of causing a great storm that destroyed many houses in a poor neighborhood of the city. Tom looked at the poor sobbing woman who knelt before him and asked, "And how did she become a witch?"

"She and her daughter made a contract with a sorceress. The contract gave her the power to make such storms," the sheriff replied.

Tom quickly fired two questions at the sheriff. First, he asked if the woman lived in the neighborhood that was wrecked by the storm. The sheriff said that she did. Next, Tom asked if her house had been destroyed by the storm. The sheriff said that it had. Then Tom concluded, "It

---

EXERCISE 5   Decoding and comprehension

1. Everybody, turn to page 396 in your textbook. *Wait. Call on a student.* What's the error limit for this chapter? **10 errors.**

2. *Call on individual students to read. Present the tasks specified for each circled letter.*

Ⓐ What was missing? *Idea:* The royal seal.
● Why was the seal important? *Idea:* It was used to make papers from the king official. The seal plays a very important part in this novel.

Ⓑ What caused the disturbance outside the gates of the palace? *Idea:* A crowd of people.
● Who did Tom send to find out what was going on? **His page.**
● When the page returned, he told Tom about the problem. What was the problem? *Idea:* Three people were accused of committing crimes.
● What did Tom order? *Idea:* To bring the three people to him.

Ⓒ What event had Tom remembered? *Idea:* The man had saved a boy from drowning.

Ⓓ The sheriff brought three people to Tom. Which person did Tom deal with first? **The man.**
● What crime was he accused of? *Idea:* Poisoning someone.
● The sheriff said a witch had predicted that the sick man would be poisoned by a stranger who wore a brown coat. How did Tom reply to this piece of evidence? *Idea:* Tom didn't think that the man was the only person in England with a brown coat.
● How many people in London do you think had brown coats? *Idea:* Many people.
● What did the judges and Hertford think of Tom's questions? *Idea:* That they were brilliant.
● Read the rest of the chapter to yourselves and be ready to answer some questions.

After all students have finished reading:
● What evidence did the man give that he was not the kind of person who would take a life? *Idea:* That he saved a drowning boy.
● So what did Tom declare? *Idea:* That the man was free.
● And how did the lords and judges respond? *Idea:* They applauded.
● Who was the next person Tom dealt with? **The woman.**
● What crime was she accused of? *Idea:* Being a witch.
● The sheriff said that she had made a contract with somebody. Who? **A sorceress.**
● What power was the sorceress supposed to have given her? *Idea:* The power to make storms.

seems as if she made a very bad deal with the sorceress, then. After she made the contract, she destroyed her own house." Again, the lords and judges applauded.

Tom continued, "Tell me what does she do to make such terrible storms?"

"She takes off her stockings, Your Highness."

Tom looked at the kneeling woman and said, "First, you are freed of all charges. Now that you are free, I want you to make a great storm for the sheriff. Take off your stockings."

The woman pleaded with Tom and explained that she had no such power. Tom explained that if she could make a storm, he would make her rich. The woman took off her stockings and obviously tried as hard as she could to create a thunderstorm or an earthquake. But she didn't even produce a cloud in the sky. The judges again applauded.

Finally, the woman's nine year old daughter was brought before Tom. The girl was accused of making a contract with the sorceress. Tom asked one of the judges if the law in England permitted children of nine years old to enter into contracts.

"No, Your Highness," the judge replied. "Children cannot make legal contracts. Only the contracts made by adults are legal."

Tom stood up and said, "This child is English and English children cannot make contracts. Therefore, I cannot see how this child could enter into a contract that is legal. She is free."

Again the lords and judges applauded. A judge said to Hertford, "The new king has more wisdom than most lawyers and judges."

• • •

Tom was supposed to eat in public that evening. Hertford and the other lords felt that it was important for the King to be seen so that there would not be rumors about his failing mind. Tom knew about this problem from Humphry, his whipping boy. Tom had dreaded the idea of eating in public, but after his experience earlier that day, he had great confidence.

That evening, Tom made a short speech at the beginning of the meal, welcoming the ladies and gentlemen to the palace. And he was quite comfortable and relaxed throughout the dinner. After the meal was over, he overheard people saying, "There is nothing wrong with our new king. He is gracious and very intelligent."

- Tom asked a question to show that the storm did not really help the woman. What did he ask? *Idea:* If the woman's house had been destroyed.
- What did the sheriff say that the woman did to create such storms? *Idea:* Took her stockings off.
- So what did Tom tell the woman after he freed her? *Idea:* To take her stockings off.
- How much of a storm did she create by taking off her stockings? *Idea:* None.
- Next Tom dealt with the last person in the group. Who was this person? *Idea:* A little girl.
- What crime was she accused of? *Idea:* Making a contract with a sorceress.
- Tom asked the judge something about contracts. What did he ask? *Idea:* If it was legal for children to make contracts.
  So, if the girl was supposed to have made a contract with a sorceress that contract was not legal.
- How did the lords and judges respond to the way that Tom handled this problem? *Idea:* They applauded.
- What did Tom do later that evening? *Idea:* Ate in public.
- How did he behave? *Idea:* Very nicely. He's learning to act like a king.
- What did the people at the meal say about the young king? *Ideas:* That there wasn't anything wrong with him.

Award 4 points or have the students reread to the error limit sign.

INDEPENDENT WORK

Do all the items in your skillbook and workbook for lesson 108.

ANSWER KEY FOR WORKBOOK

Outlining

The outline below shows three main ideas for Brown Wolf.

Write three supporting details for each main idea.

1. Brown Wolf was an unusual dog. *Idea*:
   a. He never barked.

   b. He always ran north.

   c. He was very unfriendly.

2. Skiff Miller tried to prove that Brown Wolf was his dog.
   a. Brown Wolf barked for him.
   b. Brown Wolf was friendly to him.
   c. Brown Wolf followed his commands.

3. Brown Wolf made a difficult decision.
   a. He tried to stop Skiff.
   b. He tried to make the Irvines follow Skiff.
   c. He finally ran after Skiff.

Story Items

4. If Tom wants to convince everybody that he is not crazy, he will have to stop doing certain things. Here are some things that Tom might do. Write **stop** after the things that Tom should not do.

   a. Acting as a judge. _____
   b. Answering questions about his
      past. ___*stop*___
   c. Eating dinner in public.

   d. Letting servants dress him. _____
   _____

WORKCHECK AND AWARDING POINTS

1. *Read the questions and answers for the skillbook and workbook.*

2. *Award points for independent work as follows:*

0 errors	6 points
2 errors	4 points
3, 4, or 5 errors	2 points
5 or more errors	0 points

3. *Award bonus points as follows:*

Correcting missed items or getting all items right	2 points
Doing the writing assignment acceptably	2 points

ANSWER KEY FOR SKILLBOOK

PART D

1. a. *Idea:* Official papers
   b. official
   c. Hertford
2. a. A man
   b. *Idea:* Save a boy from drowning
   c. *Idea:* Poisoning a man
   d. *Idea:* The dead man's house
   e. *Idea:* The man in the house died
   f. No
   g. *Idea:* A brown coat
   h. *Idea:* Set him free
3. a. A woman
   b. witch
   c. A storm
   d. *Idea:* By taking off her stocking
   e. *Idea:* To prove that she couldn't start storms that way
   f. Nothing
   g. *Idea:* That she had none
4. a. A little girl
   b. Nine
   c. A sorceress
   d. Yes
   e. *Idea:* English children couldn't make contracts
   f. *Idea:* It wasn't legal
   g. *Ideas:* They applauded; said he was very wise

PART E

5. a. retreat
   b. withdraw
   c. assist
   d. article of clothing
   e. suspicious
   f. mend
   g. shattered
   h. ordeal
   i. drowsy
   j. take advantage
   k. mourn

Lesson 109

Lesson 109

PART A   Word Lists

1	2
daylight	**New vocabulary**
fingernails	1. charred
innkeeper	2. sling
background	

PART B   New Vocabulary

1. **charred**—Wood that has been badly burned is **charred** wood.
   - Houses that are badly burned are _____.

2. **sling**—A **sling** is a loop of cloth that you put your arm in when it is injured.
   - What do we call a loop of cloth that you put an injured arm in?

PART C   Vocabulary Review

> official
> evidence
> suspicious
> conduct business
> drowsy
> mourn
> seal
> misplaced

1. A tool that puts a special design on a piece of paper is a _____.
2. When you do business, you _____.
3. Facts that make you conclude something are _____.

4. **a.** If you don't remember where you put something, you have _____ that thing.
   b. If you don't remember where you put your shoes, you have _____.
   c. If you don't remember where you put your keys, you have _____.

5. **a.** If rules come from an office that can make the rules, the rules are _____.
   b. A rule coming from the office of the President is an _____ rule.
   c. A rule coming from a court of law is an _____.

WORD PRACTICE AND VOCABULARY

EXERCISE 1   Word family

1. Everybody, find lesson 109, part A in your skillbook. *Wait.*
2. Column 1. All those words are made up of two shorter words.
3. Your turn. Read the first word. *Signal.* **Daylight.**
4. Next word. *Signal.* **Fingernails.**
5. *Repeat step 4 for each remaining word in column 1.*
6. *Repeat the words in column 1 until firm.*

EXERCISE 2   Vocabulary development

Task A
1. Column 2. New vocabulary.
   First you're going to read the words in column 2. Then you're going to read about what they mean.
2. Read the first word. *Signal.* **Charred.**
3. Next word. *Signal.* **Sling.**

Task B
1. Everybody, look at part B.
   You're going to read this part out loud.
2. *For each item, call on a student to:*
   - *read one item aloud*
   - *read the meaning*
   - *read the question(s) for that item*
   - *answer each question orally*

   Answer Key: **1. charred houses**
   2. A sling

EXERCISE 3   Vocabulary review

1. Everybody, look at part C. The words in the box are words you've learned.
2. Read the first word. *Signal.* **Official.**
3. Next. *Signal.* **Evidence.**
4. *Repeat step 3 for the remaining words in the box.*
5. *Repeat the words in the box until firm.*
6. I'll read the items. When I come to a blank, everybody say the part that goes in the blank.
7. Look at item 1. *Pause.* Listen.
   A tool that puts a special design on a piece of paper is a *Pause.* *Signal.* **seal.**
8. *Repeat step 7 for each remaining item.*

   Answer Key: **2. conduct business**
   3. evidence
   4. a. misplaced
   b. misplaced your shoes
   c. misplaced your keys
   5. a. official
   b. official
   c. official rule

STORY READING

EXERCISE 4   Narrative poem

1. Everybody, turn to page 442 in your textbook.
2. Everybody, read the first two stanzas out loud.
   The students read the first two stanzas aloud.

The Spider and the Fly
by Mary Howitt

"Will you walk into my parlor?" said the Spider to the Fly,
"'Tis the prettiest little parlor that ever you did spy;
The way into my parlor is up a winding stair,
And I've many curious things to show when you are there."
"Oh, no, no," said the little Fly, "to ask me is in vain,
For who goes up your winding stair can ne'er come down again."

"I'm sure you must be weary, dear, with soaring up so high;
Will you rest upon my little bed?" said the Spider to the Fly.
"There are pretty curtains drawn around; the sheets are fine and thin,
And if you like to rest a while, I'll snugly tuck you in!"
"Oh, no, no," said the little Fly, "for I've often heard it said,
They never, never wake again, who sleep upon your bed!"

Said the cunning Spider to the Fly, "Dear friend, what can I do
To prove the warm affection I've always felt for you?
I have within my pantry good store of all that's nice;
I'm sure you're very welcome—will you please to take a slice?"
"Oh no, no," said the little Fly, "kind sir, that cannot be;
I've heard what's in your pantry, and I do not wish to see!"

"Sweet creature," said the Spider, "you're witty and you're wise,
How handsome are your pearly wings, how brilliant are your eyes!
I have a little looking-glass upon my parlor shelf,
If you'll step in one moment, dear, you shall behold yourself."
"I thank you, gentle sir," she said, "for what you're pleased to say,
And bidding you good morning now, I'll call another day."

Lesson 109

CHAPTER 12
The King in the Barn (A)

Miles Hendon wormed his way along the bridge, asking questions about two youths and a ruffian. He was able to track the three past the bridge and into a crowded part of London, but then he lost the track. By now it was night. Miles was tired, hungry, and discouraged. He had supper at an inn and began to think about how he could find Edward. He figured out that the boy might be able to escape from the man who claimed to be his father. But the boy probably wouldn't return to London Bridge. Miles recalled that he had told Edward about his old home, Hendon Hall. He figured that Edward would try to reach him at Hendon Hall.(B) So he resolved to go to Hendon Hall and wait. He would start out on his journey immediately and ask questions along the way. Perhaps he would learn about where the boy was.(C)

As Miles started out on his journey, Edward was not far away. He was in a charred and deserted barn.(D) The youth that had come to Miles's room had led Edward away from the bridge. John Canty had not actually joined Edward and the youth, but had stayed a few steps behind, wearing a disguise. His left arm was in a sling, and he wore a large green patch over his left eye; he walked with a limp and used an oak stick for support.

After leaving the bridge, the two boys had taken a crooked course through a crowded part of town, past the inn where Miles would later eat.(E)

At last Edward became impatient. After all, Miles should have come to him. Edward should not be expected to go to Miles. "I'm not going any farther," he said to the youth.

The youth replied, "Your friend is lying wounded in the woods not far from here. You can stay here if you want, but . . ."

"Wounded?" Edward cried out. "Who wounded him?" Before the youth could answer, Edward exclaimed, "It doesn't matter. Move on, quickly!"

Although the woods were fairly far away, Edward and the youth covered the distance very quickly. After a while, they reached an open place, where there was a charred farmhouse, nearly burnt to the ground, and a barn that was partly burned and almost falling over from ruin. There was no sign of life anywhere, and the air was strangely silent. The youth led the way into the barn, with Edward following eagerly. No one was inside. Edward shot a suspicious glance at the youth and asked,

---

3. Listen to the first two lines of the third stanza.
**Said the cunning Spider to the Fly,
"Dear Friend, what can I do
To prove the warm affection I've always felt for you?"**
- Everybody, say those lines with me.
Read aloud with the students.
- What is **affection?** *Idea:* Love.
The spider is telling the fly that he's always had a great love for the fly.

4. Listen to the next two lines.
**"I have within my pantry good store of all that's nice;
I'm sure you're very welcome—will you please to take a slice?"**
- Everybody, say those lines with me.
Read aloud with the students.
- A pantry is a place where food is kept. The spider is offering the fly a slice of some nice food.

5. Listen to the next two lines.
**"Oh, no, no" said the little Fly, "kind sir, that cannot be;
I've heard what's in your pantry, and I do not wish to see!"**
- Everybody, say those lines with me.
Read aloud with the students.
- What do you think happens to anybody who goes into the spider's pantry? *Idea:* They don't come out.

6. Everybody, let's read the whole third stanza.
Read aloud with the students.

7. We'll read the next stanza in the next lesson.

STORY READING

EXERCISE 5   Decoding and comprehension

1. Everybody, turn to page 400 in your textbook. *Wait. Call on a student.* What's the error limit for this chapter? **8 errors.**

2. *Call on individual students to read. Present the tasks specified for each circled letter.*

(A) Where did we leave Tom at the end of the last chapter? *Idea:* He was eating dinner.
- Where was the last place that we left Miles Hendon? *Idea:* On London Bridge, looking for Edward.

(B) How long did Miles Hendon search for Edward before giving up? *Idea:* All day.
- Miles figured out what Edward would try to do. He would try to escape from John Canty. Would he go back to London Bridge? **No.**
- What place had Miles told Edward about? **Hendon Hall.**
- So what did Miles figure that Edward would try to do after he escaped? *Idea:* Go to Hendon Hall.

(C) Where was Miles going? **Hendon Hall.**

"Where is he?"

The youth answered with a mocking laugh. Edward became very angry. He picked up a large stick and was ready to attack the youth when more mocking laughter came from the barn door. Edward turned to the laughing ruffian and asked, "Who are you?"

"Stop this nonsense," John Canty said. "My disguise is not so good that you can't recognize your own father." (F)

★8 ERRORS★

"You're not my father," Edward insisted. "You have hidden my servant, Miles Hendon. Tell me where he is at once."

John Canty replied in a stern voice, "It is plain that you are mad, so I won't punish you. But don't continue with your pretending or I'll lose my temper. There's nobody around here to pay attention to your silly games, so stop play acting."

John Canty moved forward and stared into Edward's face for a moment. Then he continued, "I'm in serious trouble. I owe a lot of money to some rough seamen. They're after me, so I've changed my name. I am now Hobbs—John Hobbs. And your new name is Jack. You're always pretending. Now's your chance to do some real pretending, Jack."

Edward did not reply. He simply stared back at John Canty.

John Canty asked, "Now tell me. Where are your mother and your sisters? They didn't come to the place where they were supposed to meet me. What do you know about them?"

Edward answered solemnly, "My mother and my sister are in the royal palace."

The youth burst into laughter and started to imitate Edward. "My mother and my sister . . ."

"Stop it, Hugo!" John Canty interrupted. "There's no point in angering him. His mind is confused." Then John Canty said to Edward, "Sit down, Jack, and be quiet. We'll have a bite to eat in a while."

John Canty and Hugo began talking together in low voices, and Edward went to the far side of the barn, where he found a pile of straw. He lay down, covered himself with some straw and began to think. He was full of sorrow, but the greatest sorrow was the loss of his father. To the rest of the world, the name of Henry the Eighth brought a shiver and suggested a monster who breathed destruction and death. But to this boy, the name brought fond memories of gentleness. Edward remembered some of his experiences with his father, and tears formed in his eyes.

Edward squeezed his eyes shut to try to escape from his sadness, and he sank gradually into a deep sleep. When he woke up, he was aware of rain pattering on the roof of the old barn. For a moment he felt very snug in his bed of straw, but a moment later, his mood was broken by a loud shriek of laughter and cackling. He looked up to see who was laughing.

A bright fire was burning in the middle of the floor and around it was the most incredible company of ruffians that Ed-

Lesson 109 Textbook **401**

ward could ever have imagined. They were sprawled out around the fire, which cast a red glare on them and made them look even more frightening. There were huge men in tattered rags, with long hair hanging down their backs. There were middle-sized youths with sour expressions. There were blind beggars with bandaged eyes and crippled beggars with wooden legs and crutches. There was a peddler, a knife-grinder, and a filthy doctor. There were old wrinkled women, young women, girls, and three sore-faced babies. There were even three dogs with strings around their necks so they could lead the blind.

Edward stared blankly at this astonishing group and said to himself, "I can't believe it."

402 Lesson 109 Textbook

- Why was he going there? *Idea:* To meet Edward.
- What was he going to do along the way? *Idea:* Ask questions.
- (D) Where was Edward? *Idea:* In a barn.
- Where was Miles? *Idea:* On his way to Hendon Hall.
- (E) Did Edward know that the youth was not really a messenger from Miles Hendon? **No.**
- Did he know that Tom's father was following them? **No.**
- Why didn't he recognize Tom's father? *Idea:* Because he was in disguise.
- (F) Where did the youth take Edward? *Idea:* To a barn in the forest.
- Describe the barn. *Idea:* It was charred and falling down.
- When they got inside the barn, who laughed from the barn door? *Idea:* John Canty.
- Read the rest of the chapter to yourselves and be ready to answer some questions.

After all students have finished reading:

- John Canty gave himself and Edward new names. Why did he do that? *Idea:* Some people were after John Canty because he owed money.
- What name did John Canty give himself? **John Hobbs.**
- What name did John Canty give Edward? **Jack.**
- What was the name of the youth who brought Edward to the barn? **Hugo.**
- Where did Edward go so that he would not have to be close to John Canty and Hugo? *Idea:* To the other side of the barn.
- What person did Edward think about just before he fell asleep? *Ideas:* His father; King Henry the Eighth.
- How did Edward feel about that person? *Idea:* Sad.
- How had the rest of the world felt about Henry the Eighth? *Idea:* They feared and hated him.
- Had Henry the Eighth been cruel to Edward? **No.**
- When Edward woke up, he heard a pattering sound. What made that sound? *Idea:* Rain.
- Then he heard harsh laughter. Describe some of the people who were in the barn. *Call on individual students. Accept appropriate answers.*
- The chapter says that Edward stared blankly at this astonishing group. What does that mean: **stared blankly?** *Idea:* Stared in a shocked manner.
- What did Edward say to himself after he looked at this group? **I can't believe it.**

Award 4 points or have the students reread to the error limit sign.

ANSWER KEY FOR WORKBOOK

Main Idea and Supporting Details

Read this passage:

Michi and Fumiko got off the subway and started walking toward the baseball park. It was a beautiful Saturday afternoon. They decided to sit behind first base, because they liked watching the first baseman. During the next three hours, they saw one home run and two triples. They cheered when their team won the game. Michi and Fumiko had a great time.

Write the main idea and three supporting details. *Idea:*

1. *On Saturday, Michi and Fumiko watched a baseball game.*
   a. *They sat behind first base.*
   b. *They saw a home run and two triples.*
   c. *They cheered when their team won.*

Story Items

2. Write whether each statement describes **Edward**, **Hugo**, or **John Canty**.
   a. His new name was John Hobbs.

   John Canty

   b. He had been tricked.

   Edward

   c. He had delivered a fake message.

   Hugo

   d. He thought his son was crazy.

   John Canty

Review Items

3. Put the following events in the right order by numbering them from 1 through 4.

   _4_ Edward was tricked into following somebody.
   _1_ Edward let Tom into the palace.
   _3_ Edward stayed at an inn.
   _2_ Edward was thrown out of the palace.

INDEPENDENT WORK

Do all the items in your skillbook and workbook for lesson 109.

WORKCHECK AND AWARDING POINTS

1. *Read the questions and answers for the skillbook and workbook.*
2. *Award points for independent work as follows:*

0 errors	6 points
2 errors	4 points
3, 4, or 5 errors	2 points
5 or more errors	0 points

3. *Award bonus points as follows:*

Correcting missed items or getting all items right	2 points
Doing the writing assignment acceptably	2 points

ANSWER KEY FOR SKILLBOOK

PART D

1. **a.** Miles Hendon
   b. *Idea:* At an inn
   c. Hendon Hall
   d. Hendon Hall
2. **a.** John Canty
   b. *Idea:* He was wearing a disguise
   c. *Idea:* That he was lying wounded in the woods
   d. A barn
   e. *Ideas:* Poor; charred
   f. No
   g. John Canty
   h. *Ideas:* His son; Tom
3. **a.** Some seamen
   b. He owed them money
   c. *Idea:* To fool them
   d. John Hobbs
   e. Jack
   f. Hugo
4. **a.** *Ideas:* Sad; he loved him
   b. *Ideas:* They hated him; feared him
5. **a.** Rain
   b. Laughing
   c. *Idea:* A bright fire
   d. *Any two:* Huge men in rags; middle-sized youth; blind beggars; cripples; a peddlar; a dirty doctor; old women; girls; young women
   e. *Idea:* He couldn't believe it

PART E

6. **a.** mourn
   b. assist
   c. drowsy
   d. seal
   e. evidence
   f. official
   g. misplaced
   h. shattered
   i. garment
   j. conduct business
   k. ordeal
   l. withdraw
   m. vast

Lesson 110

Lesson 110

PART A   Word Lists

1	2	3	4	5
vagrant	eyesight	cross	**New vocabulary**	**New vocabulary**
capable	whirlwind	crisscross	1. capable of	6. vagrant
hurriedly	thundergust	string	2. brawl	7. burly
barrel	outskirts	stringy	3. brand	8. chant
	farmhouse	accident	4. prosper	9. limb
	clothesline	accidental	5. lash	
	overcast	accidentally		

PART B   New Vocabulary

1. **capable of**—If you are able to do something, you are **capable of** doing that thing. If you are able to swim, you are **capable of** swimming.
   a. If you are able to ride a horse, you are _____.
   b. If you are able to read, you are
   _____.

2. **brawl**—Another word for a **rough fight** is a **brawl**.
   • What's another word for a **rough fight**?

3. **brand**—When you **brand** an animal, you take a hot iron and press it against the animal, so that it leaves a mark that won't go away.

4. **prosper**—When you **prosper**, you earn money and do well.
   • What's another way of saying

PART C   Vocabulary Review

official
sling
evidence
garment
charred

She earned money and did well?

5. **lash**—Another word for **whip** is **lash**.
   • What's another way of saying **The man whipped his horse**.

6. **vagrant**—A **vagrant** is a person who does not have any place to live and has no job.
   • What do we call a person who does not have any place to live and has no job?

7. **burly**—Another word for **stout and strong** is **burly**.
   • What's another way of saying **He was a stout and strong man**?

8. **chant**—When you say the same thing over and over, you **chant** that thing.

9. **limb**—A **limb** is an **arm** or a **leg**.
   • What's an **arm** or a **leg**?
   • What's another word for an **arm** or a **leg**?

1. a. Houses that are badly burned are _____ houses.
   b. Wood that has been badly burned is _____.

2. A loop of cloth that you put your arm in when it is injured is called a _____.

WORD PRACTICE AND VOCABULARY

EXERCISE 1   Word practice

1. Everybody, find lesson 110, part A in your skillbook. *Wait.* Touch under each word in column 1 as I read it.
2. The first word is **vagrant.**
3. Next word. **Capable.**
4. *Repeat step 3 for each remaining word in column 1.*
5. Your turn. Read the first word. *Signal.* **Vagrant.**
6. Next word. *Signal.* **Capable.**
7. *Repeat step 6 for each remaining word in column 1.*
8. *Repeat the words in column 1 until firm.*

EXERCISE 2   Word family

1. Column 2. All those words are made up of two shorter words.
2. Your turn. Read the first word. *Signal.* **Eyesight.**
3. Next word. *Signal.* **Whirlwind.**
4. *Repeat step 3 for each remaining word in column 2.*
5. *Repeat the words in column 2 until firm.*

EXERCISE 3   Word practice

1. Column 3.
2. Your turn. Read the first word. *Signal.* **Cross.**
3. Next word. *Signal.* **Crisscross.**
4. *Repeat step 3 for each remaining word in column 3.*
5. *Repeat the words in column 3 until firm.*

EXERCISE 4   Vocabulary development

Task A

1. Columns 4 and 5. New vocabulary.
   First you're going to read the words in columns 4 and 5. Then you're going to read about what they mean.
2. Read the first line. *Signal.* **Capable of.**
3. Next word. *Signal.* **Brawl.**
4. *Repeat step 3 for each remaining word in columns 4 and 5.*
5. *Repeat the words in columns 4 and 5 until firm.*

Task B

1. Everybody, look at part B.
   You're going to read this part out loud.
2. *For each item, call on a student to:*
   • *read one item aloud*
   • *read the meaning*
   • *read the question(s) for that item*
   • *answer each question orally*

   Answer Key: **1. a. capable of riding a horse**
   b. capable of reading
   2. A brawl
   3. *No answer required.*
   4. She prospered.
   5. The man lashed his horse.
   6. A vagrant
   7. He was a burly man.
   8. *No answer required.*
   9. Limb

EXERCISE 5   Vocabulary review

1. Everybody, look at part C. The words in the box are words you've learned.
2. Read the first word. *Signal.* **Official.**
3. Next. *Signal.* **Sling.**
4. *Repeat step 3 for the remaining words in the box.*
5. *Repeat the words in the box until firm.*
6. I'll read the items. When I come to a blank, everybody say the part that goes in the blank.
7. Look at item 1a. *Pause.* Listen.
   Houses that are badly burned are *Pause.* *Signal.* **charred** houses.
8. *Repeat step 7 for each remaining item.*

   Answer Key: **1. b. charred wood**
   2. sling

STORY READING

EXERCISE 6   Narrative poem

1. Everybody, turn to page 442 in your textbook.
2. Everybody, read the first three stanzas out loud.
   The students read the first three stanzas aloud.
3. Listen to the first two lines of the fourth stanza. **"Sweet creature," said the Spider, "You're witty and you're wise, How handsome are your pearly wings, how brilliant are your eyes'."**
   - Everybody, say those lines with me.
     Read aloud with the students.
   - The spider is trying to flatter the fly by saying that the fly has pearly wings.
     Things that are pearly are white, with many other soft colors.
4. Listen to the next two lines.
   "I have a little looking-glass upon my parlor shelf, If you'll step in one moment, dear, you shall behold yourself."
   - Everybody, say those lines with me.
     Read aloud with the students.
   - Who is talking in these lines? **The spider.**
   - What does the spider say he has that might tempt the fly? *Idea:* A looking-glass.
   - What does **behold yourself** mean? *Idea:* See yourself.
     The spider said how beautiful the fly is. Now he is inviting her to look at herself.
5. Listen to the next two lines.
   "I thank you, gentle sir," she said, "for what you're pleased to say, And bidding you good morning now, I'll call another day."
   - Everybody, say those lines with me.
     Read aloud with the students.
   - When you bid somebody good morning, you say "good morning" to that person.
6. Everybody, let's read the whole fourth stanza together. *Read aloud with the students.*
7. We'll read the next stanza in the next lesson.

Lesson 110

CHAPTER 13
Foo Foo the First

As the night continued the gang started to make merry. Ⓐ The ragged group shouted and cackled and sang loud songs. One of the blind men got up and took off the patches that covered his excellent eyes. Ⓑ He tossed aside the sign that told how he had lost his eyesight. Ⓒ Another member of the gang removed a wooden leg. Underneath was a perfectly healthy limb. Ⓓ The blind man and the man with the wooden leg joined with the others in roaring out the words of a peppy song.

Conversations followed the singing. These conversations made it clear that John Canty was not a new member of the gang but that he had trained and worked with this gang at some earlier time. Somebody asked what he had been doing lately, and he said that he had become mixed up with some very rough seamen. Some of them were murderers. Canty had owed them money and when he didn't pay, they started looking for him. He feared that if they caught him they would throw him into the river with a weight tied to his feet, or send him to the other side of the world in the belly of a sailing ship. Ⓔ

Canty was asked why he had been away from the gang so many months. He answered, "London is better than the country, and safer lately because they are very strict with the laws in the country, but not in London. I would have continued to

Lesson 110   Textbook   **403**

stay there if there weren't so many seamen in London. Every time I saw a seaman, my heart would jump. I decided that it would be better to take my chances in the country." Ⓕ

Canty asked how many people were now in the gang. The chief of the gang answered. He was a large and powerful man who was called the Ruffler. "Twenty-five," the Ruffler answered, "If you count everybody. Most of them are here, but some of them are already moving eastward. We will follow the same route in the morning."

Canty said, "I do not see the Wen here. Where is he?"

The Ruffler replied, "Dead. He was killed in a brawl, sometime last summer."

"That makes me very sorry," Canty replied. "The Wen was a capable man and very brave."

"That's true," the Ruffler said. "His wife is gone, too. She was put to death by the law. But she was brave to the end."

Canty nodded thoughtfully. The Ruffler sighed. The other listeners sighed in sympathy. After a moment, Canty asked, "Have any more of our friends had a hard time?"

"Some," the Ruffler replied. "Particularly newcomers from the country. You know what they do to beggars in the country. They whipped them the first time they caught them begging. Some of them begged again. What else could they do if they had no other way to keep from starving? And when they were caught the sec-

ond time, they were branded on the cheek with a red-hot iron and sold for slaves. If they tried to run away, they were hunted down and hanged." Ⓖ ★9 ERRORS★

The Ruffler called out, "Yokel Burns, show your decorations."

A man stood up and stripped away some of his rags. He showed his back, which was crisscrossed with thick old scars left by a whip. There was also a large V that had been branded on his shoulder. The man said, "I am Yokel. Once I was a farmer who prospered. I had a loving wife and kids. Now, you can see that I am different. My wife and kids are gone. They are lucky because they do not have to live in England any more. My mother tried to earn a little bread by nursing the sick. One of the people she nursed died, and the doctors did not know why. So they put her in prison."

Yokel shook his head and yelled loudly, "English law! Let's cheer for that fine English law!" His voice was bitter as he continued. "After I could not farm, I started to beg. But you know that it's against English law to beg. The wife and I went from house to house with our hungry kids until they caught us. They lashed us through three towns. Another cheer for English law! My wife died after the last lashing. And my kids starved. Those kids never harmed any creature, but they are gone. Then I begged again, just for a crust of bread. When they caught me, I was sold for a slave. I have a brand on my cheek. It's a large letter S. A slave. Do you understand that word? I am an English <u>slave</u>,

404   Lesson 110   Textbook

1. Everybody, turn to page 403 in your textbook. *Wait. Call on a student.* What's the error limit for this chapter? **9 errors.**

2. *Call on individual students to read. Present the tasks specified for each circled letter.*

Ⓐ What kind of people are in the gang? *Idea:* Criminals and ruffians.

● What does that mean? **The gang started to make merry?** *Idea:* They started to laugh and sing.

Ⓑ What kind of eyes did he have? **Excellent.**

● So was he really blind? **No.**

Ⓒ Did that sign tell the truth? **No.**

Ⓓ What was wrong with this man's leg? *Idea:* Nothing.

Ⓔ Who had John Canty become mixed up with? **Some seamen.**

● What did he fear they would do if they caught him? *Idea:* Throw him in the river or send him to the other side of the world.

● Why were they after him? *Idea:* Because he owed them money.

Ⓕ Where is it usually safer for a person like John Canty, **in the city** or **in the country?** **In the city.**

● Why did John Canty decide to leave the city? *Idea:* Because there were so many seamen in London.

Ⓖ What happened to people who were caught begging for the first time in the country? *Idea:* They were whipped.

● What if they were caught begging again? *Idea:* They were branded and sold for slaves.

● What if they tried to run away? *Idea:* They were hunted down and hanged.

● Read the rest of the chapter to yourselves and be ready to answer some questions.

After all students have finished reading:

● Yokel told his story. What kind of work had he done before he became a beggar? **Farming.**

● What happened to his mother? *Idea:* She was put in prison.

● What happened to his wife? **She died.**

● What happened to his children? *Idea:* They starved.

● What happened to Yokel after he was caught begging? *Idea:* He was branded and sold as a slave.

and when I am found, I shall hang. Another cheer for English law!"

A ringing voice came through the gloomy air. "You shall not hang," the voice announced. "And I order an end to that law today."

Everybody turned and saw the fantastic figure of the little king approaching hurriedly. As Edward moved into the light an explosion of questions broke out. "Who is it? What is it?"

The boy stood determined in the middle of those surprised and questioning eyes. He answered their questions. "I am Edward, King of England."

A wild burst of laughter followed. Some laughed to mock, but others were laughing over the excellent joke. Edward was stung by the laughter, and said sharply, "You vagrants! Is this the way you respond to your king?" Edward continued to speak with an angry voice and excited gestures, but his words were lost in a whirlwind of laughter and mocking exclamations.

John Canty made several attempts to make himself heard above the noise, and at last he succeeded. He said, "Mates, this is my son, a dreamer and a fool. He's mad, so don't pay any attention to him. He thinks he really is the king."

"I am the king!" said Edward, turning toward Canty. "And you will be punished for your crimes."

"You would turn against your father?" Canty said as he sprang forward. "Wait till I get my hands on you!"

"Tut, tut," the burly Ruffler replied, stepping in just in time to save the king. The Ruffler knocked Canty down with his fist and continued, "You have no respect for the king nor for the Ruffler." The Ruffler then turned to Edward and said, "You must not threaten any of the mates here, lad. You can be king if you want to. And there is no one in this group that would be against the king. So, long live Edward, King of England."

The chant was taken up by the others. It came like thunder from the ragged crew. It was so loud that the building vibrated to the sound. Edward's face lighted with pleasure for an instant and then he said, "I thank you, my good people."

Edward's comment was followed by an explosion of laughter. The whole company wriggled with delight. After they quieted down, the Ruffler said firmly to Edward, "Drop it boy. It is not wise to be Edward. Choose some other title for your act."

Someone from the company shrieked out a suggestion, "Foo Foo the First, King of the Moon." The title caught on and a moment later, every throat responded, and a roaring shout went up. "Long live Foo Foo the First, King of the Moon."

Almost before Edward could draw a breath, he was robed in a tattered blanket, and throned on a barrel. His hand was holding an old iron rod, the wand of Foo Foo the First. Then the company proceeded to make fun of Edward with their mocking statements. "Oh, noble king," they cried, "have mercy on us poor worms."

One old beggar pretended to kiss Edward's foot. Edward kicked him. The beggar quickly got up and asked for a rag to cover the part of his face that had been touched by the foot of the great king. He said, "The air must not touch this precious spot on my face." The mob roared with delight.

Tears of shame and anger were in Edward's eyes. He said, "I did nothing to hurt them. I tried to help them, but see how they respond to my kindness."

- What did Edward do after he heard Yokel's story? *Idea:* He said he would change the law.
- How did the gang respond when Edward announced who he was? *Idea:* They laughed and mocked him.
- What did Edward say that angered John Canty? *Idea:* That John Canty would be punished for his crimes.
- Who saved Edward from John Canty? **The Ruffler.**
- What new title did the gang give to Edward? **Foo-foo the First, King of the Moon.**
- Name some of the things they did to make Edward look like a king. *Ideas:* Robed him in a blanket; gave him an iron wand; put him on a barrel throne.
- What did they use for a robe? *Idea:* A blanket.
- Everybody, look at the picture. It shows the king in his robe, sitting on a barrel.
- What happened when one beggar pretended to kiss Edward's foot? *Idea:* Edward kicked him.
- Then what did the beggar do to mock Edward? *Idea:* He pretended that the kick made a precious mark on his face.

Award 4 points or have the students reread to the error limit sign.

INDEPENDENT WORK

Do all the items in your skillbook and workbook for lesson 110.

ANSWER KEY FOR WORKBOOK

Main Idea and Supporting Details

Read this passage:

Beauty entered the cave and saw the Beast, sound asleep. She was glad to have found him at last. She ran up and stroked his head, but to her horror he did not move or open his eyes.

"Oh, he is dead, and it is all my fault," said Beauty, crying bitterly.

But then she looked at him again and saw that he was still breathing. Beauty got some water from the nearest fountain and sprinkled it over the Beast's face. To her great delight, he opened his eyes and woke up.

Write the main idea and three supporting details. *Idea*:

1. *Beauty saved the Beast's life.*
   a. *She found him asleep in the cave.*
   b. *She got some water.*
   c. *She sprinkled the water on him.*

Crossword Puzzle

To work the puzzle, read an item and figure out which word the item describes. Then write the word in the puzzle. Complete the entire puzzle.

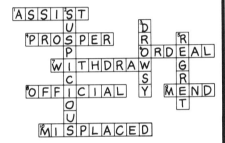

Across

1. When you help somebody, you _____ that person.
4. When you earn money and do well, you _____.
6. An extremely difficult experience is called an _____.
7. When you take something back, you _____ that thing.
8. Rules are _____ if they come from an office that can make the rules.
9. When you fix something, you _____ it.
10. If you don't remember where you put something, you have _____ that thing.

Down

2. When you don't really believe that something is true, you are _____ about that thing.
3. Another word for **sleepy** is _____.
5. When you are very sorry about something that happened, you _____ that thing.

ANSWER KEY FOR SKILLBOOK

PART D

1. a. *Idea:* Took off his eye patches
   b. *Idea:* Took off his wooden leg
2. a. John Hobbs
   b. Some seamen
   c. *Idea:* He owed them money
   d. In the country
3. a. *Idea:* The person was whipped
   b. *Idea:* The person was branded and sold as a slave
4. a. Yokel
   b. *Idea:* He would be hanged
5. a. Edward
   b. *Idea:* They laughed
   c. John Canty
   d. The Ruffler
6. a. *Idea:* King Foo-Foo, the First
   b. *Idea:* A blanket
   c. A barrel
7. Kicked him

PART E

8. a. 1918
   b. 1889
   c. 1931
   d. 1893
9. a. Blue
   b. Green
   c. Yellow
   d. Red
10. a. convince
    b. charred
    c. regret
    d. official
    e. sling
    f. evidence
    g. parlor

Lesson 111

Lesson 111

PART A   Word Lists

1	2	3
irritable	foolish	**New vocabulary**
hospitable	foolishness	1. run a risk 5. overcast
motley	assist	2. clothesline 6. hospitable
	assistant	3. motley 7. irritable
		4. eye 8. grope

PART B   New Vocabulary

1. **run a risk**—When you take a chance that may be dangerous, you **run a risk.**
   - What are you doing when you take a chance that may be dangerous?

2. **clothesline**—What is a **clothesline?**

3. **motley**—Something that is made up of many different types of things is called **motley.**
   - What kind of group is made up of many different kinds of people?

4. **eye**—When you **eye** something, you study it with your eyes. Here's another way of saying **She studied the painting with her eyes: She eyed the painting.**
   - What's another way of saying **He studied the jewels with his eyes?**

5. **overcast**—When the sky is gray and cloudy, the sky is **overcast.**
   - What's another way of saying **The day was gray and cloudy?**

6. **hospitable**—When you are **hospitable,** you show somebody hospitality.
   - A person who shows somebody hospitality is being _____ .

7. **irritable**—When you are **irritable,** you are grouchy.
   - What's another way of saying **John Canty was grouchy?**

8. **grope**—When you feel your way in the dark, you **grope.**
   - What are you doing when you feel your way in the dark?

PART C   Vocabulary Review

prosper	limb
burly	vagrant
chant	convince
charred	lash
capable of	regret
brand	brawl

1. When you earn money and do well, you _____ .

2. Another word for a **rough fight** is a _____ .

3. Another word for an **arm** or a **leg** is _____ .

4. When you take a hot iron and press it against an animal so that it leaves a mark that won't go away, you _____ that animal.

5. When you say the same thing over and over, you _____ that thing.

6. a. Another word for **whip** is _____ .
   b. What's another way of saying **The man whipped his horse?**

7. a. Another word for **stout and strong** is _____ .
   b. What's another way of saying **He was a stout and strong man?**

8. a. If you are able to do something, you are _____ doing that thing.
   b. If you are able to swim, you are _____ .
   c. If you are able to read, you are _____ .
   d. If you are able to ride a horse, you are _____ .

9. A person who does not have any place to live and has no job is a _____ .

WORD PRACTICE AND VOCABULARY

EXERCISE 1   Word practice

1. Everybody, find lesson 111, part A in your skillbook. *Wait.* Touch under each word in column 1 as I read it.
2. The first word is **irritable.**
3. Next word. **Hospitable.**
4. *Repeat step 3 for motley.*
5. Your turn. Read the first word. *Signal.* **Irritable.**
6. Next word. *Signal.* **Hospitable.**
7. *Repeat step 6 for motley.*
8. *Repeat the words in column 1 until firm.*

EXERCISE 2   Word practice

1. Column 2.
2. Your turn. Read the first word. *Signal.* **Foolish.**
3. Next word. *Signal.* **Foolishness.**
4. *Repeat step 3 for each remaining word in column 2.*
5. *Repeat the words in column 2 until firm.*

EXERCISE 3   Vocabulary development

Task A

1. Column 3. New vocabulary.
   First you're going to read the words in column 3. Then you're going to read about what they mean.
2. Read the first line. *Signal.* **Run a risk.**
3. Next word. *Signal.* **Clothesline.**
4. *Repeat step 3 for each remaining word in column 3.*
5. *Repeat the words in column 3 until firm.*

Task B

1. Everybody, look at part B.
   You're going to read this part out loud.
2. *For each item, call on a student to:*
   - *read one item aloud*
   - *read the meaning*
   - *read the question(s) for that item*
   - *answer each question orally*

   Answer Key: 1. **Running a risk**
   2. **A rope where you hang wet clothes to dry.**
   3. **A motley group of people**
   4. **He eyed the jewels.**
   5. **The day was overcast.**
   6. **hospitable**
   7. **John Canty was irritable.**
   8. **Groping**

EXERCISE 4   Vocabulary review

1. Everybody, look at part C. The words in the box are words you've learned.
2. Read the first word. *Signal.* **Prosper.**
3. Next. *Signal.* **Burly.**
4. *Repeat step 3 for the remaining words in the box.*
5. *Repeat the words in the box until firm.*
6. I'll read the items. When I come to a blank, everybody say the part that goes in the blank.
7. Look at item 1. *Pause.* Listen.
   When you earn money and do well, you *Pause.* *Signal.* **prosper.**
8. *Repeat step 7 for each remaining item.*

   Answer Key: 2. **brawl**
   3. **limb**
   4. **brand**
   5. **chant**
   6. a. **lash**
      b. **The man lashed his horse.**
   7. a. **burly**
      b. **He was a burly man.**
   8. a. **capable of**
      b. **capable of swimming**
      c. **capable of reading**
      d. **capable of riding a horse**
   9. **vagrant**

STORY READING

EXERCISE 5 Narrative poem

1. Everybody, turn to page 443 in your textbook.

2. I'll read the first four lines of the fifth stanza. Listen.

The spider then turned round about, and went into his den,
For well he knew the silly Fly would soon come back again;
So he wove a subtle web, in a little corner sly,
And set his table ready, to dine upon the Fly.

● Everybody, say those lines with me.
Read aloud with the students.

3. What is the spider's den? *Idea:* His nest.

● What did the spider know the fly would do? *Idea:* Come back.
So, the spider wove a subtle web. That is a web that is hard to see.

● Then the spider got ready to dine upon the fly. What does that mean: **dine upon the fly?** *Idea:* Eat her.

4. Everybody, read the first four lines again.
The students read aloud.

5. Listen to the last four lines of the stanza.

Then he came out to his door again, and merrily did sing,
"Come hither, hither, pretty Fly, with the pearl and silver wing;
Your robes are green and purple—there's a crest upon your head;
Your eyes are like the diamond bright, but mine are dull as lead!"

● Everybody, say those lines with me.
Read aloud with the students.

6. **Come hither** means **come here.** The spider says that the fly's wings are pearl and silver. What color are pearly wings? *Idea:* White with other soft colors.

● What is the spider referring to when he says that the fly's **robes** are green and purple? *Idea:* The colors of her body.

● The spider says that his eyes are dull as lead. Lead is a metal that is dull gray.

7. Everybody, read the last four lines again.
The students read aloud.

8. Everybody, read the entire fifth stanza.
The students read aloud.

9. We'll read the next stanza in the next lesson.

Lesson 111

CHAPTER 14
The King with the Tramps

At dawn, the troop of vagrants turned out and set forward on their march. The sky was dark with low clouds. The ground was sloppy, and the air stung with a winter chill. All merriment was gone from the company. Some were silent. Some were irritable. No one was in good humor. (A) The Ruffler put Hugo in charge of Edward. (B) Then the Ruffler commanded John Canty to stay away from the boy and let him alone. He also warned Hugo not to be too rough with the lad.

After a while, the weather grew milder and the clouds lifted somewhat. The troop ceased to shiver, and their spirits began to improve. They grew more and more cheerful and finally began to joke with each other and insult people who passed by on the road. They were once more appreciating the joy of their lives. Everybody they passed took the insults without answering, even when the members of the troop went into farmyards and snatched blankets from clotheslines. The people who owned the blankets said nothing, for they were probably glad that the troop did not take the clothesline as well as the blankets. (C)

After a while, the troop came to a small farmhouse and made themselves at home while the trembling farmer and his family brought out all the food they had to feed the motley crew breakfast. The vagrants insulted the farmer, made fun of the farmer's wife, and teased the farmer's daughters. They threw bones and vegetables at the farmer and his sons, kept them dodging all the time, and applauded loudly when a hit was made. As they left, they warned the family that they would come back and burn the house if the farmer reported them. (D)

About noon, after the troop had gone a long way, they came to the outskirts of a village. They rested outside the village for an hour. Then the crew scattered themselves so they could enter the village at different places and go about their business of stealing and begging.

Edward and Hugo went together. They wandered around for a while as Hugo watched for opportunities to do some business. (E) But there were no opportunities. (F) ★6 ERRORS★

At last, Hugo said, "I see nothing to steal in this poor place. So, we are going to try begging."

"Not _we_," Edward replied. "_You_. You may beg, but I will not."

"You won't beg?" Hugo said, scratching his head and eyeing Edward with sur-

prise. "What's wrong with you? You've begged in the streets of London all your life."

"I have never begged, you fool."

"You'll be a lot better off if you don't talk to me that way," Hugo warned. "Your father told me that you've begged. Maybe he lied."

Edward replied, "He's not even my father. Of course he lied."

Hugo shook his head. "I like your spirit," he said. "But I don't think much of your wisdom. So stop all this foolishness and let's get to work. Here's what we'll do. You will be my assistant while I do the begging. If you refuse . . ."

Edward was about to reply when Hugo interrupted. "Wait. Here comes somebody with a kindly face. Now I will fall down in a fit. When the stranger turns to me, start crying and wailing and fall down on your knees. Tell the stranger that I am your brother and that we have no friends and no home. Beg for a penny. Tell the stranger that without it we will both die. Remember, don't stop wailing until we get the penny."

The stranger was now near. Hugo stepped forward and suddenly began to moan and groan and roll his eyes. He staggered about. And when the stranger was nearly in front of him, he fell down and sprawled before him with a shriek. Then he began to squirm around as if he were experiencing great pain.

"Oh dear, oh dear," cried the kind stranger. "Oh, this poor boy, how he suffers. Here, let me help you up."

With wide eyes Hugo looked up. "Oh noble sir," he said, "please don't touch me, because it hurts too much. My brother there will tell you about my terrible condition and about these awful fits that I have. To help me just give me a penny to buy a little food. Then leave me to my sorrow."

"Penny!" the stranger exclaimed. "You shall have three pennies, you helpless creature." The stranger fumbled in his pocket with nervous haste and brought out three pennies. "There, poor lad. Take them. You are most welcome to them." The stranger turned to Edward. "Now come here, my boy, and help me carry your poor brother to my house where . . ."

"I am not his brother," said Edward.

"Oh, listen to him," groaned Hugo as he secretly ground his teeth. "He doesn't even know his own brother."

"Boy, you are indeed a hard one if this is your brother. For shame!"

Edward said, "He is pretending to be in pain. He is a begger and a thief. He has your money and he has picked your pocket. If you want to see a miracle, hit him with your staff."

Hugo did not wait for the miracle. In a moment, he was up and off like the wind, the gentlemen following after him with loud shouts.

Edward sighed a breath of relief and darted off in the other direction. He did not slow his pace until the village was far behind him. He continued to hurry along,

---

EXERCISE 6   Decoding and comprehension

1. Everybody, turn to page 407 in your textbook. *Wait. Call on a student.* What's the error limit for this chapter? **6 errors.**

2. *Call on individual students to read. Present the tasks specified for each circled letter.*

(A) What mood had the troop been in the night before? *Idea:* A good mood.

● What was the weather like in the morning? *Ideas:* Cloudy; cold.

● What kind of mood was the troop in now? *Idea:* Not so good.

(B) Who is the Ruffler? *Idea:* The leader of the gang.

(C) Why didn't the people do anything when the troop insulted them or took their blankets? *Idea:* They were afraid.

(D) This group has a very strange idea of how to have fun.

(E) What kind of business would Hugo do in this village? *Ideas:* Beg; steal.

(F) Why couldn't Hugo steal anything? *Idea:* He didn't see anything to steal.

● Read the rest of the chapter to yourselves and be ready to answer some questions.

After all students have finished reading:

● Hugo had a plan for begging. What was he going to do? *Ideas:* Pretend to have a fit; squirm on the ground.

● What did he want Edward to do? *Idea:* Beg for a penny.

● The stranger came up to Hugo. Then what did the stranger do? *Idea:* He tried to help Hugo up.

● When Hugo asked for a penny, what did the stranger do? *Idea:* Gave him three pennies.

● Where did the stranger want to take Hugo? *Idea:* To his house.

● Then what did Edward tell the stranger he could do if he wanted to see a miracle? *Idea:* Hit Hugo with his staff.

● What miracle was Edward talking about? *Idea:* That Hugo would run off.

● The story says that Hugo did not wait for the miracle. What did Hugo do? *Idea:* Jumped up and ran away.

● What did the stranger do? *Idea:* Ran after Hugo.

● What did Edward do after Hugo had left? *Idea:* Ran away in the other direction.

keeping a nervous watch over his shoulder to make sure that nobody was following him. At last his fears left him and he began to feel safe. He recognized now that he was hungry, and also very tired. So he stopped at a farmhouse, but when he was about to speak, the farmer drove him away with rude shouts. Edward then realized that his clothes created a problem for him.

He wandered on, determined that he would not beg. But hunger is the master of pride, so as the evening drew near, he approached another farmhouse. Here he was treated far more rudely than he had been treated earlier. The people in the farmhouse called him names and promised to have him arrested for a vagrant unless he moved on promptly.

The night came on, chilly and overcast. And still Edward moved slowly on, walking on very sore feet. He was forced to keep moving, for every time he sat down to rest, he was soon tormented by the cold. All his experiences as he moved through the somber gloom were strange to him. Occasionally, he heard voices approach, pass by him, and then fade into silence. Sometimes he would see a twinkling light, always far away and seemingly from another world. Now and then came the howl of a dog. He stumbled along through the night, startled from time to time by the soft rustling of dry leaves. The sounds re-minded him of whispers.

Suddenly, he noticed the light of a nearby lantern. The lantern stood by the open door of a barn. Edward waited for a long time. There was no sound and nobody stirring. Edward got so cold from standing still, and the barn looked so hospitable, that at last he resolved to risk everything and enter. He started swiftly toward the barn, and just as he was entering the door, he heard voices behind him. He darted behind a barrel inside the barn and stooped down. Two farm workers came into the barn, bringing the lantern with them. They began to work and talk at the same time. While they moved around with the lantern, Edward looked around and observed a stall at the far end of the barn. He thought that he would sneak over to the stall when it was safe. He also noticed a pile of horse blankets near the stall.

After a while, the men finished their work and left the barn, fastening the door behind them and taking the lantern with them. The shivering king quickly moved toward the blankets, gathered them up and groped his way safely to the stall. He made a bed using two of the blankets and covered himself with two more blankets. The King of England was now a very happy king, even though the blankets that covered him were old and thin and gave off a strong smell of horses.

- What did Edward do when he later became hungry? *Idea:* Stopped at a farmhouse to ask for food.
- What did the farmer do? *Idea:* Treated Edward rudely.
- The chapter says that hunger is the master of pride. So, if you become very hungry, what happens to your pride? *Idea:* You lose it.
- What did Edward do when hunger mastered his pride? *Idea:* Stopped at farmhouses to ask for food.
- Where did Edward finally find a place to spend the night? *Idea:* In a barn.
- Who came into that barn after Edward entered? *Idea:* Two farm workers.
- After they left, what did Edward do? *Idea:* Lay down and covered himself with some blankets.
- How did he feel now? *Idea:* Happy.

Award 4 points or have the students reread to the error limit sign.

EXERCISE 7   Individual reading checkout

1. *For the individual reading checkout, each student will read 150 words. The passage to be read is the shaded area on the reproduced textbook page for lesson 111 in this presentation book.*
2. Today is a reading checkout day. While you're doing your independent work, I'll call on each student to read part of yesterday's chapter.
3. When I call on you, come up to my desk and bring your textbook with you. After you have read, I'll tell you how many points you can write in the checkout box that's at the top of your workbook page.
4. *If the student finishes the passage in one minute or less, award points as follows:*

0 errors . . . .*3 points*
1 or 2 errors . . . .*1 point*
More than 2 errors . . . .*0 points*

5. *If a student takes more than one minute to read the passage, the student does not earn any points, but have the student reread the passage until he or she is able to read it in no more than one minute with no more than two errors.*

INDEPENDENT WORK

Do all the items in your skillbook and workbook for lesson 111.

ANSWER KEY FOR WORKBOOK

Review Items

1. Write the **title** of the story each statement describes.
   a. The main character was a girl who rode in horse races.
      A Horse to Remember
   b. The main character was a boy who became mayor.
      Dick Whittington
   c. The main character was a girl who asked for a rose.
      Beauty and the Beast
   d. The main character was a king who liked gold.
      The Golden Touch
   e. The main character was a dog who went north.
      Brown Wolf
   f. The main character turned into a swan. *The Ugly Duckling*
   g. The main character was a cat who made a good bargain. *The Cat that Walked by Himself*
   h. The main character was a dog who pulled a heavy sled.
      Buck
   i. The main characters were an old couple. *The Miraculous Pitcher*
   j. The main character was a girl who searched for her father.
      Adventure on the Rocky Ridge

2. Here are some events from the Jane Addams biography.
   - World War One ends
   - Hull House opens
   - Jane Addams receives the Nobel Peace Prize
   - A new factory law passes

   Write the correct event after each date on the time line.
   - 1931 *Jane Addams receives the Nobel Peace Prize*
   - 1918 *World War One ends.*
   - 1893 *A new factory law passes.*
   - 1889 *Hull House opens.*

3. You read about the game of baseball.
   a. How many innings does a game last if there's not a tie? *9*
   b. When a team is not batting, how many of its players are on the field? *9*
   c. Who was the first black man to play in the major leagues? *Jackie Robinson*

WORKCHECK AND AWARDING POINTS

1. *Read the questions and answers for the skillbook and workbook.*
2. *Award points for independent work as follows:*

0 errors	6 points
2 errors	4 points
3, 4, or 5 errors	2 points
5 or more errors	0 points

3. *Award bonus points as follows:*

Correcting missed items or getting all items right	2 points
Doing the writing assignment acceptably	2 points

4. *Remind the students to put the points they earned for their reading checkout, in the box labeled* **CO.**

ANSWER KEY FOR SKILLBOOK

PART D
1. a. *Idea:* Bad
   b. *Ideas:* Cloudy; cold
2. *Idea:* With nasty remarks
3. a. At a farmhouse
   b. *Any two:* Insulted the farmer; made fun of the farmer's wife; teased the daughters; threw food at the farmer's sons
   c. *Idea:* Burn their house
4. a. Hugo
   b. *Idea:* Hugo didn't see anything to steal
   c. *Idea:* Pretended he was having a fit
   d. A penny
   e. three pennies
   f. *Idea:* Hit Hugo with his staff
   g. *Idea:* Got up and ran off
5. a. *Idea:* Ran off
   b. *Idea:* Badly
6. a. *Idea:* Late at night
   b. barn
7. a. Two farm workers
   b. stall
   c. *Idea:* Blankets

PART E
8. a. brawl
   b. parlor
   c. burly
   d. prosper
   e. vagrant
   f. brand
   g. chant
   h. charred
   i. capable of
   j. lash
   k. limb

Lesson 112

PART A   Word Lists

1	2	3
identify	rattle	**New vocabulary**
tragic	snuggle	1. gasp
calf	trouble	2. identify
weary	cattle	3. calf
gagged	terrible	4. widow
	hospitable	5. cattle
		6. weary
		7. tragic

PART B   New Vocabulary

1. **gasp**—Show me how you **gasp**.

2. **identify**—When you tell what something is, you **identify** that thing.
   a. When you tell the name of a tree, you _____.
   b. When you tell the name of an insect, you _____.

3. **calf**—A **calf** is a cow or a bull that is not full-grown.

4. **widow**—A **widow** is a woman whose husband is dead.

• What do we call a woman whose husband is dead?

5. **cattle**—Cows and bulls are **cattle**.

6. **weary**—Something that tires you, **wearies** you.
   a. What's another way of saying **The conversation tired her?**
   b. What's another way of saying **The work made her tired?**

7. **tragic**—Something that is very sad is **tragic**.
   a. A very sad accident is a _____.
   b. A very sad story is a _____.

PART C   Vocabulary Review

eye	irritable
overcast	burly
limb	motley
hospitable	run a risk
grope	brawl

1. a. When you are grouchy, you are _____.
   b. What's another way of saying **John Canty was grouchy?**

2. a. When the sky is cloudy and gray, the sky is _____.
   b. What's another way of saying **The day was cloudy and gray?**

3. Something that is made up of many different types of things is called _____.

4. When you feel your way in the dark, you _____.

5. a. When you study something with your eyes, you _____ something.
   b. What's another way of saying **He studied the jewels with his eyes?** _____

6. When you show somebody hospitality, you are _____.

7. When you take a chance that may be dangerous, you _____.

WORD PRACTICE AND VOCABULARY

EXERCISE 1   Word practice

1. Everybody, find lesson 112, part A in your skillbook. *Wait.* Touch under each word in column 1 as I read it.
2. The first word is **identify**.
3. Next word. **Tragic.**
4. *Repeat step 3 for each remaining word in column 1.*
5. Your turn. Read the first word. *Signal.* **Identify.**
6. Next word. *Signal.* **Tragic.**
7. *Repeat step 6 for each remaining word in column 1.*
8. *Repeat the words in column 1 until firm.*

EXERCISE 2   Word family

1. Column 2. All those words end with the letters **l-e.**
2. Your turn. Read the first word. *Signal.* **Rattle.**
3. Next word. *Signal.* **Snuggle.**
4. *Repeat step 3 for each remaining word in column 2.*
5. *Repeat the words in column 2 until firm.*

EXERCISE 3   Vocabulary development

Task A

1. Column 3. New vocabulary.
   First you're going to read the words in column 3. Then you're going to read about what they mean.
2. Read the first word. *Signal.* **Gasp.**
3. Next word. *Signal.* **Identify.**
4. *Repeat step 3 for each remaining word in column 3.*
5. *Repeat the words in column 3 until firm.*

Task B

1. Everybody, look at part B. You're going to read this part out loud.
2. *For each item, call on a student to:*
   • *read one item aloud*
   • *read the meaning*
   • *read the question(s) for that item*
   • *answer each question orally*

   Answer Key: 1. *Student should gasp.*
   2. a. **identify that tree**
      b. **identify that insect**
   3. *No answer required.*
   4. **A widow**
   5. *No answer required.*
   6. a. **The conversation wearied her.**
      b. **The work made her weary.**
   7. a. **tragic accident**
      b. **tragic story**

EXERCISE 4   Vocabulary review

1. Everybody, look at part C. The words in the box are words you've learned.
2. Read the first word. *Signal.* **Eye.**
3. Next. *Signal.* **Overcast.**
4. *Repeat step 3 for the remaining words in the box.*
5. *Repeat the words in the box until firm.*
6. I'll read the items. When I come to a blank, everybody say the part that goes in the blank.
7. Look at item 1a. *Pause.* Listen.
   When you are grouchy, you are *Pause. Signal.* **irritable.**
8. *Repeat step 7 for each remaining item.*

   Answer Key: 1. b. **John Canty was irritable.**
   2. a. **overcast**
      b. **The day was overcast.**
   3. **motley**
   4. **grope**
   5. a. **eye**
      b. **He eyed the jewels.**
   6. **hospitable**
   7. **run a risk**

The Spider then turned round about, and went into his den,
For well he knew the silly Fly would soon come back again;
So he wove a subtle web, in a little corner sly,
And set his table ready, to dine upon the Fly.
Then he came out to his door again, and merrily did sing,
"Come hither, hither, pretty Fly, with the pearl and silver wing;
Your robes are green and purple—there's a crest upon your head;
Your eyes are like the diamond bright, but mine are dull as lead!"

Alas, alas! how very soon this silly little Fly,
Hearing the cunning, flattering words, came slowly flitting by;
With buzzing wings she hung aloft, then near and nearer drew,
Thinking only of her brilliant eyes, and green and purple hue—
Thinking only of her crested head—poor foolish thing! At last,
Up jumped the cunning Spider, and fiercely held her fast.
He dragged her up his winding stair, into his dismal den,
Within his little parlor—but she ne'er came out again!

And now, to all you people, who may this story read,
To idle, silly, flattering words, I pray you ne'er give heed;
And unto evil creatures close heart and ear and eye,
And take a lesson from this tale of the Spider and the Fly.

Textbook **443**

STORY READING

EXERCISE 5   Narrative poem

1. Everybody, turn to page 443 in your textbook.
2. I'll read the first four lines of the sixth stanza. Listen.
   Alas, alas! how very soon this silly little Fly,
   Hearing the cunning, flattering words, came slowly flitting by;
   With buzzing wings she hung aloft, then near and nearer drew,
   Thinking only of her brilliant eyes, and green and purple hue—
   • Everybody, say those lines with me.
     Read aloud with the students.
3. **Alas** means **too bad.**
   • The fly heard cunning, flattering words. Who said these flattering words? **The spider.**
   • Then the fly came slowly flitting by. When something flits, it moves from one place to another, the way that flies do.

   • Then with buzzing wings the fly hung aloft.
     Hung aloft means that **she hung in the air.**
   • Then she drew nearer. She was thinking only of the things the spider had told her—that she had brilliant eyes and a green and purple hue. **Hue** means **color.**
4. Everybody, read the first four lines again.
   The students read aloud.
5. Now I'll read the last four lines of the sixth stanza. Listen.
   Thinking only of her crested head—poor foolish thing! At last,
   Up jumped the cunning Spider, and fiercely held her fast.
   He dragged her up his winding stair, into his dismal den,
   Within his little parlor—but she ne'er came out again!
   • Everybody, say those lines with me.
     Read aloud with the students.
6. Everybody, read the entire sixth stanza.
   The students read aloud.
7. The last stanza tells the moral of the poem. Here's the moral: **Do not heed flattering words.** That means that you shouldn't pay attention to flattering words. Remember what happened to the fly when she started to believe the flattering words the spider told her.
8. I'll read the last stanza. Listen.
   And now, to all you people, who may this story read,
   To idle, silly, flattering words, I pray you ne'er give heed;
   And unto evil creatures close heart and ear and eye,
   And take a lesson from this tale of the Spider and the Fly.
   • Everybody, say that stanza with me.
     Read aloud with the students.
9. The poem says to close your heart and ear and eye to evil creatures. What does that mean? *Idea:* Not to pay attention to evil creatures.
10. Everybody, read the last stanza.
    The students read aloud.
11. After you finish today's work, practice reading the entire poem. In the next lesson, I'll call on different students to read each stanza.

Lesson 112

CHAPTER 15
The King with the Peasants

Edward was at the point of dropping off to sleep when he felt something touching him. The cold horror of that mysterious touch in the dark almost made his heart stand still. He lay motionless and listened, scarcely breathing. But nothing stirred and there was no sound. He continued to listen and wait for a long time, but still nothing stirred. After a few moments, Edward felt drowsy once more. Suddenly, he felt the mysterious touch again.

Edward's mind began to race as he tried to figure out what to do. Should he try to escape from the barn? The door was fastened from the outside, so there was no escape. The only thing left to do was to explore and try to find out what had touched him.

Although he resolved to do this, it is much easier to make the decision than it is to actually do it. Three times he stretched out his hand a little way into the darkness. Each time he suddenly pulled his hand back with a silent gasp, although he never touched anything. The fourth time, he groped a little farther and his hand lightly swept against something soft and warm. He imagined that it was part of a dead person. But he had to be sure. So again, his hand groped into the darkness until it found a bunch of long hair that seemed to be attached to a thick rope. Ⓐ

The king's hand slowly moved up the rope until he could identify the mysterious object. It was a calf, lying down in the stall next to him. Edward was ashamed of himself for being so frightened over a sleeping calf. Ⓑ A moment later, Edward felt delighted to have the calf's company. He petted the warm back of the calf and suddenly realized that this calf could be very useful to him on this cold night. He quickly arranged his bed so that it was right next to the calf. He then curled up and pulled his covers over himself and the calf. In a minute or two he was as warm and comfortable as he had ever been upon the splendid couches of the royal palace. Pleasant thoughts came at once. He was free from Canty, and free from the troop. He was warm and sheltered. He was happy.

The night wind was rising and blew with terrible gusts that made the old barn tremble and rattle. Then the wind would die down for a few moments before it whined and howled again. But Edward simply snuggled close to his companion and said to himself, "Let the wind blow. I am warm and comfortable." The calf slept and was not embarrassed by sleeping with

410 Lesson 112 Textbook

---

the King of England.

When Edward awoke in the early morning, he found that a wet mouse had crept under his blanket. Now that the mouse was disturbed, it scampered away. Edward smiled and said aloud, "I know now that things will get better, because they can't get any worse for a king who sleeps with a mouse." Ⓒ

Just as Edward stepped out of the stall, he heard the sound of children's voices. The barn door burst open and two little girls came in. As soon as they saw him, their talking and laughing ceased, and they stood still, eyeing him with curiosity. At last, they gathered their courage and began to discuss him. One girl said, "He has a nice face."

The other said, "And pretty hair."

"But look at those terrible clothes."

"And look how starved he seems to be."

They timidly approached Edward, circling around him and examining him as if he were some kind of strange new animal, but being very careful not to get too close to him. Finally, they stopped in front of him, holding each other's hands for protection. One of them asked, "Who are you?"

"I am the king," Edward answered.

Lesson 112   Textbook   **411**

EXERCISE 6   Decoding and comprehension

1. Everybody, turn to page 410 in your textbook. *Wait. Call on a student.* What's the error limit for this chapter? **11 errors.**

2. *Call on individual students to read. Present the tasks specified for each circled letter.*

Ⓐ Where is Edward during this part of the story? *Idea:* In a barn.

● Why didn't he just leave the barn? *Idea:* The door was locked.

● Why couldn't he see what was touching him? *Idea:* It was dark.

● When he started to try to touch the object, he kept drawing his hand back even though he didn't touch anything. Why did he keep drawing his hand back? *Idea:* He was scared.

● When he finally touched the object, what did he imagine it was? *Idea:* A dead person.

● What did the object feel like to him? *Ideas:* Soft and warm; long hair on a thick rope.

● What do you think it was? *Response:* Student preference.

Ⓑ What part of the calf had touched Edward? **The tail.**

Ⓒ Was Edward very comfortable that night? **Yes.**

● Do you think he would have been as comfortable if somebody had just taken him from the palace and had him sleep with a calf? **No.**

● Why was he so much more comfortable now than he would have been if he had just come from the palace? *Idea:* Because he had become used to terrible conditions.

Lesson 112   **227**

The children blinked, looked at each other, and then stared at Edward for a long moment before one of them asked, "The king of what?"

"The King of England."

The girls looked at each other again and one of them said, "How can that be true? It can't. So it must be a lie."

Her argument seemed to have no leaks in it. But the other girl was not convinced. She finally said to Edward, "If you are really the king, I'll believe you."

"I am truly the king."

That statement seemed to satisfy the girls and they accepted him as the true king. Ⓓ ★11 ERRORS★ The girls immediately began to question him about how he came to be in such a dreadful situation. They asked about where he planned to go and how he planned to return to the royal palace. He poured out his troubles to the girls, and as he talked he forgot his hunger. But when he told the last experiences that he had gone through and the girls learned how long he had been without food, they stopped his story and hurried him to the farmhouse to feed him breakfast.

Edward was cheerful now and said to himself, "When I return to the palace, I will always remember how these children believed in me. I'm afraid that if they were older and wiser, they would have mocked me."

The children's mother was kind to Edward and pitied him because he was in such poor condition. She was a widow and had experienced many problems herself. Although she concealed what she was

thinking, she thought that Edward was a mad boy who had wandered away from his friends. She tried to find out where he had really come from so that she would be able to return him to his friends. But he seemed to know nothing about the neighboring towns, and the boy stuck to his story about being the king.

As the woman prepared a meal for Edward, she tried to trick the boy by talking about things that a king would not know about. She talked about cattle, but he showed no interest. She talked about sheep, but the result was the same. She talked about factories, about weaving, about tinsmiths, and about merchants. But no matter what she talked about, the boy showed no knowledge of the subject and no interest in it. At last, she concluded that the boy must have been a servant. She tried to ask questions about servants, but the subject seemed to weary the boy. Finally, and quite by accident, the woman mentioned something about cooking. The boy's face lit up, and she concluded to herself that she had discovered what he had done in the past. She was very proud of herself for being so clever.

The woman's tongue now got a rest. Edward, because of his terrible hunger, made a long speech on food. After he finished this speech, he immediately started complimenting the woman on the splendid dishes that she had prepared in spattering frying pans in only a few minutes. From his talk and his manner, the woman concluded that the boy must have worked in the kitchen at the palace. As Edward de-

lighted over his breakfast, the woman left the room and secretly signaled the girls to follow her. She felt confident that the boy would show that he had worked in a kitchen by taking care of the hot cakes that were on the hot stove.

While the woman was out of the room, the hot cakes on the stove began to burn. Of course, Edward did nothing but continue to eat. When the woman returned and saw that Edward had not lifted a finger to save the cakes from becoming charred, she quickly removed them from the stove and then scolded the boy loudly.

Edward was shocked by her behavior, but before he could respond, her voice softened and once more became gentle. She was ashamed of herself for scolding someone as tragic as the ragged little boy who sat at the table.

After breakfast, the woman quietly told Edward to wash the dishes. This command stunned Edward for a moment, but then he said to himself, "Kings have had to do worse things than do dishes." With this, he went to work. After he had finished the dishes, the woman gave him and the little girls another task: peeling apples. Edward was so awkward that the girls giggled over his attempts. Finally the woman asked Edward to do some work in the backyard.

Edward went into the yard, but his work was rudely interrupted when he saw two figures approaching the front gate—John Canty, wearing a peddlar's outfit, and Hugo. They did not see Edward. So in a moment, he fled from the yard and hurried down a narrow lane.

Ⓓ Who came into the barn that morning? *Idea:* Two girls.
- What did they first ask Edward? *Idea:* Who he was.
- Did the girls believe him at first? **No.**
- Did he prove that he really was the king? **No.**
- What did he do to convince the girls he was king? *Idea:* He told them he was truly the king.
- Read the rest of the chapter to yourselves and be ready to answer some questions.

After all students have finished reading:
- When Edward was telling his story to the girls, they stopped him. Why? *Idea:* Because they realized he was hungry.
- Where did they take him? *Idea:* To the farmhouse.
- Who fixed breakfast for Edward? *Idea:* The girls' mother.
- At first, what did she think Edward really was? *Idea:* A mad boy.
- How did she try to trick Edward into giving a clue about who he really was? *Idea:* By talking about things a king wouldn't know about.
- Name some of the things she talked about. *Ideas:* Cattle; sheep; factories; weaving; tinsmiths; merchants.
- How did Edward respond to each of those subjects? *Idea:* He showed no interest.
- When she talked about one subject, Edward's face lit up. What subject was that? **Cooking.**
- So what did the woman conclude? *Idea:* That he worked in a palace kitchen.
- What was the real reason that Edward was interested in cooking? *Idea:* He was so hungry.
- When the woman left the room, she thought that she would trick Edward into doing something to show that he was really a cook. What was she confident that he would do? *Idea:* Take care of the hot cakes.
- What happened to the hot cakes? *Idea:* They burned.
- What did Edward do? *Idea:* Nothing.
- What did the woman do when she returned to the kitchen? *Idea:* Scolded Edward.
- Name some of the tasks that the woman gave Edward to do after breakfast. *Ideas:* Washing dishes; peeling apples; working in the backyard.
- Why did the girls laugh when Edward was peeling apples? *Idea:* Because he was awkward.
- When Edward was doing yard work, what did he see that made him stop working? *Idea:* Two figures coming to the gate.
- What did Edward do then? *Idea:* Ran away.

Award 4 points or have the students reread to the error limit sign.

INDEPENDENT WORK

Do all the items in your skillbook and workbook for lesson 112.

WORKCHECK AND AWARDING POINTS

1. *Read the questions and answers for the skillbook and workbook.*

2. *Award points for independent work as follows:*

0 errors	*6 points*
2 errors	*4 points*
3, 4, or 5 errors	*2 points*
5 or more errors	*0 points*

3. *Award bonus points as follows:*

Correcting missed items or getting all items right	*2 points*
Doing the writing assignment acceptably	*2 points*

ANSWER KEY FOR SKILLBOOK

PART D

1. a. In a barn
   b. *Ideas:* Cold; cloudy
   c. *Idea:* A calf's tail
   d. *Idea:* To see what it was
   e. A dead person
   f. A calf
   g. calf
   h. warm
2. a. Two girls
   b. *Idea:* I am truly the king
   c. older
   d. *Idea:* To feed him
3. a. No
   b. crazy
   c. *Idea:* To see if he's really a king
   d. No
   e. Cooking
   f. *Idea:* Because he was so hungry
   g. *Idea:* A cook's helper
4. a. Hot cakes
   b. take care of
   c. *Idea:* Nothing
5. a. *Any two:* Peeling apples; washing dishes; working in the yard
   b. John Canty and Hugo
   c. *Idea:* Ran away

PART E

6. a. withdraw
   b. shattered
   c. brawl
   d. burly
   e. irritable
   f. chant
   g. overcast
   h. ordeal
   i. grope
   j. hospitable
   k. prosper
   l. limb
   m. capable of
   n. vagrant
   o. run a risk
   p. eye
   q. motley

Lesson 113

WORD PRACTICE AND VOCABULARY

EXERCISE 1   Word family

1. Everybody, find lesson 113, part A in your skillbook. *Wait.*
2. Column 1. All those words are made up of two shorter words.
3. Your turn. Read the first word. *Signal.* **Tiptoes.**
4. Next word. *Signal.* **Fireplace.**
5. *Repeat step 4 for each remaining word in column 1.*
6. *Repeat the words in column 1 until firm.*
7. Column 2. All those words end in the letters **a-b-l-e.**
8. Read the first word. *Signal.* **Hospitable.**
9. *Repeat step 4 for each remaining word in column 2.*
10. *Repeat the words in column 2 until firm.*

EXERCISE 2   Vocabulary development

Task A

1. Column 3. New vocabulary.
   First you're going to read the words in column 3. Then you're going to read about what they mean.
2. Read the first line. *Signal.*
   Tuck somebody into bed.
3. Next line. *Signal.* **Bound and gagged.**
4. Next word. *Signal.* **Inform.**
5. *Repeat step 4 for each remaining word in column 3.*
6. *Repeat the words in column 3 until firm.*

Task B

1. Everybody, look at part B.
   You're going to read this part out loud.
2. *For each item, call on a student to:*
   • *read one item aloud*
   • *read the meaning*
   • *read the question(s) for that item*
   • *answer each question orally*

   Answer Key: **1.** *Idea:* Cover the person with blankets and tuck the blankets around the person.
   2. a. bound
   b. gagged
   3. a. Informing the girl about school.
   b. Informing the man about the weather.
   4. a. intends to go to a party
   b. intends to stop at the inn
   5. a. impulse to eat
   b. impulse to run away
   6. Confessing

The Spider and the Fly
by Mary Howitt

"Will you walk into my parlor?" said the Spider to the Fly,
"Tis the prettiest little parlor that ever you did spy;
The way into my parlor is up a winding stair,
And I've many curious things to show when you are there."
"Oh, no, no," said the little Fly, "to ask me is in vain,
For who goes up your winding stair can ne'er come down again."

"I'm sure you must be weary, dear, with soaring up so high;
Will you rest upon my little bed?" said the Spider to the Fly.
"There are pretty curtains drawn around; the sheets are fine and thin,
And if you like to rest a while, I'll snugly tuck you in!"
"Oh, no, no," said the little Fly, "for I've often heard it said,
They never, never wake again, who sleep upon your bed!"

Said the cunning Spider to the Fly, "Dear friend, what can I do
To prove the warm affection I've always felt for you?
I have within my pantry good store of all that's nice;
I'm sure you're very welcome—will you please to take a slice?"
"Oh no, no," said the little Fly, "kind sir, that cannot be;
I've heard what's in your pantry, and I do not wish to see!"

"Sweet creature," said the Spider, "you're witty and you're wise,
How handsome are your pearly wings, how brilliant are your eyes!
I have a little looking-glass upon my parlor shelf,
If you'll step in one moment, dear, you shall behold yourself."
"I thank you, gentle sir," she said, "for what you're pleased to say,
And bidding you good morning now, I'll call another day."

442 Textbook

The Spider then turned round about, and went into his den,
For well he knew the silly Fly would soon come back again;
So he wove a subtle web, in a little corner sly,
And set his table ready, to dine upon the Fly.
Then he came out to his door again, and merrily did sing,
"Come hither, hither, pretty Fly, with the pearl and silver wing;
Your robes are green and purple—there's a crest upon your head;
Your eyes are like the diamond bright, but mine are dull as lead!"

Alas, alas! how very soon this silly little Fly,
Hearing the cunning, flattering words, came slowly flitting by;
With buzzing wings she hung aloft, then near and nearer drew,
Thinking only of her brilliant eyes, and green and purple hue—
Thinking only of her crested head—poor foolish thing! At last,
Up jumped the cunning Spider, and fiercely held her fast.
He dragged her up his winding stair, into his dismal den,
Within his little parlor—but she ne'er came out again!

And now, to all you people, who may this story read,
To idle, silly, flattering words, I pray you ne'er give heed;
And unto evil creatures close heart and ear and eye,
And take a lesson from this tale of the Spider and the Fly.

Textbook **443**

EXERCISE 3   Vocabulary review

1. Everybody, look at part C. The words in the box are words you've learned.
2. Read the first word. *Signal.* **Wearies.**
3. *Next. Signal.* **Irritable.**
4. *Repeat step 3 for the remaining words in the box.*
5. *Repeat the words in the box until firm.*
6. I'll read the items. When I come to a blank, everybody say the part that goes in the blank.
7. Look at item 1. *Pause.* Listen.
   A cow or a bull that is not full-grown is a *Pause. Signal.* **calf.**
8. *Repeat step 7 for each remaining item.*

Answer Key: **2. a. identify**
                b. identify that person
                c. identify that insect
                d. identify that tree
             3. a. tragic
                b. tragic story
                c. tragic accident
             4. a. wearies
                b. The work made her weary.
                c. The conversation wearied her.
             5. cattle
             6. widow
             7. *Students should gasp.*

STORY READING

EXERCISE 4   Narrative poem

1. Everybody, turn to page 442 in your textbook. We're going to read the entire poem.
   I'll call on different students. Each student will read one stanza.
2. *The students read aloud.*

Lesson 113

CHAPTER 16
The King and the Hermit

Edward ran quickly down the path. Just before he reached a forest, he glanced back and noticed two figures behind him in the distance. He did not wait to determine who those distant figures were, but he hurried on and did not slow his pace until he was far inside the twilight of the woods. Then he stopped and listened intently. His ears heard nothing but stillness.

At first, he intended to stay where he was and rest until the following day, but a chill soon cut into his sweating body, and he again began to move so that he would feel warmer.Ⓐ He went straight through the forest, hoping that he would cross a road. But he continued farther and farther into the forest without finding a road. The gloom began to thicken, and after a while, Edward realized that night was coming. The woods were now so thick that Edward had to move very slowly. He tripped over roots and tangled himself in vines and bushes.

How glad Edward was when he caught a glimpse of light. He approached it carefully, stopping frequently to look around. The light came from an open window of a shabby little hut. He heard a voice inside, and each time it spoke, Edward had to fight the impulse to run away. Finally,

he was standing in front of the window. He raised himself on tiptoes and stared inside. The room was small. The floor was hard-packed earth. In the corner was a bed, made of sticks and a ragged blanket. In front of the fireplace an old man was holding a candle. The man was very large. His hair and beard were white, and he wore a robe of sheepskin that went from his neck to his heels.Ⓑ

Edward recognized that the man was a hermit, a man who lived by himself.Ⓒ Edward knocked on the door, and the hermit replied, "Enter." Edward entered and paused as the hermit turned with a pair of gleaming eyes. "Who are you?" the hermit inquired.

"I am the king," came the answer.

"Welcome, king," cried the hermit eagerly. Then the hermit moved a small bench to the middle of the room, seated the king on it, threw some wood on the fire, and paced back and forth as he continued to say, "Welcome, welcome."

After a few minutes, the hermit stopped talking aloud but continued to mutter. Edward took this opportunity to tell his story. But the hermit seemed to pay no attention to the story. Suddenly, he approached Edward and said, with his eyes

gleaming, "I will tell you a secret." He bent down, looked around the room suspiciously several times, and then whispered, "I am a wizard."Ⓓ ★7 ERRORS★

Edward said to himself, "I have left the company of thieves to be in the company of a madman."

The old man smiled and told the story of how he had become a wizard. He told of the bright light that had entered his hut and how two witches suddenly appeared and informed him that he was a wizard. He said, "And the witches knelt before me because I was more important than they were."

The old hermit told his fantastic story for over an hour, while Edward listened and suffered. Then the hermit's voice softened and he suddenly seemed very gentle. He set about preparing a supper, chatting pleasantly all the time. After supper, the hermit tucked Edward into bed. Edward was very sleepy. Suddenly, the hermit tapped his forehead as if he was trying to remember something. He said, "Are you the King of England?"

"Yes," came the drowsy reply.

"Then Henry is gone."

"That's true," Edward replied.

A dark frown settled over the hermit's face, and he made a hard fist. He said, "Do you know that Henry was the one who was responsible for making me take up the life of a hermit?"

Edward did not reply because he was asleep. Suddenly, a wild smile replaced the frown on the hermit's face. He went back to the fireplace and began to mutter to

himself as the winds sighed around the lonely hut. At last, he said aloud, "His father was responsible for great evil. His father can no longer be punished. But the boy shall pay for his father's evil ways."

The hermit went back to the sleeping boy. He quietly tied Edward's ankles together, and then his wrists. As Edward continued to sleep calmly, the hermit placed a rag around Edward's face and over his mouth. The old man glided away like a cat and returned with a small bench. He sat down, muttering to himself. He was like a spider who was viewing a poor insect that was caught in its web.

Suddenly, the boy woke up and stared with frozen horror at the hermit. He struggled for a moment before realizing that he was tightly bound and gagged. The old man said, "The night is nearly over and the daylight approaches. So I must take care of you now." At that moment came the sound of voices near the cabin. The hermit quickly tossed his sheepskin over the boy and stood up trembling.

Thundering knocks came to the door and a loud voice said, "Open up in there." This voice was like beautiful music to Edward's ears, for it was the voice of Miles Hendon.

The hermit moved swiftly to the door and opened it. Miles said, "Where is the boy?"

"What boy?"

"Don't lie to me," said Miles. "I'm not in the mood for it. I caught the two ruffians who were following the boy close to this cabin and I made them confess.

EXERCISE 5   Decoding and comprehension

1. Everybody, turn to page 414 in your textbook. *Wait. Call on a student.* What's the error limit for this chapter? **7 errors.**

2. *Call on individual students to read. Present the tasks specified for each circled letter.*

Ⓐ Who do you think the two figures following Edward were? *Idea:* John Canty and Hugo.

● Where did Edward finally stop? *Idea:* Inside a forest.

● What was his original plan? *Idea:* To stay in the forest until the next day.

● Why did he decide to move on?

● *Idea:* He was cold.

● Why was his body sweaty? *Idea:* He had been running.

Ⓑ When Edward followed the light, what did he come to? *Idea:* A hut.

● Describe some of the things Edward saw inside the hut. *Idea:* A small room with a dirt floor; a bed made of sticks and grass; a blanket; a fireplace; an old man.

● How did the man look? *Ideas:* Long white hair and beard; wore a long sheep skin.

Ⓒ What was the man? **A hermit.**

Ⓓ What did the hermit think that he was? **A wizard.**

● Do you think he's really a wizard? *Response:* Student preference.

● How did he respond to Edward's story? *Idea:* He didn't really listen to it.

● Do you think the hermit is crazy? *Response:* Student preference.

● Read the rest of the chapter to yourselves and be ready to answer some questions.

After all students have finished reading:

● After the hermit fed Edward, he put him to bed. Then the hermit began to figure out something. What did he figure out about Edward? *Idea:* That Henry the Eighth was Edward's father.

● What did the hermit decide to do to Edward for being the son of Henry the Eighth? *Idea:* Punish him.

● What did he do as Edward slept? *Idea:* Tied him up and gagged him.

● When Edward woke up, what did he see that frightened him? *Idea:* The hermit.

● Just as the hermit was ready to punish Edward, something happened. What was that? *Idea:* Miles knocked at the door.

They said that the boy was free and that they had followed him to the path that leads to your door. So where is he?"

"Oh," the hermit said. "You must mean the ragged vagrant that came here last night. I sent him on an errand before the dawn broke. He should return shortly."

"That's a lie," Miles declared. "He would not obey you. He wouldn't obey any man."

"But sir," the hermit said. "I am not a man. It is a deep secret, I am a wizard."

Edward tried to make as much noise as he could, but he could only manage a groan. "What was that noise?" Miles demanded.

"I heard no noise, except the wind," the hermit replied.

"I'm going to search this place," Miles said.

"I think I know what you heard," the hermit quickly said. "Come outside and I will show you." Edward heard the two go outside.

Just outside the window Miles said, "He must have lost his way in the thick woods. Which direction did he take?"

"I will go with you," the hermit said, "and show you."

The little king heard the voices and footsteps fade away. All hope left him. "My only friend has been deceived," Edward said to himself. "When that hermit returns, he will . . ."

Edward struggled with all his might and managed to shake off the sheepskin that had covered him. At that moment, he heard the door open. The sound chilled him and his imagination could already picture the cold hand of the hermit. With horror, Edward glanced at the door. Then he held his eyes open with amazement. Before him stood John Canty and Hugo. Edward would have thanked them warmly if his mouth had not been silenced with a gag. In a moment or two, his limbs were free and he was being hurried through the forest, with Hugo holding firmly onto one of his arms and John Canty holding the other.

- What story did the hermit tell Miles about Edward? *Idea:* That he had sent him on an errand.
- How did Edward try to make himself heard? *Idea:* by groaning.
- What did the hermit do to prevent Miles from searching the cabin? *Idea:* Took him outside.
- What did Edward hear the hermit tell Miles outside the window? *Idea:* That he would help Miles look for Edward.
- Why was Edward horrified about the thought of the hermit returning? *Idea:* Because the hermit would punish him.
- After Miles and the hermit left, which two people came into the cabin? *Idea:* John Canty and Hugo.
- What did they do? *Idea:* Took Edward away.

Award 4 points or have the students reread to the error limit sign.

INDEPENDENT WORK

Do all the items in your skillbook and workbook for lesson 113.

ANSWER KEY FOR WORKBOOK

Outlining

The outline below shows three main ideas for the biography of Jackie Robinson.

Write three supporting details for each main idea.

1. Jackie was a sports star at UCLA. *Idea:*
   a. *He played basketball.*
   b. *He played football.*
   c. *He played baseball.*
2. Jackie had several jobs between 1941 and 1946.
   a. *He was a construction worker.*
   b. *He was in the army.*
   c. *He played in the negro League.*
3. Jackie was a great baseball player.
   a. *He hit many home runs.*
   b. *He is in the Hall of Fame.*
   c. *He was Rookie of the Year.*

Story Items

4. Write which character each statement describes. Choose from **Edward, Miles,** or the **hermit.**
   a. Nobody believed that he was a wizard. *hermit*
   b. Very few people believed that he was the king. *Edward*
   c. He wanted to get revenge on Henry the Eighth. *hermit*
   d. He saved Edward's life by knocking on a door. *Miles*
   e. He could not cry out for help. *Edward*

Review Items

5. Put the following events in the right order by numbering them from 1 through 3.
   1 Edward and Tom changed places.
   3 Edward was almost killed by a hermit.
   2 Edward met a gang of thieves in a barn.
6. Write which Greek god each statement describes. Choose from **Apollo, Hermes, Poseidon,** or **Zeus.**
   a. He was the chief god. *Zeus*
   b. He was the messenger god. *Hermes*
   c. He was the god of the sea. *Poseidon*
   d. He was the god of light and music. *Apollo*

ANSWER KEY FOR SKILLBOOK

PART D

1. a. forest
   b. John Canty and Hugo
2. a. hut
   b. *Ideas:* A hermit; an old man
   c. Yes
   d. *Idea:* That he was a wizard
3. a. *Idea:* Made him a hermit
   b. Edward
   c. *Idea:* Tied them together
   d. *Idea:* Tied a rag over it
   e. Miles Hendon
   f. *Idea:* Because he was gagged
   g. *Idea:* A blanket
   h. The hermit
4. a. The hermit
   b. Yes
   c. John Canty and Hugo
   d. *Idea:* They saved him

PART E

5. a. official
   b. calf
   c. tragic
   d. widow
   e. motley
   f. weary
   g. identify
   h. cattle
   i. irritable

WORKCHECK AND AWARDING POINTS

1. *Read the questions and answers for the skillbook and workbook.*

2. *Award points for independent work as follows:*

   > 0 errors .6 points
   > 2 errors .4 points
   > 3, 4, or 5 errors . . . . .2 points
   > 5 or more errors . . . . .0 points

3. *Award bonus points as follows:*

   > *Correcting missed items or getting all items right . . . . .2 points*
   > *Doing the writing assignment acceptably . . . . .2 points*

Lesson 114

Lesson 114

PART A   Word Lists

1	2	3	4
innocent	troublesome	situation	**New vocabulary**
penalty	meantime	chuckle	1. band
Edith	therefore	suspicion	2. mistreat
Arthur	blacksmith	chuckling	3. betray
	courtroom	gossip	4. innocent
		daily	5. flogged

PART B   New Vocabulary

1. **band**—Another word for a **group** is a **band**.
   - A group of vagrants is a
     _____

2. **mistreat**—When somebody is treated poorly, that person is **mistreated.**
   - If a dog is treated poorly, that dog is
     _____

3. **betray**—You **betray** somebody by pretending to be that person's friend and then trick that person.
   - What are you doing to a person when you pretend to be a person's friend and then trick that person?

4. **innocent**—Someone who is not guilty of doing something wrong is **innocent.**
   - A person who is not guilty of cheating is _____

5. **flogged**—When somebody is beaten with a whip or a switch, that person is **flogged.**

PART C   Vocabulary Review

weary	intend	inform
bound	tragic	confesses
official	impulse	gagged

1. When a person tells the truth about a secret, that person _____ that secret.

2. a. When you give somebody information about something, you _____ that person about that thing.
   b. What are you doing when you give a man information about the weather?
      _____
   c. What are you doing when you give a girl information about school?
      _____

3. a. If you plan to do something, you _____ to do that thing.
   b. A person who plans to stop at the inn, _____
   c. A person who plans to go to a party, _____

4. a. A sudden, strong desire to do something is an _____ .
   b. A person who suddenly has a very strong desire to run away has an _____
   c. A person who suddenly has a very strong desire to eat has an _____

5. a. When a person is tied up, that person is _____
   b. When a person's mouth is covered, that person is _____

WORD PRACTICE AND VOCABULARY

EXERCISE 1   Word practice

1. Everybody, find lesson 114, part A in your skillbook. *Wait.* Touch under each word in column 1 as I read it.
2. The first word is **innocent.**
3. Next word. **Penalty.**
4. *Repeat step 3 for each remaining word in column 1.*
5. Your turn. Read the first word. *Signal.* **Innocent.**
6. Next word. *Signal.* **Penalty.**
7. *Repeat step 6 for each remaining word in column 1.*
8. *Repeat the words in column 1 until firm.*

EXERCISE 2   Word family

1. Column 2. All those words are made up of two shorter words.
2. Your turn. Read the first word. *Signal.* **Troublesome.**
3. Next word. *Signal.* **Meantime.**
4. *Repeat step 3 for each remaining word in column 2.*
5. *Repeat the words in column 2 until firm.*

EXERCISE 3   Word practice

1. Column 3.
2. Your turn. Read the first word. *Signal.* **Situation.**
3. Next word. *Signal.* **Chuckle.**
4. *Repeat step 3 for each remaining word in column 3.*
5. *Repeat the words in column 3 until firm.*

EXERCISE 4   Vocabulary development

Task A

1. Column 4. New vocabulary. First you're going to read the words in column 3. Then you're going to read about what they mean.
2. Read the first word. *Signal.* **Band.**
3. Next word. *Signal.* **Mistreat.**
4. *Repeat step 3 for each remaining word in column 4.*
5. *Repeat the words in column 4 until firm.*

Task B

1. Everybody, look at part B. You're going to read this part out loud.
2. *For each item, call on a student to:*
   - *read one item aloud*
   - *read the meaning*
   - *read the question(s) for that item*
   - *answer each question orally*

   Answer Key: **1. band of vagrants**
   2. mistreated
   3. Betraying that person
   4. innocent of cheating
   5. *No answer required.*

EXERCISE 5   Vocabulary review

1. Everybody, look at part C. The words in the box are words you've learned.
2. Read the first word. *Signal.* **Weary.**
3. Next. *Signal.* **Bound.**
4. *Repeat step 3 for the remaining words in the box.*
5. *Repeat the words in the box until firm.*
6. I'll read the items. When I come to a blank, everybody say the part that goes in the blank.
7. Look at item 1. *Pause.* Listen. When a person tells the truth about a secret, that person *Pause. Signal.* **confesses** that secret.
8. *Repeat step 7 for each remaining item.*

   Answer Key:
   2. a. inform
   b. Informing a man about the weather
   c. Informing a girl about school
   3. a. intend
   b. intends to stop at the inn
   c. intends to go to a party
   4. a. impulse
   b. impulse to run away
   c. impulse to eat
   5. a. bound
   b. gagged

Lesson 114

CHAPTER 17
A Victim of Treachery

Once more, King Foo Foo the First was with the wandering band of vagrants and thieves.Ⓐ They ridiculed him and teased him, but there were only two people in the entire troop that truly disliked him—John Canty and Hugo.Ⓑ Canty and Hugo were as cruel to Edward as they could be without getting caught by the Ruffler, who would send them flying to the ground if he discovered that they were trying to mistreat the boy.

Hugo would "accidentally" step on Edward's foot from time to time. One time, following one of these "accidents," Edward hit Hugo with a stout stick and sent him sprawling, much to the delight of the other members in the troop. Hugo sprang to his feet and grabbed a large stick, and immediately a ring of people formed around Hugo and Edward. The onlookers started to predict who would win the fight. But Hugo was no match for Edward, who had been trained for many years in the use of every sword or weapon that was used in battle. With graceful ease, Edward blocked the rain of blows that Hugo tried to deliver. Every time Hugo left Edward with an opening, Edward delivered a lightning-fast rap which was followed by a storm of cheers and laughter. At the end of

fifteen minutes, the bruised Hugo tossed his stick aside and pushed his way from the ring with his head down. The troop lifted the unmarked king to their shoulders and carried him to a place of honor beside the Ruffler.Ⓒ

• • •

Edward grabbed every opportunity to escape from the troop. On his first day, he was lifted through the window of an unwatched kitchen. But he didn't steal anything. Instead, he tried to wake up the people who lived in the house. Several days later, Edward was so tired of his life with the troop that he started to lose hope of escaping. Only at night, in his dreams, was he happy.

The Ruffler had decided that it was no use to require Edward to beg.Ⓓ The Ruffler therefore announced that Edward would be given work that was much better—he would steal.

The next morning, Hugo decided to get even with Edward. Hugo had many ideas for getting rid of the troublesome boy, but the one that pleased him the most was to betray Edward and turn him over to the law.Ⓔ

Hugo strolled off to a neighboring village with Edward, and the two drifted

slowly up and down one street after another. One of the boys was watching sharply for a chance to steal something, while the other watched as sharply for a chance to escape. Edward passed up several opportunities to escape, because he wanted to make sure that he would succeed. So he waited for the right opportunity.Ⓕ ★7 ERRORS★

At last, a woman approached. She carried a large package in a basket. Hugo's eyes sparkled with pleasure as he said to himself, "This is the perfect situation." He waited and watched until the woman had passed by and the time was right. Then he said to Edward, "Wait here until I return," and he darted quickly after the woman.

Edward's heart was filled with joy; he could make his escape now if Hugo contin-

ued to move farther away. But just then, Hugo snatched the package from the woman and came running back toward Edward. As Hugo ran, he wrapped the package in a blanket that he had on his arm. The woman began to scream and cry. Hugo handed the package to Edward and said, "Run after me with the others, while you cry 'Stop, thief!' "

In an instant, Hugo had turned the corner and darted down a crooked alley. In another moment or two, he came back into view again, looking very innocent. Edward threw the bundle to the ground and the blanket fell away from it just as the woman and a crowd of people approached. The woman seized Edward's wrist with one hand and her bundle with the other. She began to yell loudly at Edward.

STORY READING

EXERCISE 6 Decoding and comprehension

1. Everybody, turn to page 417 in your textbook. *Wait. Call on a student.* What's the error limit for this chapter? **7 errors.**
2. *Call on individual students to read. Present the tasks specified for each circled letter.*

Ⓐ Who is King Foo-Foo, the First? **Edward.**

• How did he get back with this band of vagrants and thieves? *Idea:* John Canty and Hugo had taken him back.

Ⓑ What other name is John Canty now using? **John Hobbs.**

• Why? *Idea:* Because he owed money.

Ⓒ Who won the fight? **Edward.**

• What does that mean: **The king was unmarked?** *Idea:* He didn't have any cuts or bruises.

• What kind of marks did Hugo have? **Bruises.**

Ⓓ Why was it no use to require Edward to beg? *Ideas:* He wouldn't beg; he was the king.

Ⓔ What was Hugo's plan for getting rid of Edward? *Idea:* To turn him over to the law.

Ⓕ The chapter says that one of the boys watched sharply for a chance to steal something. Which boy was that? **Hugo.**

• The other boy watched for a chance to escape. Which boy was that? **Edward.**

• Read the rest of the chapter to yourselves and be ready to answer some questions.

After all students have finished reading:

• Hugo tricked Edward. First, he stole something. What did he steal? *Ideas:* A package; a pig.

• What did Hugo do with the package? *Idea:* Handed it to Edward.

• Then what did Hugo do? *Idea:* Ran away.

• What did Edward do with the package? *Idea:* Threw it on the ground.

• What did the woman do? *Idea:* Grabbed Edward.

Hugo had seen enough. His enemy was captured and the law would take care of him now. So Hugo slipped away, chuckling to himself as he started back toward the camp, ready to tell the Ruffler a lie about what had actually happened.

In the meantime, Edward continued to struggle in the woman's grasp. The crowd closed in around Edward, threatening him and calling him names. A burly blacksmith approached Edward and spoke of some of the things he would do to him when he got his hands on him. But the blacksmith stopped short as a long sword flashed in the air and came down with its flat side on the man's arm. Edward's eyes grew wide as the man holding the sword spoke in a pleasant tone. "Good people," he said, "let's not be hasty. This is a matter for the law. Let go of the boy's arm, good woman."

The blacksmith glanced at the stranger and then went away muttering and rubbing his arm. The woman released the boy's wrist as the crowd eyed the stranger with suspicion. Edward quickly sprang to the side of the person who had saved him. He said, "It took you long enough to get here, Sir Miles. Now let's get out of here."

Miles Hendon smiled and looked down at the pitiful little boy. Miles said, "That's right. I had almost forgotten that I was now Sir Miles, a knight." At that moment, the crowd opened and a police officer approached. He was about to lay his hand on Edward's shoulder when Miles said, "Go easy, good friend. I am responsi-ble for the boy. So lead the way and we will follow."

The officer led, with the woman, Miles and Edward following. Behind them was the crowd. Edward wanted to fight but Miles said to him in a low voice, "Be patient, my king. One of your laws has been broken, and if you expect others to obey the law, you should obey it also."

"You're right," Edward said after thinking over the matter for a moment. The officer led Edward and the others to a judge. He ordered everybody but Miles, Edward, and the woman to leave. Then he asked the woman whether the bundle that had been stolen was worth more than thirteen pennies.

"Indeed it is," she replied firmly. "It is a pig and it is worth over twice the amount."

The judge turned to the woman and said, "You can see that this poor lad stole because he was hungry. You know that these are terrible times, and you can see that he does not have an evil face." He paused and then continued, "Good woman, do you know that when somebody steals something that is worth more than thirteen pennies, the law says that the person shall hang for it?"

The little king's eyes popped open wide with amazement. The woman cried out, "That's horrible! I would not hang the poor thing for the whole world. What shall I do?"

The judge said, "Well, maybe you were mistaken about how much the bundle was worth."

"Yes," the woman said, "I was mistaken. The bundle was worth only eight pennies. Only eight pennies." Without thinking, Miles threw his arms around Edward in delight. The judge thanked the woman and she left the courtroom. The officer followed her into a narrow hall.

Miles wondered why the officer had followed the woman, so he softly slipped into the hall and listened. The officer was saying to the woman, "That pig you have will make some fine meals. So I will buy it from you. Here are eight pennies."

"Eight pennies," the woman cried. "You will not buy it for that amount, and you know very well that it cost a lot more."

"Oh," the officer said slowly. "So you lied when you swore that it cost only eight cents. You have committed a terrible crime. Come back with me and answer for that crime. And then the lad will hang."

The woman smiled and shook her head. "There, there," she said. "Say no more. Just give me the eight pennies and take the pig."

The woman went off crying. Miles slipped back into the courtroom and the officer followed after he had hidden his prize. Inside the courtroom, the judge sentenced Edward to be sent to jail where he would be kept and flogged for his crime. Edward was ready to respond to that order, but Miles told him to be quiet.

Soon, Miles and Edward were following the officer toward the jail. Suddenly, Edward stopped and told Miles that he would not enter the jail. Miles whispered in a sharp voice, "Be patient. We'll have a chance to escape, but be patient."

- Somebody stopped the crowd from attacking Edward. Who was that? *Idea:* Miles Hendon.
- What did he do to stop the blacksmith? *Idea:* Brought his sword down on the blacksmith's arm.
- Where did the police officer take Miles, Edward, and the woman? *Idea:* To a judge.
- What was in the package that Hugo had stolen? **A pig.**
- The judge asked the woman if the package was worth more than thirteen pennies. What was the penalty for stealing something worth more than thirteen pennies? *Idea:* Hanging.
- Was the package really worth more than thirteen pennies? **Yes.**
- After the woman heard about the penalty that faced Edward, what did she say the package was worth? **Eight pennies.**
- When she left, who followed her into the hall? *Idea:* The police officer.
- What did the officer want from her? *Idea:* The pig.
- How much did he want to give her for the pig? **Eight pennies.**
- What did he say he would do if she did not let him have the pig for eight pennies? *Idea:* Tell the judge she had lied.
- What sentence did the judge give to Edward? *Idea:* Time in jail and a flogging.
- What did Miles tell Edward at the end of this chapter? *Ideas:* To be patient; they would have a chance to escape.

Award 4 points or have the students reread to the error limit sign.

INDEPENDENT WORK

Do all the items in your skillbook and workbook for lesson 114.

ANSWER KEY FOR WORKBOOK

Story Items

1. Put the following events in the right order by numbering them from 1 through 4.

   _4_ Edward went to jail.

   _1_ Edward and Hugo had a fight.

   _2_ Miles rescued Edward.

   _3_ Edward was accused of being a thief.

3. Write whether each animal is **wild** or **domestic**.

   a. Rattlesnake ___wild___

   b. Poodle ___domestic___

   c. Whale ___wild___

   d. Giraffe ___wild___

   e. Goat ___domestic___

Review Items

2. Write the story that each moral fits.
   a. Be kind to strangers.

   The Miraculous Pitcher

   b. Do not trust appearances.

   Beauty and the Beast

   c. Love is better than gold.

   The Golden Touch

4. Write whether each statement is **true** or **false**.
   a. California is north of Alaska.

   false

   b. Gold was discovered near Dawson in 1891. _false_

   c. The Yukon river flows through San Francisco. _false_

   d. California is south of Alaska.

   true

   e. Brown Wolf took place in Canada.

   true

WORKCHECK AND AWARDING POINTS

1. Read the questions and answers for the skillbook and workbook.

2. Award points for independent work as follows:

0 errors	6 points
2 errors	4 points
3, 4, or 5 errors	2 points
5 or more errors	0 points

3. Award bonus points as follows:

Correcting missed items or getting all items right	2 points
Doing the writing assignment acceptably	2 points

ANSWER KEY FOR SKILLBOOK

PART D

1. **a.** John Canty and Hugo
   b. *Idea:* Stepped on his foot
   c. A stick
   d. *Idea:* Because he had been trained
2. Hugo
3. **a.** A woman
   b. *Idea:* A bundle
   c. Edward
   d. Edward
   e. A blacksmith
   f. Miles Hendon
   g. *Idea:* With his sword
4. **a.** A police officer
   b. *Idea:* To a court
   c. A pig
   d. thirteen
   e. thirteen / hanged
   f. eight
   g. The police officer
   h. Miles Hendon
   i. Eight pennies
5. *Idea:* Time in jail and a flogging

PART E

6. **a.** intend
   b. confesses
   c. weary
   d. gagged
   e. tragic
   f. impulse
   g. identify
   h. bound
   i. widow
   j. inform

Lesson 115

Lesson 115

PART A   Word Lists

1	2
irritable	**New vocabulary**
comfortable	1. duties
hospitable	2. reel
disagreeable	3. bind
	4. armed
	5. penalty
	6. slumber

PART B   New Vocabulary

1. **duties**–Your **duties** are the things that you must do. If a person must be at school on time, that person has a **duty** to be at school on time.
   - If a person must fix dinner, that person _____.

2. **reel**–Another word for **stagger** is **reel**. If a person **staggered** from a blow, that person **reeled** from the blow.
   - If the person staggered around the room, that person _____.

3. **bind**–If you **tie** somebody up, you **bind** that person. If you **tied** somebody up, you **bound** that person.
   a. What do you do if you **tie** somebody up?
   b. What did you do if you **tied** somebody up?

4. **armed**–Somebody who has a weapon is **armed**.

5. **penalty**–A **penalty** is the punishment somebody receives for breaking the rules.
   - What do we call the punishment somebody receives for breaking the rules?

6. **slumber**–Another word for **sleep** is **slumber**.
   a. What's another way of saying **He slept in the afternoon?**
   b. What's another way of saying **She slept for hours?**

PART C   Vocabulary Review

innocent	band
mistreated	bound
impulse	inform
flogged	betray

1. When somebody is beaten with a whip or a switch, that person is _____.
2. a. Someone who is not guilty of doing something wrong is _____.
   b. A person who is not guilty of stealing is _____.
   c. A person who is not guilty of cheating is _____.
3. a. Another word for a **group** is a _____.
   b. A group of vagrants is a _____.
4. a. When somebody is treated poorly, the person is _____.
   b. If a dog is treated poorly, that dog is _____.
5. When you pretend to be somebody's friend and then trick that person, you _____ that person.

WORD PRACTICE AND VOCABULARY

EXERCISE 1   Word family

1. Everybody, find lesson 115, part A in your skillbook. *Wait.*
2. Column 1. All those words end with the letters **a-b-l-e.**
3. Your turn. Read the first word. *Signal.* **Irritable.**
4. Next word. *Signal.* **Comfortable.**
5. *Repeat step 4 for each remaining word in column 1.*
6. *Repeat the words in column 1 until firm.*

EXERCISE 2   Vocabulary development

Task A

1. Column 2. New vocabulary.
   First you're going to read the words in column 2. Then you're going to read about what they mean.
2. Read the first word. *Signal.* **Duty.**
3. Next word. *Signal.* **Reel.**
4. *Repeat step 3 for each remaining word in column 2.*
5. *Repeat the words in column 2 until firm.*

Task B

1. Everybody, look at part B.
   You're going to read this part out loud.
2. *For each item, call on a student to:*
   - *read one item aloud*
   - *read the meaning*
   - *read the question(s) for that item*
   - *answer each question orally*

   Answer Key:
   1. **has a duty to fix dinner**
   2. **reeled around the room**
   3. a. **bind that person**
      b. **bound that person**
   4. *No answer required.*
   5. **The penalty**
   6. a. **He slumbered in the afternoon.**
      b. **She slumbered for hours.**

EXERCISE 3   Vocabulary review

1. Everybody, look at part C. The words in the box are words you've learned.
2. Read the first word. *Signal.* **Innocent.**
3. Next. *Signal.* **Mistreated.**
4. *Repeat step 3 for the remaining words in the box.*
5. *Repeat the words in the box until firm.*
6. I'll read the items. When I come to a blank, everybody say the part that goes in the blank.
7. Look at item 1. *Pause.* Listen.
   When somebody is beaten with a whip or a switch, that person is *Pause. Signal.* **flogged.**
8. *Repeat step 7 for each remaining item.*

   Answer Key:
   2. a. **innocent**
      b. **innocent of stealing**
      c. **innocent of cheating**
   3. a. **band**
      b. **band of vagrants**
   4. a. **mistreated**
      b. **mistreated**
   5. **betray**

Lesson 115

CHAPTER 18
The Escape

The short winter day had nearly ended as Edward, Miles and the police officer approached the jail. There were only a few people on the street and nobody paid any attention to the party. Edward wondered if the sight of the King of England going to jail had ever received so little interest before. (A)

Near the steps of the jail, Miles put his hand on the officer's shoulder and said, "Slow down a minute. I would like to have a word with you."

"I cannot do that," the officer said. "I must do my duty. Now take your hand off me."

"This matter concerns you," Miles said. "I want you to turn your back and let the boy escape."

"How dare you suggest such a thing!" the officer replied. "I should arrest you in the . . ."

"Don't be so hasty," Miles said. Then he lowered his voice to a whisper. "You may have to pay a great deal for the pig that you purchased for eight pennies." (B)

The poor officer was speechless at first. When he found his tongue, he began to say threatening things to Miles, but Miles remained calm until the officer had finished. Then Miles said, "I like you,

friend, and I would not harm you if I didn't have to. But I heard it all—every word. I will prove it to you." Miles repeated the conversation the officer had with the woman in the hall. He ended by saying, "Haven't I told it correctly? I can tell that story the same way to the judge, if that's what you want."

The officer said nothing for a moment. Then he laughed nervously and said, "You're making a great deal over a little joke that I played on that woman."

"It was a pretty good joke, because you kept the pig."

The officer insisted that it was an innocent joke. Miles replied, "Well, why don't you just wait here a moment while I run back to the courtroom and ask the judge what he thinks of that kind of joke." (C) ★6 ERRORS★

"Wait a minute," the officer said as Miles started to move away. "That judge doesn't understand jokes very well." The officer explained that he had a wife and family. Then he asked, "What do you want of me?"

"Just close your eyes and count to a thousand—very slowly."

The officer muttered, "This will ruin me. I . . ."

In a sharp voice, Miles said, "Just remember that the penalty for your little joke is <u>death</u>, according to the law."

"Oh, good sir," the officer said. "Go with the boy. I will see nothing. I will say that you snatched the boy from me and ran off."

Miles and Edward fled. As soon as they were out of sight of the officer, Miles and Edward sat down to figure out what they were going to do. Edward wanted to go back to London, but Miles longed to see his father at Hendon Hall. Finally, he convinced Edward to go with him. Half an hour later, the two friends were riding toward Hendon Hall on a horse that Miles had bought. Edward was warm. He was no longer wearing rags, but rather a used suit that Miles had brought along.

When Miles and Edward had journeyed about ten miles, they reached a very large village and stopped there for the night. They stayed in a comfortable inn. Miles had the same duties that he had performed earlier at the other inn. He waited on Edward, helped him get ready for bed, and then slept on the floor in front of the door as the king slumbered in the bed.

The next day, as the two rode along on the horse, Miles told the story of how he had searched for Edward with the hermit. He told Edward that when the hermit returned with him to the cabin and discovered the sheepskin on the floor, he had seemed brokenhearted.

"I'm sure he was disappointed," Edward said, and then explained why the hermit was saddened when he didn't find him

in the cabin.

Miles and Edward were on their way to Hendon Hall, and as they approached it, Miles's spirits rose. He talked and talked about his father, about his brother Arthur, his brother Hugh, and Edith, the woman that Miles was going to marry. As the horse made its way over the top of a hill, Miles pointed excitedly and said, "There, my king, is the village. And you can see Hendon Hall nearby. It's a splendid place. All those woods you see belong to Hendon Hall—a mansion with seventy rooms, and twenty-seven servants."

Miles urged the horse to speed its pace, but it was after three o'clock before the horse reached the village. As the travelers moved through the village, Miles's tongue went constantly, explaining every building to Edward. Soon, the horse stopped before a noble mansion. "Welcome to Hendon Hall, my king!" Miles exclaimed, and then sprang to the ground. He helped Edward down, then took him by the hand and rushed inside. He led Edward to a spacious apartment, seated him, and then ran toward a young man who sat at a writing table.

"Hugh, it's me!" Miles cried. "I'm home again. Give me a hug."

But Hugh drew backward and stared firmly at Miles. Presently, Hugh said in a mild voice, "I'm sorry, stranger. You must think that I am someone else."

"No," Miles said, sharply. "I think that you are Hugh Hendon."

Hugh said, "And who do you think you are?"

STORY READING

EXERCISE 4   Decoding and comprehension

1. Everybody, turn to page 421 in your textbook. *Wait. Call on a student.* What's the error limit for this chapter? **6 errors.**
2. *Call on individual students to read. Present the tasks specified for each circled letter.*

(A) What punishment was waiting for Edward when he got to the jail? *Idea:* A flogging.

(B) How does Miles know about that pig? *Idea:* Because he overheard the officer talking to the woman.

● Does the officer know that Miles had seen him cheat the woman? **No.**

(C) What do you think the judge would do if he heard about this "joke?" *Idea:* Put the officer in jail.

● Read the rest of the chapter to yourselves and be ready to answer some questions.

After all students have finished reading:

● When Miles talked to the officer, he reminded him of the penalty for cheating the woman out of her pig. What was the penalty according to law? *Idea:* Death.

● What did the officer agree to do? *Idea:* Let Miles and Edward escape.

● Where did Miles and Edward go after they spent the night in an inn? *Idea:* Hendon Hall.

● How did Miles feel as he and Edward approached Hendon Hall? *Ideas:* Happy; excited.

● Inside Hendon Hall, they met a young man at a writing table. What was his name? **Hugh Hendon.**

Miles replied, "What are you doing, pretending that you don't even know your own brother?"

Hugh smiled with mock surprise. "How could you be my brother if he is dead?" He stood up and slowly circled Miles as he examined him. At last he sighed and said, "This is very disappointing."

"Why?" Miles demanded.

"Because you are not my brother. We received a letter six years ago that brought the sad news of my brother's death."

Miles replied excitedly, "Call our father. He will know me."

"It's not possible to call someone who is dead," Hugh said.

In a soft voice, Miles said, "Dead . . . my father dead. This is terrible news . . ." Looking down, Miles continued, "Call our brother Arthur, He will know me."

"He is also dead."

"Oh no," Miles said and slumped into a chair, holding his hands over his face. "And what about Lady Edith? Is she . . .?"

"No, she lives," Hugh answered flatly.

"Bring her to me," Miles said. "And bring the servants. They will know me."

A few moments later, a richly dressed, beautiful young lady followed Hugh into the room, and after her came several servants. "Oh, Edith, my darling," Miles said and began to move toward her.

But Hugh raised his hand and said to Edith, "Look at him. Do you know him?"

The woman's face was flushed and she was trembling. Slowly, she lifted her head and looked into Miles's eyes with a frightened gaze, as her face turned deathly pale. With a voice as dead as her face, she said, "I don't know him." She turned away with a slight sob and ran from the room.

Miles sank into a chair and covered his face with his hands. After a pause, Hugh said to the servants, "You have observed him. Do you know him?" They shook their heads no, and Hugh said, "You have made a mistake. Neither the servants nor my wife know you."

"Your wife?" Miles said, and in an instant pinned Hugh to the wall with an iron grip on his throat. "Now I get it. You wrote the letter about my death so that you could marry Edith. Get away from me before I give you the punishment you deserve!"

Hugh reeled to a chair and commanded the servants to seize and bind the stranger. They hesitated and one of them said, "But he is armed."

"Don't tell me that. There is only one of him and many of you."

Miles warned them to be careful. He said, "You remember from the old days. I have not changed. Attack me and you will find out." The servants stood frozen.

Hugh shouted, "Go arm yourselves and guard the doors!" Then he turned to Miles, "You will find out that you cannot escape."

"Escape?" said Miles. "I am master of Hendon Hall and all its belongings. I will remain here, where I belong."

- Who did Miles try to convince Hugh that he was? *Idea:* His brother.
- Did Hugh act convinced? **No.**
- Why didn't Miles's father identify Miles? *Idea:* Because he was dead.
- Why didn't Miles brother, Arthur, identify Miles? *Idea:* Because he was dead.
- Name the woman that Miles wanted to see. **Lady Edith.**
- What did she say when Hugh asked her if she recognized Miles? *Idea:* She didn't know him.
- What did Miles do when Hugh indicated that Edith was his wife? *Idea:* He started to choke Hugh.
- What did Miles figure out about the story that Hugh had told him? *Idea:* That Hugh had written the letter saying Miles was dead.
- Why didn't Miles try to escape from Hendon Hall? *Idea:* Because he belonged there.

Award 4 points or have the students reread to the error limit sign.

INDEPENDENT WORK

Do all the items in your skillbook and workbook for lesson 115.

ANSWER KEY FOR WORKBOOK

Main Idea and Supporting Details

Read this passage:

It was six o'clock in the morning. Birds were beginning to chirp, and squirrels were starting to come out of their holes to look for food. The eastern sky was growing lighter and lighter. There was not a cloud to be seen, nor did any wind rustle the leaves. Suddenly, the first glimmer of sunlight lit up the houses and trees. The birds began to chirp more loudly, and the eastern sky was filled with light. Another day had begun.

Write the main idea and three supporting details. *Idea:*

1. *The sun rose in the east.*
   a. *It was six in the morning.*
   b. *Sunlight lit up the houses.*
   c. *The eastern sky was filled with light.*

Review Items

2. Write the correct dates on the time line.

   1931 Jane Addams receives the Nobel Peace Prize.
   1918 World War One ends.
   1893 A new factory law passes.
   1889 Hull House opens.

WORKCHECK AND AWARDING POINTS

1. *Read the questions and answers for the skillbook and workbook.*
2. *Award points for independent work as follows:*

0 errors	6 points
2 errors	4 points
3, 4, or 5 errors	2 points
5 or more errors	0 points

3. *Award bonus points as follows:*

Correcting missed items or getting all items right	2 points
Doing the writing assignment acceptably	2 points

ANSWER KEY FOR SKILLBOOK

PART D

1. a. prison
   b. *Idea:* Let Edward escape
   c. *Idea:* Bought the pig
   d. The judge
   e. *Idea:* He would be hanged
2. a. In an inn
   b. To Hendon Hall
   c. Seventy
   d. *Idea:* Because his palace was much bigger
3. a. Hugh Hendon
   b. No
   c. Yes
   d. *Idea:* He died
   e. A letter
   f. *Idea:* His father and brother
4. a. Lady Edith
   b. Get married
   c. No
   d. *Idea:* Written the letter
   e. *Idea:* To marry Edith
   f. *Idea:* Capture him
   g. *Idea:* They were afraid of Miles

5. a. Yes
   b. Yes
   c. No
   d. No
   e. Yes

PART E

6. a. vagrant
   b. intend
   c. prosper
   d. inform
   e. betray
   f. capable of
   g. confesses
   h. impulse
   i. innocent
   j. band
   k. mistreated
   l. flogged

Lesson 116

Lesson 116

PART A   Word Lists

1	2	3
deny	overpowered	**New vocabulary**
coronation	tormented	1. prison cell
	parted	2. smuggle
	remembered	3. deny
	horrified	4. daily
	treated	5. stall

6. deathbeds
7. gossip
8. coronation

PART B   New Vocabulary

1. **prison cell**—A **prison cell** is a small room that prisoners live in.

2. **smuggle**—When you **smuggle** something, you hide it and take it to some place. If somebody hides some money and takes it into a prison cell, the person **smuggles** the money into the cell.

3. **deny**—When you say that something is not true, you **deny** that thing. When you say that you do not know a person, you **deny** knowing that person.
   - When you say you do not know a fact, you _____ .

4. **daily**—Another word for **everyday** is **daily**.
   a. What's another way of saying **He ate everyday?**
   b. What's another way of saying **She visited her grandmother everyday?**

5. **stall**—When you **stall,** you try to put off doing something.
   - How could you **stall** if you were trying to put off going to the dentist?

6. **deathbeds**—People who are on their **deathbeds** are dying.

7. **gossip**—When you **gossip** about something, you tell rumors about that thing. When you tell rumors about a new person in school, you **gossip** about a new person in school.
   - When you tell rumors about something you don't like, you

8. **coronation**—A **coronation** is an important event in which a crown is officially placed on the head of a new king. A new king is not officially a king until the **coronation.**

PART C   Vocabulary Review

bind	betray
slumber	bound
innocent	impulse
penalty	duties
armed	reel

1. The punishment somebody receives for breaking the rules is the _____

2. If you tie somebody up, you _____ that person.

3. a. Another word for **stagger** is _____
   b. If a person staggered from a blow, that person _____ .
   c. If a person staggered around the room, that person _____ .

4. a. Another word for **sleep** is _____
   b. What's another way of saying **She slept for hours?** _____
   c. What's another way of saying **He slept in the afternoon?**

5. Somebody who has a weapon is _____

6. a. The things that you should do are your _____ .
   b. If a person should be at school on time, that person has a _____
   c. If a person should fix dinner, that person has a _____ .

7. If you tied somebody up, you _____ that person.

WORD PRACTICE AND VOCABULARY

EXERCISE 1   Word practice

1. Everybody, find lesson 116, part A in your skillbook. *Wait.* Touch under each word in column 1 as I read it.
2. The first word is **deny.**
3. Next word. **Coronation.**
4. Your turn. Read the first word. *Signal.* **Deny.**
5. Next word. *Signal.* **Coronation.**

EXERCISE 2   Word family

1. Column 2. All those words end in the letters **e-d.** But be careful, because **e-d** makes different sounds in the words.
2. Your turn. Read the first word. *Signal.* **Overpowered.**
3. Next word. *Signal.* **Tormented.**
4. *Repeat step 3 for each remaining word in column 2.*
5. *Repeat the words in column 2 until firm.*

EXERCISE 3   Vocabulary development

Task A

1. Column 3. New vocabulary.
   First you're going to read the words in column 3. Then you're going to read about what they mean.
2. Read the first line. *Signal.* **Prison cell.**
3. Next word. *Signal.* **Smuggle.**
4. *Repeat step 3 for each remaining word in column 3.*
5. *Repeat the words in column 3 until firm.*

Task B

1. Everybody, look at part B.
   You're going to read this part out loud.
2. *For each item, call on a student to:*
   - *read one item aloud*
   - *read the meaning*
   - *read the question(s) for that item*
   - *answer each question orally*

   Answer Key: 1. *No answer required.*
   2. *No answer required.*
   3. **deny knowing that fact**
   4. a. **He ate daily.**
      b. **She visited her grandmother daily.**
   5. *Ideas:* Say you were sick; forget your appointment.
   6. *No answer required.*
   7. **gossip about something you don't like**
   8. *No answer required.*

EXERCISE 4   Vocabulary review

1. Everybody, look at part C. The words in the box are words you've learned.
2. Read the first word. *Signal.* **Bind.**
3. Next. *Signal.* **Slumber.**
4. *Repeat step 3 for the remaining words in the box.*
5. *Repeat the words in the box until firm.*
6. I'll read the items. When I come to a blank, everybody say the part that goes in the blank.
7. Look at item 1. *Pause.* Listen.
   The punishment somebody receives for breaking the rules is the *Pause. Signal.* **penalty.**
8. *Repeat step 7 for each remaining item.*

   Answer Key:
   2. **bind**
   3. a. **reel**
      b. **reeled from a blow**
      c. **reeled around the room**
   4. a. **slumber**
      b. **She slumbered for hours.**
      c. **He slumbered in the afternoon.**
   5. **armed**
   6. a. **duties**
      b. **duty to be at school on time**
      c. **duty to fix dinner**
   7. **bound**

Lesson 116

CHAPTER 19
Prison

Hugo and the servants left the room. Edward sat thoughtfully for a few moments, then observed, "It is strange that there are no soldiers out looking for me."

Miles said to himself, "His mind is ruined."(A)

Edward then announced a plan. He said, "I will write a letter in three languages—English, Latin, and Greek. Take that letter to the palace and deliver it to one person—Hertford. When he reads it, he will know that it comes from the real king."

Miles said, "Wouldn't it be better for us to wait here until I prove who I really am?"

Edward became very angry and began to scold Miles for worrying about such small matters. Just then Lady Edith entered. She was very pale, but she walked with a firm step. Miles sprang forward, but she stopped him with a gesture. She sat down and asked him to do the same. Then she said, "I have come to warn you. If I can't persuade you to forget your mad dream, then I would like to persuade you to save yourself. You are in great danger." She stared steadily at Miles. Slowly, she continued, "I know my husband. He will deny you, and he will see to it that you are

424   Lesson 116   Textbook

destroyed."(B)

Miles tried to explain that he was Miles Hendon, but she stopped him with a gesture and said, "Arthur and his father are free from the terror of Hugh. If you stay here, you will suffer the same fate they suffered. So, please go and do not hesitate. Take this purse of money and leave at once, while you still can."

Miles did not accept the purse. He rose and stood before her. "Look me in the eyes and tell me if I am Miles Hendon."

"I do not know you," she replied in a steady voice. "Now leave, while you can."

At that moment, four officers burst into the room and a terrible struggle began. Miles was soon overpowered and dragged away. A few minutes later, Miles and Edward were being led to prison.(C)

★6 ERRORS★

The cells inside the prison were crowded, so the two friends were chained together in a large room. With them in this room were over twenty other prisoners, both men and women. All the prisoners were chained together in pairs. Edward complained loudly over the way he had been treated, but nobody paid much attention to him. Miles became solemn. He was

confused, after being so joyful at the thought of coming home and now finding himself in prison. He felt like somebody who had stepped outside to see a beautiful rainbow and been struck by lightning.

But gradually his tormented thoughts settled down into order, and then his mind focused on Edith. He couldn't understand why she wouldn't remember him.

• • •

The first week went by very slowly. During the days, there was very little to do, except think. At night the gang of people inside the room became very loud and made it hard for Miles and Edward to sleep.

A week after Miles and Edward had entered the prison, the prison guard brought another prisoner into the room, an old man. The guard said to him, "The person who claims to be Miles Hendon is in this room. Look around and see if you can identify that person."

Miles looked at the old man and recognized him instantly. He was Blake Andrews, who had been a servant all his life at Hendon Hall. At first Miles experienced a spark of hope, but then he concluded that Blake Andrews would lie the same way the others lied.

The old man gazed around the room, glanced at each face, and then said, "I don't see Miles Hendon in this motley bunch. Which one claims to be Miles Hendon?"

The prison guard laughed, "Here," he said, pointing to Miles. "This big animal is the one."

The old man approached Miles, examined him, then shook his head and said, "This man is not Miles Hendon and has never been Miles Hendon."

The guard laughed and left the room. As soon as he was out of sight, the old man dropped to his knees and whispered, "I am thankful that you have come back, my master. I denied that it was you, but if you say the word, I will tell the truth, even though I will be hanged for it."

"No," said Miles. "There is no need for that. I am grateful enough that you are still true to me."

The old servant became very valuable to Miles and Edward. He visited them everyday and smuggled in things for them to eat. He also brought them news. Through these daily visits, Miles learned the true story of his family. His brother, Arthur had been dead for six years. After Arthur's death, Miles's father became ill and believed that he was going to die. He wanted to see Hugh and Edith married before he died, but Edith begged for a delay in the marriage, hoping that Miles would return. Then the letter about Miles's death came. The letter shocked Miles's father and Edith. Miles's father was convinced that he was ready to die, and Hugh urged him to insist on the marriage. Edith kept stalling by asking for one more month before making a decision. But after the third time she stalled, Miles's father was on his deathbed and the marriage finally took place. It was not a very happy marriage. Rumors around the countryside said that Edith had discovered that the letter about Miles's death had

Lesson 116   Textbook   425

244   Lesson 116

STORY READING

EXERCISE 5   Decoding and comprehension

1. Everybody, turn to page 424 in your textbook. *Wait. Call on a student.* What's the error limit for this chapter? **6 errors.**

2. *Call on individual students to read. Present the tasks specified for each circled letter.*

(A) Why would Edward think that soldiers should be looking for him? *Idea:* Because he was the missing king.

• If they're not looking for him, do they think he is missing? **No.**

(B) What does that mean: **Her husband will deny him?** *Idea:* Her husband will say that he doesn't know him.

(C) Do you think Lady Edith really recognizes Miles? *Response:* Student preference.

• Why do you think she denies that she knows him? *Response:* Student preference.

• Where are Edward and Miles going now? *Idea:* To prison.

• Read the rest of the chapter to yourselves and be ready to answer some questions.

After all students have finished reading:

• The chapter says that Miles was confused over what had happened. It said he felt like somebody who had stepped outside to see a rainbow and got struck by lightning. When did Miles feel like somebody stepping outside to see a rainbow? *Idea:* When he arrived at Hendon Hall.

• When did Miles feel like somebody who got struck by lightning? *Idea:* When everybody at Hendon Hall denied knowing him.

• Who did the prison guard bring to the room after Miles and Edward had been in prison for a week? **Blake Andrews.**

• Where had Blake Andrews worked all his life? **At Hendon Hall.**

• What did the guard want to see if Blake Andrews could do? *Idea:* Identify Miles.

• Did Blake Andrews identify Miles for the guard? **No.**

• Did Blake Andrews actually know Miles? **Yes.**

• Blake Andrews told the story of what had happened at Hendon Hall. Who was Arthur? *Idea:* Miles' brother.

• What happened to him? *Idea:* He died.

• What did Miles's father want to happen before he died? *Idea:* He wanted Lady Edith and Hugh to get married.

• How did Edith feel about the plan? *Idea:* She didn't like it.

been written by Hugh. Other rumors told of Hugh's cruelty to Lady Edith. After the death of his father, Hugh did not disguise his cruelty any longer. He got rid of the servants who had been faithful to his father and replaced them with servants who would be loyal to him.

One bit of gossip that the old man delivered interested Edward greatly. The old man reported that other people who had been to London were saying that the king was mad. Edward objected loudly to that comment, pointing out that he was not even slightly mad. After Miles managed to quiet Edward, the old servant continued with his gossip. He said that Hugh was planning to go to the coronation of the new king. The servant explained that Hugh was planning to become friendly with Hertford so that he would be treated well by the new king.

Again Edward became angry and tried to explain that _he_ was the real king. Miles asked the old man to go on, and the old man explained that although the new king was supposed to be mad, he had done some very good things, and that everybody was talking about how intelligent he was. The old man concluded by saying, "The king is now working on changing the cruel laws that threaten the people."

This news amazed Edward so much that he stopped listening to the old man and turned to his own thoughts. As the day dragged on, these thoughts bothered Edward so much that he could not be stirred

from his sadness. When he was feeling his gloomiest, a prison guard entered the room and announced that the prisoners were going into the prison yard for a little while. That announcement raised Edward's spirits, and he tried to hurry the other prisoners so that he could get outside quickly and again look at the sky, rather than the dark walls of his prison room. But outside, Edward was horrified to learn the reason for going out. The prison guards grabbed Miles and with a mob of cackling prisoners following, they led Miles to the stocks. They placed him in the stocks, and the mob then proceeded to throw things at him and hurl insults. "What is the meaning of this?" Edward demanded, as he pushed through the mob.

One of the prisoners explained, "That's his punishment for pretending to be Miles Hendon."

Edward rushed forward and announced angrily to a guard, "Take him out of those stocks immediately. He is my servant and you shall not treat him this way!"

"Who do you think you're talking to?" the guard said and grabbed Edward. "You will talk differently after you have felt the sting of my whip."

At that moment, Hugh Hendon rode up on a fine horse, and the mob parted to let him through. "Yes," Hugh said with a smile, "I think the boy should be flogged so that he will learn some manners."

- What did Edith later discover about the letter that told of Miles's death? _Idea:_ That Hugh had written it.
- What event was Hugh planning to attend? _Idea:_ The coronation.
- Who did he hope to become friends with at the coronation? **Hertford.**
- Why? _Idea:_ So that the new king would treat him well.
- How did Edward feel when he found out that the prisoners were going outside? _Idea:_ Happy.
- What did the guards do outside? _Idea:_ Put Miles in the stocks.
- What happened when Edward objected to the way they were treating Miles? _Idea:_ The guard threatened to whip Edward.
- Who rode up on a fine horse?
- What did he say? _Idea:_ That Edward should be flogged.

**Award 4 points or have the students reread to the error limit sign.**

EXERCISE 6 Special projects

1. Everybody, turn to lesson 116 in your workbook. Read the special projects section to yourself. Read it carefully so that you can decide what you want to do. After you finish, we'll discuss the projects.

2. *After all students have finished reading:* Every student should work on at least one project. I'll name the projects, and you raise your hand if the project I name is the one you want to work on.
   - **Project 1:** Making a list of all the kings and queens of England. Who wants to work on that project? *List students who volunteer.*
   - **Project 2:** Writing your own ending for The Prince and the Pauper. Who wants to work on that project? *List students who volunteer.*

3. *Allow the students extra time to carry out their projects.*

INDEPENDENT WORK

Do all the items in your skillbook and workbook for lesson 116.

ANSWER KEY FOR WORKBOOK

Story Items

1. Write which character each statement describes. Choose from **Edward, Hugh, Miles,** or **Tom.**
   a. He had written a false letter.
   Hugh
   b. Edith had wanted to marry him.
   Miles
   c. He wanted to write a letter in three languages. *Edward*
   d. People thought he was the new king.
   Tom
   e. He was put in the stocks.
   Miles
   f. He ruled Hendon Hall after his father died. *Hugh*

Special Projects

1. England has had many kings and queens. Look in an encyclopedia or other reference books and find the names of all the kings and queens since William the First. On a large piece of paper, make a time line that shows all the kings and queens of England and the years they ruled. Circle the kings and queens that were more important than the others. If you want, you can put other important dates in English history on the time line.

2. There are only four chapters left in The Prince and the Pauper. Without reading ahead, write your own ending for the novel. Tell what will happen to Edward, to Miles and to Tom. Tell what will happen to the other characters. Make your story at least three pages long. Then turn your stories into the teacher. The teacher will read them out loud after the class finishes the novel.

WORKCHECK AND AWARDING POINTS

1. *Read the questions and answers for the skillbook and workbook.*

2. *Award points for independent work as follows:*

0 errors	6 points
2 errors	4 points
3, 4, or 5 errors	2 points
5 or more errors	0 points

3. *Award bonus points as follows:*

Correcting missed items or getting all items right	2 points
Doing the writing assignment acceptably	2 points

ANSWER KEY FOR SKILLBOOK

PART D
1. a. A letter
   b. Three
2. a. Lady Edith
   b. *Idea:* He was in danger
   c. *Idea:* To see if she recognized him
   d. *Idea:* Some officers
   e. To prison
   f. *Idea:* With chains
3. a. Blake Andrews
   b. Hendon Hall
   c. No
   d. Yes
4. a. Miles's father
   b. *Idea:* The letter
   c. *Idea:* Cruelly
   d. Hugh Hendon
5. a. The stocks
   b. *Idea:* He was being punished
   c. Whip him
   d. Hugh Hendon

PART E
6. a. irritable
   b. innocent
   c. flogged
   d. armed
   e. duties
   f. betray
   g. reel
   h. bind
   i. slumber
   j. penalty

Lesson 117

Lesson 117

PART A   Word Lists

1	2	3	4
ceremony	imagination	deafen	**New vocabulary**
procession	coronation	broken	1. riot
riot	concentration	brokenhearted	2. procession
imposter	expression	deafening	3. ceremony
aisle	hesitation	cannon	
	procession		

PART B   New Vocabulary

1. **riot**—A **riot** is a great fight that involves a mob of people.
● What do we call a great fight that involves a mob of people?

2. **procession**—A **procession** is a group of people who go from one place to another.
A line of people going through the lunchroom is a **procession** of people going through the lunchroom.
● A line of people going on a fire drill is a _____.

3. **ceremony**—A **ceremony** is an important event that always takes place in the same way.
A marriage is a **ceremony**. A graduation is a **ceremony**.

PART C   Vocabulary Review

gossip	penalty
reel	armed
stocks	prison cell
deathbeds	deny
coronation	stall
smuggle	daily

1. a. When you hide something and take it to some place, you _____ something.
   b. If somebody hides some money and takes it into a prison cell, the person _____.

2. a. Another word for everyday is _____.
   b. What's another way of saying **She visited her grandmother everyday?** _____
   c. What's another way of saying **He ate everyday?** _____

3. People who are dying are on their _____

4. A small room that prisoners live in is a _____.

5. An important event in which the crown is officially placed on the head of a new king is a _____.

6. a. When you say that something is not true, you _____ that thing.
   b. When you say you do not know a fact, you _____.
   c. When you say that you do not know a person, you _____.

7. a. When you tell rumors about something, you _____ about that thing.
   b. When you tell rumors about something you don't like, you _____
   c. When you tell rumors about a new person in school, you _____.

8. When you try to put off doing something, you _____.

WORD PRACTICE AND VOCABULARY

EXERCISE 1   Word practice

1. Everybody, find lesson 117, part A in your skillbook. *Wait.* Touch under each word in column 1 as I read it.
2. The first word is **ceremony.**
3. Next word. **Procession.**
4. *Repeat step 3 for each remaining word in column 1.*
5. Your turn. Read the first word. *Signal.* **Ceremony.**
6. Next word. *Signal.* **Procession.**
7. *Repeat step 6 for each remaining word in column 1.*
8. *Repeat the words in column 1 until firm.*

EXERCISE 2   Word family

1. Column 2. All those words end in the sound **shun.**
2. Your turn. Read the first word. *Signal.* **Imagination.**
3. Next word. *Signal.* **Coronation.**
4. *Repeat step 3 for each remaining word in column 2.*
5. *Repeat the words in column 2 until firm.*

EXERCISE 3   Word practice

1. Column 3.
2. Your turn. Read the first word. *Signal.* **Deafen.**

3. Next word. *Signal.* **Broken.**
4. *Repeat step 3 for each remaining word in column 3*
5. *Repeat the words in column 3 until firm.*

EXERCISE 4   Vocabulary development

Task A

1. Column 4. New vocabulary.
   First you're going to read the words in column 4. Then you're going to read about what they mean.
2. Read the first line. *Signal.* **Riot.**
3. Next word. **Procession.**
4. *Repeat step 3 for ceremony.*
5. *Repeat the words in column 4 until firm.*

Task B

1. Everybody, look at part B.
   You're going to read this part out loud.
2. *For each item, call on a student to:*
   ● *read one item aloud*
   ● *read the meaning*
   ● *read the question(s) for that item*
   ● *answer each question orally*

   Answer Key: **1. A riot**
   2. procession of people going on a fire drill
   3. *No answer required.*

EXERCISE 5   Vocabulary review

1. Everybody, look at part C. The words in the box are words you've learned.
2. Read the first word. *Signal.* **Gossip.**
3. Next. *Signal.* **Reel.**
4. *Repeat step 3 for the remaining words in the box.*
5. *Repeat the words in the box until firm.*
6. I'll read the items. When I come to a blank, everybody say the part that goes in the blank.
7. Look at item 1a. *Pause.* Listen.
   When you hide something and take it to some place, you *Pause. Signal.* **smuggle** something.
8. *Repeat step 7 for each remaining item.*

   Answer Key:
   1. b. smuggles some money
   2. a. daily
   b. She visited her grandmother daily.
   c. He ate daily.
   3. deathbeds
   4. prison cell
   5. coronation
   6. a. deny
   b. deny knowing that fact
   c. deny knowing that person
   7. a. gossip
   b. gossip about something you don't like
   c. gossip about a new person in school
   8. stall

Lesson 117   **247**

Lesson 117

CHAPTER 20
London

The guard was holding Edward as Hugh Hendon smiled from his horse. Just as the guard was ready to strip off the boy's shirt, Miles said, "No, do not strike that boy. He is mad, and not well. I will take his punishment." Ⓐ

Hugh's smile grew larger. "Indeed," he exclaimed. "Let that man take the boy's punishment. And make the punishment something he will remember for a long time." Ⓑ

So Edward watched with empty horror as the guards removed Miles from the stocks, stripped off his shirt, and struck him with the terrible whip.

Miles Hendon did not cry out. His face kept the same hard expression. When the beating was finished, Hugh Hendon turned his horse around, and the crowd quickly parted to let him leave. The guards again placed Miles in the stocks, and soon the crowd left. Edward slowly approached Miles and knelt down beside him. He picked up a small stick from the ground. "You are very brave," Miles said through his tears.

Edward touched Miles lightly on his bleeding shoulder with the stick. "I, the King of England, make you an earl. You are now Earl Miles Hendon." Ⓒ

Poor Miles didn't know whether to laugh or cry. He felt tears forming in his eyes, but he couldn't tell whether they came from the terrible pain or from the terrible humor of being a prisoner who is both a knight and an earl.

Miles was kept in the stocks all that day and all the following day. On the morning of the next day, the guards released him, and gave him back his horse and his sword. They gave him a paper stating that he had paid for his crime. They then announced that he and Edward were free and could leave the prison. Ⓓ

★6 ERRORS★

As Edward and Miles left the prison yard on Miles's horse, the other prisoners stared silently at them. Once outside the walls of the prison, Miles began to wonder where he should go. He remembered what his servant had told him about the new king, and Miles thought that he might go to this intelligent boy and tell him what had happened at Hendon Hall. But then Miles wondered how someone who looked like a vagrant could ever get inside the palace to talk to the king. After thinking about other possible plans, Miles decided to head for the palace. "I'll find some way to get inside," he said to himself. Once

428   Lesson 117   Textbook

Miles made that decision, his mood changed. He forgot about his terrible experience in the prison and began concentrating on plans to see the young king.

Several days later, Miles and the real king reached London Bridge, around ten o'clock at night. The bridge was swarming with a struggling mob of howling people. Edward shouted to Miles, above the roaring crowd, "Why is this mob celebrating?"

Miles shouted back, "Because tomorrow is coronation day. Edward becomes the official king tomorrow."

Before Edward could remind Miles that the real king was riding on the horse with him, a fight started among some men on the bridge. One person had tripped and fallen into another person, who had fallen into another, and another. In a few moments, the fight spread until it became a riot. As the fight spread around Miles's horse, the horse reared up and threw Edward to the street. Within a few moments, Miles and Edward were hopelessly separated from each other and lost in the roaring mob. And that is where we leave them.

• • •

When we left Tom Canty, he was beginning to enjoy playing the part of a king. As time passed, he enjoyed it even more. His fears faded and died. His embarrassment left him and was replaced with quiet confidence. He enjoyed hearing the horns sound as he approached and the distant voices announce, "Make way for the king!" From time to time, Tom Canty was

troubled when he thought about the real king and what might have happened to him. But as time passed and Edward did not return, Tom thought less about him and more about his own new experiences, until the thoughts about Edward nearly vanished from his mind.

Tom's feelings about his mother, his sisters, and his grandmother changed in the same way. At first, he missed them greatly, but later he began to hope that he would never see them again. He was afraid that if he saw them again he would have to return to Pudding Lane and the life he had known before he was king. When he thought about them in this way, he hated himself for having such heartless thoughts. He would picture their poor faces in his imagination, and they made him feel lower than the worms that wriggle along the ground.

While the real king was caught in the middle of a riot and was being pushed along by an angry crowd, Tom Canty was lying on his silk sheets feeling very satisfied. Tomorrow was coronation day—the day that he would become the official King of England.

When Tom awoke the next morning, he could hear the voices of thousands of people in the distance. They lined the river, waiting for the king to enter his royal barge and move down the river to the Tower of London. At the Tower of London, the king would ride a horse through the streets of London to a splendid church, where the coronation ceremony would be held.

Lesson 117   Textbook   **429**

STORY READING

EXERCISE 6   Decoding and comprehension

1. Everybody, turn to page 428 in your textbook. *Wait. Call on a student.* What's the error limit for this chapter? **6 errors.**

2. *Call on individual students to read. Present the tasks specified for each circled letter.*

Ⓐ What punishment is Edward supposed to receive? *Idea:* A flogging.

Ⓑ Do you think Hugh Hendon would mind it if Miles took the punishment? **No.**

Ⓒ What new title did Edward give to Miles? **Earl.**

● What title had Edward given Miles earlier? *Idea:* Knight.

● How do you think Miles feels about being an earl? *Idea:* Confused.

Ⓓ What did the guards give Miles to show that he had paid for his crime? *Idea:* A paper.

● What had Miles gone to prison for? *Idea:* Pretending to be Miles Hendon.

● Read the rest of the chapter to yourselves and be ready to answer some questions.

After all students have finished reading:

● Where did Miles decide to go after he was freed from prison? *Idea:* To the royal palace.

● Who did he want to see? *Idea:* The king.

● Several days later, Miles and Edward arrived at a place that was swarming with howling people. What place was that? **London Bridge.**

● What was the mob celebrating? *Idea:* The coronation.

● When was the coronation of the new king to take place? *Idea:* The next day.

● What happened on the bridge that separated Miles and Edward? *Idea:* A riot.

● Tom's thoughts about the real king changed as Tom got used to playing the part of the king. Tell how his thoughts changed. *Idea:* He stopped thinking about the real king.

● Tom's thoughts about some other people changed in the same way. Who were these people? *Idea:* His mother and sisters.

● When he pictured their poor faces, how would he feel? *Idea:* Lower than a worm.

● Why did he feel that way? *Idea:* Because he knew they were still living on Pudding Lane.

● The next morning, Tom went to the coronation ceremony. How did he get from the palace to the Tower of London? *Idea:* On the royal barge.

Within an hour Tom and the royal party were floating down the river to the Tower of London. When Tom arrived, cannons in the tower shot out hot tongues of flame and white clouds of smoke, followed by deafening explosions that made the ground tremble. The cannons fired again and again, until the Tower of London disappeared in a great cloud of smoke.

Tom Canty was dressed in splendid clothes. He mounted a magnificent war horse that pranced nervously. Next to Tom was Hertford, riding a horse like Tom's. Behind Tom and Hertford followed a line of lords, including the Mayor of London. It was a splendid sight, and as the troop moved slowly down the streets, people bowed, and cheered, and cried out encouragement for the new king. Tom responded by holding his head high and smiling.

Just as Tom was at the height of enjoyment, he caught sight of a pale, puzzled face that strained forward from the second row of the crowd that lined the street. The eyes of that face were fixed on Tom, and Tom suddenly felt sick as he recognized the face. It belonged to his mother. Almost without thinking, Tom waved to her. An instant later, she tore through the crowd of people, past the guards, and was at Tom's side. She embraced his leg, and covered it with kisses as she cried, "Oh, my child, my darling!" Her expression showed pure joy.

An instant later, an officer of the king's guard snatched her away and sent her reeling back into the crowd. Tom felt himself saying, "I do not know you, woman," but at the same time, his heart was very heavy to see her treated in that way. As the troop moved on, and the crowd swallowed up the sight of his mother, Tom took a last glimpse of her. She looked brokenhearted, and a feeling of shame came over Tom Canty. He wondered why he had betrayed her for the worthless robes and the empty life of a king. As the splendid, shining procession moved down the streets, Hertford was quick to notice the change that had occurred in the king. Tom rode with his head down as he kept hearing the words that he had said, "I do not know you, woman."

Hertford reminded Tom that everybody was looking at him and that he should smile. Hertford added, "We should punish that pauper. She was the one who disturbed you."

The handsome figure of the king turned his eyes to Hertford and said, in a dead voice, "She is my mother."

"Oh, no!" Hertford exclaimed. "He's gone mad again!"

- How did he get from the Tower of London to the church? *Idea:* On a horse.
- What happened at the Tower of London to signal that the king had arrived? *Idea:* Cannons were fired.
- Then Tom and the troop moved down the streets of London. How did Tom feel at first? *Idea:* Good.
- What happened to make him feel very sad? *Idea:* He saw his mother.
- What did Tom's mother do when Tom waved at her without thinking? *Idea:* She ran through the crowd and embraced him.
- What did the officer do? *Ideas:* Grabbed her and shoved her back into the crowd.
- What did Tom say? *Idea:* That he didn't know her.
- Who noticed that Tom's mood had changed? **Hertford.**
- What did Tom tell Hertford? *Idea:* That the woman was his mother.
- What did Hertford think when Tom said that? *Idea:* That the king had gone crazy again.

Award 4 points or have the students reread to the error limit sign.

INDEPENDENT WORK

Do all the items in your skillbook and workbook for lesson 117.

ANSWER KEY FOR WORKBOOK

Outlining

The outline shows three main ideas for <u>The Golden Touch.</u>

Write three supporting details for each main idea.

1. Midas had an insane desire for gold.

Idea:

a. *He collected all the gold he could.*

b. *He spent all his time with his gold.*

c. *He asked for the Golden Touch.*

2. The Golden Touch created problems.

a. *Midas could not see through his glasses.*

b. *Midas could not eat.*

c. *Midas turned Marygold into gold.*

3. Midas solved his problems.

a. *Midas admitted his mistake.*

b. *Midas dove into the river.*

c. *Midas sprinkled water on all the golden things.*

WORKCHECK AND AWARDING POINTS

1. *Read the questions and answers for the skillbook and workbook.*
2. *Award points for independent work as follows:*

0 errors	6 points
2 errors	4 points
3, 4, or 5 errors	2 points
5 or more errors	0 points

3. *Award bonus points as follows:*

Correcting missed items or getting all items right	2 points
Doing the writing assignment acceptably	2 points

ANSWER KEY FOR SKILLBOOK

PART D

1. a. *Idea:* In the courtyard
   b. A guard
   c. Hugh Hendon
   d. Miles Hendon
   e. Miles Hendon
   f. *Idea:* He cared for Edward
   g. Earl
   h. Knight
   i. pain
2. a. The king
   b. London
   c. Ten o'clock at night
   d. The coronation
   e. The next day
   f. On London Bridge
   g. Edward and Miles
3. a. *Idea:* Seldom
   b. *Idea:* His mother and sisters
4. a. The coronation
   b. Cannons
   c. *Idea:* A church
   d. Hertford
5. a. His mother
   b. *Idea:* Ran up to him
   c. *Idea:* I don't know you
   d. *Idea:* Bad
   e. *Idea:* That she was his mother
   f. *Idea:* He had gone crazy again

PART E

6. a. deathbeds
   b. smuggle
   c. slumber
   d. deny
   e. identify
   f. stocks
   g. duties
   h. coronation
   i. penalty
   j. stall
   k. gossip
   l. tragic
   m. daily
   n. prison cell

Lesson 118

Lesson 118

PART A   **Word Lists**

1	2	3
worthless	form	**New vocabulary**
heartless	platform	1. under arrest
hopeless	loud	2. imposter
motionless	aloud	
speechless	suspicious	
	suspicion	

PART B   **New Vocabulary**

1. **under arrest**—When a police officer places somebody **under arrest,** the officer accuses that person of committing a crime.

2. **imposter**—Someone who pretends to be somebody else is an **imposter.**
   • What do we call someone who pretends to be somebody else?

PART C   **Vocabulary Review**

| deny |
| ceremony |
| stall |
| daily |
| procession |
| riot |

1. a. A group of people who go from one place to another is a _____.
   b. A line of people going on a fire drill is a _____.
   c. A line of people going through the lunchroom is a _____.
2. An important event that always takes place in the same way is a _____.
3. A great fight that involves a mob of people is a _____.

WORD PRACTICE AND VOCABULARY

EXERCISE 1   Word family

1. Everybody, find lesson 118, part A in your skillbook. *Wait.*
2. Column 1. All those words have the same ending.
3. Your turn. Read the first word. *Signal.* **Worthless.**
4. Next word. *Signal.* **Heartless.**
5. *Repeat step 4 for each remaining word in column 1.*
6. *Repeat the words in column 1 until firm.*

EXERCISE 2   Word practice

1. Column 2.
2. Your turn. Read the first word. *Signal.* **Form.**
3. Next word. *Signal.* **Platform.**
4. *Repeat step 3 for each remaining word in column 2.*
5. *Repeat the words in column 2 until firm.*

EXERCISE 3   Vocabulary development

Task A

1. Column 3. New vocabulary.
   First you're going to read the words in column 3. Then you're going to read about what they mean.
2. Read the first line. *Signal.* **Under arrest.**
3. Next word. *Signal.* **Imposter.**

Task B

1. Everybody, look at part B.
   You're going to read this part out loud.
2. *For each item, call on a student to:*
   • *read one item aloud*
   • *read the meaning*
   • *read the question(s) for that item*
   • *answer each question orally*

   Answer Key: **1.** *No answer required.*
   2. An imposter

EXERCISE 4   Vocabulary review

1. Everybody, look at part C. The words in the box are words you've learned.
2. Read the first word. *Signal.* **Deny.**
3. Next. *Signal.* **Ceremony.**
4. *Repeat step 3 for the remaining words in the box.*
5. *Repeat the words in the box until firm.*
6. I'll read the items. When I come to a blank, everybody say the part that goes in the blank.
7. Look at item 1a. *Pause.* Listen.
   A group of people who go from one place to another is a *Pause. Signal.* **procession.**
8. *Repeat step 7 for each remaining item.*

   Answer Key: **1. b. procession of people going on a fire drill**
   c. procession of people going through the lunchroom
   2. ceremony
   3. riot

The Spider and the Fly
by Mary Howitt

"Will you walk into my parlor?" said the Spider to the Fly,
"Tis the prettiest little parlor that ever you did spy;
The way into my parlor is up a winding stair,
And I've many curious things to show when you are there."
"Oh, no, no," said the little Fly, "to ask me is in vain,
For who goes up your winding stair can ne'er come down again."

"I'm sure you must be weary, dear, with soaring up so high;
Will you rest upon my little bed?" said the Spider to the Fly.
"There are pretty curtains drawn around; the sheets are fine and thin,
And if you like to rest a while, I'll snugly tuck you in!"
"Oh, no, no," said the little Fly, "for I've often heard it said,
They never, never wake again, who sleep upon your bed!"

Said the cunning Spider to the Fly, "Dear friend, what can I do
To prove the warm affection I've always felt for you?
I have within my pantry good store of all that's nice;
I'm sure you're very welcome—will you please to take a slice?"
"Oh no, no," said the little Fly, "kind sir, that cannot be;
I've heard what's in your pantry, and I do not wish to see!"

"Sweet creature," said the Spider, "you're witty and you're wise,
How handsome are your pearly wings, how brilliant are your eyes!
I have a little looking-glass upon my parlor shelf,
If you'll step in one moment, dear, you shall behold yourself."
"I thank you, gentle sir," she said, "for what you're pleased to say,
And bidding you good morning now, I'll call another day."

The Spider then turned round about, and went into his den,
For well he knew the silly Fly would soon come back again;
So he wove a subtle web, in a little corner sly,
And set his table ready, to dine upon the Fly.
Then he came out to his door again, and merrily did sing,
"Come hither, hither, pretty Fly, with the pearl and silver wing;
Your robes are green and purple—there's a crest upon your head;
Your eyes are like the diamond bright, but mine are dull as lead!"

Alas, alas! how very soon this silly little Fly,
Hearing the cunning, flattering words, came slowly flitting by;
With buzzing wings she hung aloft, then near and nearer drew,
Thinking only of her brilliant eyes, and green and purple hue—
Thinking only of her crested head—poor foolish thing! At last,
Up jumped the cunning Spider, and fiercely held her fast.
He dragged her up his winding stair, into his dismal den,
Within his little parlor—but she ne'er came out again!

And now, to all you people, who may this story read,
To idle, silly, flattering words, I pray you ne'er give heed;
And unto evil creatures close heart and ear and eye,
And take a lesson from this tale of the Spider and the Fly.

STORY READING

EXERCISE 5 Narrative poem

1. Everybody, turn to page 442 in your textbook. We're going to read the entire poem. I'll call on different students. Each student will read one stanza. *The students read aloud.*

Lesson 118

CHAPTER 21
Coronation Day

At last the procession reached the towering church where the coronation ceremony would take place. Ⓐ Kings and queens from other countries in Europe filed inside and took their places. They were followed by a long line of dukes and earls and ladies and judges. Next came the king's sister, Elizabeth. At last, the horns sounded to announce the king. As the entire group stood motionless, Tom Canty slowly moved forward and stepped up on the platform at the front of the church. Two judges led Tom to the throne in the middle of the platform, while the audience gazed. With each step toward the throne, Tom's face grew more pale. He was confused and ashamed as he sat on the throne. Silent moments passed as the head of the English Church walked toward Tom, holding the crown that could be worn only by the King of England. Once that crown was placed on Tom's head, he would be the official king. Ⓑ ★6 ERRORS★

At the moment that the crown was just over Tom's head and was being lowered slowly, the ceremony was interrupted by an incredible sight. A young boy, wearing an old suit, was standing in the middle aisle of the church. He raised his hand and announced loudly, "Do not place the crown on that imposter, for I am the real King of England!"

In an instant, guards grabbed the boy, but in the same instant, Tom Canty jumped from the throne and cried out in a ringing voice, "Take your hands off him! He is the king!"

The huge audience was shocked. People wondered whether they were awake or having some sort of terrible dream. Hertford stepped forward and said above the mumbling of the crowd, "Don't pay any attention to the king. He is suffering from an illness that he's had for a while."

Before anybody had a chance to obey Hertford, Tom Canty stamped his foot and cried out, "I told you not to touch him! He is the real king!"

The hands that had held Edward moved back, and the audience fell into such a deep silence that it was possible to hear Edward breathing. The people watching this amazing event were lost in confusion as the true king walked confidently forward and stepped up on the platform. Tom Canty, the mock king, ran with a glad face to meet him. Tom fell to his knees and said, "Oh, my king, let poor Tom Canty be the first to say, "Put on the crown and take your place as King of England."

Hertford turned his sharp eyes toward the shabbily dressed boy who stood in front of the kneeling Tom Canty. Hertford's eyes quickly softened and gave way to an expression of wondering surprise. The others who were close to the two boys had the same experience as they observed that the boys seemed to be identical. Hertford approached the real king and said in a gentle voice, "Excuse me sir, would you mind if I asked you a few questions?"

"I will answer them, my lord."

Hertford asked many questions about the king's duties, and about princes and princesses. The boy answered every question correctly, without the slightest hesitation. He described the rooms in the palace, including the king's apartment. All who listened were amazed. People turned to each other and said, "Perhaps he is the real king."

Tom Canty smiled broadly. But Hertford slowly shook his head, and then said, "You have shown great knowledge, but your knowledge is no greater than that of the king you see robed before you. He could also tell about the things you have described." This statement saddened Tom, and he felt his hopes fall.

There was a sudden shift in the crowd, as people began to repeat what Hertford had just said. "Yes, his answers to the questions don't prove that he is the true king."

Hertford expressed his thoughts aloud. "This situation is very dangerous," he said. "We cannot have any doubt about who the real king is. Such doubt could divide the country and ruin it." Before

EXERCISE 6   Decoding and comprehension

1. Everybody, turn to page 431 in your textbook. *Wait. Call on a student.* What's the error limit for this chapter? **6 errors.**
2. *Call on individual students to read. Present the tasks specified for each circled letter.*

Ⓐ Where did this procession begin? *Idea:* At the Tower of London.

Ⓑ The picture shows Tom Canty during the coronation ceremony. You can see the platform that he and the others are on.

- What is the judge holding above Tom's head? **A crown.**
- What happens when that crown is placed on his head? *Idea:* He is King of England.
- Why do you think Tom has such a sad expression? *Idea:* Because he isn't really the king.
- Read the rest of the story to yourselves and be ready to answer some questions.

After all students have finished reading:

- Who asked Edward questions about the palace and the duties of the king? **Hertford.**
- How well did Edward answer those questions? *Idea:* Very well.
- Was Hertford convinced that Edward was the real king? **No.**
- Why wasn't Hertford convinced? *Idea:* Because Tom Canty knew all those things too.

Tom could again object and point out that Edward was the real king, Hertford turned to a judge and said, "Arrest this young . . . No, wait." Hertford's face lighted and he said to the shabbily dressed boy, "I have one more question for you. If you answer it correctly, you will prove that you are indeed the King of England."

"I will answer it," Edward said.

"Ever since Henry's death, we have been unable to find the royal seal. As far as we know, the last person to have this seal was the real prince. If you can tell me where the seal is, you will tell us something that only the true King of England could know."

This question was such a good one that some of the officials applauded Hertford. The officials looked at each other and nodded with approving smiles. They were saying to themselves, "Yes, this young man has been very carefully taught information about the palace, but an imposter could not possibly know where the seal is."

The officials expected to see the foolish boy stand speechless and confused. But nothing like that happened. How they marveled when the lad answered promptly in a confident voice, "This puzzle is not difficult." He turned to Lord Saint John and gave a command with the manner of a person who was used to giving commands. "Go to the private cabinet in my apartment. You'll find a secret door just above the bottom shelf. Press the button over the secret door and the door will open. You will see some of my jewels inside and the

royal seal is there also."

The entire company was struck with wonder over this speech. Lord Saint John started to carry out the command and then stopped with embarrassment as he realized that he was taking orders from a young vagrant. When Lord Saint John stopped, Tom Canty turned and said sharply, "What are you waiting for? Didn't you hear the king's command? Go!"

Lord Saint John obeyed the command and left. As the group waited for his return, a strange change came over the lords, ladies, and officials. One by one, they moved toward Edward, staring at him with wonder, until Tom Canty stood alone on the platform, outside the thick ring of people that surrounded the king.

Soon, the announcement came that Lord Saint John was returning. As he moved down the middle aisle of the church, the interest was so great that the low murmurings of the crowd died out and were followed by a deep silence. Every eye was fixed on Lord Saint John. At last, he reached the platform, paused a moment, and then moved toward Tom Canty. Quietly, he announced, "Your Highness, the seal is not there."

In an instant the crowd that had circled the king melted, and Edward stood alone, without friend or supporter. The eyes that had looked at him with wonder now stared with anger. Hertford called out angrily, "Throw this beggar into the street, and make sure that he leaves the city!"

Guards sprang forward to grab Edward, but Tom waved them off. "Get

Lesson 118   Textbook   **433**

- Just before Hertford was ready to tell a judge to arrest Edward, he thought of another test for the boy. What object did he ask Edward about? *Idea:* The royal seal.
- Did Hertford or any of the others know where the seal was? **No.**
- Where did Edward tell Lord Saint John to look for the seal? *Idea:* In a cabinet in his apartment.
- When Lord Saint John was on his way to look for the seal, who did the crowd of important people surround? **Edward.**
- What news did Lord Saint John bring about the seal? *Idea:* That it was not where Edward said it was.
- At the end of the chapter, Tom Canty sprang forward with a question. What did he ask? *Idea:* If somebody could describe the seal.

Award 4 points or have the students reread to the error limit sign.

INDEPENDENT WORK

Do all the items in your skillbook and workbook for lesson 118.

back! Any person who touches him will be punished."

Hertford was angry and confused. He turned to Lord Saint John and asked, "Did you search the cabinet carefully?"

Lord Saint John nodded. "Yes, very carefully. And it is not . . ."

Tom interrupted with beaming eyes.

He sprang forward and shouted, "Can you describe this thing that you are looking for—this royal seal?"

Hertford and Lord Saint John looked at each other and blinked. Then Hertford turned to Tom Canty and said, "Of course, Your Majesty."

ANSWER KEY FOR WORKBOOK

Review Items

1. Write **fact** or **fiction** after each statement.
   a. Henry Tudor was the King of England. _fact_
   b. Tom Canty was the King of England. _fiction_
   c. A dog named Brown Wolf ran north. _fiction_
   d. A dog named Buck pulled a thousand-pound sled. _fiction_
   e. Dogs were used to pull sleds in the Yukon. _fact_
   f. A man was able to change objects into gold. _fiction_
   g. Some people think that gold is evil. _fact_

2. Write **where** each story took place. Choose from **Canada, England,** or the **United States.**
   a. Adventure on the Rocky Ridge _United States_
   b. Brown Wolf _United States_
   c. The Prince and the Pauper _England_
   d. Buck _Canada_
   e. A Horse to Remember _England_

3. You read about a baseball player.
   a. What was his name? _Jackie Robinson_
   b. Which team did he play for? _Dodgers_
   c. Which city was that team located in? _Brooklyn_

WORKCHECK AND AWARDING POINTS

1. *Read the questions and answers for the skillbook and workbook.*
2. *Award points for independent work as follows:*

0 errors	6 points
2 errors	4 points
3, 4, or 5 errors	2 points
5 or more errors	0 points

3. *Award bonus points as follows:*

Correcting missed items or getting all items right	2 points
Doing the writing assignment acceptably	2 points

ANSWER KEY FOR SKILLBOOK

PART D

1. a. church
   b. *Idea:* Royalty
   c. Horns
   d. *Ideas:* He had denied his mother; he wasn't the real king
   e. *Idea:* He would become king
2. a. Edward
   b. The real king
   c. Tom
   d. *Idea:* They looked alike
   e. *Idea:* To see if he really was the king
3. a. *Idea:* Very well
   b. Tom
   c. The royal seal
   d. the real king
   e. *Idea:* That he was the real king
   f. *Idea:* A secret compartment
   g. Lord Saint John
4. a. Edward
   b. Tom
   c. *Idea:* The royal seal was not there
   d. Edward
   e. *Idea:* Arrest him
   f. Tom stopped him
   g. The royal seal

PART E

5. a. coronation
   b. impulse
   c. smuggle
   d. deny
   e. procession
   f. intend
   g. riot
   h. stall
   i. gossip
   j. ceremonies

Lesson 119

Lesson 119

PART A   Word Lists

1	2
incredible	product
impossible	produce
terrible	giant
horrible	garage
	garbage

PART B   Vocabulary Review

riot
ceremony
under arrest
procession
imposter

1. Someone who pretends to be somebody else is an _____.
2. When a police officer accuses a person of committing a crime, the officer places that person _____.

Lesson 119

CHAPTER 22
The Royal Seal

Tom Canty asked eager questions about the royal seal: "Was it large and round? . . . Was it very heavy ? . . . Did it have letters on it?" After the questions were answered, Tom said, "So that thing is the royal seal. If you had described it to me earlier, you could have had it three weeks ago. I know where the royal seal is, but I was not the one who put it there . . ."Ⓐ

Tom quickly turned to Edward. Pointing to him, Tom continued, "The true king put it there. And he will tell you where it is. Then you will believe him."

Tom now spoke quietly to Edward. "Think about the day that we met. Remember that you rushed out to scold the soldier when you were dressed in my rags. Now think very carefully about the last thing you did before you rushed from the room. You did something with the royal seal."

A silence followed. During the silence nobody moved or whispered, and all eyes were fixed on the beggar, who was frowning and groping through his memories to recall the event. One small event, but an event so important that it could make a difference about who sat on the throne of England. Moment after moment passed, and the moments became minutes. Still

Edward struggled silently and gave no sign of remembering what had happened. At last, he said in a trembling voice, "I can remember the scene, but I can't remember anything about the seal." He continued in a calm voice, "I'm sorry that I cannot recall the event, and so I must face the fate of being robbed of the throne."Ⓑ

★6 ERRORS★

"Stop that crazy talk, my king!" cried Tom. "Think, and do not give up." Tom looked sternly at the young king before continuing, "I will describe some of the things that happened. Listen carefully to what I say and I'm sure that your memory will return. When we were in your apartment I told you about where I lived. I told you of my sisters—Bet and Nan. I told you of Pudding Lane and the games that we played. Do you remember that part?" Tom paused before continuing. "Now follow this next part. You gave me something to eat and drink. You sent the servant out of the room so that I would not be embarrassed over my poor manners. Do you remember that . . .?"

Edward nodded. Tom continued as the others listened with amazement. The story sounded true to them, but it was impossible that they could not bring them-

Lesson 119   Textbook   **435**

WORD PRACTICE AND VOCABULARY

EXERCISE 1   Word family

1. Everybody, find lesson 119, part A in your skillbook. *Wait.*
2. Column 1. All those words have the same ending.
3. Your turn. Read the first word. *Signal.* **Incredible.**
4. Next word. *Signal.* **Impossible.**
5. *Repeat step 4 for each remaining word in column 1.*
6. *Repeat the words in column 1 until firm.*

EXERCISE 2   Word practice

1. Column 2.
2. Your turn. Read the first word. *Signal.* **Product.**
3. Next word. *Signal.* **Produce.**
4. *Repeat step 3 for each remaining word in column 2.*
5. *Repeat the words in column 2 until firm.*

EXERCISE 3   Vocabulary review

1. Everybody, look at part B. The words in the box are words you've learned.
2. Read the first word. *Signal.* **Riot.**
3. Next. *Signal.* **Ceremony.**
4. *Repeat step 3 for the remaining words in the box.*
5. *Repeat the words in the box until firm.*
6. I'll read the items. When I come to a blank, everybody say the part that goes in the blank.
7. Look at item 1. *Pause.* Listen. Someone who pretends to be somebody else in an *Pause. Signal.* **imposter.**
8. *Repeat step 7 for the remaining item.*

   Answer Key: **2. under arrest**

STORY READING

EXERCISE 4   Decoding and comprehension

1. Everybody, turn to page 435 in your textbook. *Wait. Call on a student.* What's the error limit for this chapter? **6 errors.**
2. *Call on individual students to read. Present the tasks specified for each circled letter.*
Ⓐ How long had people in the palace been looking for the royal seal? *Idea:* Ever since Henry the Eighth died.
● Who said that he knew where the seal was? **Tom Canty.**
● Why didn't he tell people where it was a long time before? *Idea:* He didn't know what it was.

selves to believe it. There was probably never a large group of people so interested in what they heard—and so puzzled—as the group that listened to Tom as he said, "Do you remember that I had a wish to dress like a prince and you had a dream of being as free as the other lads from Pudding Lane? So, we exchanged clothes."

Edward nodded again. "Then," Tom said, "as we stood in front of the mirror, wearing each other's clothes, we noticed that we looked so much like each other that it was almost impossible to see that a change had taken place. You noticed the only difference, a bruise that I had received from the soldier at the gate."

"Yes, I remember," Edward replied.

"You became very angry over the bruise and started toward the door of the room. You passed the table, and the seal was on that table. You picked it up, and looked nervously around the room, as if you were trying to think of where to hide it. Your eye suddenly caught sight of . . ."

"That's enough, thank you," Edward said with a confident voice. He turned to Lord Saint John and said, "Inside my apartment is a suit of armor, standing next to the door. If you look inside the helmet you will find the royal seal."

"Right, my king!" Tom exclaimed. "Now everybody will know who the true king is. Go, Lord Saint John. Go as if you had wings on your feet!"

Everybody in the great church was standing, dumb with confusion. This confusion burst into a sudden deafening buzz of conversation so loud that people had to shout to be heard by their neighbors. The buzzing conversations continued until Lord Saint John returned. Then a hush came over the crowd. Lord Saint John moved to the platform and without saying anything held the royal seal over his head. Immediately, a deafening shout went up from the audience, "Long live the true king!"

The chant went on for about five minutes. During this entire time, all the lords and ladies that were on the platform knelt in front of the little king, who was smiling broadly. At last Tom approached the king and said, "Now these splendid clothes belong to you."

No sooner were the words out of Tom's mouth than the chief judge pointed to Tom and said, "Strip the clothes from that imposter and throw him in prison."

Edward said, "No! If it weren't for him I would not be recognized as the true king." Edward turned to Tom and said, "Why were you able to remember where the seal was, when I couldn't remember it myself?"

"That was easy. I have used it on many occasions."

"Used it? How could you use it if you didn't know how it was supposed to be used?"

Tom replied, "I did not use it to mark letters."

"Then how did you use it?"

Tom blushed and looked down. Edward repeated the question. At last, Tom looked up and managed to say, "I used the seal to crack nuts."

436   Lesson 119   Textbook

The audience broke into thunderous laughter.

The royal robe was removed from Tom's shoulders and placed on Edward's. Then the coronation ceremony continued. The crown was placed upon the new king's head, while cannons thundered to announce the coronation, and the entire city of London rocked with applause.

• • •

We left Miles Hendon on London Bridge the night before the coronation. After escaping from the riot on the bridge, Miles searched for Edward. He had lost his horse, and he groped through dark alleys and empty streets, but he could not find a trace of the boy. He continued his search all night and until noon the next day. At that time, he came to the large crowds that were lining the streets, waiting for the coronation procession. He drifted here and there among the crowd, hoping to find a sign of the boy, but at last he gave up and wandered from the city to a quiet place where he could make better plans for finding his strange, brave friend. When he finally stopped to rest, he was far from the city, near the river. He stretched out on the cool ground and listened to the distant cannons that announced the crowning of the new king.

In a few moments, Miles fell asleep. He slept until the middle of the next morning. When he awoke, he was very stiff and cold. He washed his face in the river, drank some of the river water, and formed a plan. He knew one of the lords that stayed at Westminster Palace. If he could somehow get inside, he would borrow a little money from this lord. Miles Hendon was so hungry that he didn't care if he got a lot of money; he wanted just enough for a hearty meal.

Miles walked back to the city. He went to the large gates of the palace and stood outside, hoping to find the friendly face of somebody who could carry a message to the lord. As he stood there, Humphry, the whipping boy, left the palace grounds and paused as he looked at Miles. To himself, Humphry said, "That man looks exactly like the one King Edward has described." As he stared at Miles, Miles turned to him and asked, "Do you work inside the palace?"

"Yes, I do."

"Do you know Sir Humphry Marlow?"

The boy knew him very well, because Sir Humphry Marlow was the boy's dead father. "I know him," Humphry said.

"Is he inside?" Miles asked.

"Yes he is," Humphry replied, and then said to himself, "inside his grave."

Miles asked the boy to tell Sir Humphry Marlow that Miles Hendon wanted to see him, if that was possible.

Humphry told Miles to wait there while he delivered the message. After Humphry left, Miles sat down on a stone bench. No sooner had he seated himself than a guard walked past him, paused, eyed him for a moment, and then said, "Come with me. You are under arrest for being a suspicious-looking person."

Lesson 119   Textbook   437

(B) What do you think will happen if Edward cannot remember what he did with the seal? *Idea:* He will be thrown in jail; he won't be king.

- Read the rest of the chapter to yourselves and be ready to answer some questions.

After all students have finished reading:

- Tom Canty recalled the events that took place in Edward's apartment. When did Edward do something with the seal? *Idea:* Just before he left Tom.
- Edward told Lord Saint John where to find the seal. Where was it? *Idea:* Inside a suit of armor.
- When Lord Saint John returned, what did he do to announce what he had found? *Idea:* He held the royal seal over his head.
- How did the audience react when the people saw the seal? *Idea:* They shouted, "Long live the king."
- Tom remembered where the seal was because he had used it on many occasions. How had he used it? *Idea:* To crack nuts.
- When he made this announcement, how did the people react? *Idea:* They laughed.
- How long did Miles continue to search for Edward? *Idea:* All night and half the next day.
- Where did he go the next day to make better plans? *Idea:* Outside the city.
- How did Miles know that the new king had been crowned? *Idea:* The cannons were booming.
- Miles went to sleep. When did he wake up? *Idea:* The next morning.
- Where did Miles go? *Idea:* To the palace.
- What was his plan? *Idea:* To borrow money from one of the lords.
- Who did he talk to outside the gates? **Humphry.**
- Why did Humphry recognize Hendon? *Idea:* Edward had described him.
- Miles asked about Sir Humphry Marlow. Did Humphry know this person? **Yes.**
- Why? *Idea:* Marlow was his father.
- Was Sir Humphry Marlow really inside the palace? **No.**
- Why not? *Idea:* Because he was dead.
- Where did Miles wait while Humphry went inside? *Idea:* On a stone bench.
- What happened just as Miles sat down? *Idea:* He was arrested.

Award 4 points or have the students reread to the error limit sign.

INDEPENDENT WORK

Do all the items in your skillbook and workbook for lesson 119.

ANSWER KEY FOR WORKBOOK

Main Idea and Supporting Details

Read this passage:
Alas, alas! how very soon this silly little
   fly,
Hearing the cunning, flattering words,
   came slowly flitting by;
With buzzing wings she hung aloft, then
   near and nearer drew,
Thinking only of her brilliant eyes, and
   green and purple hue—
Thinking only of her crested head—poor
   foolish thing! At last,
Up jumped the cunning spider, and
   fiercely held her fast.
He dragged her up his winding stair, into
   his dismal den,
Within his little parlor—but she ne'er
   came out again!

Write the main idea and three
supporting details. *Idea:*

1. *The spider caught*
   the fly.
a. *The fly came*
   flitting by.
b. *The spider jumped*
   up.
c. *The spider dragged*
   her into his web.

Crossword Puzzle

To work the puzzle, read an item and
figure out which word the item describes.
Then write the word in the puzzle.
Complete the entire puzzle.

Across

4. When you give somebody information
   about something, you _____ that
   person about that thing.
6. If you plan to do something, you
   _____ to do that thing.
7. Someone who pretends to be
   somebody else is an _____.
8. Someone who is not guilty of doing
   something wrong is _____.
10. When you are grouchy, you are
   _____.
11. When you pretend to be somebody's
   friend and then trick that person,
   you _____ that person.

Down

1. When you show someone hospitality,
   you are _____.
2. Something that makes you tired
   makes you _____.
3. When somebody tells the truth about
   a secret, that person _____.
5. When you tell what something is, you
   _____ that thing.
9. When you say that something is not
   true, you _____ that thing.

1. *Read the questions and answers for the skillbook*
   and workbook.
2. *Award points for independent work as follows:*

0 errors	6 points
2 errors	4 points
3, 4, or 5 errors	2 points
5 or more errors	0 points

3. *Award bonus points as follows:*

Correcting missed items or getting all items right	2 points
Doing the writing assignment acceptably	2 points

ANSWER KEY FOR SKILLBOOK

PART C

1. **a.** the royal seal
   b. Yes
2. **a.** *Idea:* He would not become the king
   b. No
   c. *Idea:* Inside a suit of armor
   d. Lord Saint John
   e. the royal seal
   f. *Idea:* That Edward was the real king
   g. *Idea:* Stamping official papers
   h. Cracking nuts
3. **a.** Edward
   b. *Idea:* Near a stream
   c. *Idea:* the royal palace
   d. Money
   e. Humphry
   f. *Idea:* He was arrested

PART D

4. **a.** Brains
   b. *Idea:* A trip back to Kansas
   c. A heart
   d. Courage
5. **a.** Greyhound
   b. Collie
   c. Hound
   d. Poodle
   e. Airedale
6. **a.** innocent
   b. betray
   c. under arrest
   d. riot
   e. procession
   f. imposter
   g. ceremony

Lesson 120

Lesson 120

PART A   **Word Lists**

1	2
delicious	gaze
suspicious	glaze
prosperous	desolate
dangerous	poverty
	ridicule
	ridiculous

Lesson 120

CHAPTER 23

King Edward

A guard had placed Miles under arrest. He ordered Miles to follow him and then marched toward two other guards. "Search him," the first guard commanded, and the others began to search Miles. One of them found the paper that showed that Miles had been in prison for pretending to be Miles Hendon.

Miles shook his head and said to himself, "They will probably hang me now."

A moment later, a messenger came from the palace and whispered something to the first guard. The guard immediately ordered the other guards to leave Miles alone. He then bowed to Miles and said, "Would you please follow me inside, sir?"Ⓐ

Miles couldn't figure out why the guard was suddenly so polite, but he followed the guard through the gates, across the great lawn, up the steps of the palace, and then inside. Miles passed splendidly dressed men and women. He could hear them laughing over the costume that he wore. The guard delivered Miles to another guard, one who was dressed in a very bright uniform. This guard took Miles up a broad stairway, past groups of richly dressed people, and into a huge and crowded room. The guard bowed and left

Miles standing in the middle of this room.

Miles Hendon was completely confused. In front of him was the throne of England, and on the throne sat the young king with his face turned away as he talked to a lord. After a few moments, the king turned his head and Miles saw it clearly, although the king had not yet seen Miles. The sight of the king's face nearly took Miles's breath away. He stood in stunned silence, gazing at the fair young face. Without thinking, he said aloud, "It's the lord of the kingdom of dreams!"Ⓑ

★6 ERRORS★

Miles quickly looked around the magnificent room. "Is this a dream?" he asked himself. To test whether it was a dream, Miles walked to the wall, picked up a chair, brought it back, placed it on the floor in front of the king, and sat down.

Two guards shot forward and grabbed Miles as one guard said, "How dare you sit in the presence of the king!"

Suddenly the king looked up. His face sparkled with delight for a moment. Then he raised his hand and said, "Don't touch him. He has the right to sit in my presence."

The audience became silent as Ed-

438   Lesson 120   Textbook

WORD PRACTICE AND VOCABULARY

EXERCISE 1   Word family

1. Everybody, find lesson 120, part A in your skillbook. *Wait.*
2. Column 1. All those words end in the sound **us.**
3. Your turn. Read the first word. *Signal.* **Delicious.**
4. Next word. *Signal.* **Suspicious.**
5. *Repeat step 4 for each remaining word in column 1.*
6. *Repeat the words in column 1 until firm.*

EXERCISE 2   Word practice

1. Column 2.
2. Your turn. Read the first word. *Signal.* **Gaze.**
3. Next word. *Signal.* **Glaze.**
4. *Repeat step 3 for each remaining word in column 2.*
5. *Repeat the words in column 2 until firm.*

STORY READING

EXERCISE 3   Decoding and comprehension

1. Everybody, turn to page 438 in your textbook. *Wait. Call on a student.* What's the error limit for this chapter? **6 errors.**
2. *Call on individual students to read. Present the tasks specified for each circled letter.*

Ⓐ Is the guard still being rude to Miles? **No.**
● Something happened just before the guard changed the way he treated Miles. What happened? *Idea:* A messenger whispered something to the guard.
● What do you think the messenger said to the guard? *Idea:* Student preference.
Ⓑ Where is Miles now? *Idea:* In the throne room.
● Has Edward looked up at Miles yet? **No.**
● How do you think Miles feels to see Edward on the throne? *Idea:* Amazed.
● Read the rest of the chapter to yourselves and be ready to answer some questions.

After all students have finished reading:
● What did Miles do to test whether or not he was having a dream? *Idea:* Sat down in front of the king.
● Who grabbed him when he sat down? *Idea:* Two guards.
● What did Edward say to the guards who grabbed Miles? *Idea:* Not to touch Miles.

ward continued. "This man is my trusted servant, Miles Hendon. He saved my life and for his bravery I made him a knight. He took punishment for me in prison, and for that brave act, I made him an earl. He will have all the land and all the riches of an earl. And he may sit in my presence for the rest of his life."

The people in the audience looked with puzzled eyes, first at the king, then at this ragged figure standing before him, then back to the king. Miles shook his head and muttered to himself, "This is the boy I tried to impress with the seventy rooms of Hendon Hall." Miles shook his head in embarrassment. "I should hide my head in a bag," he thought.

But a moment later, Miles's manners returned to him. He dropped to one knee. He gripped Edward's hands in his and said, "I am your servant, my king."

Lesson 120 Textbook **439**

Miles rose, stepped to one side and turned toward the audience. His expression suddenly became startled, and the king looked to see what caused this change in expression. There, near the back of the room, sat Sir Hugh Hendon and Lady Edith. Standing up, the king pointed to Sir Hugh and said, "Strip that robber of Hendon Hall and of all the other things that he has stolen! Then lock him up inside the palace until I have time to deal with him."

As the guards were leading Hugh Hendon away, Tom Canty entered the room. He was wearing a rich outfit. He knelt before the king. Edward said, "I have learned the story of these past weeks and I am very pleased with you. You have ruled with intelligence and kindness. And for the rest of your life, you will be recognized as one who had been king. You will wear a special costume that nobody can copy. You will live with your mother and grandmother and sisters in a fine cottage. At any important meeting or celebration, you will sit with the lords, where you belong. And you will have the title of the King's Ward. Thank you."

The proud and happy Tom rose and kissed Edward's hand. After he was led from the throne room, he wasted no time in going to Pudding Lane to tell his mother and his grandmother and his sisters about their good fortune.

It took days for all the mysteries to be cleared up. But within a few hours, Sir Miles Hendon and the king discovered why Edith had denied knowing Miles. When she had caught a glimpse of Miles in Hendon Hall, she had known instantly who he was. At first she had refused to lie, but Hugh had told her that if she didn't lie, he would have Miles killed. So she pretended not to know Miles.

Miles refused to have Hugh brought to court for his terrible crimes. When Hugh was released, he left England and went to Spain. Miles married Edith and returned to Hendon village, where there was great rejoicing.

Tom Canty's father was never heard of again.

The king later found Yokel, the poor farmer who had been branded, sold as a slave, and escaped to travel with the Ruffler. He gave Yokel a small farm. The king found the judge who had kept him from hanging because of the stolen pig. Edward made that judge more important. Edward sent gifts to the woman who had made breakfast for him and he also sent gifts to her two young daughters. Finally he sent a gift to the woman who had lost her pig.

King Edward the Sixth died a few years later, when he was only sixteen. But until he died, he was fond of telling the story of his adventures. Miles Hendon and Tom Canty were his favorite people. When Edward died, they were both very sad. Tom Canty lived to be a very old man. He became a handsome, white-haired old fellow who was known for his kindness. He was known to everybody by the costume that he wore. It reminded everybody that

440 Lesson 120 Textbook

- Who did Miles notice sitting in the back of the audience in the throne room? *Idea:* Hugh Hendon and Lady Edith.
- What had Hugh planned to accomplish by going to the palace? *Idea:* To get favors from the king.
- Edward gave Tom Canty some rewards for the things that he had done. Name those rewards. *Ideas:* He could wear a special costume; he could live in a cottage; he would have a special title; he could sit with lords.
- Had Edith recognized Miles at Hendon Hall? **Yes.**
- Why had she denied knowing him? *Idea:* Because Hugh had threatened to kill Miles.
- What happened to Hugh after the king released him? *Idea:* He went to Spain.
- What happened to Lady Edith? *Idea:* She married Miles.
- What happened to Tom Canty's father? *Idea:* Nobody ever heard from him again.
- Name some things Edward did for the people who had helped him. *Ideas:* Gave Yokel a small farm; made the judge more important; sent gifts to the other people.
- What did Edward tell lords who argued for strict laws? *Idea:* That they didn't know anything about suffering.
- How old was Edward the Sixth when he died? **Sixteen.**

he had once been king. Wherever he went, people parted, bowed, and took off their hats.

Yes, King Edward the Sixth lived only a few years. But he lived his years well. He changed the laws so that the poor would not suffer as much. More than once, lords tried to tell him that he was too kind and that he should make strict laws, like the ones of Henry the Eighth. But young Edward had lived through suffering and evil, and he knew that the terribly strict laws caused many problems. So, when a lord argued for strict laws, the young king would answer by saying, "What do you know about suffering? I know, and the people of England know. But you don't."

Edward the Sixth was a merciful king who ruled in Europe during a cruel time. Although he is now gone, we should try to remember his mercy and recognize the strength that he showed by being merciful.

THE END

- How was Edward different from the other kings of Europe at that time? *Idea:* He was merciful.
- The chapter says that although Edward is now gone, we should try to remember his mercy and recognize the strength that he showed by being merciful. Why would it require great strength for a king to be merciful? *Response:* Student preference.

Award 4 points or have the students reread to the error limit sign.

INDEPENDENT WORK

Do all the items in your skillbook and workbook for lesson 120.

ANSWER KEY FOR WORKBOOK

Outlining

The outline below shows three main ideas for The Prince and the Pauper.

Write three supporting details for each main idea.

1. Tom and Edward changed places. *Idea:*
   a. *Tom came to the palace.*
   b. *Tom and Edward talked to each other.*
   c. *Tom and Edward changed clothes.*

2. Tom found out what it was like to be a king.
   a. *He gave orders.*
   b. *He acted as a judge.*
   c. *He ate in public.*

3. Edward found out what it was like to be a pauper.
   a. *He walked around London.*
   b. *He wore rags.*
   c. *He was hungry.*

Review Items

4. Here are some events from the Jane Addams biography.
   - World War One ends
   - Hull House opens
   - Jane Addams receives the Nobel Peace Prize
   - A new factory law passes

Write the correct event after each date on the time line.

1931 *Jane Addams receives the Nobel Peace Prize*

1918 *World War One ends*

1893 *A new factory law passes*

1889 *Hull House opens*

WORKCHECK AND AWARDING POINTS

1. *Read the questions and answers for the skillbook and workbook.*

2. *Award points for independent work as follows:*

0 errors	6 points
2 errors	4 points
3, 4, or 5 errors	2 points
5 or more errors	0 points

3. *Award bonus points as follows:*

Correcting missed items or getting all items right	2 points
Doing the writing assignment acceptably	2 points

ANSWER KEY FOR SKILLBOOK

PART B

1. a. Edward
   b. *Idea:* Sat down in front of Edward
   c. *Idea:* Grabbed him
   d. Edward
   e. *Idea:* Because of their agreement
2. a. *Idea:* Knight and Earl
   b. Hendon Hall
   c. Hugh Hendon
   d. Hendon Hall
3. a. *Idea:* He had ruled well
   b. *Idea:* A special costume
   c. *Idea:* In a cottage
   d. His mother, grandmother, and sisters
4. a. Spain
   b. John Canty
   c. *Ideas:* Yokel; the woman; the mother and her two daughters
5. a. laws
   b. suffering
   c. 16
   d. *Idea:* He was merciful

PART C

6. a. irritable
   b. regret
   c. intend
   d. merciful
   e. tragic
   f. take advantage
   g. impulse
   h. retreat
   i. betray
   j. vagrant
   k. innocent
   l. prosper
   m. convince
   n. identify